MOTION PICTURE PARADISE

UNIVERSITY PRESS OF FLORIDA

Florida A&M University, Tallahassee
Florida Atlantic University, Boca Raton
Florida Gulf Coast University, Ft. Myers
Florida International University, Miami
Florida State University, Tallahassee
New College of Florida, Sarasota
University of Central Florida, Orlando
University of Florida, Gainesville
University of North Florida, Jacksonville
University of South Florida, Tampa
University of West Florida, Pensacola

MOTION PICTURE
Paradise

A History of Florida's Film and Television Industry

David Morton

UNIVERSITY PRESS OF FLORIDA

Gainesville · Tallahassee · Tampa · Boca Raton
Pensacola · Orlando · Miami · Jacksonville · Ft. Myers · Sarasota

Cover: Florida-shaped swimming pool at Cypress Gardens in Winter Haven, 1959. The Esther Williams Swimming Pool was built in the shape of the map of Florida, projecting out in Lake Eloise as a set for the film *Easy to Love* (1953) which was partly filmed at Cypress Gardens. Founded in 1936 by Dick and Julie Pope, Cypress Gardens was one of the state's first theme parks. State Archives of Florida, Florida Memory.

Copyright 2024 by David Morton
All rights reserved
Published in the United States of America

First cloth printing, 2024
First paperback printing, 2025

30 29 28 27 26 25   6 5 4 3 2 1

Library of Congress Cataloging-in-Publication Data
Names: Morton, David D., author.
Title: Motion picture paradise : a history of Florida's film and television
   industry / David Morton.
Other titles: History of Florida's film and television industry
Description: 1. | Gainesville : University Press of Florida, [2024] |
   Includes bibliographical references and index.
Identifiers: LCCN 2023044837 (print) | LCCN 2023044838 (ebook) | ISBN
   9780813069999 (hardback) | ISBN 9780813081250 (pbk.) | ISBN 9780813070742 (pdf)
Subjects: LCSH: Motion picture industry—Florida—History. | Motion picture
   locations—Florida—History. | Florida—In motion pictures. | BISAC:
   HISTORY / United States / State & Local / South (AL, AR, FL, GA, KY, LA,
   MS, NC, SC, TN, VA, WV) | SOCIAL SCIENCE / Media Studies
Classification: LCC PN1993.5.U73 M67 2024 (print) | LCC PN1993.5.U73
   (ebook) | DDC 384/.8509759—dc23/eng/20231019
LC record available at https://lccn.loc.gov/2023044837
LC ebook record available at https://lccn.loc.gov/2023044838

The University Press of Florida is the scholarly publishing agency for the State University System of Florida, comprising Florida A&M University, Florida Atlantic University, Florida Gulf Coast University, Florida International University, Florida State University, New College of Florida, University of Central Florida, University of Florida, University of North Florida, University of South Florida, and University of West Florida.

University Press of Florida
2046 NE Waldo Road
Suite 2100
Gainesville, FL 32609
http://upress.ufl.edu

GPSR EU Authorized Representative: Mare Nostrum Group B.V., Mauritskade 21D, 1091 GC Amsterdam, The Netherlands, gpsr@mare-nostrum.co.uk

Contents

List of Figures   vii

Acknowledgments   ix

Abbreviations   xiii

Opening Credits: "The Sun of Florida's Destiny"   1

1. "This Venture Was Epoch-Making": Florida's Early Twentieth-Century Movie Boom, 1898–1925   21

2. "Of Course They Please the Southern People": Florida Becomes Home to the Cinematic "Lost Cause" and Race Film Industry, 1908–1928   72

3. "Motion Pictures at a Great Saving!": Florida Attempts to Build a "Second Los Angeles," 1922–1945   114

4. "The Business Can Kill You Anyway": Hollywood Comes to Florida, 1938–1971   155

5. "Assurances of Full Cooperation": Florida Becomes a National Film and Television Capital, 1971–2005   203

End Credits: "The Flip of a Switch"; The Sun Sets on Florida's Motion Picture Industry (Can it Rise Again?), 2006–Present   255

Notes   271

Index   321

Index to Films and Television Shows   329

Figures

1. Ocala Drive-In (2020) 10
2. "Movies Move On" (2017) 14
3. Gene Gauntier and the Kalem Stock Company (1908) 20
4. Spanish-American War film reels (1898) 23
5. Film set in Jacksonville (1912) 35
6. Charles Field's Miami film studio under construction (1914) 42
7. J.E.T. Bowden after Jacksonville's Great Fire (1901) 47
8. *The Clarion* advertisement (1916) 52
9. Klutho Fine Arts City (1919) 61
10. D. W. Griffith and G. W. "Billy" Bitzer in South Florida (1919) 69
11. Gene Gauntier as a southern belle (1911) 77
12. United Confederate Veterans parade program (1914) 85
13. Frank Crowd's Globe Theatre (1915) 98
14. Sidney Catts campaign pamphlet (1916) 101
15. *The Flying Ace,* Richard Norman Studios (1926) 110
16. Theda Bara in *A Woman There Was* (1919) 118
17. Henry King, Lupe Vélez, and Governor Doyle Carlton (1929) 130
18. *Tarzan Finds a Son!* (1939) film crew at Silver Springs 154
19. Nancy Tribble receives key to the City of Tampa (1948) 165
20. Ginger Stanley and Ricou Browning in *Creature from the Black Lagoon* (1954) 171
21. Governor Fuller Warren carrying film reels (1951) 174
22. Premiere of *Follow That Dream* in Ocala (1962) 178
23. Ricou Browning and the dolphin Mitzi (1963) 193
24. Governor Haydon Burns with Walt Disney and Roy Disney (1965) 201
25. Bob Graham and Burt Reynolds on the set of *Stick* (1985) 217

26. *Miami Vice* promo (1984) 223
27. "Hollywood Weather without Hollywood Overhead" (1986) 226
28. Universal Studios promotion (1989/1990) 247
29. John Watzke at Ocala Drive-In (2021) 256
30. Film Florida incentive map (2024) 266

Acknowledgments

To properly tell the fascinating 125-year story of Florida's relationship to the motion picture industry, this book has relied on incredibly dedicated research from the many Florida film scholars and enthusiasts who have come before me. *Motion Picture Paradise* would not have been possible without the depth of research materials assembled by Richard Alan Nelson. The veracity of his writing combined with the treasure trove of correspondence, government documents, interviews, newspaper clippings, and trade press articles he donated to Florida State University's Special Collections are not only the backbone of this book but also where all future research projects on Florida film must begin. Dr. Nelson was a great source of advice and encouragement as I pieced together the puzzle of the story of Florida's turbulent relationship with the American motion picture industry from its beginnings to today.

The research that went into this book would not have been possible without the diligent support of scholars, researchers, archivists, and librarians across Florida. I could not have come close to reviewing the endless array of documents donated by Dr. Nelson without the coordinated assistance of Hannah Davis at the Florida State University Libraries, Jim Cusick of the University of Florida Library, Ben DiBiase of the Florida Historical Society, and Lisa Dunbar of the Florida Department of State, who were indispensable in directing me to contacts and identifying the collections that I would later incorporate into my research.

Isabella Formar of the State Archives of Florida helped me access various governors' papers and documents related to the Florida motion picture industry. Jessica Morio and John Wilson at the Jacksonville Public Library assisted in providing me with daily uploads of early editions of the *Florida Times-Union* and *Florida Metropolis*. Mitchell Hermann of the Jacksonville Historical Society directed me to a multitude of collections and sources on Jacksonville's early cinema history. Devan Stuart Lesley and Rita Regan at the Norman Studios Silent Film Museum were generous enough to offer me a tour of their grounds.

Barbara Tepa Lupack of the University of Rochester gave me an important crash course in the history of film production in Jacksonville. James Crooks of the University of North Florida and Mark Woods of the *Florida Times-Union* also helped me achieve a greater understanding of Jacksonville's complicated political history at the turn of the twentieth century. Jennifer Dietz, the archives and records manager for the City of Tampa, was an enormous help in providing scans for film programs of motion pictures produced in Tampa in the 1930s. Lou Kramer of the Lynn and Louis Wolfson II Moving Image Archive at Miami-Dade College graciously provided a tour of the facilities and insight into the long history of film and television production in South Florida. Ashley Trujillo of the HistoryMiami Museum was also incredibly helpful assembling the pieces of the puzzle to South Florida's fascinating film history. John Lux, the executive director of Film Florida, was another tremendous source of help in getting me up to speed about the gallant effort of lobbyists and community organizers to gain support for increased tax incentives and government support from the Florida Legislature.

This book would not have been possible without support from my colleagues at the University of Central Florida. Joanie Reynolds of UCF's Interlibrary Loan managed to help me track down a vast array of obscure pamphlets, government papers, and documents that I had all but relegated to my wish list. Mary Rubin and Rebecca Hammond of UCF Special Collections provided me with an excellent environment to review delicate documents and pages from Florida's past. Barry Mauer and Patty Hurter of the UCF Texts and Technology program were frequent sources of support in my writing process.

I would like to individually thank each of my mentors, without whom I could not have completed this book. Daniel Biltereyst of Ghent University's Centre for Cinema Studies has set an incredibly high bar of quality scholarship that I hope to emulate in my career as an emerging film and media scholar. My lunches with Phil Peters of the UCF Digital Media Department helped me to untangle a series of incredibly complicated episodes of Florida's motion picture history into a cohesive narrative. Dr. Lisa Mills, Assistant Director of the UCF Film Department was a major source of support and encouragement both in my writing and where to showcase my research.

My interest in Florida's film history was initially inspired from classes taught by both Dr. Bruce Janz and Professor Elizabeth Kritzer during my first semester as PhD candidate in UCF's Texts and Technology Program. Dr. Scot French has also been another incredible mentor and source of encouragement at UCF. A special thank-you to Dr. Jim Clark, who helped advise me on how to approach such a challenging and nuanced story in an entertaining and engaging way. I also would like to thank Susan Doll, who provided instrumental feedback to a very rough early draft of this manuscript. My editor, Sian Hunter, deserves an enormous amount of credit for patiently abiding through pandemic-related delays and her constant encouragement to help get me to the finish line. I especially would like to thank Marthe Walters and Susan Murray of UPF for their eagle-eyed copyedits and enduring through multiple redrafts to help this text reach its full potential. This book is dedicated to my family—to my parents, who instilled in me a curiosity and unwillingness to accept what appear to be unanswerable questions, and last, but certainly not least, to my wife Freyza, who tolerated so many stolen evenings and weekends as I pieced this fascinating, but complex puzzle "together."

Abbreviations

AFP	Americans for Prosperity
AIP	American International Pictures
AMPC	Advance Motion Picture Company
BRPC	Birth of a Race Photoplay Corporation
CDC	Centers for Disease Control
CDMP	Committee for the Development of the Motion Picture
COMPASS	Congress of Motion Picture Associations
EMC	Edison Manufacturing Company
EPCOT	Experimental Prototype Community of Tomorrow
EPIC	End Poverty in California
FECR	Florida East Coast Railway
FETC	Florida Educational Television Commission
FCC	Federal Communications Commission
FFFC	Field Feature Film Company
FICUS	Florida Institute for Continuing University Studies
FMPTA	Florida Motion Picture and Television Association
FMPTB	Florida Motion Picture and Television Bureau
FPC	Foster Photoplay Company
FWP	Federal Writers' Project
IDC	Industrial Development Commission
JCC	Jacksonville Chamber of Commerce
KPC	Kennedy Picture Corporation
MBCC	Miami Metropolitan Board of County Commissioners
MCA	Music Corporation of America
MOFTO	Metro Orlando Film and Television Office
MPIC	Motion Picture Industry Committee

MPPA	Motion Picture Producers of America
MPPC	Motion Picture Patents Company
MPPDA	Motion Picture Producers and Distributors of America
MRMA	Ministry for the Recovery of Misappropriated Assets
NAACP	National Association for the Advancement of Colored People
NNBL	National Negro Business League
NYBC	New York Board of Censorship
OFE	Office of Film and Entertainment
OSS	Office of Strategic Services
RFC	Reconstruction Finance Corporation
RNMC	Richard Norman Manufacturing Company
SFFTPA	South Florida Film and Tape Producers Association
SHC	State Hotel Commission
SMPC	Special Motion Picture Committee
TCT	Tin Can Tourist Association
TFI	Tampa Films Incorporated
TOBA	Theater Owners Booking Association

OPENING CREDITS

"The Sun of Florida's Destiny"

Oldest of all in its history, it is the youngest of all in its development. But as the facts of Florida's unmatchable climate, its unrivaled agricultural and horticultural possibilities and its limitless opportunities in commerce and industry become known of all men, it cannot fail to become one of the richest, most populous, and influential in the whole family of commonwealths which make up our nation. The sun of Florida's destiny has arisen and only the malicious and the short-sighted contend or believe it will ever set.
    Florida governor John W. Martin, foreword to *Florida in the Making*, 1926

March 2020: "The Show Must Go On"

In the spring of 2020, the world came to a standstill as the spread of COVID-19 shuttered airports, businesses, concert halls, restaurants, schools, and of course, movie theaters. With the sudden closure of movie theaters, major studios including Disney, DreamWorks, Universal, Warner Brothers, scrapped their releases and began mobilizing to offer home-streaming options. The motion picture industry was shaken to its very foundation: at the box office. As theaters across the United States were impacted by temporary closures, the premieres of nearly all first-run films were either delayed or scheduled for purchase by way of video-on-demand. During this unprecedented moment in motion picture history, in a tucked-away corner of North Central Florida, there was still one theater that offered moviegoers a bit of relief.

In early April 2020, almost all box-office receipts in the country came from just one place: the Ocala Drive-In in Marion County, Florida. Of the fourteen theaters known to show movies that weekend, the Ocala Drive-In was the only one to contribute to the national box office.[1] The screenings of two arthouse horror flicks: *The Other Lamb* (2020) and *Swallow* (2020) grossed a whopping total of $1,194 on the weekend of April 3, and $1,710 on the weekend of April 10, respectively.[2]

As the COVID-19 pandemic raged into the summer of 2020, drive-in theaters provided a much-needed and unexpected source of salvation for both producers and moviegoers alike. John Watkze, owner of the Ocala Drive-In, made headlines across the country for running the last theater in America to screen new movies. In an interview with *Vice*, Watkze justified his decision to remain open: "Anybody that knows me and knows the drive-in knows I don't close. I've had hurricanes come, I've stayed open until the power went off and I had no one in the parking lot."[3] The story of the Ocala Drive-In's holdout soon went viral, and the following week, Watzke was featured in a special segment on NPR's *All Things Considered*, where he discussed his surprise at being at the top of the box office:

> Kind of like the last dinosaur standing, you know? Never in the day [*sic*] thought that I would be the top in the box office. But I ended up the only one in the box office, so it's not hard to be the top if you're the only one. . . . Coming from the family that's worked theaters for over a hundred years, the old cliché the show must go on is not a cliché. It's a way of life. So, the show must go on.[4]

Despite the Ocala Drive-In's unlikely newfound fame, Watzke continued to charge the same price for admission, even after reducing the theater's car capacity by half to meet the social-distancing guidelines of the Centers for Disease Control (CDC). Although the Ocala Drive-In was not "raking it in by any means," Watzke saw an opportunity to provide an essential service to the Ocala community. In addition to offering screenings of first-run and classic films, Watzke allowed the use of his drive-in, free of any charge, for church services, city hall meetings, and high school graduations. Attendees just needed to sit in their cars and listen on the radio while the presenters either spoke onstage or had their message projected on the big screen.[5] With tickets priced at six dollars for adults, three dollars for children under twelve, and free admission for kids under five, the drive-in's pricing was a refreshing alternative to the bloated charges typical of most megaplexes. To accommodate his customers' precarious financial circumstances, the Ocala Drive-In offered promotions such as "Take You Back to the 1950's Ticket Prices," where drive-in patrons were able to attend a double feature for just fifty cents per person.[6]

Of the 321 remaining drive-in theaters that existed in the United States in 2020, few were able to turn a profit on ticket sales alone. Before the pandemic, the Ocala Drive-In only made $1.20 from a full-price ticket, with almost all profits coming from concessions. "What I make off of ticket sales would barely cover the electric bill and the light bulbs," Watzke explained in a 2019 interview with WUFT.[7] To meet the increasingly costly demands from distributors, in 2013 the Ocala Drive-In had to make the switch from film to digital projection, after the major studios ceased offering film stock as an option.

John Watzke had built a second screen projector in 2016 after Disney and the other majors adjusted their distribution plans to require theaters to keep their movies on a set number of screens for at least three to four weeks during their first run.[8] In the uncertainty during the first days of the COVID-19 pandemic, as all major film releases were shelved, and only a handful of low-budget independent films were left in circulation, the Ocala Drive-In was able to go its own way. IFC Films, which produced both *The Other Lamb* and *Swallow*, allowed both films to be screened at the Ocala Drive-In, thus turning these two indie films into the unlikely top contenders at the box office in April 2020.

Originally from Waveland, Mississippi, John Watzke and his brother Charlie are third-generation members of a family of movie projectionists with roots in film exhibition that can be traced back to 1913. Charles Alexander Watzke Sr., John and Charlie Watzke's grandfather, worked as a projectionist in movie houses in New Orleans during the 1910s. Charles Watzke worked tirelessly to help his community weather the fallout from the 1918–19 Spanish influenza pandemic, just as his grandson would do in Ocala during the COVID-19 pandemic more than one hundred years later.[9] The period from November 1918 to March 1919 was remembered by film exhibitors as "the funless season," when celebrities fell ill, productions halted, and theaters were shut down across the country.[10] When New Orleans was ravaged by the pandemic and movies theaters closed, Charles Watzke helped found the city's first projectionist union and worked to ensure that exhibitors were able to keep food on their table.[11]

The Ocala Drive-In has its own long and unique history as well. It first opened in 1948 as the Dyer Drive-In, owned and operated by its namesake, Ira Dyer. At the time it was only one of twenty-two drive-ins in all of Florida and of 820 across the country.[12] After several slow years, Ira Dyer sold the property to Johnny West, who renamed it the Ocala Drive-In, which soon tapped into the growing appeal that the B-movie market and late-night screenings had to teenagers. Johnny West eventually became known by Ocala teens as the "scourge of lovers" for his nightly patrols during the late-night screenings. "We all feared Johnny West," said Steve Mosley, a 1959 graduate of Ocala High School and frequent drive-in patron as a teen, in a 2002 interview with the *Ocala Star-Banner*: "He used to patrol the lanes with a flashlight, shining it into your car. If he caught you messing around with a girl in the back seat, you were thrown out."[13]

By 1960, there were over four thousand drive-ins across the United States, and the Ocala Drive-In too became a weekend fixture for grind-house double features—many of which were filmed in Florida. That same year, West, who had decided to pursue a career in law enforcement, sold his drive-in to a partnership made between a husband and wife, Lou and Sheri Williams, and brothers George and Brad Tomlinson. For the next half century, the drive-in was operated by the Williams-Tomlinson families until its sudden closure in 2002. Unlike most drive-ins, which declined due to a downturn in attendance, urban encroachment, rising land prices, and the advent of Daylight Savings Time (which caused even later showtimes), the Ocala Drive-In continued to thrive right up until the end of its first closure.[14] Lou Williams, who served as the drive-in's resident owner, explained that, although his "popular family night-spot could have run forever," forty-two years had been long enough. Co-owner George Tomlinson felt the drive-in's switch to second-run features did not have much of a place in the early 2000s exhibition market: "There's just not much of a window for second-run theaters like this anymore. If people miss a movie at the theater, they just say they'll catch it on video."[15]

In 2010, John and Charlie Watzke purchased the property and officially reopened the Ocala Drive-In the following year. After working with his brother on restoring and remodeling the drive-in, Charlie returned to Mississippi to purchase and restore their hometown Beacon Theater in Waveland, which had been destroyed during Hurricane Katrina.[16] John Watzke stayed on in Ocala and continued to work to revitalize the drive-in's place as a community fixture. In addition to reintroducing first-run screenings at the Ocala Drive-In, he has aided customers in projecting wedding proposals and high school "promposal" messages and has rented out the grounds for boy scout and girl scout camping weekends.

One hundred years after their grandfather helped theater employees and moviegoers endure the Spanish influenza pandemic, both Watzke brothers did their part to see their communities through another pandemic. In Waveland, Charlie Watzke opened a "Temporary Drive-In" where he projected movies on the exterior wall of the Beacon Theater. Although on the first night of showing the screen experienced a few mishaps, including poor weather and a swarm of termites that covered the screen, he took it all in stride, quipping to the *Seacoast Echo*, "We still have a few bugs to work out."[17] The following evening he purchased a fogger to keep mosquitoes and termites away, and held out for better weather. With the blessing of the Mississippi governor's office, the Beacon was able to screen second-run films such as *Jaws* (1975), *Ghost Rider* (2007), *Terminator* (1984), and *Aliens* (1979) at the cost of five dollars per person. The only condition was that customers purchase concessions "so we can afford to pay the bills and keep this going."[18] Throughout the tumultuous spring and summer of 2020, Charlie Watzke used the magic of the movies to give members of the Waveland community a needed moment of relief and respite.

Meanwhile in Ocala, John Watkze worked with smaller film distributors to secure new releases, a wider disruption had started to occur across the entire motion picture industry. In April 2020, *Trolls World Tour* (2020) premiered on video-on-demand to an estimated $100 million in box-office receipts from its first weekend alone. For the premium price of twenty dollars, customers could purchase the film to view anytime within a forty-eight-hour window. The financial return was not far behind the initial $116 million that *Trolls* (2016) grossed during its first three weeks at the box office. In response to Universal Studios' decision to premiere the film digitally, AMC Theaters issued a ban against exhibiting all Universal-affiliated productions at its theaters.[19] Unfazed by AMC's action and more than pleased by the success of *Trolls World Tour*'s digital premiere, NBCUniversal CEO Jeff Shell told the *Wall Street Journal*, "As soon as theaters reopen, we expect to release movies on both formats."[20]

One of the first testing grounds for this mixed-mode digital/in-person premiere was none other than the Ocala Drive-In, which was one of twenty-five drive-in theaters that contributed an additional $60,000 in revenue to the film's on-demand premiere.[21] Industry presses initially decried this mixed-distribution method could mean that *Trolls World Tour* would go down in film history as "the movie that killed theaters."[22] The pandemic has simply accelerated ongoing changes in how films are distributed and exhibited. Meanwhile the ascent of streaming platforms has since caused the further decentering of Hollywood's place as the center of gravity of the American motion picture industry.

"The Last Dinosaur Standing"

The story of the Ocala Drive-In helping the domestic box office to persevere through the worst days of the COVID-19 lockdown was not the first (and certainly will not be the last) time all eyes turned to Florida as a major transition occurred in the American motion picture industry. Often overlooked in its contribution to the history of motion pictures, Florida has a long and contentious relationship with the motion picture industry. This relationship has produced iconic entertainment that played an essential role in establishing trends within the American motion picture industry and would define how state and local governments ultimately influence the trajectory of how visual entertainment is produced and consumed in the United States.

This book will examine the sometimes cooperative and often combative efforts made by film producers and local movie boosters to turn Florida into a "third coast" of the American motion picture industry, as assorted Florida communities hosted major and minor film and television productions over the past 125 years. The story of filmmaking in Florida raises the question, what might the American motion picture industry have looked like if it had not been encumbered by the hegemony of the Hollywood studio system? Unlike California, where production has consistently been centered around Los Angeles, at different times over the past one hundred years Florida has had several different major production hubs.

It is important to state upfront that in no way does this book suggest that Florida could have become an "Almost Hollywood" or "Hollywood East." Instead, the statewide effort to create an integrated network of film offices with an emphasis on community building offers a fascinating glimpse into what a decentralized motion picture industry could look like in the United States. As the entertainment industry grapples with the implications of the COVID-19 pandemic and streaming revolution, the story of Florida's motion picture industry provides an exciting alternative narrative for American film history and a potential roadmap for the future.

For more than 125 years, different Florida communities emerged as important film production centers. In the 1910s, Jacksonville outproduced Los Angeles nearly 2–1 in the number of films made in North Florida and the number of production companies active in the city. In the 1930s, Tampa Bay set out to convince Hollywood studios to build a "second West Coast" on Weedon Island. A decade later, in the 1940s and 1950s, when Hollywood again came calling, Ocala and its surrounding environs became an important testing ground for on-location shooting that would later become the template for present-day "runaway" productions. In the 1950s and 1960s, Miami hosted one of the largest concentrations of television studios outside of Burbank, while the state's beaches, swamplands, and natural landscape inspired a generation of iconic B movies. After repeatedly losing productions to its rival Georgia in the 1970s, the creation of a statewide production agency would eventually culminate, in the 1980s and 1990s, with Florida emerging as the third-largest production center in the United States.

During the first decades of the twenty-first century, the state experienced an incredible boom in film and television productions, despite increasing competition from emerging film industries in Canada and other southern

U.S. states. However, a drastic shift in policy toward tax incentives and the collapse of industry support from the Florida Legislature in the 2010s signaled a decline in the statewide motion picture industry, which, at the time of writing this book, remains in recovery. If there is one thing that has remained constant in Florida's motion picture industry, from the 1910s to the 2020s, it is the moving image's vital role in community building and ability to offer much-needed reassurance to audiences in need of a momentary escape.

"It's really nice to see the families getting out here and they feel normal, and that's the thing. To me mental stability is just as important as physical stability," John Watzke explained in an April 2020 interview with WCJB-TV News in Gainesville.[23] Even as a relative newcomer to the state, John Watzke helped to create a sense of community and purpose during a time of crisis and need. In this narrative history of the Florida film industry, which includes business owners, community organizers, educators, filmmakers, and local politicians, one recurring theme comes to light: that visionary outsiders who understood viewers' universal desire for escapism exploited, with the state's support, the ambiguities and hypocrisies of the motion picture industry to help make the Sunshine State shine.

While this book will showcase plenty of moments when Florida's motion picture industry basked in the sun, we will also need to weather more than a fair share of sudden summer storms. The relationship between Florida and the motion picture industry is just as stormy and unpredictable as the state's weather. The promise of "fun in the sun" and never-ending summer has been what has brought tourists, snowbirds, and an ever-increasing number of new arrivals (almost 1,000 new residents per day starting in 2000) have brought with them new streams of commerce and development.[24]

The story of Florida's relationship with the motion picture industry overlaps with the most pivotal moments in its rise as one of the most consequential states in terms of demographics, economics, and politics in modern America. At the turn of the twentieth century, when the first movie cameras turned their lenses toward Florida, the thirty-second-most-populous U.S. state, with an estimated half million inhabitants, and no major town or city with a population of over 35,000 people.[25] In one hundred years, Florida's population grew from just over a half million in 1900 to over 16 million in 2000, and over 21 million in 2020, becoming the third-most-populous state in the country.

The demographic explosion Florida has experienced over the past half century, combined with the state's $1 trillion economy, have turned Florida into one of the most essential players in American cultural, economic, and political life.[26] The state's rapid evolution has in turn been shaped by real estate, transportation, and tourism, all influenced in varying degrees by the image of Florida that has been cultivated in visual media.

This book attempts to explain why Florida has failed to maintain a stable statewide film and television production industry while states such as New York and California (and, to a lesser extent, Louisiana, Georgia, North Carolina, Montana, Utah, and Texas) have flourished. Although Florida is geographically the southernmost state in the continental United States, its development has a trajectory more like that of the western frontier. The comparison between "sister sunbelt states" Florida and California is especially enlightening in the context of the parallels between both state's histories. Both were admitted as states within five years of one another, in 1845 and 1850, respectively, and although California experienced a population boom following the 1848 Gold Rush, it had a comparatively slow but steady population growth until the twentieth century. At the turn of the twentieth century, just as the first filmmakers arrived in Southern California and North Florida, both states experienced massive population and economic surges, as each state cultivated its own distinct image as a fair-weather playground.

Between 1908 and 1910, a small California village called Hollywood, which at the time was best known for its orange groves, produced only two confirmed short films: *The Count of Monte Cristo* (1908) and *In Old California* (1910), while the film studios in Florida, founded by subsidiaries of the Edison Manufacturing Company (EMC), produced over one hundred short subjects during two successful seasons, earning Jacksonville the nickname the "World's Winter Film Capital."[27] In less than ten years, Hollywood would come to dominate the American film industry, while motion picture production in Jacksonville—and across Florida—had all but collapsed, with many of the producers who first filmed in Florida for its distinct climate and environment opting for California instead.

The rise and sudden fall of North Florida's film industry in the early twentieth century set a pattern that has since repeated itself across the history of motion picture production in Florida ever since. Since Jacksonville's heyday as a film production hub in the 1910s, other parts of Florida have also sought to win back the producers it had lost: Tampa Bay in the 1930s, Ocala in the 1940s–50s, Miami during the 1960s–80s, and Orlando in the 1990s.

During times of major disturbances in the American motion picture industry, the spotlight would occasionally return to Florida. In the early 1930s, the transition to sound temporarily made the sprawling studio backlots obsolete in favor of self-contained soundstages. In the 1940s–50s, the widespread availability of Technicolor and improvements in camera mobility allowed for a return to location-based filmmaking. Labor unrest in the film and television industry between the 1960s and 1980s, along with the onset of "runaway" productions in the 1990s, provided the state with distinctive opportunities to build up a strong regional production industry.

By the 2000s and 2010s, Miami had emerged as a regularly sought-after location for cable and premium television networks. Miami was hit hard, however, by the advent of streaming platforms, and the city couldn't compete with the tax incentives that emerging film centers in such cities as Atlanta, New Orleans, and Wilmington offered for "runaway" productions. In other words, the history of motion picture production in Florida has continually cycled between moments of opportunity and loss. The state's role as a "year-round playground" has attracted filmmakers for over a century. As the motion picture industry continues to reorient itself from the COVID-19 pandemic, the story of the relationship between the state of Florida and the American motion picture industry can serve as an important point of reference toward understanding what happens next.

Although the Ocala Drive-In's place at the top of the U.S. box office was momentary and minimal, at least from the perspective of the motion picture industry in a larger sense, its contribution to moviegoers offered an intrinsic value on an individual level that cannot be measured. Moments like John Watzke's publicity stunt at the Ocala Drive-In during the spring of 2020 have defined Florida's role in the wider workings of the American motion picture industry. Regardless of changing industry dynamics, disruptions to distribution networks, and even a global pandemic, audiences will continue to seek respite from the uncertainty of the world beyond the screen.

History Repeats Itself

For the past one hundred years, Florida's motion picture industry has experienced several major boom-bust cycles. It has usually gone something like this: A Florida city starts to draw interest from outside producers, and the industry begins to take off, gaining local financial and community support. Eventually, either because of political obstruction, bad business, or due to institutional changes in the motion picture industry itself, the momentum slows, relations between producers and local politicians deteriorate, and Florida again experiences an exodus of film and television productions.

The first and perhaps best example of the tug-pull relationship between Florida politicians and the motion picture industry can be found in the political career of John Wellborn Martin, who was elected mayor of Jacksonville from 1917 to 1923, and governor of Florida from 1925 to 1929. During Martin's three terms as mayor, he introduced three recurring themes into his approach

Figure 1. James Adkins (*right*), 33, and a friend chat before the movie begins while remaining socially distant at the Ocala Drive-In, April 2020. Copyright WUFT News/ University of Florida. Photographer: Hope Hathcock. Reprinted with permission.

to government: "demands for liberality, common sense, and a businessman's administration."[28] When Martin won a surprise victory in the Florida gubernatorial election, he called for balanced representation between Florida's urban and rural areas and made sure to cultivate relationships with out-of-state investors to help build the state's infrastructure.

In his appraisal of John W. Martin's time in office, Florida historian William Cash has described the achievements of Martin's governorship as closely resembling "the hero of one of Horatio Alger's stories so that it made voters believe his election would greatly stimulate the development and progress of Florida."[29] Historian Victoria McDonell further credits Martin's "businessman's administration" as one of the defining reasons that Florida moved toward embracing "the prospects of increased industry and tourism," which helped the state "leap from its past agricultural orientation into a modern, urban-oriented future."[30] Governor Martin's opening message to the Florida Congress in 1925 clearly expresses his views on how to organize the state budget and economy: "Florida needs capital, and must have it, in the building and establishing of her industries. She needs labor, also, and must have it. One without the other, though in abundance, will not suffice. No statute should be enacted inimical to either."[31]

According to John Martin, the source for an infusion of capital was simple—the legislature needed to revamp the state's corporation laws: "Consideration should be given to amending our general corporation laws so as to make it attractive for businesspeople to incorporate and transact business in Florida under the most favorable conditions."[32] Such legislation would play an instrumental role in keeping Florida financially solvent after the collapse of the state economy with the end of the Florida Land Boom, followed by the destruction wrought by two calamitous hurricanes in 1926 and 1928. Governor Martin's ability to bridge Florida's urban-rural political divide through his infrastructure initiatives, have historically placed him as one of the most important figures to help trigger Florida's transformation from "from Old South to New South, to Sunbelt South" and as the "catalyst for the emergence of modern Florida."[33] These policies eventually helped the state endure the trials and tribulations of the Great Depression and create the conditions that would bring about Florida's post–World War II economic and population boom.[34]

Yet, even as Governor Martin created the conditions that promoted industries Florida is best known for today (aerospace, agriculture, information technology, manufacturing, tourism), his seemingly forward-thinking vision for the state's destiny did not include motion pictures. If a label can be assigned to his views, it would be that of a moderate with "a mix of progressive and conservative stands." When asked about his politics directly, Martin would simply respond, "Governments should be supported by men and not men by governments."[35] Given this mindset, it could be argued that Martin's disagreement with the motion picture producers was rooted in the early film industry's innate dependency on financial and institutional support from taxpayers and civic organizers.

When Martin was elected mayor of Jacksonville in 1917, the city was home to dozens of films studios, which he played an instrumental role in dismantling. In terms of cash flow, movies were the third-most-profitable business in the city, right after the steel and oil industries.[36] According to a report in the *Florida Metropolis* from 1923, one year before Martin's election, the growing number of production companies in North Florida would in due time become "one of the biggest factors in the future prosperity of Florida, a factor which gives us an endless amount of free advertising, which is worth millions of dollars to the State."[37]

John Martin's election as mayor of Jacksonville in 1917 was the spark that led to the collapse of North Florida's burgeoning film industry.[38] To defeat incumbent mayor J.E.T. Bowden in the 1917 mayoral election, the Martin campaign sought the support from a small but vocal faction of virulent anti-movie crusaders who expressed their ire at the disturbances caused by the so-called movie people. Bowden, for his part, had meanwhile earned the nickname of "Movie Mayor" and was known throughout the city for his close ties to the producers and filmmakers who had built their studios in his city.

Since much of J.E.T. Bowden's campaign was financially sponsored by film producers who had built a profitable working relationship with the Bowden administration, Jacksonville's mayoral race became a proxy referendum on how the city felt about the "movie people." Martin defeated Bowden by a narrow margin, and as soon as he took office, all the goodwill between the studios and the city evaporated. In his first week as mayor, Martin initiated a series of "anti-vice" crackdowns in line with the state's ruling Prohibition Party, which by the end of the year had sent filmmakers and producers running for the exit.[39]

During the mid-1920s, then governor Martin was lobbied by real estate speculators who were frenetically selling shares in proposed "studio cities" intended to rival California communities such as Burbank, Culver City, Hollywood, and Universal City, to name a few. Although the overspeculation that accompanied the 1920s Florida Land Boom was in part fueled by the Martin administration's support for the relentless pace of development across the state, it is interesting to note his continued reluctance to support incentives that could have promoted Florida's entertainment industry at the same time.

In contrast to his carefully constructed image as the "pro-business politician," Governor Martin refused to lend support to one of the few real estate deals during the land boom that, with the proper oversight, could have truly benefited the state. Throughout his political career, Martin remained an ardent opponent of incentivizing what was formerly his home city's third-largest industry to return to the state. It is difficult to fully gauge how Martin's personal political beliefs may have influenced his seemingly antagonistic policy choices concerning the film industry.

With every bust, a boom soon followed. Florida's film industry has had many notable champions in the Governor's Mansion as well. In an abrupt policy change toward the film industry, Martin's immediate successors as governor, Doyle Carlton (1929–33) and David Sholtz (1933–37), both supported the creation of a statewide motion picture committee, and each regularly corresponded with Hollywood producers who were interested in building a permanent studio city near Tampa Bay. Later in the 1960s and 1970s, Governors Claude Kirk (1967–71) and Reubin Askew (1971–79) both battled with an initially skeptical legislature in their efforts to turn the state into a "Hollywood

South." In the process, they helped to encourage a boon for independent film producers and television networks filming in the state.

By 1978, Florida boasted the third-largest statewide motion picture production industry in the United States, behind only New York and California, and the following year, with the inauguration of Governor Bob Graham (1979–87), the state motion picture industry acquired one of its greatest allies yet. During his eight years as governor, Graham made dozens of trips to Los Angeles, even helping to convince NBC to shoot *Miami Vice* (1984–89) on location in South Florida, inspiring both Miami's rise as major television production center, and the creation of Universal Studios Florida, and Disney-MGM Studios in Orlando.

Going into the 2000s, Florida's role as a major regional contributor to the American film and television industry seemed unassailable. In 2007, Governor Jeb Bush (1999–2007) continued this support by sponsoring $25 million in funding for the Florida Entertainment Industry Incentive Program (FEIIP), to "encourage the use of this state as a site for filming and to develop and sustain the workforce and infrastructure for film and entertainment production."[40] Bush's successor, Charlie Crist (2007–11), followed this with a bipartisan $242 million tax incentive plan to support producers interested in filming in Florida, one of the most sweeping pieces of pro-movie legislation the state had seen in one hundred years.[41]

The collapse of film and television production in Florida during the 2010s and 2020s eerily parallels the exodus of film producers that the state experienced a hundred years earlier in the 1910s and 1920s. This most recent downturn began when the Florida Legislature refused to renew the incentive programs that the Bush and Crist administrations had introduced, instead opting to let the tax breaks expire. In 2014, a powerful libertarian-leaning lobby organization known as Americans for Prosperity (AFP), sponsored by billionaire lobbyists Charles and David Koch, directly provided the maximum number of campaign donations for more than fifty members of the Florida House of Representatives who opposed incentives during that year's election. Then governor Rick Scott (2011–19) also echoed many of the fiscally conservative attitudes utilized during John Martin's "businessman's administration" in the 1920s.

During Governor Scott's reelection campaign in 2014, he promised voters to oversee a state government that was centered around "rebuilding the economy and slashing government spending."[42] In October 2016, a group of dedicated film lobbyists began a campaign to extend the Crist and Bush–era incentive programs, to which Florida Speaker of the House Richard Corcoran (2016–18) responded by launching a destructive anti-incentive platform,

Figure 2. Eric Raddatz's cover article in *Florida Weekly* from June 2017 highlights the collapse of Florida's motion picture industry following the legislature's refusal to approve any further statewide tax incentives for big-budget film and television productions. Eric Raddatz/Florida Weekly

describing the previous administration's support for film incentives by referring to such policies as "corporate welfare."[43] Corcoran's successor, José Oliva (2018–20), similarly labeled such policies "de facto socialism."[44] Corcoran, Oliva, and Florida's two most recent House Speakers, Chris Sprowls (2020–22) and Paul Renner (2022–Present), each earned an A+ on AFP-Florida's

"Economic Freedom Scorecard," receiving substantial campaign support from the organization.[45]

According to AFP communications director Andrew Malave, "It's not the government's role to pick winners and losers. The film industry is an important part of the economy, but the legislature should implement policies that benefit businesses across the board."[46] As we will see in the pages ahead, it is this ongoing ideological divide in Florida politics that has led to the question of whether the state should take on a facilitative or assistive role toward supporting a statewide motion picture industry. The answer will depend on the economic and political context of life in Florida at any given time.

The "Florida Imaginary" on the Screen

Florida's role in the American film industry has certainly had more than its fair share of ups and downs. Since the first images of Florida flickered across viewfinders in kinetoscope parlors and flimsy screens at vaudeville houses in the 1890s, the state has experienced a continual cycle of moments of cooperation and conflict between Florida's government and the motion picture industry.

This book examines how the state of Florida and the American motion picture industry have intrinsically influenced one other. To adequately relay this over-a-century-long narrative history of filmmaking in Florida, this book will examine trade press sources, periodicals, local newspapers, and the personal papers of filmmakers and politicians to help explain the various factors behind the repeated rise, fall, and resurrection of the state's motion picture industry. By exploring selected moments in the history of Florida's motion picture industry, this work will showcase the men and women who have helped to make sure the Sunshine State has continued to stay in the spotlight.

Since the first cameras started rolling in Key West in 1898, Florida has consistently boasted five basic advantages that have made it a competitive film center: (1) weather/climate, (2) transportation, (3) government relations, (4) labor costs, and (5) land costs.[47] Unlike other leading industries in the state like real estate, transportation, or tourism, where Florida's state and local governments have been able to leverage a certain degree of control over how new businesses were managed, the motion picture industry has proven to operate as an entity unto itself. Quite often, the motion picture industry's relationship with Florida was just as often influenced by industry developments happening outside of the state in New York or California.[48]

The Florida state government has historically sought to institute major incentives for filmmaking and empower administrative agencies to implement them.[49] The adoption or rejection of legislation that benefits filmmakers, as well as providing easy-to-use permitting forms, and with abundance of grants and assistance have contributed to the failure or success of Florida's film industry.[50] In periods when the state worked closely with producers and filmmakers to create a cooperative environment for their projects, Florida became one of the most sought-after destinations for filmmakers outside of California or New York.

Whenever state politicians turned ambivalent or outright hostile to the "movie people," producers immediately began to look elsewhere. In 1917, the result was a mass exodus of filmmakers from Florida to California. By 2016, many producers looked to Georgia, Louisiana, and North Carolina, so that Florida-set films and television shows like *Live by Night* (2016), *Gifted* (2017), *On Becoming a God in Central Florida* (2019), *Killing It* (2022–Present), and, perhaps most astonishingly of all, *Florida Man* (2023), used Florida as a setting but operated their productions from out of state. *Motion Picture Paradise* will set out to explain the environmental characteristics that inspired filmmakers to come to Florida, along with examining sociopolitical circumstances that shaped the success and failure of the state's motion picture industry over the past century.

This work is the sum of decades of impressive scholarship carried out by an incredibly dedicated array of film scholars and enthusiasts. In the 1950s, James C. Craig, a journalist for the *Florida Times-Union*, helped compile one of the first narrative accounts of Florida's early film history. In addition to his PhD dissertation, "Florida and the American Motion Picture Industry" (1980), Richard Alan Nelson has also contributed dozens of articles and a book, *Lights! Camera! Florida!* (1991), that has helped to draw an essential road map to Florida film history, with which all future studies must start. James Ponti's *Hollywood East* (1992) also provides an excellent snapshot of an incredibly exciting moment in Central Florida's film and television industry, as well as a thorough catalogue of films and TV shows made in Florida from the early twentieth century to the early 1990s. Robert Ingalls and Susan Fernández's *Sunshine in the Dark* (2006), Susan Doll and David Morrow's *Florida on Film* (2007), and Shawn Bean's *The First Hollywood* (2008) each contributed substantially to an understanding of the state's deep and nuanced film history. More recently, Barbara Tepa Lupack's *Richard E. Norman and Race Filmmaking* (2014) and Thomas Graham's *Silent Films in St. Augustine* (2017) have provided essential new insights into the state's early film history.

Although *Motion Picture Paradise* will by no means attempt to tell a "total history" of motion picture production in Florida, it does seek to synthesize many competing accounts of the state's film and television industry into a comprehensive narrative from its beginnings to the relative present. This is a story that can be told in five acts:

Chapter 1, "This Venture Was Epoch-Making" (1898–1925), addresses the history of silent film production in North Florida from the arrival of the Edison Manufacturing Company in Jacksonville in 1908 on through to the ill-fated attempts to build "motion picture cities" in South Florida and on the Gulf Coast during the 1920s land boom. By 1916, the city of Jacksonville had become a major center of film production for the emerging American motion picture industry. The election of Governor Sidney Catts in 1916 made film producers wary of taking advantage of Florida's natural landscape and film-friendly environment. The controversial election of John Martin as Jacksonville mayor ended North Florida's reign as a regional film center, while the erratic nature of the Catts administration discouraged investors from attempting to relocate elsewhere in the state. The completion of Henry Flagler's East Florida Railway and Governor Napoleon Broward's Everglades drainage project essentially turned the small fishing village of Miami into an "instant city" as affiliates of the Edison Manufacturing Company (EMC) traveled to South Florida for location-based filming. Despite these efforts, early attempts by local boosters to attract the film industry to Florida during the silent era were all met with departure and disappointment.

Chapter 2, "Of Course They Please the Southern People" (1908–1928), examines the contrasts in racial representation in films produced in Jacksonville during the Jim Crow segregation era. These tensions will be examined through exploring how motion picture consumption factored into the politics of race in one of the largest cities in the New South during cinema's silent era. This will be accomplished by exploring how marginalized and disenfranchised people attempted to assert agency in public and private spaces despite living in an environment of white supremacy and social inequities. Through tracing the lived experiences of African American moviegoers in Florida at the onset of the Jim Crow era, the early American film industry's dismissiveness and, at times, outright insensitivity toward acts of political terror against African Americans can be better understood. Meanwhile, the abandoned studio grounds of Jacksonville's Arlington neighborhood became home to Richard Norman Studios—the first and only studio dedicated to the production of race films in the country. At roughly the same time in Tampa, activists from the National Association for the Advancement of Colored People (NAACP) and Florida-based civil rights organizers set out to upend the horrific stereotypes and caricatures of Black life portrayed in films such as D. W. Griffith's *Birth of a Nation* (1915). This chapter will track the intersection between identity and agency in storytelling from the perspective of African American filmmakers and their allies during the most of oppressive years of the Jim Crow system.

Chapter 3, "Motion Pictures at a Great Saving!" (1922–1945), opens with the 1920s Florida Land Boom and how it influenced the creation of Associated Authors Productions in Orlando and to build a proposed "second Universal City" in Miami. Riding on the crest of the Florida Land Boom, local boosters attempted to create various studio cities across Central Florida and along the state's West Coast. Each of these fly-by-night ventures succumbed almost as quickly as they began due to misappropriation of funds, investor fraud, or lack of interest either by filmmakers or the local communities. To complicate matters further, Florida suffered a series of successive disasters caused by the 1926 Miami and 1928 Okeechobee hurricanes followed by the onset of the Great Depression. Unchecked development inspired several questionable film promoters in the Tampa Bay area to pledge that they could turn Florida's West Coast into a "Second Los Angeles." Through the efforts of real estate promoter Trenton Collins, several producers would attempt to build a permanent studio in Tampa Bay. A combination of unprofessionalism and an overall lack of structural organization caused each of these ventures to eventually fail. Following the failure of the Davis and Weedon Island studios in the 1930s, Florida once more became an only occasionally sought-after location for filmmakers.

Chapter 4, "The Business Can Kill You Anyway" (1938–1971), tells how filmmaking at Silver Springs and Ocala National Forest helped to inspire a statewide "movie tourism" industry. With the advent of the grind-house and B-movie film craze of the 1950s, Florida became a lucrative location to offer a cheap and affordable alternative for low-budget producers. The unexpected box-office success of *Creature from the Black Lagoon* (1954) brought on a series of low-budget, independently produced horror and comedy films across the state. Orlando-based filmmaker R. John Hugh's Empire Studios and Thomas Casey's Shamrock Studios worked to turn Winter Park into an entertainment center several years before Walt Disney announced plans for his "Florida Project." At the same time, another popular children's entertainer, a Hungarian-born immigrant named Ivan Tors, built his own studio in South Florida, while CBS and NBC each began to develop their own studio cities in the greater Miami area. The popularity of Tors's children's television programming and films such as *Flipper* (1963), *Zebra in the Kitchen* (1965), and *Gentle*

Ben (1967–69) helped popularize the idea of Florida as a place of adventure and wonder for a new generation of audiences.

Chapter 5, "Assurances of Full Cooperation" (1971–2005), examines how Governor Reubin Askew's (1971–79) "Open Letter to the Motion Picture Industry" initiated an unprecedented moment of statewide cooperation with the motion picture industry. Working in tandem with his predecessor Governor Claude Kirk's (1967–71) courtship of the Walt Disney Corporation, Askew sought to increase the prevalence and presence of film and television productions in the state to help bolster its fledgling economy following the onset of the 1973–75 recession. Meanwhile, social upheavals in South Florida in 1980 (including the Mariel Boatlift and McDuffie Rebellion) created the perception of South Florida as a "Paradise Lost," bringing negative publicity to the region, but also captivated the imagination of filmmakers and television producers who hoped to create iconic programming around this perceived image. The additional funding and tourism inspired by such programs led to an economic resurgence across South Florida. Organizations such as the Florida Motion Picture and Television Association (FMPTA) and Florida Motion Picture and Television Bureau (FMPTB) sought to further reinforce Governor Bob Graham's lobbying efforts with film producers. This in turn would lead to the creation of Disney-MGM and Universal Studios in Orlando, which both allowed their visitors and national film and television audiences to "ride the movies."

The End Credits, "Like a Flip of a Switch" (2006–Present), picks up just as production activity winds down in Central Florida during the mid-2000s, and the center of gravity of the statewide production industry once again shifts to South Florida. As the South Florida television industry experienced a resurgence after a series of tax incentives were initiated during the Jeb Bush and Charlie Crist administrations, Florida established an open policy of cooperation with the Office of Film and Entertainment (OFE). These efforts toward cooperation came to a grinding halt when the Florida Legislature denied requests to extend the incentives legislation after the funds were completely spent in 2016. This shift in disposition would again spark a heated debate between politicians and lobbyists over Florida's future as a motion picture production center.

Since this is a developing story that will continue beyond the publication of this book, this final segment will address only the major beats of the state's decline in production following the expiration of production tax incentives as Florida continues to come to terms with the rise of rival regional film centers across the South such as Georgia, Louisiana, North Carolina, and Texas.

The sensational history of Florida's motion picture industry includes within it a well-drawn storyboard of how Florida could once more return to

Figure 3. Gene Gauntier and the Kalem Players at the start of production for their *Sunny South* series in Jacksonville during the 1908–9 winter season. Courtesy of Academy of Motion Picture Arts and Sciences/Margaret Herrick Library.

the spotlight in the post pandemic world. During the 1908–9 winter season, a troupe of actors and crew members from the Kalem Company arrived in Jacksonville to shoot their *Florida Series* of short films. Twenty years later, long after Jacksonville was abandoned as a film center, the company's lead actress and director, Gene Gauntier, fondly recollected her time in North Florida. In a short autobiography written for *Woman's Home Companion,* Gauntier noted that, despite her initial misgivings over Jacksonville's relative isolation from the metropolises of the Northeast, she was won over by the warmth and hospitality of her Floridian hosts. In reflecting on her time in Florida during those early years, she remarked, "[W]e discovered a moving picture paradise."[51] In short, the story of Florida on film is one of a paradise found and lost by mainstream filmmakers and showrunners, but it is also one of a refuge where only the most creative and rebellious visual storytellers can find their voice and bring the American motion picture industry firmly into the twenty-first century.

1

"This Venture Was Epoch-Making"

Florida's Early Twentieth-Century Movie Boom, 1898–1925

> For the moving picture industry this venture was almost epoch-making, establishing as it did new artistic standards, particularly in atmosphere and inaugurating the custom of traveling far and wide in search of effective and authentic backgrounds . . . Our departure created a sensation in the industry. Partly because of the significant influence exerted by this venture on the making of motion pictures and partly because the story of our life in Florida presents such a contrast to life as it is now led in Hollywood.
>
> Gene Gauntier, "Blazing the Trail," 1928

March 1898: Florida Enters the Picture

Florida's relationship with the moving image is nearly as old as the American motion picture industry itself. The first images of Florida flashed across the screen in April 1898, when the Edison Manufacturing Company (EMC) traveled to Key West and Tampa to capture footage of the impending U.S. invasion of Cuba during the Spanish-American War. Five years earlier, in August 1893, inventor William Kennedy Laurie (W.K.L.) Dickson's Kinetoscope first premiered at the Brooklyn Institute of Arts and Sciences. Dickson was a protégé of Thomas Edison and first perfected his device while under contract at Edison's West Orange Laboratory in New Jersey. Unveiled as "Edison's Greatest Marvel" despite the Wizard of Menlo Park's limited involvement in the device's invention process, Edison did provide financial support and the resources Dickson needed to come up with increasingly engaging and interesting short film subjects. Between 1892 and 1896, Dickson's short subjects were filmed on the grounds of Edison's West Orange Laboratories in a tar-paper-covered dark studio room with a retractable roof, which loosely resembled a police paddy wagon, or, as it was popularly nicknamed at the time, the "Black Maria."[1] These early self-contained subjects with seconds-long images that gradually increased in narrative complexity.[2] In the years to come, W.K.L. Dickson continued to tinker with his novel new invention and add new components to it.

On April 23, 1896, Dickson's latest invention, a device that was unveiled as "Edison's Greatest Wonder" at Koster and Bial's Music Hall in New York City. The sensation in the press over Dickson's short film subjects, left both he and Edison to contemplate where else they could turn their cameras. One of the earliest opportunities Dickson had to take his Vitagraph camera into the field came surely enough on February 15, 1898, when the naval cruiser USS *Maine* mysteriously exploded in Havana Harbor, killing 266 American sailors.[3] Growing tensions between the United States and the Spanish Empire presented a prime opportunity to show the full extent of what the motion picture was capable of. Yellow journalists Joseph Pulitzer and William Randolph Hearst had, since 1895, inflamed public opinion in the United States toward war with Spain. In the aftermath of the *Maine* crisis, Hearst, especially, jumped to the conclusion that the *Maine* had been sunk by a Spanish mine, and plastered across his *New York Journal* the slogan, "Remember the Maine, To Hell With Spain!"[4] To help excite public support for an American invasion of Cuba, Hearst's *Journal* hired cameraman William Paley, who had previously worked with Dickson at the Black Maria, to travel to Florida and survey the reaction of Tampa's large Cuban expatriate community. With this new mission in mind, Dickson and Edison rebranded their Vitagraph as the "Wargraph" and requested that Hearst grant the use of his yachts to send their Wargraph cameramen to the front lines. The plan was to travel to Florida and film a series of short one-shot films capturing the movements of American troops in Tampa, then travel to the Florida Keys to record the departure of the USS *Iowa* from the Dry Tortugas.

On March 27, 1898, five weeks after the *Maine* sunk, a military funeral was held for the fallen sailors in Key West, Florida. William Paley was on the scene with Hearst journalist Karl C. Decker to make sure the cameras were there rolling as the funeral procession progressed toward Key West Cemetery. *Burial of the "Maine" Victims* (1898) became the first moving images of Florida to flash across the screen.[5] A month after the funeral of the *Maine* sailors, the United States officially declared war on Spain on April 21, 1898. As soon as war was announced, the Port of Tampa became the key strategic point of departure for the American invasion of Cuba. Dozens more motion picture cameramen soon arrived in Florida during the spring and summer of 1898 to

Figure 4. Spanish-American War film reels, 1898. The first three film subjects shot in Florida were by William Paley for Thomas Edison's "Wargraph." *From top to bottom: Burial of the "Maine" Victims, War Correspondents,* and *Rough Riders Embarking for Santiago.* Courtesy of Motion Picture, Broadcasting, and Recorded Sound Division, Library of Congress

document the departure of thirty thousand U.S. servicemen as they embarked for Cuba during the Spanish-American War.

Newsreels like *U.S. Calvary Supplies Unloading at Tampa, Florida* (1898) are an early example of "visual newspapers" intent on keeping American moviegoers up to date on the progression of the Spanish-American War.[6] These short, unassuming wartime "actualities" were barely over a minute long, but played a pivotal role in shaping public support for what U.S Secretary of State John Hay would later call "A Splendid Little War." These crude newsreels dispatched from Florida were displayed in vaudeville houses, kinescope parlors, and storefront theaters across the country, granting large parts of the American public their first glimpses of the country's little-known tropical appendage.

In December 1908, a decade after Edison's Wargraph first came to Florida, Kalem Studios, another Edison-affiliated film company, arrived in Jacksonville to shoot their *Sunny South* series. Kalem came to Jacksonville to take advantage of the city's advertised "272 days of 'clear-cut' sunlight."[7] Jacksonville's accommodating atmosphere, along with its unique landscape (compared to the mostly industrial New York metro area) offered plenty of untapped opportunities to film new and exciting stories that could take full advantage of its tropical environment. Kalem returned to Florida for the 1909–10 winter season, and several more EMC-associated studios followed suit, as Jacksonville in the 1910s became the "World's Winter Film Capital."[8] Like the Spanish-American War "actualities" made in the 1890s, the films produced in Jacksonville during the 1900s and 1910s captured the national imagination and helped introduce Florida to a nation of eager moviegoers.

This chapter traces the story of early filmmaking in Florida against the backdrop of Florida's turbulent economic and political environment during the 1910s and 1920s. It was during this pivotal moment, years before Southern California became the center of gravity for the film industry, that the movies produced in North Florida offered filmmakers an alluring alternative to the corporate consolidation and vertical integration business model that had become popular with early movie moguls like William Fox, Carl Laemmle, Marcus Loew, and Adolph Zukor, among others. Years before the first studio cities were established in Southern California, studios affiliated with the Motion Picture Patents Company (MPPC) like Kalem blazed an entirely different trail in North Florida.

Previous studies on the early history of Florida's motion picture industry have tried to depict Jacksonville in the 1900s and 1910s as "Almost Hollywood," or even "The First Hollywood," however, it is important not to draw a direct comparison between what were two fundamentally different regional production industries (as nice as it would be to imagine Jacksonville neighborhoods such as Arlington, Fairfield, LaVilla, Riverside, or Springfield would have replaced Beverly Hills, Burbank, Culver City, or Venice Beach, as the most filmed neighborhoods in the country).[9] These works on North Florida's early film history have attempted to explain how Florida ultimately "lost out" to California as the capital of the American motion picture industry. This narrative typically pits Jacksonville against Los Angeles as "quite literally a tale of two cities," arguing that Jacksonville "was *this close* to becoming the country's premiere destination for movie production" and could have wrested control of the American motion picture industry away from "that other film town."[10] The problem with this approach is that it relies on the counterfactual assumption that had events gone slightly differently, Hollywood would have somehow replicated itself in Florida. This leaves out the fact that the film industries that emerged in Los Angeles and those that faded from Jacksonville were fundamentally different both in their structure and business model.

The so-called independent producers who would go on to found major Hollywood studios were quite different from the Edison-affiliated MPPC studios that settled in North Florida. Studios like Kalem were from their inception fiercely independent and itinerant. For example, right after completing the 1908–9 winter filming season in Jacksonville, Gene Gauntier and company immediately set sail for Ireland and the Middle East to shoot another series of shorts before returning to Florida the following winter. In other words, the approach to filmmaking that emerged in Florida during the first decades of the twentieth century looked a lot more like the modern-day film industry, and was far more decentralized than the films produced in Hollywood. The story of the first attempt to build a lasting base of operations for film producers in Florida should be seen as a fascinating alternative glimpse into what the American motion picture industry was like before it was consolidated by the Hollywood studio system.

In the two decades after Kalem's first winter stay in Jacksonville, a succession of ambitious filmmakers, producers, investors, and land developers followed in the studio's wake to attempt to build permanent studios and production headquarters in Florida. In its heyday between 1910 and 1917, North Florida consistently outproduced Southern California in its output of films. Ultimately, however, a decisive political shift in state and local politics in 1916 and 1917 sparked an exodus of film studios that put an end to Jacksonville's promise as a major film production center. After the collapse of North Florida's production industry in the 1910s, a series of con men and real estate speculators promised on paper and at times feebly attempted to build flimsy production facilities across the state. These so-called studio cities were modeled after the far more successful Universal City or Paramount Village in Los Angeles. The result was often the same as the ill-fated investments made during the Florida Land Boom of the 1920s: bankruptcy, financial disgrace, and suicide.

"Beyond Them Lay Real Wilderness"

On December 17, 1908, a specially catered Pullman sleeping car steamed ahead into Jacksonville's Flagler Depot after completing its grueling overnight journey along the Atlantic coast. As throngs of tourists, leisure-seekers, and businessmen disembarked, a small cadre of actors and film technicians stepped off the train, where they were met with a balmy brush of mild air that would have been a welcome reprieve from the winter weather they had left behind in New York. There was no stir or fanfare at the station when the "movie people" arrived in Jacksonville. Instead, this small troupe of bohemian performers was, if noticed at all, just another collection of faces amid the city's nearly 100,000 annual winter visitors.[11] The American motion picture industry was still in its infancy, without stars or celebrity filmmakers; in most cases, performers and directors were known only as names that accompanied the short one- or two-reel short subjects that would play primarily in secondhand vaudeville houses and nickelodeons across the country.

The cast and crew of the Kalem Company who set out for Florida during the winter of 1908 did not come simply for leisure or a winter-weather respite. Instead, they were eager to take advantage of the clear skies and temperate climate that could allow the company to meet their high production quota. Gene Gauntier, Kalem's signature "Kalem Girl," who also served as part-time producer and director, recalled her first impressions of the city in her memoir: "We detrained at Jacksonville, which in 1908 was vastly different from the bustling metropolis it is today. The main street was more like a country village than the artery of a town containing some sixty thousand people."[12]

The "country village" that Gauntier and company had arrived in was a community still recovering from a devastating fire that took place in May 1901, which destroyed 466 acres of the city, 146 city blocks, and immolated more than 2,300 buildings.[13] When Kalem came to town in 1908, Jacksonville was just starting to emerge from the ashes of the Great Fire of 1901. In seven short years, the city had become the financial center of Florida and commissioned four skyscrapers that were simultaneously under construction. Jacksonville was still in the process of developing a road network that would extend the paved roads between Jacksonville and the rest of the state. In terms of entertainment, Jacksonville only had two segregated storefront theaters that played films regularly in 1908. The more "respectable" Pastime and Duval theaters, which served as the center of the city's cultural life, hosted art exhibitions, music festivals, performances by the New York Symphony Orchestra, and had even once hosted Broadway luminary Lillian Russell for a special engagement.[14]

Before 1908, North Florida had hosted cameramen who filmed various travelogues and "visual newspaper" short films, but few filmmakers stuck around for an extended stay. Many of the earliest productions that were partially filmed in Florida were made by film crews often on their way to The Bahamas and Cuba. When Kalem arrived in North Florida, it was a relatively new and upcoming film company in the process of rehabilitating itself after a string of financial and legal disasters. Kalem was formed a year earlier, in 1907, as part of a collaboration between film distributor George Kleine and producers Samuel Long and Frank Marion, the company's name being an amalgam of the names of its three founders: Ka (Kleine), Le (Long), M (Marion).[15] In its first summer of operation, the studio shot several short subjects in Upstate New York and New England and soon attracted talent from other New York–based studios such as Biograph, from which director Sidney Olcott and actress Gene Gauntier defected to join the Kalem Players.[16]

The new studio very quickly found itself in hot water, however, when it attempted to adapt Lew Wallace's 1880 novel *Ben-Hur* into a short film. Gene Gauntier wrote the adaptation—she at times carried out double duty both in front of and behind the camera—but the studio failed to secure the adaptation rights either from the Wallace estate or Harper and Brothers, the book's publisher. According to film historian Terry Ramsaye, the consequences of the *Ben-Hur* lawsuit against Kalem had earned the distinction of being "the most costly one reel scenario in the history of the business," and despite favorable box office returns, the company not see any return on investment and instead was "sued with great completeness and vigor."[17] The case would ultimately help to establish the necessity of film studios obtaining motion picture rights to the properties they used for their stories. Although an official court ruling would not be passed down until 1911, the cost of the ongoing legal battle over *Ben-Hur* placed Kalem on unsure footing going into the winter of 1908–9.[18]

The only hope the fledgling production company had to survive another winter would be to lawyer up. As the studio struggled to find funding for both its legal fees, two major shake-ups in the American film industry occurred that presented Kalem with an unexpected (but welcome) chance for redemption. The first such opportunity came in early December 1908, when Thomas Edison and W.K.L. Dickson put an end to a nearly decade-long period of intensive competition and legal disputes between rival film producers, distributors, and manufacturers. The result, known as "the great peace," was a collective of production companies that would pool their patents under the Edison umbrella, with complete financial and legal support from the Wizard of Menlo Park.[19] The newly created Motion Pictures Patents Company (MPPC) was intended to protect producers from potential financial loss in litigation either brought against them by vindictive exhibitors or local politicians or involving charges of copyright infringement. That winter, Kalem also joined the MPPC to cover its legal challenges during its lawsuit against the Wallace estate.

When Kalem joined the Edison Trust, it merged with an impressive roster of New York–based production companies, which also gave the company access to one of the most extensive film distribution networks in the country.

By 1908, however, film producers and exhibitors in New York had become a scapegoat by so-called moral crusaders who railed against the motion picture as an unwanted distraction to the working public and a deterrent from attending church on Sundays. By December 1908, the political attitude toward New York's motion picture industry had grown increasingly hostile as New York mayor George McClellan Jr. (son of Civil War general George McClellan) prepared to revoke the licenses of the city's almost six hundred movie theaters. Just one week after Kalem's arrival in Florida, on Christmas Eve, under orders of the mayor, the New York Police Department began a crackdown campaign that resulted in arrests and fines issued against dozens of exhibitors and producers across the city. The Kalem Players' decision to flee to Florida could not have been better timed.

During the winter of 1908, both MPPC-affiliated studios and Edison's rival "independent" filmmakers started to send scouting expeditions outside of the city, anticipating the mayor's nickelodeon ban. As the political situation against motion picture producers in New York continued to deteriorate, studio owners started to reconsider whether to continue to base their operations in the Northeast.[20] If a city government turned against the industry, both MPPC affiliates and their rival "independent" producers felt the only solution was to spread out their operation either southward to Florida or westward to California. Aside from the unfavorable and increasingly hostile political environment, filming in New York presented other unwanted challenges for producers. Terry Ramsaye recalled, "The motion picture world was widening its horizons. It had outgrown the little rooftop studios of Manhattan and now was fairly started toward making in reality 'all the world's a stage,'" and soon "the studios of New York and Chicago" went "hunting sunshine" with "tentative exploring expeditions to sunnier regions began, including Florida, Cuba, and California."[21]

At the time there were no expensive lighting systems, and indoor studio work relied on available sunlight through glass roof skylights. The growing demand by audiences for content increased the stress on companies in cities whose seasonal weather patterns limited the number of productions they could complete.[22] The harsh cold was especially disruptive to hand-cranked cameras, and the shortened winter daylight hours in northern cities limited the number of hours in which scenarios could be shot. While the New York–based "independents" such as William Fox, Carl Laemmle, and Adolph Zukor would eventually break for Southern California and found studios that continue to dominate the global film industry today, little attention has been paid in the story of early American film to names such as George Kleine, Gene

Gauntier, Frank Marion, and Sidney Olcott, who inspired one of the first attempts to build an active film colony outside the Northeast.[23]

Although Florida had its share of lavish coastal hotels and resorts that catered to the country's Gilded Age elite, the state was still seen by most working- and middle-class Americans as a seemingly inaccessible wilderness. Kalem's decision to film on location in Florida set their productions apart from what Marion described as the "theatrical films of their competitors."[24] An added benefit of location shooting was that productions were not nearly as cost-prohibitive as films that required a fixed studio setting. Samuel Long and Frank Marion both believed their company's films could appeal to an audience eager to see "movies that aspire to reality."[25] Kalem distinguished itself from its rival production companies by offering a novel approach to filmmaking that incorporated "outdoor scenes that were actually filmed outdoors rather than in front of crudely painted scenery."[26] Just as the orange groves of Hollywood became a backdrop to Fox, Universal, and Paramount Studios, the unencumbered landscape outside of Jacksonville offered Kalem and its MPPC affiliates a boundless array of opportunities to tell stories that filming in the New York–New Jersey metro area could not provide.

The Kalem Company's first experiments with outdoor location-based filmmaking in Florida would go on to become a catalyst for the decentering of the motion picture industry during cinema's transitional period and to inaugurate the custom of traveling long distances for aesthetically striking backgrounds.[27] On December 19, one day after Kalem arrived in Florida, the company announced its agreement with the MPPC, and the motion picture trade periodical *Moving Picture World* flashed an image of the small troupe of twelve Kalem Company actors with the headline "The Sunny South in Motion Pictures."[28] The article revealed that Sidney Olcott and Frank Marion anticipated the move months earlier when they traveled to Jacksonville to meet with A. S. Hoyt of the Pastime Theater, who helped the troupe secure a lease for the Roseland House in Fairfield, a small suburb that was about a fifteen-minute trolley ride from Jacksonville's downtown district.[29] In his official press release, Sidney Olcott optimistically described the "beautiful estate" on the St. Johns River as providing "almost everything that is dear to the heart of the artistic producer . . . and every feature of Southern life that might be required."[30]

Not everyone in the Kalem Players saw Roseland through the same rose-tinted glasses. Gene Gauntier recalled the estate as "a big rambling ramshackle old hotel set in three acres of ground."[31] She described the surroundings along the riverbank as having a broken pier that remained unrepaired for the entire season, while her fellow crew members complained of mosquito bites and frightening late-night noises that often reminded them that "beyond them lay real wilderness."[32] However, Gauntier did write fondly of her memories of "real southern style" cooking and the innate hospitable nature of the Floridians she met. During that first winter at Roseland the Kalem Company had a relatively bare-bones operation. Without a working film set, support crew, wardrobe, or carpenters, all the films Kalem produced in the 1908–9 season were filmed entirely outside. North Florida's primitive road network also caused the production to primarily scout locations up and down the St. Johns River on a rented motorboat.

Despite these early challenges, the "Kalem Invasion" of 1908 helped spark a "movie boom" across North Florida that would turn the state into one of the most important film production hubs in the United States in the first decades of the twentieth century. The economic and environmental factors that turned Jacksonville into an emerging city in the New South, were exactly what early filmmakers were in search for. As Jacksonville chronicler Fredrick Davis, acknowledged about the city's growth during this period, "Jacksonville did not spring up by accident. A careful analysis shows that the forces operating in its behalf in the beginning were founded on sound principles of climate, health, and location for trade."[33]

Kalem Studios Sparks "A Florida Feud"

By all appearances, Jacksonvillians seem to have thoroughly enjoyed hosting the Kalem Players during their winter stay in December 1908 and January 1909. However, the first sign of tension between Kalem and its Florida hosts occurred as soon as the troupe sent the results of their first scenarios north, while continuing to film additional short reel subjects in Florida. On January 8, 1909, the Kalem Players premiered the first of their *Sunny South* releases, *A Florida Feud; Or, Love in the Everglades* (1909). Directed by Sidney Olcott and written by Gene Gauntier, the film was one of the first new releases to be screened in New York after mayor George McClellan Jr.'s short-lived citywide nickelodeon ban had been lifted. Promotions for *Florida Feud* appear especially aware of the fraught political climate in which it would be screened to its audiences. An advertisement for the film in the *New York Dramatic Mirror* reassured moviegoers that Kalem had produced "a film that should meet with the approval of the clergymen who have lately severely criticized the class of subjects shown in moving picture theaters."[34] While *Moving Picture World* heralded the film as "the first of the great Southern series, the biggest novelty of the season. A strong dramatic story in real tropical scenery."[35] The advertisement also promised that the next addition to the southern series, *The Sponge Fishers of Cuba* (1909), would be ready for distribution the following week.[36]

Between January and March 1909, Kalem exhibited eighteen short subjects from its stay in Jacksonville, which were well received by the industry during a period of great uncertainty for motion picture exhibitors. The films produced by Kalem in Florida leaned heavily on either the available tropical or southern landscape, as well as numerous Civil War–themed productions that featured battle reenactments and sometimes former Union and Confederate army veterans who served as extras and advisors on set.[37] Despite the national box-office success for Kalem's *Sunny South* releases, Floridians were less enthused. For example, while *Florida Feud* was celebrated in the North as "a most charming representation of tropical foliage and Southern home life and customs," Jacksonville residents objected to the film's assertion that in certain parts of Florida, "Feuds are common, more so perhaps than any other section of the country." The film's negative portrayal of the "Florida cracker" made Sidney Olcott for a time "very unpopular with civic authorities."[38] A *Variety* review described another Kalem release, *The Cracker's Bride* (1909)—a story that featured adultery and murder in the Florida swamps—as likely to attract the ire of the film censors. According to the review, the film offered "the kind of 'uplift' which justifies the police whenever shown in stepping in to prohibit demoralizing exhibition."[39]

Just as *Cracker's Bride* debuted in theaters, movie mogul William Fox had successfully filed an injunction against McClellan's nickelodeon ban. In a sweeping edict by New York Supreme Court Justice William Gaynor (who would succeed McClellan as mayor of New York), the court ruled in favor of the Fox Amusement Company and effectively silenced the controversy over the enforcement of Sunday blue laws in New York City's movie houses.[40] In April 1909, the first Kalem Stock Company in Florida disbanded and the players returned to New York to resume operations in the now more favorable northern spring weather.[41]

By the end of that first winter season, Kalem's profits had reached $5,000 per week as its status "continued to rise with the MPPC."[42] Despite some local tension, the success of the 1908–9 winter season compelled Sidney Olcott and the Kalem Company to return to North Florida the following winter with an even larger operation. Soon Kalem's fellow members of the MPPC began to send scouting expeditions southward toward Florida. This first experience between the American motion picture industry in the state of Florida would, according to film historian Richard Alan Nelson, establish "the ambivalent interplay between the native Floridians and the new industry that would be reflected through the years in a continuing love-hate relationship."[43] Over the course of the next century, this dynamic would continue to play out in a myriad of different forms in multiple cities and communities across the industry's newly discovered "motion picture paradise."

The positive reports Kalem relayed about its first winter excursion to Jacksonville encouraged both their fellow MPPC affiliates and independent filmmakers to take advantage of Florida's unique natural environment and climate. These early movie producers saw boundless opportunities to film compelling outdoor sequences featuring Spanish moss–draped forests, white sand beaches, tropical islands, open plains, and the unique ancient architecture of St. Augustine.[44] This environment offered a stark contrast to the winter climate in New York, where most of the major production companies were based and that industry insiders considered "treacherous and sunless." Even as developments of indoor studio lighting "became a reality, [it was] more the realization of a nightmare than an aesthetic dream."[45] While the Kalem Company was initially drawn to Florida to take advantage of its landscape for location-based filming, other MPPC affiliates saw an opportunity in Florida to purchase cheap land to meet increased industry-wide demand for one- and two-reel subjects. To meet this demand, production companies had to depend on early cinema's most essential natural resource: sunlight.

In the winter of 1909–10, Edison Trust producer Siegmund Lubin followed Kalem's lead and sent his own acting troupe to film on location in Florida and the Caribbean while he oversaw construction of a new studio for the company's new headquarters in Philadelphia.[46] Florida's geographic position as a gateway to the Caribbean helped to expand the Edison Trust's efforts to keep up with increasing demands for one-reel film subjects from the rapidly growing number of nickelodeons and storefront theaters nationwide. In January 1910, the Lubin Manufacturing Company arrived in Florida to film *A Honeymoon through Snow to Sunshine* (1910).[47] Lubin first set up in Jacksonville to film sequences at the Yacht Club before moving to St. Augustine's Florida House. The closing scenes in the film were shot in Palm Beach and Miami, before pushing farther on toward The Bahamas.[48]

While Lubin's itinerant production team traversed the length of Henry Flagler's Florida East Coast Railway (FECR), the Baltimore-based Motograph Company of America arrived in South Jacksonville to build the first official film studio facilities in Florida. The site Motograph settled on was the Dixieland Amusement Park, located along the St. Johns River and connected to

Jacksonville by ferryboat.[49] Dixieland had opened in March 1907, and at the time of its completion was remembered as "a place of general amusement for the people of Jacksonville and vicinity, a place where entertainments, fairs, theatricals, athletics, and contests of every character could be held."[50] The park was part of an initiative encouraged by Governor Napoleon Broward to increase development in communities across the state by "advertising of their attractions to bring the tourists who frequently became settlers."[51] To further bolster his settlement initiative, Governor Broward incorporated the City of South Jacksonville in June 1907.

At the time of its incorporation, the area surrounding what would become the grounds for Dixieland Park appeared quite unassuming. With a population of 251 people in 1907, South Jacksonville was then described as "little more than a small dirty place, [with] no paved streets or sidewalks, no lights, and poor water service."[52] Billed by South Jacksonville's first mayor, S. M. Scruggs, as the "Coney Island of the South," Dixieland's array of attractions ranged from a 160-foot rollercoaster, a merry-go-round called a "Flying Jenny," an ostrich park, a wild animal arena, and 20,000 electric lights.[53] The adjacent Dixie Theater was fully equipped for stage and film presentations but struggled to compete with the Duval, Pastime, and Orpheum theaters in Jacksonville's downtown.[54]

After Dixieland closed for good in February 1910, the property was purchased by Elmer Walters of the Motograph Company. Walters told the *Florida Times-Union,* "This is the ideal spot for us. No use in going in any further . . . Here [sic] me, boys; we'll sure turn out a few films around this man's burg that will create a sensation with the picter [sic] men of this blooming hemisphere."[55] He then negotiated a plan to rent out the space to other studios and refit the park's Dixie Theater into the first functioning film studio in Florida. However, before Motograph was able to produce a single film at Dixieland, the studio, which had been beleaguered by suits carried out by Thomas Edison's patent attorney Frank Dyer. The cost of the patent suits against Motograph ultimately forced Walters to retreat back to its headquarters Baltimore.[56]

Conveniently enough for Edison, once Motograph abandoned its studio plans, the MPPC-affiliated Selig Polyscope Company took over the studio grounds for the season. Founded by Colonel William Selig, the company had first distinguished itself by filming unauthorized reenactments of the Smithsonian–Roosevelt African Expedition, which commenced two weeks after the end of Theodore Roosevelt's presidency in March 1909. Although filmmakers were commissioned to follow Roosevelt on location in Africa, Selig elected to hire an actor to impersonate the ex-president and rented circus animals to give the impression he had acquired actual footage from the expedition. The financial success that accompanied Selig's safari films attracted the attention of the MPPC, which absorbed Selig into its rapidly growing patent pool.

Freed from costly litigation from the Edison Trust, Selig was able to invest in opening studio facilities in Chicago, Los Angeles, New Orleans, and Jacksonville.[57] A great deal of enthusiasm was expressed in the *Florida Times-Union* when Selig announced his plans to set up a studio at Dixieland. An October 1910 article heralded that with the arrival of the Selig Company, Jacksonville now "had the honor of being a home of the moving picture industry."[58] That same month, a special train arrived from Chicago fully equipped with a collection of 160 trained animals, camera equipment, a mobile film processing lab, as well as a troupe of actors and crewmen that dwarfed the small exploratory crew Kalem had sent to North Florida just two years earlier.[59]

Despite local excitement, Selig viewed its South Jacksonville studio as just one of several production facilities the company operated. Colonel Selig's interests were divided between the company's flagship studio in Chicago and another studio it had recently completed in Edendale, California. Florida film boosters were less concerned with whether Selig had studios located elsewhere and instead saw the company's interest in South Jacksonville as chance to entice more producers to come film in their city.

A November 1910 update on Selig's progress notes, "It is supposed that Jacksonville will furnish a good base of supplies and action for camera excursions over the state and islands about the coast."[60] During Selig's production of *Lost in the Jungle* (1911), the company brought elephants, tigers, lions, camels, and horses to Dixieland, with South Jacksonville serving as a stand-in for the African Serengeti. Despite passing mention of an on-set accident involving the film's lead actress, Kathlyn Williams, who was attacked by a leopard during a stunt sequence, the trade presses labeled the production as "quite successful," noting that "the studio was reliant on Florida as a setting."[61] To prepare for the winter season of 1911–12, Selig brought in a group of Native American actors from their Western stock company to appear in "authentic Seminole roles" in films to be produced at Dixieland. The Seminole War films Selig produced there were among the studio's top audience draws.

The momentum that Selig had hoped to carry into the next winter filming season was abruptly cut short on October 27, 1911, when the first of what would be many lurid Hollywood murders occurred. That day William Selig's California point-man, Francis Boggs, was murdered by Frank Minnimatsu, his property caretaker. Allegedly, the murder occurred after Boggs fired Min-

Figure 5. Unknown production filmed in Jacksonville during the 1912–13 winter season. Courtesy of Jacksonville Public Library.

nimatsu for smoking in his car garage. The disgruntled caretaker responded by pulling a gun on both Boggs and Selig, who was visiting Boggs at home. Boggs was shot and killed instantly; Selig was shot in the arm while wrestling the gun away from Minnimatsu.[62] While Selig recovered from his injuries in California, he started to seriously reconsider whether to keep his Edendale studio open.[63]

Ironically, just as William Selig considered cutting his ties with his California studio, Frank Marion from Kalem Studios, who had been a driving force behind the first filming expedition to Jacksonville in December 1908, sent a large crew to Glendale, California, with instructions to construct temporary studio facilities to be used to produce "historical Indian subjects."[64] Focused on his West Coast studio, Marion ordered Kalem's Florida unit to be reduced to ten members. Soon producers from both independent and Edison Trust–affiliated studios alike started to invest their time and money into creating a "movie metropolis" that could bring to life their most vivid dreams and fantasies.

"It Started with Pictures of Interesting Florida Sites": Silent Films in St. Augustine

As the industry's attention homed in on Southern California in the early 1910s, Florida-based producers were far more intrepid than their West Coast counterparts in sending their production troupes to all ends of the state. Although Jacksonville served as an essential gateway for producers interested in filming in Florida, there was little incentive to stay firmly fixed in one place. Unlike the concentrated studio cities in Los Angeles, Florida filmmakers were not tethered to a specific portion of the state.

St. Augustine was one such favorite secondary location for filmmakers in Florida. Located just forty miles south of Jacksonville, a short ride along Henry Flagler's Florida East Coast Railway, St. Augustine had the distinction of hosting producers two years before Gene Gauntier and the Kalem Company wintered in Jacksonville. In 1906, the Selig Polyscope Company bypassed Jacksonville to film a short travelogue titled *A Trip to St. Augustine* (1906).[65] What made St. Augustine so compelling for filmmakers and audiences alike were its preserved fort and Spanish-style houses from the 1700s, which provided a perfect set for films about the exotic far-off lands of Egypt, South America, and India.[66]

Between 1908 and 1911, Kalem, Lubin, and Selig each made regular excursions from Jacksonville to St. Augustine. Two prominent early St. Augustine–set films, Kalem's *In Old Florida* (1911) and Selig's *The Rose of St. Augustine* (1911), could be seen as Florida's attempt to answer the heightened attention to California brought on by D. W. Griffith's *In Old California* (1910). Both Kalem's and Selig's films were reported to have "attracted a lot of attention in the movie world and turned a spotlight on St. Augustine as a place to make movies."[67]

Following up on the positive reports and box-office returns of St. Augustine–set productions, the French-based Pathé-Frères built one of Florida's first production studios in St. Augustine in 1914. Fredrick E. Wright, of Pathé-Frères, remarked in an interview with the *Florida Times-Union* that he had come "to the conclusion that the State of Florida offered the most advantages of the pictures I have been commissioned to make."[68] Wright was especially impressed with North Florida's environment as an effective stand-in for exotic locales and boasted that an even expert might have thought that "the pictures had been made in the old world—India, Egypt, Morocco, Persia—instead of the State of Florida."[69] This notion is further reinforced by historian Thomas Graham, who expresses how, as producers continued to gravitate to North Florida, "St. Augustine's experience paralleled that of the whole industry: It started with pictures of interesting Florida sites and progressed to films that used drama and action to tell a story."[70]

The Rise and Fall of Tampa Films Incorporated

On the state's west coast, Tampa could be considered a compelling competitor to Jacksonville as a film hub. Unlike Jacksonville, which still was in the process of electrifying and completing its paved road network, Tampa Bay boasted over one hundred miles of well-paved and lighted streets. The City of Tampa also had much to offer filmmakers: the multimillion-dollar Tampa Bay Hotel, a convenient location as the terminus of Henry Plant's Atlantic Coast Line Railroad, an array of unique Arabian Nights–inspired architecture, stunning local attractions such as Sulphur Springs Park (known as Tampa's Coney Island), along with multiple scenic locales along the Hillsborough River—was ideally situated to become a vibrant film production center.

In 1910, Tampa mayor Donald B. McKay and the local Board of Trade began an active drive to promote new industries.[71] The first film company to "heed the call of Tampa" was the World's Best Film Company—a subsidiary of Carl Laemmle's Universal Pictures—which arrived in Tampa with the goal to capture "authentic backgrounds to make stirring jungle pictures with Captain Jack Bonavita," a world-renowned animal trainer.[72] During production of *Wizard of the Jungle* (1913), Bonavita and producer Frank Whitman expressed their interest in remaining in Tampa after production was set to wrap in April 1913 and forming their own production company. After acquiring nearly $50,000 in capital stock investments from local investors, Bonavita and Whitman formed Tampa Films Incorporated (TFI) and pledged to the Tampa community that their company would inevitably become a valuable "advertisement of this city."[73]

With community cooperation assured and a strong base of local capital, TFI sought to form two stock groups of actors and produce a series of three- to five-reel feature films (ranging from thirty-three to fifty-five minutes in length), at three-week intervals, and at least one single-reel short each week. The company also looked to hire local would-be screenwriters to develop scenarios with Florida-specific stories. Willis Powell, the secretary of the Tampa Board of Trade, excitedly announced the potential for profits TFI could provide for the surrounding community: "The prospective films, instead of carrying money out of the city will bring money into it making a draft on picture shows of the forty-five states for a share of the dimes the picture show takes in."[74] By July 1913, Bonavita and Whitman had commenced with the production of their proposed film series, as H. C. Dorsey the manager of Tampa's Montgomery Theater, became the new president of TFI.[75]

Although TFI did succeed in producing several short films, the studio's overall lack of organization and inability to attract a national distributor set a tone for the many failures of other would-be film ventures throughout Florida in the years to come. Bonavita and Whitman reorganized the company to fit the financial reality of a rapidly changing production industry as they abandoned their weekly single-reel concept and decided to focus solely on feature films. By the end of the summer of 1913, Selig had completed several three-reel films including *The Island of Lions, The Diamond Smugglers,* and *Love's Justice* (1913), along with a series of other short reel subjects. These films superbly demonstrated the potential for showcasing the exhilarating natural beauty of the countryside along the Hillsborough River. TFI also used the Tampa Bay Hotel for a thrilling stunt dive in *The Diamond Smugglers* (1913), which helped demonstrate the profound potential of Tampa's urban backdrop to out-of-state producers.[76] Unfortunately for Bonavita and Whitman, they continued to struggle to find a distributor.

The death knell for TFI came when Bonavita and Whitman signed a distribution agreement with the recently incorporated Warner Films; however, Warner canceled the agreement at the last minute, and the company folded entirely.[77] The sudden failure of TFI was by no means uncommon for film studios during this period. As one of TFI's sponsors, E. D. Horkheimer, remarked in an interview with *Motography* after the company's collapse, "The formation of fly-by-night production companies [had become] one of the popular sports in the country."[78] Horkheimer went on to caution other would-be investors, "In almost every city of any size the promoters are busy. They work upon the home pride calling upon local capital to get together and exploit the scenery and advantages to be found peculiar to each place in pictures written to bring them out." In the end, "Lots of people have lived to regret their investing in 'dusters.' Unhappily, there have been many flivvers among the picture companies."[79]

Even though Tampa's first dalliance in bringing the motion picture industry to the city ended in failure and thousands of dollars siphoned from would-be investors, the city continued to serve as a satellite for production companies based in North Florida. During the summer of 1913, the Lubin Company traveled to Tampa from its headquarters in Jacksonville to film *The Wine of Madness* (1913), a comedic short featuring a northerner who purchases an orange grove in Florida and falls into an ill-fated romance with a local gypsy girl. The film was quickly dismissed in the trade presses, with *Moving Picture World* offering the single line, "This is not entertainment."[80] For all intents and purposes, *The Wine of Madness* would have soon been forgotten as one of dozens of weekly short reels that failed to resonate with audiences had it not been for James E. Mears, the acting secretary for the Tampa Board of Trade.

A month after *The Wine of Madness* premiered, Mears wrote a strongly worded editorial condemning the Lubin Company's portrayal of Floridians:

> To one who has neither lived in nor visited Florida, the impression would be created that not only is all of Florida worthless, but that it is inhabited exclusively by the lowest class of citizens and land sharks. The evil effects of such a film, shown throughout the country, could not be counteracted in a year by the combined efforts of all the commercial organizations and newspapers in the state. Such a picture is welcomed by those who endeavor to prevent migration to Florida.[81]

The public pressure campaign appeared to have worked. In the end, Lubin agreed to pull the film from its distribution circuit the following month. In a follow-up article published in August 1913, aptly titled "A Victory for Florida," the *Tampa Morning Tribune* relished the sudden about-face. Mears also issued a public apology that was reprinted by the *Tribune* in which he acknowledged, "There is in Florida ample setting for beautiful and inspiring motion pictures and there is no occasion for portraying false impressions."[82]

Miami Becomes the "Hub of the Hemisphere"

As Tampa Bay vied to stake its claim within the American motion picture industry, farther along the FECR, the recently incorporated City of Miami emerged as America's newest frontier metropolis. Miami's position 500 miles south of Los Angeles's latitude and 350 miles south of Jacksonville offered film crews longer wintertime sunlight hours and an even milder climate than its northern counterparts.[83] The extension of the FECR into South Florida also made Miami accessible to the rest of the country. The construction work needed helped to bring in a large influx of workers and attracted a service sector to meet the needs of the construction crews.[84] By the 1910s, what was once a small fishing village had become an "instant city, a winter resort for rich, a depot for agricultural goods, and a home for railroad workers."[85] The combination of rail building, land speculation, and the explosion of winter resort communities all contributed to Miami's emerging reputation as the "Magic City."[86] With its new reputation as a "Tropical New York" and "Hub of the Hemisphere," America's latest urban center captured the popular imagination.[87]

Unlike St. Augustine and Tampa, where the state's Spanish colonial history remained wholly visible, the identity and imagery associated with Miami was separate from the rest of Florida. What distinguished Miami from other emerging metropolises in the New South was its newness. As North America's newest frontier, South Florida became, in essence, a screen on which the national imagination could be projected. In other words, Miami was a place "where lies could become truths within a single day."[88] The physical transformation of the state's southern fringes helped forge Florida into a fantasy-scape, while mass media itself played an ever-increasing role in the transformation of "open land" into owned, lived, or imagined territory.[89] It is no surprise that Miami's position on this new American frontier caught the attention of the motion picture industry.

The Lubin Manufacturing Company was the first film studio to arrive in South Florida during the winter of 1910. The company's stay was a short pit stop as part its southward journey to The Bahamas in *A Honeymoon through Snow to Sunshine* (1910), with the film's closing sequence including scenes shot in both Palm Beach and Miami. Although this film could be considered little more than a "glorified travelogue," Siegmund Lubin expressed an interest in establishing a regular series of one- to three-reel productions filmed on location in the Caribbean.[90]

The appeal of South Florida as a film location resonated strongly with Lubin director Arthur Hotaling, who in 1912 announced his plans to establish a permanent production studio in Miami and expressed to the *Weekly Miami Metropolis* that he "could find no better place anywhere for the production of moving pictures than in and around Miami."[91] Despite his initial flourishes, Hotaling later changed his mind and instead decided to join the growing ranks of film producers who were shooting in Jacksonville. It is likely that Miami's still primitive urban infrastructure and the 350-mile additional distance (700 miles round-trip) from New York were deciding factors in Hotaling's last-minute recalibration. Even so, Miami remained a popular location for travelogues and newsreel subjects during the first half of the 1910s.

The first concerted effort to establish a film production studio in Miami came in 1914, when Charles Field, president of the Prismatic Film Company, decided to relocate his operation from New York to Miami. With a $65,000 investment, which was mostly contributed by the Miami Board of Trade, Field produced a two-reel booster film called *The Magic City of the South* (1914). Field went as far as to promise that "Miamians could expect to see a burgeoning local film industry with three or more picture companies active before the close of the winter season."[92] Similar to Jack Bonavita and Frank Whitman's collaboration with the Tampa Board of Trade, Charles Field and company had bitten off more than they could chew. The film followed the approach of an increasingly popular genre of "home-talent" moving pictures, which incorporated either prerecorded footage or an on-location reproduction of a simple plot with establishing shots that featured prominent town landmarks and occasionally scenes that included local citizens. The final product was screened to Miamians on December 6, 1914, in two tandem showings at the city's two theaters: the Fotoshow in the afternoon and an outdoor screening at the Miami Airdome in the evening.[93]

Following the screenings of *The Magic City of the South*, several Board of Trade members suggested enlarging the scope of the film into a melodramatic feature that could "increase the potential audience for the film" by adding a sequence "showing a Seminole Indian burning a white man, or something similar to arouse interest." After concerned citizens expressed concerns that such creative liberties would "give a wrong impression of life in and around Miami," the production was ultimately scrapped.[94] Whether put off by the reception of his film by local investors or the city's primitive infrastructure, within two days of the premiere for *The Magic City of the South*, Field stunned the city when he announced Prismatic would relocate to Los Angeles for the remainder of the winter season. According to Field, he needed access to a credit line and to ensure his films had an urban backdrop, "which can only be obtained in a great city."[95] The *Miami Herald* noted that "this sudden change of plans comes as a decided surprise."[96] Field's time in Los Angeles proved to be short-lived. Less than five months later, he was back in Miami with another production scheme in the works. In a May 1915 interview with the *Miami Herald*, Field explained that if he found a suitable location (and funding) could be secured, "within a few weeks [we can] have a company here for the purpose of taking motion pictures connecting our scenarios with scenes around Miami."[97]

It would take nearly a year, but Field eventually was eventually able to secure the funding he sought. The company rebranded itself as the Field Feature Film Company (FFFC) in August 1916. In a series of exaggerated boasts to the industry trade press, Field claimed his new venture was "composed of men of wide experience and reputation and backed by their own capital exclusively to the extent of several million dollars."[98] In truth, the FFFC was valued at $100,000, with most of its financial backing coming from local investors such as Thomas J. Peters, the self-described "Tomato King of Florida." Using the funding provided by Peters and other prominent South Florida businessmen, Field oversaw the construction of Miami's first film studio at the intersection of Twenty-Fifth Street and South Miami Avenue. The concrete-and-tile structure cost a total of $15,000 and was noted in the trade press *Motography* to have been "equipped with the newest lighting systems and . . . complete stock

Figure 6. Construction of Charles Field's short-lived film studio on South Miami Avenue, 1914. Courtesy of State Archives of Florida, Florida Memory.

of scenery and props."[99] Despite the newly built Miami studio's positive portrayal in the trade presses, the reality of the facilities was less than glamorous. In a 1977 interview, Norma Stevens, the receptionist for FFFC, recalled, "The plant area was roughly built and really wasn't a finished building at all. It was a one-story affair with glass roofing and banks of windows on three sides."[100] Even in its incomplete state, the Field Studio eventually housed two full companies of forty-four performers, technicians, and production staff.

In June 1916, the studio's first feature film, *The Human Orchid* (1916), was distributed for a nationwide release. The film received mixed reviews, with criticism on the film's reliance on "crude sensationalism" and a story that "offers little or nothing original" and in which "the arm of coincidence is stretched almost to the breaking point."[101] A silver lining could be found in *The Human Orchid*'s review in *Variety*, which optimistically predicted that the studio could improve for future productions: "Mr. Field says he has a number of other features, eighty-five percent of them better than *The Human Orchid*."[102] Unfortunately, Field's next feature, *Fate's Chessboard* (1916), was met with even more damning reviews than its predecessor. After another trouncing in the trade presses, Charles Field lost the support of his most important financial backer, Thomas J. Peters, who subsequently withdrew his stake in the FFFC. Once the Tomato King withdrew his financial support, Field's hopes to turn Miami into a film center all but faded by year's end.[103]

Charles Field's short-lived studio venture was one of many largely unsuccessful efforts during the 1910s to construct a lasting motion picture industry presence in Florida. Studio promoters with inadequate access to distribution and long-term capital investments, even when well-intentioned as was the case with the FFFC, failed to rise above the headlines and advertising they generated in local newspapers.[104] In a retrospective on Miami's film history, *Miami Herald* columnist John Dorschner referred to Field as "part producer, part con man."[105] In truth, with every advancement in the early American film industry, whether it be in New York, California, or Florida, there was an equal or greater number of failed promoters and local promotions.

The overzealousness of Miami's Board of Trade and Chamber of Commerce can also bear part of the blame, combined with the city's still primitive urban infrastructure, which prevented South Florida's further expansion as a film production center in the 1910s. Yet, just as Charles Field and company prepared to leave Miami for good, 350 miles to the north, film production in Jacksonville was about to experience its own dramatic ascent, only to face a tense political showdown that would irrevocably change the fate of Florida's film industry.

"Just Easy Times Boys": Jacksonville Emerges as a Film Production Hub

Charles Field's ill-fated efforts to boost Miami as a film production center proved little more than a temporary challenge to Jacksonville's previous position as the "World's Winter Film Capital." Although the MPPC-affiliated studios Kalem, Lubin, Selig, and Edison had established inroads with the North Florida community, few of these companies remained in North Florida any longer than they needed to. With the onset of a local recession in 1914, the Jacksonville Board of Trade became increasingly interested in attracting production companies to boost the local economy. In January 1914, the previously rootless Kalem Company strengthened its ties with Jacksonville by constructing a permanent studio at a cost of nearly $20,000.[106] Kalem's choice to build a studio in Jacksonville (by now Kalem already had permanent studios in New Orleans and Glendale, California) was more or less indicative of the increasing demands for multireel film productions that emerged the last phase of cinema's transitional period, in particular for sophisticated single-story subjects of forty-five minutes or longer.

With longer running times, higher budgets, and greater visibility through the advent of movie fan magazines and a wider distribution network, the motion picture industry had come a long way in a very short time. To keep up with increased audience demand for new subjects with lavish settings and backdrops, more motion picture communities started to emerge across the United States. Filmmakers who were interested in establishing a base of operations during this time, whether it be in New Jersey, Louisiana, California, or Florida, needed vast enclosed stages, space for prop and wardrobe rooms, access to processing labs, and homes for studio workers. As studios became increasingly self-contained, they also presented cities across the country with the prospect of supporting a low-cost and low-maintenance industry, which could yield high returns both in terms of tourism and expenditures by "movie people" dependent on community cooperation to complete their respective productions.

In March 1914, the Jacksonville Board of Trade sponsored a municipal advertising film called *Jacksonville in Motion*. Director Ernest Day coined the slogan "Get in the movies and boost Jacksonville," to show producers "all the busy and interesting parts of the city."[107] With the mantra "anything which helps Florida helps Jacksonville," the Board of Trade began to actively court the film industry in greater earnest.[108] In a series of ads published in the *Florida Times-Union* and *Metropolis*, Day extolled the virtues of Florida's landscape and winter climate as well as the cooperative relationship between the production companies and Jacksonville community.

The making of *A Florida Enchantment*, a feature-length comedy directed by Sidney Drew and produced by the Brooklyn-based Vitagraph Company is especially instructive understanding this relationship. Just before production Sidney Drew had lost his wife and performance partner Gladys Rankin. Producer J. Stuart Blackton decided to send Drew and contract actress Edith Storey to film on location in Florida. Sequences for the film were shot in Jacksonville, St. Augustine, and St. Petersburg likely between March and April 1914. The film has since widely been considered by film historians as one of the earliest portrayals of homosexuality and cross-dressing on screen. Although, as film historian Maggie Hennefeld acknowledges, the film entirely missed the mark of "codified deviance or sexual subversion," its subject matter did stir a great deal of controversy in the New York presses.[109] Upon the film's release, *Variety* stated that film should have "never been put out," the *New York Clipper* criticized Sidney Drew's film for selecting "a most disagreeable theme," while the *New York Times* described it as "vile stuff" and "nauseating."[110]

At the time of writing, there are no available reviews of *A Florida Enchantment* in either the *Florida Times-Union* or *Metropolis* but considering the backlash that followed Kalem's *Florida Series* in 1909, it is likely that it may have at the very least caused consternation from Jacksonville's civic leaders. Shortly after *A Florida Enchantment* premiered, the Jacksonville Board of Trade announced that moving forward each film produced in the Jacksonville metro area was required to have a special "Made in Jacksonville" title card placed at the beginning of each reel. The *Times-Union* expressed that such a label could grant North Florida "the sort of publicity that attracts favorable attention to the state and the vicinity about Jacksonville, so the city proudly includes the studios among its worthy enterprises."[111]

By May 1914, the Jacksonville press pronounced its campaign a success, asserting that "the movie people in Jacksonville" had already made "hundreds of friends, personally and on the screen," and that the "establishment of the studios here has been a vast benefit to the city in many ways."[112] To support Jacksonville's potential as a "headquarters for motion picture companies, especially during the winter season," the Board of Trade distributed a series of promotional booklets expressing the city's willingness to cooperate and collaborate with incoming film producers.[113]

As the Board of Trade issued their formal invitation to motion picture production companies to bring their operations to Jacksonville, the city geared up for a contentious mayor's race that could change its destiny. In late 1914, former Jacksonville mayor James Edward Theodore (J.E.T.) Bowden surprised voters by announcing his plans to return to city politics and run against the incumbent mayor Van C. Swearingen. Bowden had previously served as mayor of Jacksonville between 1899 and 1901, overseeing leadership of the city during one its darkest moments: the Great Fire of 1901. Mayor Bowden heroically worked with local fire brigades to stem the worst of the Jacksonville fire and personally opened his home to Jacksonvillians displaced by the fire. As the flames of the Great Fire smoldered and the work to rebuild the city commenced, Bowden surprised the city by announcing that he would not seek reelection as mayor and returned to his law practice.

The catalyst for his decision to run for mayor again in 1915 came after Swearingen started to crack down on brothels and the lively bar culture in the city's LaVilla neighborhood. Bowden, who was also mayor of LaVilla when it was an independent town in the 1880s, had a far more relaxed outlook on the so-called vices that conservative crusaders such as Swearingen and others railed against. When asked his thoughts on the city's emerging reputation as a nightlife hotspot, Bowden was straightforward:

> This "social evil" is not such a terrible evil after all. These poor unfortunates are the greatest safety valves to our society . . . Let us not persecute

these women to conduct their business in the secret of the night under dangerous conditions and circumstances but instead embrace a culture of merciful toleration and respect.[114]

With a campaign slogan that played on his initials "J.E.T.B.," Bowden promised his voters that as mayor there would be "Just Easy Times Boys." He also pledged that if reelected, "he would run the city like a business" and uphold the virtues of the "separation of church and state," which his political opponents had seemingly ignored.[115] He argued that Swearingen's anti-vice crusade, which sought to excessively regulate Jacksonville's entertainment industry, had a severely negative impact the city's economy and hindered its growth.[116] In the end, the race between Bowden and Swearingen was a referendum on the political turmoil that had been persistent in statewide politics since the end of Reconstruction.

The underlying divisions in Florida's Democratic Party were represented by two primary factions, the "Antis," or anti-corporation Democrats (Swearingen), and the "Straightouts," or corporation Democrats (Bowden).[117] The political tug and pull between the Antis and Straightouts, not only in Jacksonville but across the state level, left a fraught foundation for film producers who had any interest in setting up a permanent studio in Florida during this period.

"Anti" politicians like Van Swearingen saw North Florida's motion picture industry as being comprised of so-called "menacing elements that this faction of the Democratic Party was staunchly outspoken against."[118] Although a vocal minority of Swearingen supporters were certainly mobilized by "Anti" fears of the outsider influence that would come with the increased presence of northern business interests, Jacksonville's business community expressed their own set of concerns in regard to Bowden's supposed get-rich-quick campaign promises. One of Bowden's most outspoken skeptics was Jacksonville's preeminent architect and New York transplant Henry John Klutho, who arrived in the city following the 1901 fire. In an editorial letter to the *Times-Union*, Klutho expressed his doubts as to whether Bowden was truly sensitive "to the needs of Jacksonville and an opportunist."[119]

The tense race between Jacksonville's former and current mayor came to a decisive head during the first Democratic primary on January 26, 1915. Aside from Bowden and Swearingen, ninety second-tier candidates also ran for the Democrat Party nomination for mayor. That evening, the results were tallied on a massive screen draped outside the *Metropolis* office. As each election tally was announced, the screen counted votes for the nearly eight thousand

Figure 7. Jacksonville mayor J.E.T. Bowden personally oversaw the relief and rebuilding efforts following Jacksonville's Great Fire of 1901. Courtesy of University of North Florida PALMM Collections.

Jacksonvillians who had gathered to witness the results of the contentious ninety-two-man race.

Although Swearingen won the plurality vote, the margin was narrow enough that a runoff election needed to be called between the two top contenders for the following month. When the runoff was announced, Bowden ran a letter thanking voters and promised that he sought to serve as mayor "for all of Jacksonville."[120] The outcome of the second primary election, held on February 23, was first announced to audiences in attendance at the Keith Vaudeville Show at Jacksonville's Orpheum Theatre. Cheers erupted from the crowd as the messenger interrupted the performance to proclaim Bowden's victory over Swearingen by a 58 percent margin.

The following day Bowden issued a message to his constituents that his return to the mayor's office in 1915 centered on a mandate to attract "industry, tourism, and new settlement." To restore confidence in local businesses and help create new jobs, Bowden joined the Board of Trade in an aggressive attempt to expand upon the organization's efforts to attract filmmakers to the city.[121] Coinciding with this effort, the Jacksonville Board of Trade formally changed its name to the Jacksonville Chamber of Commerce (JCC) one week after Bowden's election victory.[122]

After taking office, Bowden and the JCC formed a permanent Motion Picture Commission "to look after the interests of the producing companies and to assist them in obtaining sites and equipment."[123] The premise of the initiative was to encourage complete cooperation with arriving production companies, while at the same time severely undercutting the day-to-day expenses that cities with much larger film colonies demanded from their movie tenants. In what seemed like no time at all, the JCC reeled in their first big fish, when the Thanhouser Film Corporation announced its plans to open a production branch in Jacksonville instead of California. Company president Edwin Thanhouser complimented the Chamber of Commerce on its persuasiveness and promised that his southern branch would invest more than $30,000 in constructing an elaborate glass-and-steel studio. As an additional boon to the city's recession economy, he also announced that the daily payroll would exceed one thousand dollars, creating several hundred more jobs. According to Thanhouser, a combination of persuasion from the Chamber of Commerce and the proximity to other film studios in the city also influenced his decision to select Jacksonville.[124]

The following month, in November 1915, the French-based studios Gaumont and Pathé chose Jacksonville as the site for their American studios. Not interested in traversing a longer sea voyage to California, European film companies certainly saw cities such as New York and Jacksonville as alluring alternatives for a North American base of operation. Shortly after setting up shop, Gaumont's general manager, Richard Garrick, placed a call for five thousand to six thousand extras to be ferried across the St. Johns River to Dixieland for a theater scene for his film *The Actor* (1916). Garrick dispersed funds to pay the first 555 extra actors who arrived at Dixieland a dollar each. News of the payout soon spread across the city and Garrick's casting call was fully met. The *Florida Times-Union* reported, "It was an unusual day for Jacksonville and a treat for those who availed themselves of Mr. Garrick's invitation. When night came there were nearly 6,000 citizens who knew more about motion picture making than they had ever read, dreamed, or thought about and some longing for a career."[125] The successful one-day production of *The Actor* and the enthusiasm expressed from the Jacksonville community showcased the prestige and possibilities that local businessmen, would-be entertainers, and politicians could achieve if they were to become movie boosters.

As news of the thousands of both paid and unpaid extras who gathered at Dixieland to perform in Richard Garrick's *The Actor* spread in the Jacksonville, a sense of optimism could be felt by many of North Florida's newest filmmakers. Thanhouser expressed his hope that very soon other studios would likely locate in Jacksonville and foresaw "the time when this city will become the Los Angeles of the Southeast as a moving picture center," suggesting that Jacksonville could imitate how "Los Angeles and many sections of California hold the moving picture industry above all others in value and revenue."[126] This quote is especially instructive toward understanding how Jacksonville was perceived by the motion picture industry during its greatest period of activity. Meanwhile Mayor Bowden commenced his concerted effort to convince the movers and shakers in the motion picture industry to "quit Los Angeles."[127]

During J.E.T. Bowden's tenure as mayor, there was a heightened interest across the city in North Florida's potential role as a movie capital. The crux of the "quit Los Angeles" campaign rested on Jacksonville's relative proximity to New York City, which at the time was the uncontested entertainment capital of the United States. H. S. Kealhofer of the JCC followed up on Mayor Bowden's "quit Los Angeles" campaign by developing an *Industrial Survey of Jacksonville*, which lauded the city's remarkable short-term growth from the wreckage of the 1901 fire to become, in just over a decade, the "Queen City of the South."[128] Kealhofer marveled, "The development of the port of Jacksonville from a small town next to a wide but shallow river, to a metropolitan city handling every year a deep-water commerce worth millions of dollars along a splendidly charted channel, is the story of the efforts of earnest men, foreseeing the possibilities of the magnificent future and bending every effort to hasten its coming."[129]

North Florida's overstated role as a film colony for smaller independent film studios and MPPC affiliates has since perpetuated an underlying "founding myth" in the telling of Florida's film history.[130] Daniel Pleasant Gold first advanced the idea of a so-called rivalry between the Jacksonville and Los Angeles production industries during the 1910s. According to Gold: "It was during this period that Jacksonville made an effort to compete with Los Angeles as the center of the motion picture industry, contending that the sunlight of Florida was equal in photographic prosperities if not superior to California's."[131] There is plenty of room to speculate on what could have been, but the travails of J.E.T. Bowden's "quit Los Angeles" campaign do not offer enough details or insights on how Jacksonville could have disrupted the American motion picture industry in the long term.

Regardless, J.E.T. Bowden's second term as the mayor of Jacksonville did offer several exciting developments for Florida's motion picture industry. In January 1916, Jacksonville experienced a dramatic breakthrough when Bowden called a meeting with the JCC, the Tourist and Convention Bureau, the Real Estate Board, and the Port Commission to form an open trust between the city's the banking interests and its resident motion picture producers. The *Florida Times-Union* reported that if this collaboration were to be successfully coordinated, it would by year's end "pour in at least $30,000,000 annually into local coffers and increase the resident population by over 6,000 persons."[132] Perhaps most promising of all, Bowden had telegraphed the Board of Directors of the Los Angeles Photo Players Screen Club with an open invitation "to the moving picture fraternity of this country" to "personally inspect the advantages of North Florida."[133] With the support of city business leaders and the interest of filmmakers piqued, it seemed Jacksonville was on the cusp of fulfilling its aspiration to become the "Motion Picture Producing Mecca of the Atlantic Coast."[134]

"Shucks Who Cares? It Was Only the Movies"

On a seemingly unremarkable Sunday afternoon on January 2, 1916, nearly 1,400 Jacksonvillians and forty municipal police officers armed with rubber billy clubs assembled in front of a secondhand saloon in the city's LaVilla neighborhood. The location was previously part of the city's "restricted district" and reserved for bordellos euphemistically called "female boarding houses." Several months earlier, Mayor Bowden had initiated an effort to transform the neighborhood into a burgeoning entertainment district. LaVilla's lurid atmosphere was a favorite setting for production companies that wanted to depict "all the squalor and hopelessness of chronic poverty" as suggested "in the scenes of the town's disease breeding slums."[135] On that particular day, the Equitable Film Company, one among an ever-growing number of production studios that chose Jacksonville as their winter headquarters, placed a casting call for a "mob sequence" for the climactic final scene of their latest film, *The Clarion* (1916).

In the weeks leading up to the filming of this sequence, Equitable's on-site manager, Clifford Robertson, posted several advertisements in the *Florida Times-Union* calling for a large gathering of men, boys, and women with "whom he wanted to form a mob."[136] Interest in participating in the mob scene was so great that Robertson and *The Clarion*'s director, James Durkin, opened a temporary office at the Hotel Mason arcade in downtown Jacksonville to accommodate all of the requests. The saloon's owner further intensified interest by allowing the extras "the privilege of smashing every window in his place as well as the stock of liquor on display in the front end."[137] Durkin knew he would attract the largest possible crowd if he timed the shoot to begin just after church had let out, even if this was in blatant disregard of Jacksonville's Sunday blue laws.

The thousand-plus-person gathering of volunteers amassed at the intersection of Davis and Monroe Streets. The cameras started to roll, and Durkin signaled to the mob to rush down the street "hurling bricks, sticks and every missile they could find."[138] However, the mob's momentum did not stop after the initial charge, and when they reached the saloon, the young men in the crowd rushed the bar and ransacked the two-story building in a desperate frenzy to steal a drink from the bottles of wine and whiskey that were left out as props. They snapped off the necks of the bottles and "flung away the glass corks without ado."[139]

This scene of wanton destruction, debauchery, and Sunday drinking brought on by Jacksonville's rogue film colony was remembered as a travesty, mobilizing a growing contingent of reformers who sought to eliminate the corrupting influence of those wild and licentious "movie people."[140] The legacy of "The Clarion Riot" resonated to such an extent that, nearly thirty years later in 1954, *Florida Times-Union* reporter James C. Craig used this account in his own retrospective on the Florida film industry: "Because the mob became unruly and almost uncontrollable, it gave a tainted name to motion picture producing and furnished fuel for those who had opposed the film industry being here all along. From then on opposition to the film producers gained in strength."[141] Craig's account of "The Clarion Riot" has since become local folklore.

Each subsequent history of Jacksonville's role as a "movie capital" has relied on this event as the catalyst to explain what caused a downturn in relations between Jacksonville and its incipient motion picture industry. The political implications of Jacksonville's so-called disfavor toward the disruptive "movie people" came to a head one year later in a decisive mayoral runoff election that removed Mayor Bowden from office and "ended the honeymoon once and for all."[142] Such a story, however, ignores the many factors that truly contribute to the success or failure of regional production industry.

A closer reading into the original *Times-Union* account of the filming of the mob scene paints a much different portrait of events than previously has been given. A *Times-Union* article from January 4, 1916, titled "Mob Destroys

Figure 8. *New York Tribune* advertisement promoting James Durkin's *The Clarion* (1916), which later was mythologized as the catalyst for the souring of relations between filmmakers and Jacksonvillians. Courtesy of Library of Congress.

Building on Davis Street and the Wrecks Saloon," certainly creates the initial impression of the author's concern that a dangerous combination of heedless filmmakers and unrestrained civilians could lead to a direct threat against the city's staunchly conservative moral values. A look at the article's subtitle, however, shows that the *Times-Union* was clearly on Equitable's side: "Forty Jacksonville Policemen unable to stop rush of 1,300 men and boys who show hatred of the establishment's owner. Although they used clubs vigorously—but who cares? It was only the movies, and the clubs were made of rubber—Each Bluecoat got $5 a week."[143]

The paper goes to great lengths to clarify for concerned citizens what actually happened during the filming of *The Clarion*, making special mention that Clifford Robertson reimbursed the damages to the saloon's owner caused by the filming "to the extent of about $2,000."[144] To further assure readers, the article shifts to a more tongue-in-cheek tone by speculating, "Maybe the accumulating crowd of spectators along the sidewalks and at the street crossings thought the mob was an awful hard-headed one. But shucks, who cares? It was only the movies."[145] As far as Equitable and Jacksonville's movie boosters were concerned, the filming of *The Clarion* was a tremendous success. *The Moving Picture World*'s review of *The Clarion* published in February 1916 expressed awe at the impressive saloon sequence and indicated that James Durkin's "handling of this mob is admirable."[146]

Undeterred by any perceived negative reaction from disapproving Jacksonvillians, ten days after the so-called Clarion Riot, Clifford Robertson, along with dozens of boosters and representatives from each of Jacksonville's part-time production companies, participated in a "state of the industry" meeting at the Hotel Mason, that was presided by J.E.T. Bowden. The purpose of the meeting was to extend an open invitation "to the moving picture fraternity of this country to personally inspect the advantages of North Florida."[147] Bowden's invitation for New York and Los Angeles film producers to relocate their companies to Jacksonville was the next major step in a cooperation campaign he initiated to increase business and industrial development throughout the city. In an open letter printed on the front page of the *Metropolis*, on January 22, 1916, Bowden reiterated his invitation:

> I, J.E.T. Bowden, as Mayor of the City of Jacksonville, Fla., do hereby extend a hearty invitation to the Motion Picture Producers, to make this city their center of production, assuring them a hearty welcome and every co-operation in facilitating their work. Our morning sun permits a longer working day than any other part of the country.[148]

J.E.T Bowden's continuing effort to foster year-round film productions in Jacksonville was the latest part of his broader political campaign to fulfill his campaign promise to "restore business confidence and create new jobs."[149] This initiative yielded incredibly positive results. By the end of 1916, more than one thousand actors and thirty companies were based in Jacksonville on a regular or semi-regular basis.[150] In combination with a supportive local government, the recent upsurge in activity by major production companies such as Metro and Gaumont in Jacksonville helped to further reinforce North Florida's position as an attractive winter film production haven and encouraged the city's movie boosters' aspirations to turn their city into a permanent film production center.

If there was any tension between Jacksonvillians and the "movie people," it was not the result of disruptions caused by filming in the city. Instead, a series of dramatic shifts within the American motion picture industry would signal both the downfall of J.E.T. Bowden's political career and, with it, Jacksonville's movie dreams. During this brief window between 1915 and 1917, it appeared that Jacksonville under Mayor Bowden had convinced at least a few high-profile producers to "quit Los Angeles" and relocate to North Florida. Bowden seemed more focused than ever on bringing more studios to the city. In a February 1916 letter to film producers published in the trade journal *Motography*, he wrote: "Jacksonville wanted to win the patronage of the motion picture people through their building plants in Jacksonville it was essential that the city profit through the mistakes of other cities by avoiding these troubles."[151] The tragedy of the situation is that just as soon as Bowden and the JCC were able to get Jacksonville up and running as a competitive film town, the rug would be pulled out from under him by his political rivals. Meanwhile, the rise of a dangerous demagogue who utilized populist politics to upend the political establishment in Florida would also sow the seeds of the film industry's downfall.

"A Referendum on Film Production in Jacksonville"

Despite J.E.T. Bowden's best efforts, by the time he came to office in 1915, it was quite unlikely that any major California-based film studios would ever fully "quit Los Angeles." Most of the studios that filmed in North Florida between 1908 and 1915 were affiliated with Thomas Edison and his motion picture trust. As we have seen, Kalem had joined the MPPC just days before arriving at Roseland to film their *Florida Series*. Since that first winter season, most of the companies that shot in Florida were associated with the Fort Lee,

New Jersey, studios allied with Edison. Most of the emerging Los Angeles studios were instead established by a rebellious group of "independents" who challenged Edison's patent claims and the dirty tactics he used to prevent patent violations. Since Jacksonville had such close ties to Edison and the Fort Lee film industry, its fate was closely entwined with Edison's. Ultimately, the most persistent reason for Jacksonville's perceived "failure" was that its studios lacked affiliation with the rising vertical integration occurring outside the state.[152]

The seeds for Jacksonville's downfall as a film center were already sown in October 1915, the same month J.E.T. Bowden took office, when the Supreme Court ruled against Edison and the MPPC in *United States v. Motion Picture Patents Co.* (1915). In its ruling the Supreme Court declared the Edison Trust was in direct violation of the Sherman Anti-Trust Act and ordered the dismantlement of the MPPC.[153] With the breakup of the Edison Trust, many the now former MPPC affiliates such as Kalem, Lubin, and Selig were without a stable source of financial backing and access to their New Jersey film processing labs.

Prior to the MPPC's breakup, MPPC-affiliated studios had provided Jacksonville with a steady cash flow from the company's corporate headquarters directly into the pockets of shopkeepers, realtors, hotel managers, police officers, and Jacksonvillians interested in a day's extra work. Following the breakup of the MPPC, numerous fly-by-night independent operations briefly appeared in Jacksonville, and as rapidly as they had attracted the interest of would-be investors, they disappeared without the slightest hope of a financial return.[154] Increased suspicion against unlicensed film promoters served as the basis for much of the existing distrust of the motion picture industry. Since Jacksonville's connection to the motion picture industry was tied to film distribution networks in New York and New Jersey, once the East Coast studios were sacrificed as production centers to consolidate on the West Coast, economic controls could be more efficiently maintained.[155]

Jacksonville's comparable proximity to New York, which was advertised by the JCC as just a short "Twenty-Seven Hours from Broadway," indirectly brought about the city's downfall as a film center.[156] The only hope film studios in North Florida had of sustaining even a part-time regional industry would have been to develop a massive production and distribution infrastructure supplied by local capital. Since the Jacksonville studios did not have their own processing laboratories or distribution exchanges in the city, the companies were entirely reliant on sending their footage north to New York for editing and distribution. In contrast, the five-day train journey to California required the studios that established operations on the West Coast to be entirely self-sufficient. This advantage factored heavily in Los Angeles's favor during this period of industry-wide consolidation.

The popularity of multireel films such as D. W. Griffith's first Hollywood production, *In Old California* (1910), sparked demands for larger-budget and longer-sequence productions. Few Florida filmmakers had links to the major events reshaping American film into a theatrical model, in which the producer organizations would obtain control over distribution and achieve more certain access to theater screens.[157] Although it can be said that between 1912 and 1914 there were more production units working in Jacksonville and St. Augustine than in Los Angeles, this should not be considered the basis for an imagined "competition" between two aspirational film centers.[158]

Another deciding factor that kept Jacksonville from at the very least staying on as an influential regional motion picture hub was an unfortunate change in Florida politics, which took place at the height of J.E.T. Bowden's "quit Los Angeles" campaign.[159] If there was one politician who permanently changed the fate of Florida's entertainment industry, it was a one-eyed Alabama pastor by the name of Sidney J. Catts. In 1904, following a failed bid to win a congressional seat in Alabama, Catts relocated to Florida.[160] Ten years later, Catts returned to politics, this time as a candidate for governor of Florida. Applying similar grievances to those that the "Anti" wing of Florida's Democratic Party had previously voiced, Catts pledged to regulate what he considered to be "Godless entertainment and vices," which included both liquor and the movies. Although Catts had won the statewide Democratic primary, his extremist views were seen as too radical even for southern Democrats at the time, and he was denied the party's nomination. He responded by launching an insurgent third-party bid with the Prohibition Party, promising as governor to ban the sale and distribution of alcohol in Florida.

Catts found eager support from white-supremacist and anti-immigrant organizations that included the Ku Klux Klan and the Guardians of Liberty. According to Catts biographer Wayne Flynt, he was "an intuitively accurate observer of the cracker mentality," and in particular he used the state's agricultural sector's increasing suspicion of industrial growth as a talking point to tap into a constituency that had until then been ignored by the establishment.[161] His supporters remarked, "the Florida cracker had three friends: Jesus Christ, Sears Roebuck, and Sidney J. Catts."[162] The *New York Times* called his upset victory "one of the most spectacular gubernatorial campaigns ever waged in the United States. He won, without money, and only with the aid of a Bible and two revolvers."[163]

Riding on Sidney Catts's surprise victory as the Prohibition Party candidate, Florida's Democratic party's "Anti" wing quickly aligned behind the governor. By 1917, this alliance morphed into a newly formed "Cattocrat" wing of Florida's Democratic Party swept through the state's municipal elections.[164] According to Florida historian William Cash, after the election of Sidney Catts "there was little heard of the old 'corporation' and 'anti-corporation' issues of other days."[165] The upending of the established political order in Florida, combined with the disruptions in the American film industry at large, could not have come at a worse time for J.E.T Bowden or Jacksonville's movie boosters.

Catts's sudden rise to political power gave rise to supposedly "reform"-minded Florida Democrats who were fixated on expelling so-called undesirable outside influences from the state.[166] With the U.S. entrance into World War I, Florida teemed with a never-before-seen wave of anti-German sentiment, and Catts attempted to exploit this to further his own anti-Catholic and racist agendas. At one rally, the governor publicly theorized to his supporters that the monks of Saint Leo Abbey near Tampa were planning to arm Florida's Black community for a popular revolt in favor of Kaiser Wilhelm II, after which Pope Benedict XV would move the Holy See to nearby San Antonio, Florida, and close all Protestant churches. Such extremist rhetoric surely frightened the bohemian colony of filmmakers in North Florida, who were firmly put on notice by the Catts administration.[167]

The example set by Sidney Catts was soon copied by other politicians across the state such as, in Jacksonville, an upstart thirty-one-year-old lawyer named John Wellborn Martin. As Martin prepared to challenge J.E.T. Bowden for his seat as mayor of Jacksonville, he modeled much of his campaign after Catts's playbook. Although Martin's political disposition did not fit into the categories of "Anti," "Straightout," or "Cattocrat," he did apply a scorched-earth campaign like the approach Catts had used during the 1916 gubernatorial race. Capitalizing on his stance as a politically unknown outsider, Martin synthesized a message that appealed directly to the city's fiscal conservatives along with addressing the xenophobic concerns over supposed "undesirable foreign influences" that encouraged "Cattocrats" to the polls by the droves.[168]

In a series of direct appeals to the citizens of Jacksonville, Bowden responded to his opponent by expressing his continuing support of the motion picture industry not as a key campaign issue but instead as an expression of the successes his pro-business administration had to date provided for the city. In an open letter published in the *Times-Union*, he appealed to his fellow Jacksonvillians:

To promote extended development of local business enterprise, I did interest, among other industries, a rich, thrifty, cultured and delightful community of incoming producers of moving picture film companies and players. Ignoring considerations of culture and refinement, valuable as they are, can we yet afford to ignore and disparage a cash payroll of $40,000–$50,000 a week from the film industry in order to exclude some mighty good new citizenship from our midst?[169]

The day before the Democratic Party primary on February 6, Bowden pled to his constituents that they should "Think and reason with yourself, see if it would not be foolish to make an experiment now while Jacksonville is on the upward road to prosperity, the financial and moral interests of the city are being protected most thoroughly."[170] In his final message, Bowden warned voters that he had "been preyed upon by misrepresentation and harangues that have nothing to do with municipal government and should have no part in government."[171] Mayor Bowden's pleas to Jacksonville's citizenry seem to have fallen on mostly deaf ears, and the following day Martin won a decisive victory against Bowden by a margin of more than 800 votes, and in June 1917, Martin ran unopposed in the general election.[172]

Far from being simply a "referendum on film production in Jacksonville," the 1917 mayor's race is an effective meter for understanding the changing dimensions of Florida politics that happened during the Sidney Catts administration. After 1917, Florida experienced a period that witnessed a combination of infrastructural regression and financial stagnation brought on by mismanagement and corruption from within the Catts administration. In terms of motion picture production, the combined anti-Catholicism and anti-Semitism of the Cattocrats and organizations like the Guardians of Liberty kept the predominantly foreign-born movie moguls from considering to use the studios in Jacksonville, leading to a de facto boycott of North Florida's production industry.

Another setback came from federally imposed wartime rationing that followed the U.S. entrance into World War I, which caused many low-budget producers based in Jacksonville to either go out of business or become absorbed into larger production companies. A shift toward feature film production, reactionary city politics, price gouging against producers by Jacksonville merchants, the refusal of banks to finance Florida-made pictures, the devastation caused by the 1918 Spanish influenza pandemic, a succession of freezes that same winter, and a general apathy by local filmmakers all combined to drive production studios in North Florida toward the West Coast.[173]

Klutho's Fine Arts City and Jacksonville's Fate as a Movie Capital

Just two weeks after J.E.T. Bowden's loss to John Martin, Gaumont announced that it would abandon its Jacksonville facilities and scrapped the plans for the construction of Richard Garrick's proposed $500,000 film processing plant and distribution exchange on Union Street. Following the announcement of Gaumont's departure, the city's banks denied other independent filmmakers any further loans for their productions.[174] The timing of the announcement was by no means coincidental. Garrick's close affiliation with the Bowden administration was well-known, and now that he was faced with an antagonistic city government and a mayor with a penchant for holding a grudge, his business prospects in Jacksonville had become quite bleak. The speed of Gaumont's exit suggests that Garrick probably had one foot out the door anyway, but the election of John Martin sealed the deal. The loss of Gaumount's proposed Union Street Studio, along with J.E.T. Bowden's removal from office, effectively left Jacksonville's movie booster movement "leaderless and flounder[ing]."[175] Without J.E.T. Bowden and Richard Garrick, the JCC continued to actively seek out additional business as well as court its existing studios.

Kalem, Jacksonville's oldest operating film company, stayed in the city through the 1917–18 winter season, before financial difficulties caused the company to entirely relocate to California, only to fold shortly afterward. Following the departure of Gaumont, Henry Klutho, a Martin supporter, sought to pick up where Richard Garrick and J.E.T. Bowden had left off and sought to develop his own production venture. Klutho bought the abandoned property along Dixieland Park and set out to develop a million-dollar studio facility capable of housing forty different production companies.[176] If successful, Klutho's Fine Arts City could have sustained North Florida's position as an important regional center of production, but not a direct competitor with Hollywood.[177]

Whereas Bowden supporters such as Sidney Olcott of the Gene Gauntier Players, or GGs, and Richard Garrick with Gaumount were iced out by the mayor's office once John Martin took control, Henry Klutho, who had supported Martin's campaign, was at least given tacit support for his proposed Fine Arts City. Initially, Klutho was able to gain investors and financial backing, but the increasingly assertive anti-German rhetoric that came from the governor's office forced Martin and others to reconsider supporting a business owned and operated by a second-generation German American. A subsequent statewide boycott of German-made products led by Governor Catts made it increasingly difficult for Klutho to raise funds. Despite being born and raised in Illinois, Klutho was viewed by Catts and his supporters as compromised by his German heritage. In the end, it was impossible for Klutho to secure the loans he needed from Florida banks or local investors.

The outbreak of Spanish influenza pandemic in 1918 and 1919, along with the post–World War I depression of 1920–21, depleted any remaining savings Klutho had set aside for his Fine Arts City. By 1922, Klutho closed his Fine Arts City and sold the property to Richard Norman, an independent producer, who also purchased the site of the former Lubin/Eagle Studios and went on to develop the first (and ultimately the only) studio dedicated entirely to the production of race films during the silent period.[178] In an interview given toward the end of his life, Klutho bitterly reflected that the business leaders and politicians in Florida "were not prepared emotionally or intellectually to deal with the opportunity that the motion picture industry offered."[179] Instead, "All left for Los Angeles because people there had more vision and a willingness to gamble a bit for a large stake. At one time I was pointed to as a man of vision and ideas for the good of the town. Later I was often told I was a bit of a fool."[180]

Tampa Bay as the "Movie Center of the Country"

At the height of J.E.T. Bowden's "Twenty-Seven Hours from Broadway" campaign to attract producers to North Florida, Tampa mayor D. B. McKay jumped on the bandwagon and pledged his support through the *Tampa Times* (of which he was also the editor) to ensure "South Florida would soon become the 'movie' center of the country."[181] McKay's call was answered by comedian William "Smiling Bill" Parsons and actor Paul Gilmore, who sought to take advantage of Florida's loose state incorporation laws and form the National Film Corporation of America. Initially, Parsons and Gilmore proposed to build a $300,000 facility in Jacksonville in 1915. However, when the JCC refused to provide an upfront inducement, they took their proposal to the Tampa Board of Trade instead.

With the support of Mayor McKay and other civic leaders, Parsons and Gilmore next made a hard press to prominent businessmen in the city to invest $1,000 worth of stock in their company and an additional 200,000 shares that could be bought by middle-class Tampans at five dollars each. Shortly after their $300,000 goal was reached, Gilmore abruptly left the company, and by June 1916, it had been discovered that Parsons sold nearly $102,000 of his shares in National's stock. The studio building that he and Gilmore had

Figure 9. In 1919, Briggs Pictures, Inc., moved to Jacksonville and occupied Henry Klutho's proposed "Fine Arts City." Several Paramount-Briggs Comedies were produced at the studio between 1919 and 1922. Courtesy of State Archives of Florida, Florida Memory.

raised the funds for went into receivership, and after Parsons refused to return to Florida, a negotiated settlement was made for partial repayment to their defrauded stockholders.

Thousands of dollars were lost in the ill-fated venture, and any further attempts to recoup the misspent funds through litigation ended with Parsons's mysterious death (a supposed suicide) in 1919.[182] This second attempt at fostering an industry through "frenzied promotion and disastrous collapse" became a typical pattern in Tampa Bay's film production industry during the 1920s and 1930s.[183]

Following the inauguration of Sidney Catts in 1917, his administration set out to lift his predecessor's restrictive statewide regulations toward investment and fundraising practices. This legislation opened the floodgates to allow another wave of shady speculators to descend into the state. Many such promoters were drawn to Tampa in the wake of the collapse of Jacksonville's motion picture production industry. Among the most notorious of these film speculators was a former Florida East Coast Railway photographer named Harry Kelly. He initially entered the industry in 1915 with the Eagle Film Manufacturing and Producing Company in Jacksonville. After the Eagle property was sold to Henry Klutho in 1917, Kelly disappeared from the public record for two years and resurfaced again in Tampa in July 1919 with a brand-new company.

A *Tampa Morning Tribune* advertisement announced the formation of the Superb Film Corporation and Kelly's plans "to construct a new mammoth studio facility in Tampa," which would "do the developing and printing for any other companies which may desire to locate in the city."[184] He called for "inducements" from the leading citizens of Tampa, including the head of Tampa's First National Bank, to produce a featured cityscape called the *Tip Top of Tampa* (1919), a hastily put-together film that starred investors from Tampa's Kiwanis Club. By September 1919, Kelly had attracted enough local capital that he could afford to purchase a forty-acre site in Palma Ceia Park for his studio and developing plant.[185] In a hearty endorsement from the *Tampa Tribune*, the Board of Trade called for a campaign of cooperation to ensure the success of Kelly's venture.

The inexorable link between the aspirations of Florida's incipient tourism industry and the motion picture industry can be seen in a *Tampa Tribune* advertisement from October 1919 that expressed the need for such a collaboration: "With the early completion of the studios, we see an added interest to the visit of many visitors this winter, men and women, who are 'fans' when it comes to the movies and who will welcome the opportunity to see the movie man and the movie star in their native lair."[186]

Whether or not Harry Kelly intended to construct his studio is up for debate. Kelly seems to have been first and foremost an opportunist who saw in Tampa an assembly of politicians and businessmen blinded by their optimism that each new investment would bring more studios to the city.[187] With perpetual construction delays and without a professional acting troupe, Superb eventually folded without producing a single film. Several months later, in September 1920, Kelly rebounded with a concerted campaign in the trade presses to create a location-referral service based in Tampa for producers interested in filming on location in Florida. Despite his previous missteps, he was able to garner support from the directors of the boards of trades in communities across the Gulf Coast to form the Florida West Coast Association. Kelly's plan was to circulate a series of photographs he had taken or collected from potential film location sites and have them circulated among prominent film producers in New York and California. At first, he received a warm reception in the trade presses. An October 1920 *Moving Picture World* article went as far as to call his location-finding service "a bomb brought from Florida," and posed the question, "Will 'coast' mean Florida West Coast?"[188]

Just as Harry Kelly's promotional campaign had started to garner momentum, the Tampa Board of Trade refused to advance the four thousand dollars needed to pay for the film negatives for the films he intended to distribute to producers. Further suspicions were raised by Board member Charles H. Brown over the fact that Kelly had adamantly insisted that the city finance the construction of a large studio complex before any major studios were attached to produce their films in Florida. Relations between Kelly and the Tampa Board of Trade soon deteriorated to such an extent that by November 1920 he abandoned his Tampa plans and instead attempted to build his film studio in Jacksonville. However, by then the prospect of competition with Klutho's Fine Arts City prevented Kelly from getting any real traction from investors in the city.

Kelly then returned to Tampa in April 1921 with a proposal to the Board of Trade to secure 750 acres of land on Tampa Bay for use by his proposed Florida West Coast Studios syndicate. Interested in the proposal but skeptical of Kelly's reputation and his refusal to name the New York financiers who would supposedly invest in the project, the board surprisingly committed $150,000 for the purchase of a 350-acre site suitable for use by affiliates within the Florida West Coast Association. Kelly's proposal once again ended without any of the concrete accomplishments ballyhooed in a series of promotional news releases.[189]

What is most astounding about the shady dealings carried out by promoters such as Parsons, Gilmore, and Kelly is not that their schemes ended in failure and thousands of dollars lost in ill-advised investments, but that, despite all warning signs to the contrary, Tampans time and again were willing to place their faith in promoters who had no verifiable financial backing. Either these investors were blinded by optimism from promising sales pitches, or they severely underestimated the effort it would take to establish a permanent regional film industry. In the aftermath of the 1917 mayoral election and the subsequent failure of Henry Klutho's Fine Arts City in Jacksonville, it was quite natural that the center of gravity of motion picture production in Florida shifted down the Atlantic Coast Line Railroad to Tampa Bay. Despite the city's ill-executed promotions during the 1910s, Tampa's promotional office would eventually become a model for the future state-supported film offices in Florida in the 1930s.[190]

"We Will Do This Thing Somehow, with No Foolishness"

The unchecked and unregulated speculation associated with Florida's land and tourism boom during the 1920s captured the national imagination. As increased land promotions brought new arrivals and investors to settle along America's newest frontier, it also attracted opportunistic con men in search of their next scheme to steal from hopeful Floridians. As perennial presidential candidate William Jennings Bryan once remarked after retiring to Miami, "In Florida, a lie told at breakfast could become the truth by lunch."[191] Unlike the movie boosters of the 1910s, this new set of would-be producers were mostly realtors who had little or no understanding of the inner workings of the film industry. In a recurring pattern, these realtors would make their pitch to eager and naive investors who expected that these proposed "film cities" would have filmmakers simply "flock[ing] to Florida," bringing with them the glitz and glamour that only movies could offer.

The "film cities" projects were intended as a draw for tourists, which would then lead to the construction of more resorts and housing settlements and subsequently create thousands of jobs in the service sector. In the end, all that any of these so-called part-time producers managed to accomplish was to entice enough local support to collect several thousands of dollars in investment, then make a halfhearted effort toward building a studio, possibly even producing a low-budget film or two, before abruptly closing shop, fleeing town with the profits, and leaving their dumbfounded Florida investors to clean up their mess.[192]

In the summer and fall of 1922, Orlando was hoodwinked in just such a way. Motivated by ongoing speculation in new industries throughout the state, a Boston-based film promoter named John O'Loughlin arrived in town and proposed the construction of a studio facility in the vicinity of Orange Avenue in downtown Orlando. After meeting with twenty-five of Central Florida's top-tier business leaders, he began his search for a pool of funding for his proposed studio.[193] By June 1922, O'Loughlin announced the formation of the Associated Authors Productions, which, he promised in an *Orlando Sentinel* interview, would bring to the city "visions of palaces being erected one day and torn down the next almost within the city limits and of Orlando's fame spreading far and wide."[194] The appeal worked, and within several weeks O'Loughlin managed to raise nearly $85,000 from local investors by promising he had already secured a six-picture distribution deal with Pathé-Frères. He expanded on this claim by requesting that the Orlando Chamber of Commerce invest an additional $60,000 to build a studio that he promised would be "equal to the finest estate in the country."[195]

O'Loughlin next teamed up with Orlando-based writer Hapsburg Liebe to write a series of six feature films to be produced by Authors. After a set of fits and starts, production began on first film in their proposed film series: *The Broad Road* (1922). However, almost as soon as production for the film kicked off, it appears O'Loughlin had already burned through all his initial savings. As he scrambled to secure funding for the other five films, the Authors executive team announced that their plans for the promised studio were held off until production on *The Broad Road* finished.[196] He reached out to community investors once again to secure an extra $100,000 to produce the films he pledged to develop with Hapsburg Liebe. On October 6, he penned "An Letter of Importance to the People of Orlando," which he published in both the *Orlando Sentinel* and *Orlando Evening Star*:

> Fortunes can be made from the present urgent demand in the motion picture industry for good productions. Orlando is ideally situated as the home of motion picture production. And here thousands of dollars will be spent that we earn in the making of our pictures. No merchant can help but see the larger totals in his daily sales and weekly profits increase through the presence of this industry here, and its expenditures among the people whose farsightedness and progressiveness have furnished the capital that has made the company a success. Nor have we just joined together and said, "We will do this thing somehow," no such foolishness.[197]

With an estimated cost of $40,000–$50,000 for each of the six promised films, O'Loughlin and company guaranteed investors an over $100,000 return per film. The appeal was also extended to civic boosters and local politicians in the hope to increase the city's visibility and draw tourism. They contended,

"Orlando itself presents every opportunity for city pictures, either north, east, west, or south."[198]

Even with the initial windfall Authors received to produce *The Broad Road*, it seems that Orlando's would-be movie producers became increasingly skeptical of the high-hatted promises of the Authors Executive Committee. The following month, after shooting for *The Broad Road* wrapped, and without additional capital for his proposed studio or to produce any further films, O'Loughlin abruptly left Orlando and disappears from the record. Upon abandoning Orlando, he sold his shares to R. E. Grable, a member of the Orlando Chamber of Commerce, who had remained on as one of Authors' primary investors.

For his part, Grable described his ascent to company president as "very hurried," saying that even though he "had not attended a single board meeting and was only given the company as an evidence of my faith in its success by taking the bulk share of stocks, . . . almost immediately I was told I had been made president."[199] Without industry experience or the know-how to run a film studio, he overoptimistically predicted that with the success of Authors, the motion picture industry would soon shift from California to Florida.[200]

The Broad Road premiered on January 17, 1923, to a sold-out crowd at the Beacham Theater in downtown Orlando. However, by the time of its premiere, Grable no longer expressed the same national aspirations for his studio as he had in the local papers a year earlier in 1922. Rebilled by Grable as a home-talent production, *The Broad Road* had a modest local exhibition around Central Florida and was later distributed across the country by First National (the forerunner of Warner Brothers).[201] Despite the film selling out local movie houses and securing a national distribution deal, the realities of independent film production soon hit home to the remaining members of Associated Authors Productions. In the end, *The Broad Road* came nowhere near recouping its expenses, and, most astounding of all, John O'Loughlin absconded with tens of thousands of dollars, never to be heard from by Orlandoans again.[202]

R. E. Grable continued to hold out hope that positive word of mouth for *The Broad Road* could help supplement the costs for the company's next film. After they paid off the editing firm that processed the film stock, and the film's distribution fees were deducted by First National, the net profits for *The Broad Road* failed to come anywhere close to O'Loughlin's promises. Several months later Grable was left to cut his losses, and he sold off his shares to State Senator Moses Overstreet. Senator Overstreet outlined his own plan to produce several additional comedy films that utilized local funding. He also promised to reedit footage from several loose-ended comedy films that were shot earlier in the year.[203]

Associated Authors' vice president, Donald Cheney, shared his hopes that "the future of the company and the motion picture industry in Florida was promising," but in the end, Authors would produce no further films, and its proposed downtown Orlando studio never materialized.[204]

D. W. Griffith in South Florida

At the end of the 1910s, David Wark Griffith was regarded as the master of silent melodrama. In 1919, he formed the United Artists Corporation (UA) with silent film icons Charlie Chaplin, Douglas Fairbanks Sr., and Mary Pickford. As an independent studio, UA provided directors like Griffith the opportunity to follow their own creative vision for projects without the commercial oversight that had started to dog other filmmakers as they fell under the umbrella of major Hollywood studios. After the widespread financial success of *Broken Blossoms* (1919), his first UA outing, Griffith expressed his desire to return to return to big-budget, epic storytelling. After leaving California behind, he moved his company from Los Angeles to Upstate New York, where he built a studio facility.

In October 1919, Griffith purchased a $375,000, 28-acre estate in Mamaroneck, New York, formerly owned by Florida rail magnate Henry Flagler. It would later be remembered as "the home Griffith never had."[205] In order to update the property into a fully functioning studio that he hoped would one day become his own proposed "Hollywood East," Griffith needed to raise an additional $500,000.[206] To raise the funds he needed to pay for the new studio, Griffith contracted with the First National Company to film two South Seas romances, *The Idol Dancer* (1920) and *The Love Flower* (1920). With his focus primarily on his next big-budget spectacle, *Way Down East* (1920), Griffith's collaboration with First National in Florida was remembered by his cinematographer and frequent collaborator Billy Bitzer as "little more than routine productions that [would] do nothing for Griffith's reputation as a director."[207]

In November 1919, Griffith and company traveled to Fort Lauderdale and commenced filming *The Idol Dancer* and *Love Flower* simultaneously. Hoping to get the most out of his Florida detour, Griffith also traveled north to shoot near Jacksonville to pick up secondary location footage near the St. Johns River for *Way Down East* (1920).[208] While Griffith presided over filming for *Idol Dancer* and *Love Flower*, his concentration was clearly on his New York studio and building up publicity for *Way Down East* instead of on the day-today demands his Florida productions needed. Meanwhile, Fort Lauderdale responded by rolling out the red carpet for the director and his high-profile silent stars Richard Barthelmess and Ford Sterling. Local papers reported how "the whole town turned out to watch the filming, with many Seminole Indians and other residents typically working as extras."[209] Griffith may have been a sight seldom seen outside of the Las Olas Inn, but Philip Wielding of the Fort Lauderdale Historical Society recalled, "The actors turned out to be friendly and seemed really interested in the townsfolk. Some of them dated local young men and one even married here. All of the people of the town watched at least a few scenes being shot."[210]

Even with the positive relations between the Fort Lauderdale community and the films' cast and crew, both productions were marred by tragedy and disaster. While filming a sequence in a coconut grove near the Las Olas Inn, Clarine Seymour, the lead actress for *Idol Dancer*, fell from a tree. Plagued by abdominal pains, Seymour managed to push through and complete her scenes, but she soon after took a turn for the worse and was rushed by train back to New York. Seymour was diagnosed with having a twisted intestine, and when her condition failed to improve, she underwent emergency surgery. Although the surgery was initially successful, Seymour soon came down with pneumonia and died from complications of the infection. The unexpected passing of Clarine Seymour would have the ominous distinction of becoming one of the earliest celebrity deaths to shake the American film industry to its core.[211] Before her untimely death, Seymour filmed several scenes for a supporting role in Griffith's *Way Down East*, which, along with her star turn in *Idol Dancer*, could have given her the breakout role that might have set her on the path to Hollywood stardom.

Production on *Love Flower* was also fraught with peril and nearly resulted in the deaths of the entire production company. While scouting locations on a boating trip between Fort Lauderdale and The Bahamas, Griffith and his cast and crew sailed into an unexpected storm that caused their ship to run aground against a desert island. The production team was stranded on the island for three days, capturing national headlines with hourly updates as the U.S. Coast Guard searched for the missing production team. After three days of being stranded in the middle of the Caribbean Sea, the *Love Flower* cast and crew were found and safely returned to Fort Lauderdale, where the staff of the Las Olmas Inn and town leaders threw a party to celebrate the misbegotten troupe.[212] Ignoring the hospitality and friendly accommodations provided by the people of Fort Lauderdale, Griffith announced shortly after the shipwreck incident that he did not believe "the city provided the backdrop he needed,"

Figure 10. G. W. "Billy" Bitzer (*left*), acclaimed as one of the first and greatest early camera artists, with director D. W. Griffith on the set of *Idol Dancer* outside of Fort Lauderdale, 1919. Courtesy of State Archives of Florida, Florida Memory.

and he relocated to New Providence Island in The Bahamas to complete the remainder of his location shooting.[213]

Following the premiere of Griffith's Fort Lauderdale films, critics dismissed the films for their "overly maudlin sentimentality," while praising the use of authentic landscape and scenery that came with filming on location in South Florida. Several months after completing his work on *Idol Dancer* and *Love Flower*, Griffith's *Way Down East* premiered to rave reviews, becoming one of his greatest financial successes and giving United Artists much sought-after industry-wide acclaim.[214] While Griffith continued to attempt to establish his studio in Mamaroneck in the early 1920s, his company was hit with several box-office failures in a row. Even contemporary critics began to complain that his later films were "too long in both unfolding and concluding" and that stories had become "rather worn and thin."[215]

By the winter season of 1922–23, Griffith once again returned to South Florida to take advantage of its temperate winter weather and abundant sunshine to film *The White Rose* (1923). At the same time, Vitagraph director John S. Robertson came to Fort Lauderdale to film several scenes for *Classmates* (1924), which was mostly shot at the Mamaroneck studio in New York, with Fort Lauderdale used as a stand-in for scenes set in the jungles of South America.[216] During the filming of *White Rose*, Griffith coordinated with E. G. Sewell of the fledgling Miami Studios to negotiate a leasing arrangement in which he would bring his own cast (notably silent stars Mae Marsh and Carol Dempster) and his longtime collaborator Billy Bitzer but promised to hire a local crew for all other production-related tasks.

In their films made in Florida D. W. Griffith and Billy Bitzer conveyed a spirit of inventiveness and creativity in form and style that had eluded many of their films over the past decade. In these films Griffith broke from his conventional aesthetic of close-ups and cropped-in sequences in favor of long shots and wide-frame views that showcased the location. It was remarked that his time in Florida had a rejuvenating on the beleaguered film pioneer.[217] As promising as the process of filming at Miami Studios may have seemed during production, Griffith's initial enthusiasm for the visual potential of the film was deflated after he returned to Mamaroneck to process the raw footage he had shot and discovered that the bright Florida sun had overexposed many of the film's sequences. Even though this was a technical error on the part of the Griffith team, he expressed his frustration in the trade presses and his displeasure at not being able to adequately capture the vibrant shades and shadows that had initially caught his eye.[218] At this point in time, cameras were not yet able to fully capture the awe-inspiring range of colors and landscape details that the South Florida coastline could offer filmmakers.

The White Rose and *Classmates* turned out to be yet another pair of financial failures for Griffith, which contributed toward his ouster at UA and the eventual closure of his New York studio the following year, in 1924.[219] As film historians Susan Doll and David Morrow have observed, "*The White Rose* signaled the beginning of a permanent decline for Griffith, in which his films and production methods were increasingly out of step with the times."[220] Historian Jan-Christopher Horak agrees that the flawed approach to storytelling that characterizes Griffith's later films certainly accelerated his decline, but he added that the film's adventurous approach toward capturing its subtropical setting contributes to the "compositional grace of Griffith's camera" and moves the film into "the realms of Griffith's best work."[221]

Even by 1920s standards, Griffith's efforts to spark a cultural conversation over race and history were severely outdated. In the opening scenes of *The White Rose*, Mae Marsh's character is taken in by "two kindly black folks," played by renowned vaudeville comedian Porter Strong and Lucille La Verne (a white actress in blackface).[222] Contemporary critics dismissed Griffith's feeble attempt to overcome the criticisms associated with his stereotyping of freed people in *The Birth of a Nation* (1915). Reviews for Griffith's Florida films were critical of their "mawkish sickening sentimentality" and Griffith's "refusal to take ideas from the trend of the day." In the critics' view, Griffith was working "in isolation, surrounded by minor advisors, a genius out of touch with the world."[223] As historian of the early race film industry Thomas Cripps observed, "Griffith lived out his life learning nothing and forgetting nothing."[224] Even as his career plummeted to its nadir, Griffith failed to let go of his "old Southern attitude" and take advantage of the range of possibilities that America's newest frontier could have provided in the way of the rejuvenation and reinvention of his career.

Unbeknownst to Griffith, as he struggled to complete his ill-fated Fort Lauderdale films, three hundred miles to the north in Jacksonville, a collective of African American entertainers and their white allies joined forces to resurrect Jacksonville's defunct film industry and establish the first—and ultimately only—production studio solely dedicated to the making of race films. These films would attempt to diminish the malicious racial stereotypes that had come to dominate the early American motion picture industry. In so doing, they would turn the eyes of the national film industry back to Florida.

2

"Of Course They Please the Southern People"

Florida Becomes Home to the Cinematic "Lost Cause" and Race Film Industry, 1908–1928

> Southern stockholders [from Jacksonville] in the Kalem Company were in the majority, and . . . audiences in the North are now all or nearly all interested in the Southern version, and . . . of course they please the Southern people. The success of Kalem's Civil War films will inspire other studios to travel to Florida for the purposes of authentic narrative filmmaking.
> Kenean Buell, of the Kalem Company, to the *Florida Times-Union*, 1911

"A Civic Life Reflecting the Community's Vitality"

In his sweeping autobiography *Along This Way*, James Weldon Johnson describes his eventful career as a central fixture of the Harlem Renaissance, NAACP leader, diplomat, and visionary educator. In this introspective and self-effacing story of his life, Johnson provides his readers with a comprehensive look into the ebbing tides of race relations in the United States from the Reconstruction period to the onset of the Red Summer of 1919. Johnson tells his story through personal experiences that paint a narrative of striving and success against the backdrop of the adoption of segregationist laws at the state and national level, and the resurrection of the Ku Klux Klan. By 1933, the year Johnson's memoir was published, he had witnessed a systematic rollback of the promises put forth by the Reconstruction amendments. Johnson recalled, "When I was growing up [in the 1880s], most of the city policemen were Negroes; several members of the city council were Negroes."[1] Yet by the 1930s, Johnson lamented that Jacksonville essentially "ate Jim Crow in their segregated restaurants, taught Jim Crow in their segregated schools, preached Jim Crow from their segregated pulpits, and lived Jim Crow in their segregated neighborhoods."[2]

The acrimony in Johnson's words, combined with his sharp repudiation of the imposition of Jim Crow segregation by Jacksonville's all-white city government, lays bare how the city's African American population were effectively stripped of the civil rights gains that stemmed from the Reconstruction era. Personal testimonies from authors and activists such as James Weldon Johnson provide important insight into the lived experiences of marginalized groups during the early twentieth century—especially the way social spaces and visual culture engaged with political and discourse in the Jim Crow South.

Jacksonville offers a compelling case study as a New South city that underwent a drastic shift from being a city with a Black-majority population that had widespread political agency to the epitome of a white-supremacist stronghold. This transformation was brought on by a series of restrictions to Black people's access to public spaces and the implementation of a legally sanctioned American apartheid regime. As civil and voting rights were systematically denied to the city's Black population, Jacksonville's Ashley Street—located in the primarily African American neighborhood of LaVilla—became an important place of dissent and resistance, with the lively theater district emerging as the "Harlem of the South." Jacksonville's Ashley Street theater district also later helped to inspire an itinerant film producer named Richard Norman to build the first and only film studio dedicated solely to the production of race films among the ruins of Jacksonville's abandoned film studios in Arlington.

Decades earlier, Kalem had created the template for Civil War dramas that were sympathetic to the Confederate cause, most notoriously adapted later by D. W. Griffith in *The Birth of a Nation* (1915). Such films inspired the resurrection of the Ku Klux Klan and in turn a new wave of racially motivated terrorism in the United States. Although Griffith's role in resurrecting the Klan and inspiring racial violence through his film has been duly documented, without exploring the context of the films that preceded *The Birth of a Nation*, the full extent of the early American film industry's involvement in perpetuating white-supremacist ideologies cannot be fully understood.

In the 1910s and 1920s, Black voting rights organizers and performers in Jacksonville aligned themselves with members of the NAACP, led by James Weldon Johnson as its executive director. Johnson and the NAACP effectively served as "the tip of its spear for piercing one-party rule in the South."[3] The on-the-ground coordination of Johnson's voting rights campaign would not have been possible without the efforts of Mary McLeod Bethune, an educator from Daytona Beach, Florida, known as the "First Lady of the Struggle." Bethune's efforts as activist and organizer who would establish a template for the nonviolent direct-action campaigns carried out by Martin Luther King Jr.

and the Southern Christian Leadership Conference (SCLC) in the 1950s and 1960s.[4]

At the turn of the twentieth century, Jacksonville was a city with an African American–majority population and a small but aspirational African American middle class, but most of the wealth and power in the city remained concentrated in a relatively small white aristocracy. According to Jacksonville historian James Crooks, "Black Jacksonville, despite varying degrees of segregation, discrimination, and exclusion from voting, education, entertainment, and work opportunities, pursued a varied civic life reflecting the community's vitality."[5]

Jacksonville's political and demographic transformation was part of a broader political shift that took place in the American South at the turn of the twentieth century. In 1907, Jacksonville's African American–majority Sixth Ward, which had consistently elected Black Republicans to the City Council, was gerrymandered out of existence. The redistricting of Jacksonville's last bastion of African American political agency was soon followed by the removal of the city's last two African American city councillors in 1907. Over the next fifty years, African Americans were effectively barred from holding public office in Jacksonville.[6] That same year, Governor Napoleon Broward, a self-described "unapologetic segregationist," proposed to the U.S. Congress that it "purchase [a] territory, either domestic or foreign, and provide means to purchase the property of the negroes at a reasonable price and to transport them to the territory purchased by the United States."[7]

Taking the hint from Florida's governor, more than forty thousand Florida Blacks fled in search of more congenial surroundings.[8] Between 1900 and 1910, Jacksonville's slight African American majority had systematically eroded with the arrival of whites from neighboring Georgia, Alabama, and South Carolina. It is no surprise that with the migration of an increased number of whites from surrounding Deep South states, their segregationist sentiments soon followed.[9]

Florida in the early twentieth century served as both a wellspring for the return of white-supremacist terrorist organizations such as the Ku Klux Klan and as one of the most important early battlegrounds of the civil rights movement. Jacksonville's brief heyday as the "World's Winter Film Capital" led to its numerous contributions toward the technical and narrative conventions that would later be adopted by the feature film industry that eventually consolidated in Hollywood. One of the most lasting—and damaging—influences, however, was the way the region's racial politics ultimately influenced its filmmakers and, in turn, defined the portrayals of race relations in American film during the first half of the twentieth century. A closer look into how the politics of the Jim Crow era in Jacksonville shaped the national discussion on race highlights a fascinating interplay between the social power of the motion picture as an apparatus that reinforced the worst impulses of the Jim Crow system, while at the same time served as an instrument of resistance and self-determination by Jacksonville's Black community.

This chapter will revisit many of the same film producers and studios discussed in chapter 1, although this time we will investigate how early Florida filmmakers formed relationships with activists and community organizers who did their best to stem the tide of Jim Crow. In doing so, this chapter seeks to uncover the intersection between race and the early American film industry. As such, this portion of the book is a response to film historian Daniel Bernardi's call "to begin revising the revisionist, with an eye to expanding the history of U.S. cinema to uncover, deconstruct, or defamiliarize its racial practices."[10] This approach can be accomplished by exploring the complications and contradictions in play as Florida-based filmmakers became increasingly entwined in local politics in the first decades of the twentieth century.

Kalem Introduces the "Southern" as Florida's First Motion Picture Genre

In his seminal work on African American cinema, *Slow Fade to Black*, Thomas Cripps established the conventional narrative surrounding portrayals of the Confederacy and racial politics in film that have remained in place to this day. According to Cripps, "Until the release of *The Birth of a Nation*, the races never confronted each other on equal terms, the rulers versus the aggrieved."[11] This dialectic of oppression and resistance has yielded important discussions on the film's role in "transposing the national myth of the South into terms congruent with the mythology of White American nationalism."[12] In other words, by examining motion picture production and spectatorship into a dynamic between what Cara Caddoo terms as "the rulers" and "the aggrieved," a template can be established to explain how "the mass protest movement against *The Birth of a Nation* continued to develop in dialogue with modern Black life with the emergence of the race film industry."[13]

The "Southern" genre films effectively established the grounds for a cultural conversation in early American film that would notoriously meet its apex with the distribution of *The Birth of a Nation*. What is missing both from Cripps's initial observation and subsequent works on the pervading influence of "Lost Cause" redemption narratives is an explanation of the influence place has on the genre's inception. Understanding how the motion picture *inspired* and was *influenced by* the social transformation of Florida politics during the first decades of the twentieth century provides an essential component of Florida's early film history.

As discussed in chapter 1, between 1908 and 1914, Jacksonville, Florida, became home to the first Civil War–themed films to be told from an exclusively southern perspective. Although studios such as Kalem, Lubin, Selig, and Vim Comedy Company were all originally from the North, the films produced during their wintertime expeditions to North Florida were without doubt influenced by the culture and community there. The "Southern" film genre depended extensively on reductionist representations of race first introduced through Kalem Studios' *Florida Series*. The looming presence of the city's motion picture industry shaped the community and national discussion on race and memory during cinema's silent era.

It was the combined arrival of northern entertainers, displaced Deep South white planters, and aspirational New South businessmen that created the terse dynamic in the films made *in* and *about* the South in a period that has been called "the nadir of race relations in America."[14] The perversion of Civil War–era memory on film first appeared in Kalem's *Florida Series* during the 1900s and 1910s. These early serials helped establish a narrative that romanticized the South and misrepresented race relations by picturing a world that presented a distorted and dangerous depiction of Southern life in films set during the antebellum and Reconstruction eras.[15]

During the summer of 1907, Kalem filmed several historically based films on location in Upstate New York, New Jersey, and Connecticut. The indoor scenes for Kalem's Civil War–set *The Days of '61* (1907) were filmed on location in Connecticut, while the battle scenes were shot on the grounds of St. John's Military Academy in Manlius, New York. According to Gene Gauntier, the studio's most popular films during this time were "Western" and "Southern" stories. She remarked, "Taverns doubled for western saloons, for Civil War recruiting stations, and dozens of other sets," and with simple "costumes and props, we turned out pictures which were things of beauty even in those crude days."[16] The financial success that followed *The Days of '61* inspired Kalem's general manager Frank Marion to produce even more Civil War–themed films. Marion, for that matter, "suggested it would be a novel thing to make pictures from the Confederate side."[17] Kalem's absorption into the MPPC in December 1908 was followed a week later by their first expedition to Florida. The additional financial and legal security provided by Kalem's membership in the Edison Trust helped the company pursue on-location filming for a proposed a series of Civil War films as a part of their *Sunny South* releases.[18]

Figure 11. An actor profile in *Motion Picture Story Magazine* featuring Gene Gauntier and her upcoming film *Sailor Jack's Reformation* (1911), for which she also wrote the scenario. Courtesy of Media History Digital Library.

When Kalem's Civil War films were produced in New York and Connecticut, their films usually had Union characters as the protagonists. Yet, after arriving in Florida, the studio's perspective shifted to increasingly sympathize with the Confederacy. This shift in perspective from northern-themed to southern-themed Civil War films can be traced to their first season in Jacksonville during the winter of 1908–9. Two of Kalem's films from their initial excursion to Jacksonville, *A Florida Feud: Or, Love in the Everglades* and *The Cracker's Bride* (1909), were marketed to northern audiences as "a very faithful portrayal of conditions which exist in certain portions of Florida today."[19]

Ironically, it was Kalem's initial Florida-set films that received a less-than-enthusiastic reception in Jacksonville. Following the debut of Kalem's *Florida Series*, the *Florida Times-Union* carped, "*A Florida Feud* presented a rather unfavorable picturization of poor whites residing outside of Jacksonville," while *The Cracker's Bride* was condemned by one local reviewer as "misshapen, shuddering, disgusting, and revolting, as well as totally unfit for showing."[20] The animosity against Kalem became so great that "Jacksonville whites threatened to throttle future Kalem's productions unless the studio ceased making such movies as *Florida Crackers* [*The Cracker's Bride*]."[21] The community-wide backlash was a likely factor in Kalem's decision to shift the content of their scenarios toward more southern friendly topics during future filming seasons.

Kalem's mission to create "authentic" location-based stories showcases the complicated race and class dynamics in North Florida during this period. A film that best encapsulates Kalem's shifting ideology from that same winter season is the studio's adaptation of Irish playwright Dion Boucicault's antebellum antislavery melodrama *The Octoroon* (1859). Although the original play concerned the residents of a pre–Civil War Louisiana plantation, Sidney Olcott's adaptation, *The Octoroon: A Story of the Turpentine Forest* (1909), relocated the story to the Florida Pines. In a synopsis published in *Moving Picture World*, Olcott expressed, "we are going to try to teach you something about our great country while we are entertaining you with our dramatic story."[22]

Dion Boucicault's original version of *The Octoroon* set out to provide an explicit commentary on the moral evils of slavery, while Olcott's 1909 adaptation sidesteps any mention of slavery and instead focuses on the interracial relationship between "a beautiful young octoroon named Zoe and her lover, who is the owner of the turpentine still."[23] In the film adaptation, the owner of the turpentine still is described as "a man of Spanish descent, a cruel vindictive brute of little principle."[24] By changing the ethnicity of the film's characters and placing greater emphasis on showing "the principal features of the turpentine industry," Olcott and the Kalem Players appear to have avoided another unfavorable response from Jacksonville civic leaders.

Perhaps as a capitulation to its northern urban audiences, Kalem producers made an unexpected choice to present the interracial relationship central to the film's premise in line with the original British version. This version ends with "a colored boy confessing to the crime" and "love triumphant [as] the mixed-race couple are united."[25] The film adaptation deviates further from the American version of Boucicault's stage version of *The Octoroon*, where the story initially had to be changed to have a tragic ending in which Zoe dies. In the nineteenth century the "original American ending" of *The Octoroon* was required by theater owners before the play could be performed.[26]

It is uncertain why Sidney Olcott specifically preferred the original British ending to the more familiar American ending of *The Octoroon*, but it indicates the Kalem Company was at the time indifferent to any potential backlash to an overt display of miscegenation on the screen. It is unlikely that Olcott and company intended to make an explicit social commentary in their films, however there was quite an extensive diffused commentary on slavery and racial violence in many of the films in Kalem's *Florida Series*.

Another notable multireel film serial in Kalem's first *Florida Series*, written and directed by Gene Gauntier, was *The Northern Schoolmaster* (1909). Produced six years before the premiere of *The Birth of a Nation* (1915), Gauntier's film may have been the first to feature the Ku Klux Klan on the screen.[27] The film was promoted in *Moving Picture World* as "a true-to-the-life story of the scorn of the Southern gentleman for the negro and their ill-treatment of a northern schoolmaster who takes the part of the one who is being persecuted."[28] Unlike D. W. Griffith, however, Gene Gauntier depicted the Klan as antagonists who assault the northern teacher and set fire to a southern mansion. The film concludes with "the heroic rescue of a young lady [ostensibly from the Klan] by the schoolmaster which lets the people see what courage is in him and they are quick to atone for their past misdeeds."[29]

Both *The Octoroon* and *Northern Schoolmaster* demonstrate a meager effort on the producers' part to portray slaveholders and Klansmen as amoral villains. Both films also serve as an ominous predictor of things to come regarding depictions of race on film. As the 1910s progressed, an increasing number of films began to adopt the pro-Confederate "Lost Cause" narrative. This distorted account of Civil War history, which historian Eric Foner considers "the edifice of the Jim Crow system," was used as a means "for the white South [to resist] outside efforts in changing race relations because of the worry of having another Reconstruction."[30]

Ultimately, "Southern" genre films demonstrated the sincerity of the southern cause by presenting the Confederacy in sacrificial terms as the cycle of war movies shaped the outlines of heroism and villainy in purely southern terms.[31] Even if early "Southern" genre films focused on the villainy of slave masters and Klansmen, the agency of its African American characters was severely compromised. In Kalem's Civil War-set films, Black characters were invariably pawns in the conflict rather than independent individuals with minds and wills of their own.[32]

Kalem's *Florida Series* introduced key concepts that would later be mimicked and repeated by other film studios across the country. One such film that truly set the tone for the genre was *The Girl Spy* (1909), written by and starring Gene Gauntier, this was the first of a series of films that were a loosely adapted depiction of the exploits of real-life Confederate spy Belle Boyd.[33] Although the *Girl Spy* films fell in line with Kalem's mission of producing location-based stories, the film also represents an important turning point in the Civil War genre. Gene Gauntier's *Girl Spy* films attempted to counter the image of stodgy Union-focused stage adaptations, in favor of using a southern heroine, a Confederate point of view, and southern locations.

A recurring theme started to appear in the releases in Kalem's *Florida Series:* the films placed their emphasis on authenticity and the use of the local landscape to portray what white southerners considered to be "real history." Promotions published in *Moving Picture World* and other exhibitor-approved synopses offered in trade presses like *Kalem Kalendar* showcase these familiar tropes. *Moving Picture World* describes Gauntier's eponymous character as a daring young girl who "had consecrated her entire life to the cause of their beloved Southland."[34] While the films' synopses emphasized the use of authentic costumes and props (actual period uniforms and weapons) that includes a "plucky heroine."[35]

Several films in the *Girl Spy* series demonstrate the narrative conventions that would go on to define the "Southern" as a film genre. *A Daughter of Dixie* (1910) focuses on a love triangle between the "Girl Spy" and a Northern and Southern officer. As she "wavers between love and duty," the film resolves with the heroine saving the life of her Unionist beau. The film's emphasis on reconciliation further plays out when, upon the heroine professing her love, the Union officer and his Confederate rival shake hands and pledge "to forget the past and renew the friendship of the Blue and Gray."[36] *The Confederate Spy: A Story of the Civil War* (1910) takes on a more shaded perspective on North-South relations. The film tells of a Confederate officer who infiltrates the Union army and his wife—played by Gauntier—who is chased from her home after a Union soldier attempts to assault her and burns their plantation to the ground. Gauntier's heroine is rescued from her near rape by her slave "Uncle Daniel," who attacks the soldier and helps her escape. Daniel later aids the eponymous Confederate spy after he is captured behind enemy lines and delivers the young family to safety from the "lawless men who made the war their excuse for plunder and robbery." The film concludes with the couple holding hands with their slave as they gaze at him affectionately.[37]

The archetype of the "faithful slave narrative" was yet another disturbing aspect of the "Cinematic Lost Cause" that Kalem had adopted. Characters such as Uncle Daniel often embodied the notion that certain slaves (and later free domestic workers) were seen by slaveholders as one of the family.[38] Similar characters would reoccur in Lost Cause narrative films such as *The Birth of a Nation* and be echoed in the unquestioning loyalty of characters such as Hattie McDaniel's Mammy and Butterfly McQueen's Prissy in *Gone with the Wind* (1939).[39]

What is most confounding about Kalem's predilection to tell stories from a Confederate perspective in Florida is that Jacksonville itself was not a traditional Old South City. Furthermore, very few military engagements took place in Florida during the Civil War. Regardless, the aspiration of Kalem's early Civil War narratives was to showcase "historical fact," and producing such stories in the South certainly influenced the shape these narratives took. The imposition of the city's Jim Crow regime in 1907 exacerbated the existing racial disparities in Jacksonville, creating an atmosphere of racial animosity that contradicted the image of a prosperous Jacksonville that the Chamber of Commerce was promoting.[40]

Behind the affluence of Jacksonville's Main Street and prosperous neighborhoods such as Riverside and Springfield, the city's segregationist regime produced widespread poverty in African American neighborhoods such as Oakland, Hansontown, LaVilla, and Brooklyn.[41] As James Crooks has remarked, "Observers of the New South rightly saw boards of trade and chambers of commerce as engines for economic development. They also welcomed northern capitalists and upheld white supremacy."[42] Ultimately, the spending that came from northern capital in Florida's motion picture industry would further reinforce the darkest aspects of life in Florida during the Jim Crow era.

"A New Elan to the Old Tradition": Florida and the Cinematic Lost Cause

During the 1910s Jacksonville experienced a dramatic decade of demographic and economic growth, the city's motion picture industry served as an important chronicler of the broader cultural shifts taking place within the city.[43] In addition to experiencing a drastic demographic shift, Jacksonville soon had new arrivals from the Edison Manufacturing Company eager to establish seasonal residence in the city that had been labeled the "World's Winter Film Capital."[44]

As discussed in chapter 1, in the fall of 1909, the Selig Polyscope Company of Chicago leased a portion of South Jacksonville's Dixieland Amusement Park to make motion pictures using elephants, lions, tigers, and camels. Several more studios, including Majestic, Vim Studios, the Thanhouser Film Corporation, Gaumont, and Metro, soon followed Selig's lead.[45] By the end of 1910, eight theaters offered a combination of movies, vaudeville, minstrel shows, and touring stock companies for the community. The *Florida Times-Union* slightly exaggerated in describing Jacksonville's Main Street as the new "Great White Way." Although the city's Black theatergoers were allowed entry to Main Street theaters, they were relegated to segregated balconies. The only exception where Black moviegoers were able to freely sit where they wished was in the Black-only Bijou and Globe theaters.[46]

Despite the full imposition of segregation ordinances and increasing disenfranchisement, Jacksonville's African American community had marginally expanded its economic and cultural life during the decade as well. The 1910 City Directory listed 342 small businesses owned by Blacks, almost double the number listed nine years earlier. However, there were notable barriers to opportunities for employment, education, and social mobility that hindered the city's economic and physical development.[47] Jacksonville's motion picture industry represents a stark metric of the self-imposed limitations its Jim Crow regime had placed on its own growth. The de facto economic boycott against the first would-be Black film producers eventually led to the creation of a separate distribution network that would cater to theaters for Black audiences with little distribution anywhere else.[48]

Rising racial tensions in Jacksonville came to a decisive head on July 4, 1910, in the aftermath of the heavyweight showdown between the Galveston Giant Jack Johnson and the so-called Great White Hope, Jim Jefferies. Jacksonville's African American community celebrated Johnson's win; white Floridians seethed. Incensed local whites responded to the news of Jefferies' defeat by forming street gangs to attack any revelers seen celebrating Johnson's victory in the ring. Although the overall extent of injuries and property destruction remains highly contested (a common issue in calculating racial violence during the period), insights as to its extent come, ironically, from the response of the city's white leadership.

The following day, Mayor William S. Jordan called for the arrest of more than forty whites for their participation in the riot, which is all the more indication of the severity of the violence inflicted on Jacksonville's Black community.[49] Meanwhile, the *Florida Times-Union* sought to exonerate the rioters by reporting that Black Jacksonvillians "clashed in the streets with whites enraged over 'their manner and manifestations of joy' after Johnson's victory."[50]

Just as the initial outbreak of violence started to subside, the announced distribution of film footage from the fight threatened to reignite tensions. J. Stuart Blackton of the Vitagraph Company made sure to have his cameras rolling in Reno on that fateful Fourth of July, and his *Johnson-Jefferies Fight* (1910) threatened to ignite a political maelstrom across the United States. Two days after the Johnson-Jefferies match, nine states had already banned the exhibition of the film outright, and by the end of the week every southern city (including Jacksonville) joined in the ban.[51]

Film historian Dan Streible astutely argues, "No discussion of race and early cinema in the United States would be complete without considering the impact of Jack Johnson's cinematic image on the racial order of things."[52] Perhaps the most lasting influence that stemmed from subsequent efforts to censor the film is that the motion picture industry became complicit in "imposing segregation of theatrical space[, which] remained a defining reminder of white rule."[53] The visceral reaction of white Americans against the Johnson revelers through both mob violence and the publication of manifestos was not limited to North Florida but was a common occurrence throughout the summer of 1910.

Jack Johnson's victory in the boxing ring sparked a coordinated backlash by white Americans keen to reassert their cultural dominance, and his open defiance of miscegenation codes that dictated that Black people could not have children with white people would later bring about Johnson's own downfall and exile.[54] In the aftermath of the efforts to ban the screening of the *Johnson-Jefferies Fight*, filmmakers established several tropes that were central to how the southern imaginary was portrayed in ensuing decades. In Jacksonville, the fallout from the Johnson Riots led Mayor Jordan and the city Board of Trade to turn to the city's motion picture industry to help create films that could effectively undermine the images of Black excellence that the distribution of the *Johnson-Jeffries Fight* had briefly succeeded in flashing across the screen.

In April 1912, the Kalem Company built what was at the time the world's largest outdoor stage for "yard pictures" right in Jacksonville.[55] By the time Kalem's Jacksonville studio was under construction, Kalem already had two other studios in New Jersey and California and a new roster of "Kalem Girls," including early silent stars such as Alice Joyce, Anna Nilsson, and Ruth Roland. During the 1912–13 winter season, Kalem revisited several of its most popular pro-Confederate–themed films, including an updated three-reel version of *The Octoroon* (1913), this time including the original American stage ending, which concludes in the tragic death of Zoe, the titular "Octoroon," and a repudiation of the film's presumed interracial romance.[56]

By the time the new *Octoroon* premiered, Gene Gauntier and Sidney Olcott had broken with Kalem and signed with the newly formed Warner's Features distribution business, owned by brothers Harry, Albert, and Sam Warner. That same winter, they arrived in Jacksonville with plans to form their own production company, the Gene Gauntier Players, or "the GGs."[57] Like their former Kalem counterparts, once they arrived in Jacksonville, Gauntier and Olcott would return to their "southern" roots.[58] While Sidney Olcott convalesced from a bout of appendicitis, Gauntier's husband, Jack J. Clark, assumed charge of the company's day-to-day operations.

The first film Clark and Gauntier produced under this new arrangement was yet another Klan-themed drama, *In the Clutches of the Ku Klux Klan* (1913). A thinly veiled remake of Kalem's earlier *The Northern Schoolmaster* (1909), the film explores the terrorism that the Klan carried out against other whites. In the film, Jack Clark played the role of a white lynching victim, while at least one scene implied the violence the Klan carried out against Blacks. In a *Moving Picture World* interview promoting the film, Clark callously recalls how a Duval County sheriff "induced a gentleman of color" to perform in a scene where he would be chased by bloodhounds. After he was given what Clark described as a "safe start," "The hounds jumped at the scent and in full cry were away like the wind[;] you could have played checkers on his coattails."[59] Although the antagonist role the Klan played in Gauntier's Florida films offers an insightful contrast to the disturbing historic revision that would come following the premiere of Griffith's *The Birth of a Nation*, the filmmakers were clearly dismissive of the full scope of violence the organization had inflicted on freed people. The dilution of the Klan's terrorism found in *In the Clutches of the Ku Klux Klan* demonstrated a decisive turn in Florida's film industry's toward the "southern" perspective on the American Civil War.

Jacksonville's film studios became increasingly influenced by efforts to perpetuate a cinematic telling of the Lost Cause narrative. The local "cooperation" between Jacksonville's film studios and Lost Cause revisionists can best be seen when the Edison, Lubin, Kalem, GGs, and Sid Olcott Players all came together to film the annual meeting of the United Confederate Veterans, on May 6–8, 1914. The event was intended to commemorate the fiftieth anniversary of the nearby Battle of Olustee, which occurred on February 20, 1864, and provided an opportunity for more than 48,000 Confederate soldiers to celebrate a reunion in Jacksonville.[60] That day the cameras captured the proceedings as Jacksonville experienced an "invasion" of Confederate battalions who had been renamed "The Legion of the Lost Cause." With the addition

Figure 12. Pamphlet promoting the United Confederate Veterans meeting, which featured Jacksonville's "invasion" by members of the "Legion of the Lost Cause," 1914. Cameramen from Edison, Lubin, Kalem, GGs, and the Sid Olcott Players all contributed footage of the event. Courtesy of Florida Historical Society.

of 12,000 members of the Sons and Daughters of the Confederacy, the parade's numbers swelled to more than 60,000 bystanders and marchers. The procession was then greeted by Florida governor Park Trammell, who took the time to shake the hand of every battalion commander. The *Florida Times-Union* marveled as "Bands and bunting and open arms greeted the Sons of the South, now being gracefully supplanted by their sons and daughters, progeny sustaining and lending a new elan to the old tradition."[61]

The United Confederate Veterans parade was a moment of valediction for Jacksonville's white civic leaders and their burgeoning partnership with the city's motion picture producers. As Kalem and subsequent production companies entrenched themselves as a cultural and economic fixture in the North Florida community, they also adopted and echoed the ideologies of Florida's Jim Crow government. The shared timing of the arrival of the first film production companies in Jacksonville and their shift toward pro-Confederate narratives, with the imposition of a citywide segregationist regime was not coincidental.

The influence that North Florida–based business leaders and politicians had either directly, through community organizing, or indirectly, through exposing northern filmmakers to "the South's perspective," would come to shape how the Civil War and Reconstruction would be portrayed on the screen for decades to come.

Selig Polyscope and the Lubin Company's "Colored Comedies" and "Jungle Adventures"

While most of Florida's "southern" Civil War dramas relied on either the suppression or outright absence of Black images on the screen, a new genre of films placed Black characters front and center. Whereas in Civil War dramas, most Black characters were shown not as individuals but as a "living background," a proposed series of "fast break comedy films" featured Black characters (portrayed by both white actors in blackface and African Americans) in adaptations of minstrel shows that had become popular along the whites-only vaudeville circuit.[62]

During the 1909–10 winter season, Florida's most notorious purveyor of such films was Arthur Hotaling, the chief comedy producer for the Lubin Company, who formed a partnership with local film exhibitor Frank Montgomery in order to create a series of "comedies" with an "exotic" tropical setting.[63] Hotaling and Montgomery's films adopted two core elements of segregationist ideology: the notion that African Americans benefited from their affiliation with whites, along with an emphasis on their perceived "otherness" and inferiority. In his assessment of the denigration of Black images on the screen, historian Donald Bogle considers Hotaling's films to have produced "the most blatantly degrading of all Black stereotypes," as "subhuman creatures good for nothing."⁶⁴

Arthur Hotaling's personal views on race are clearly documented. As Richard Alan Nelson remarks, "That he was a racist is amply demonstrated by the publicity the Lubin Studios released to the motion picture trade press."⁶⁵ In a series of interviews describing his work on productions such as *Rastus in Zululand* (1910), followed by *Zulu King, Zeb, Zack and the Zulus,* and *Rastus among the Zulus* (1913), Hotaling disparaged his Black actors and expressed his preference for white actors in blackface. "It would be possible to do four times as much work with white extras," he said, noting that "it required repeated rehearsals to drill an idea of the simple business into their heads. But the results justify the trouble, and three capital comedies are the result."⁶⁶ Despite holding deep-seated animosity toward his Black cast members, Hotaling attempted to increase Lubin's market share by attracting African American audiences. Hotaling regularly advertised in Black presses such as the *New York Age, Chicago Defender,* and *Indianapolis Recorder* to hire authors and actors to write and perform in "characteristic stories" that "will be a credit to the race."⁶⁷ It should be noted that any supposed notions of "uplift" Hotaling promised in such ads are further evidence of his open disdain for the very audiences upon whom who his career depended.

At the time of writing, there are no available critical reviews of Lubin's Jacksonville films, so it is difficult to assess how Black audiences responded to the films, or if they watched them at all. It does appear that Hotaling's films had a limited distribution run, since Black moviegoers were unlikely to find much comedy in Hotaling's "parodies," while the restrictions of Black bodies on screen would have prevented white audiences from accessing such "satires."⁶⁸

During the 1913–14 winter season, the Selig Polyscope Company jumped on the bandwagon of "Jungle Adventure" films, by transporting a menagerie of animals into the Florida wilderness to re-create "the wilds of Africa." These films produced by Selig with jarring titles like *Back to the Primitive, Wizard of the Jungle,* and *Voodoo Vengeance* (1913) each depicted their African characters in a similarly paternalistic and negative light as their Lubin counterparts.⁶⁹ Despite the degrading and derogatory characters featured in such films, hundreds of Black men and women vied to work as extras for Selig and Lubin, sometimes at their own peril. For example, during production of *Wizard of the Jungle* (1913), an actor was burned to death after an on-set explosion; while another actor drowned while performing a stunt dive. The *Tampa Morning Tribune* made a passing mention of these startling film casualties, along with the ominous prediction that "unquestionably there are more to come."⁷⁰

Hotaling and Montgomery also recalled that, although they "have been having fun with their fellow-colored citizens[;] lately the darkies have been having their turn and unconsciously avenged the wrongs of their fellows."[71]

Arthur Hotaling's disturbingly titled "comedy," *Coon Town Suffragettes* (1914), includes one of the most explicit attacks against Black Floridians on film. Produced with the financial backing of the Jacksonville Board of Trade, Hotaling's film attempted to make light of the diligent voting rights efforts made by Black Floridians.[72] The film's main character, "Mandy Jackson," was written as a composite of two prominent Jacksonville civil rights organizers: Mary McLeod Bethune, the president of the Florida chapter of the NAACP, and Eartha White, director of the Negro Republican Women Voters in Jacksonville.[73] The overall aim of this film was to undermine the ongoing advocacy carried out by Bethune, White, and the Black women of Jacksonville for voting rights and civil rights.[74]

Overshadowed by D. W. Griffith's *The Birth of a Nation* (1915), Arthur Hotaling's inclusion of caricatured versions of real-life civil rights leaders in his Florida films established an especially troubling trend of trivializing Black agency on the screen. *The Birth of a Nation* has since become an apocryphal lightning rod that both inspired the Ku Klux Klan's second reign of terror in the 1920s and also became a rallying cry for a new generation of African American filmmakers to create their own counternarratives against. In his foundational study on southern audiences, *Main Street Amusements,* Gregory Waller argues, "Griffith's melodramatic celebration of Jim Crow's founding principles might well be the most telling indication of the movie's place and role in a small biracial city and a racist society."[75] Michelle Faith Wallace reinforces Waller's acknowledgment of Griffith's film's unfortunate staying power: "It would be one thing if *The Birth of a Nation* were merely the best of a thousand or even a hundred similarly racist or similarly virulent films and therefore represented a larger trend in silent film production. But as far as we know, it is the only historical epic focused on the fear of so-called Negro domination in the Reconstruction era."[76]

As we have seen in examining the problematic portrayals of Black characters in Kalem, Lubin and Selig's Florida-made films, D. W. Griffith already had an established template to draw from by the time he sought perpetuate his own distorted telling of life in the post–Civil War South in *The Birth of a Nation*. Further research will need to be done to better comprehend Florida's role in perpetuating the "Cinematic Lost Cause" on screen. The more that is learned on the subject, a greater understanding of how the motion picture served both as a tool to perpetuate white-supremacist propaganda and also an instrument of resistance by Black filmmakers against unrealistic portrayals and unreasonable stereotypes on screen can be achieved.

"An Untapped Global Market for 'Authentic' Black Film"

The organized backlash against *The Birth of a Nation* helped place the NAACP in the national spotlight. In January 1917, newly appointed NAACP Field Secretary James Weldon Johnson commented on the organizing efforts of Florida's civil rights movement with a revived spirit of hope. In a letter to voting rights organizer Margaret Downs McCleary, Johnson remarked, "Circumstances were combining to put a higher premium on Negro muscle, Negro hands, and Negro brains than ever before; all these forces had a quickening effect that was running through the entire mass of the race."[77] Unfortunately, Johnson's overstated optimism proved to be premature.

Jacksonville's white community was equally dismissive of Johnson's aspirations. When *City of Jacksonville* (1916), the Board of Trade's promotional documentary, premiered, Jacksonville's African American majority population was little more than an afterthought. The only mention in the film of the city's African American community's contributions toward Jacksonville's progress comes with reference to a sequence where "a little comedy was added to the reel by photographing a negro pie eating contest."[78]

In contrast to the reductive racial stereotypes propagated by mainstream producers in Florida and California, independent race film companies like the Foster Photoplay Company (FPC), Lincoln Motion Picture Company, and the Micheaux Film Corporation, produced hundreds of motion pictures that aspired to access an "untapped global market for 'authentic' Black film."[79] In African American communities across the United States, churches and lodges arranged film exhibitions not only for their own members but also for the wider community at large.[80]

An opportunity for Black Floridians to refute the illicit stereotypes found in the films of Gene Gauntier and Arthur Hotaling, among others, came when William D. Foster, one of the first independent Black producers in the country, visited the state in the hopes of building a production facility in Jacksonville to "off-set so many insults of the race" and "tell their side of the birth of this great race."[81] However, his stay in Florida would be extremely short-lived. As he searched for a suitable studio site, Foster was barred from purchasing property every which way by the Board of Trade. He was also informed that the city's film stock rental companies would not take his money, and distributors would refuse to screen his films in white theaters. Given the hostility he was met with from Jacksonville civic leaders and filmmakers, Foster returned to Chicago, where he founded the Foster Photoplay Company, one of the first film companies exclusively dedicated to the production and distribution of race films.[82]

Established in 1910, the FPC was the first film studio founded by an African American. From the start, Foster announced his goal to break the cycle of stereotyping of African American characters on film and expressed a vision for the Black community in which they portrayed themselves as they wanted to be seen, not as someone else depicted them. Between 1910 and 1913, the FPC produced four short silent comedies that loosely imitated the pacing and styling of Mack Sennett's Keystone Cops.[83] What distinguishes Foster's films is that his productions were the first to be written and directed by and to star an all-Black troupe. His debut comedy, *The Railroad Porter* (1912), incorporated a similar series of madcap comedy sequences as depicted in the Lubin Company's "comedies," but unlike the movies of Arthur Hotaling, Foster's photoplays sought to tell stories from a distinctively Black perspective for a Black audience who were quite tired of reductionist stereotypes and brazenly offensive "satires."[84]

Whether Foster's comedies were intended as a direct challenge to the filmmakers he encountered while in Jacksonville is impossible to tell, but one cannot help but wonder whether Arthur Hotaling's films would have had a marketplace at all if Foster had been successful in forming a Black-owned and -operated film studio in Jacksonville.

Despite the FPC's early success in Chicago, however, the studio struggled to find stable financial backing. When the FPC defaulted on the lease of its Chicago property in 1913, Foster once again attempted to set up operations in Florida, only to experience the same hostility Foster had experienced three years earlier. A year later, the FPC reincorporated with an ambitious plan to distribute its comedies in Europe. Foster's aspiration was for international audiences to "see what he was trying to do back home in the States to help the fight for racial equality."[85] With the onset of World War I, however, which led to the collapse of exhibition networks across Continental Europe, Foster's plan never fully took off.[86]

The Making of *The Birth of a Race*: "A Tale of Black Sufferings and Strivings"

Although Jim Crow remained a pivotal facet of Florida's political institutions throughout the first half of the twentieth century, following the collapse of Jacksonville's movie boom in the 1910s, Florida also became a bastion for social and cultural resistance against the white-supremacist imagery in American films. In the summer of 1915, two civil rights groups, the NAACP and the Tuskegee Institute had each taken steps to "make a cinematic statement with the power and conviction of [*The*] *Birth of a Nation*" that would be a "plea for mutual respect between the races."[87] Although the NAACP originally expressed support for the project, it was the Tuskegee Institute that followed through on the production. Led by Tuskegee's founder, Booker T. Washington, and his secretary, Emmett J. Scott, the organization began to raise funds from the National Negro Business League (NNBL) to produce a film on the Tuskegee campus.[88] Ironically, the NNBL initially suggested that D. W. Griffith should serve as the director of the as yet untitled film, which could be shown at once as both "a conciliatory prologue to [*The*] *Birth of a Nation*" and a "pageant of [Black] history."[89]

Following the premiere of *Birth of a Nation*, NAACP cofounder Mary White Ovington expressed the urgent need to produce a film that would directly challenge D. W. Griffith's notorious depiction of southern Blacks in the form of "a tale of Black sufferings and strivings that would meet with favor from conservative and radical alike."[90] At Tuskegee, Booker T. Washington and Emmett Scott were of a different opinion, suggesting that by collaborating with D. W. Griffith directly, they could instead focus less on the "race problem" and produce a "story of universal human progress." The solution would be to convince the director to adapt Booker T. Washington's bestselling autobiography, *Up from Slavery* (1901), as "a story of interest and value to all races."[91]

For his part, D. W. Griffith obviously had no interest in directing a film funded by Black investors. Griffith instead replied to the widespread protests and criticisms that followed the racial violence *Birth of a Nation* inspired by producing a tone-deaf response in his historical epic *Intolerance: Love's Struggle through the Ages* (1916). *Intolerance* was not an apology, since Griffith felt he had nothing to apologize for. Until his death in 1948, Griffith made it abundantly clear in interviews that his second feature was instead a rebuttal to his critics and that, in his view, "they were, in fact, the intolerant ones."[92] None of the four intersecting stories depicted in *Intolerance* address any examples of racial intolerance. Since, by 1916, Griffith felt he had succeeded in telling his own "story of universal human progress," he entirely dismissed the NNBL and Tuskegee's overtures.

While Tuskegee's efforts to adapt *Up from Slavery* stalled, Ovington joined with her fellow NAACP member W.E.B. Du Bois, author of *The Souls of Black Folk* (1903), to form a scenario committee that would develop a script. Creative differences on the direction of the film soon caused Du Bois to drop out of the project. Ovington then turned to NAACP secretary Mary Childs Nerney to oversee the scenario committee. Nerney then contacted screenwriter Elaine Sterne of Universal Studios to draft "a sketch of a scenario—or plot or whatever you call it."[93] This now left the proposed NAACP film in the hands of a trio of white women: two wealthy socialites and a twenty-four-year-old Ivy League school graduate.

Ovington, Nerney, and Sterne took their proposal to Carl Laemmle, the owner of Universal. Initially intrigued, Laemmle agreed to contribute $150,000 to the film's budget if the NAACP could raise $50,000, one-quarter of the film's stake. Struggling to secure the necessary funds, Elaine Sterne next reached out to Emmett Scott and the NNBL for funding. With Tuskegee still in pursuit of funding for their own project, Sterne's proposal was swiftly dismissed. Whether Scott was bluffing, or D. W. Griffith had a sudden uncharacteristic change of heart, Sterne reported back to Nerney that "the Griffith crowd were actively planning something of the sort with the active support of Tuskegee."[94]

Without the limited financial support of NAACP members and with little to go on other than a flimsy verbal agreement from Carl Laemmle, Sterne revised her proposed feature film from its original twelve-reel treatment to a five-reel film titled *Lincoln's Dream*. The project further mutated away from its original intent when the film's primary backer, Carl Laemmle, suggested that the revised film remove any "parts favorable to the Negro" and that it should instead engage "white attention by defining Black aspiration."[95] Even with concessions made to the prejudice of Universal's southern shareholders, the lack of additional funding eventually led Laemmle to entirely withdraw from the film in August 1915.[96] With Universal out, Sterne again tried to get support for her project from Tuskegee, but in the end, as she recalled, a combination of "mutual suspicion and bad faith" effectively brought an end to *Lincoln's Dream*.[97]

Meanwhile, the Tuskegee Institute's efforts to adapt *Up from Slavery* ended abruptly with the death of Booker T. Washington from kidney failure in November 1915. After Washington's death, the NNBL dropped plans for adapting his autobiography. Emmett Scott, who was Washington's presumed heir apparent at Tuskegee, continued to push for a film production that "would uplift the race," but when he was passed over by the board of trustees in favor of Robert Russa Moton, Scott decided to take his project elsewhere.[98] He soon found an interested partner in Edwin L. Barker of the white-owned, Chicago-based Advance Motion Picture Company (AMPC). Scott felt that if he was able succeed in producing a film through this coloration, it could have "broken the Hollywood monopoly and kept open the door of hope for aspiring Black filmmakers."[99]

With both the NAACP's hope of producing Elaine Sterne's *Lincoln's Dream* and the Tuskegee Institute's plan to adapt Booker T. Washington's *Up from Slavery* all but abandoned, Scott and Barker set out to combine elements from both proposed projects into a new film called *The Birth of a Race*. The treatment for this new film had little resemblance to either the NAACP's or Tuskegee's original vision.[100] In his haste to sign with Barker and the AMPC, Emmett Scott was manipulated into selling the rights to the film entirely to Edwin Barker. With this sleight of hand, the production intended for African American audiences now fell under the control of a white production company. To further capitalize on the fundraising drive that the NAACP and Tuskegee had initially started, Barker rebranded his studio as the Birth of a Race Photoplay Corporation (BRPC), declared himself president of the company, and issued eighty thousand shares valued at ten dollars each to be publicly sold to finance the film.[101]

Scott remained loosely involved in the BRPC as a financial officer who courted potential "fiscal agents" and sought to market *The Birth of a Race* stock. Both Scott and Barker appealed to would-be investors to develop a film that "would tell the true story of the Negro—his life in Africa, his transportation to America, his enslavement, his freedom, his achievements, together with the past, present and future relations to his white neighbor and to the world in which both live and labor."[102] Barker and his business partners followed up on this proposal with a regular series of advertisements in the Black presses to help promote financing to produce an "entertaining motion picture of racial understanding."[103] Enthusiasm for the project continued to escalate: it received the support of nearly ten thousand individual investors who purchased almost fifty thousand of the eighty thousand shares offered, and nearly $1 million worth of stock sold.[104]

Ironically, the largest would-be financial contributor to *The Birth of a Race* was the Selig Company, which invested more than $140,000 toward the film.[105] Even with its broad support from the Black press, production was hampered by a series of false starts, as well as what Thomas Cripps describes as "chicanery and mismanagement, which for two years was camouflaged under periodic stockholder's newsletters."[106] The troubled production was undermined further in early 1917, when the Selig Company pulled its funding from the project entirely. It is likely that William Selig was not fully aware of the film's original mission until about halfway through the production, when the first reels of the film's scenario were developed at the studio's processing lab. After receiving the first rushes, Selig, who, as we have seen previously, sponsored the explicitly racist "Jungle Adventure" and "Colored Comedies" in Jacksonville, was not pleased "the character of its propaganda."

In a heated exchange of letters with Edwin Barker, he wrote of his extreme displeasure toward the film and that he would not contribute another cent toward the production.[107] Publicly, the Selig Company reasoned that its choice to no longer back *The Birth of a Race* was due to the studio's decision to redirect its focus toward making war bond promotions for the U.S. government. Only after World War I ended was the truth revealed in the trade presses. A December 1918 article in *Variety* explains how Selig called for "the character of the picture to be altered," in particular to remove "certain phrases of the advancement of the Negro race."[108] When Selig's demands were met with resistance, he decided to pull funding from the film.

At this point an exhausted Emmett Scott started to lose interest in the project, and after "the virtual junking of his ideas for a scenario by Barker," he decided to take a position in the War Department instead. During World War I, Scott became the highest-ranking African American official in President Woodrow Wilson's notoriously segregated administration.[109] Following Scott's resignation, the last remaining African American involved with the film withdrew from *The Birth of a Race*. Control of the production once again changed hands, this time passing to the all-white Frohman Amusement Corporation.[110] Edwin Barker remained on as the film's producer and expressed to his investors that the sudden shake-up in production would only increase audience appeal and "that the theme of *The Birth of a Race* has broadened tremendously."[111] He followed this statement up in an October 1917 interview with *Variety* where he announced, "The movie would not be about the Negro at all," and he went to even greater lengths to outright deny the fact that "the majority of the stock had been sold to Negroes."[112] As Barker downplayed their film's connection to civil rights groups and support from African American investors, he set out to finish the now seemingly "colorblind" version of *The Birth of a Race*.

To accommodate his reduced budget and complete the film, Barker announced that he would relocate the remainder of the production from Chicago to Florida. In a statement to the *Tampa Morning Tribune*, Barker expressed how *The Birth of a Race* could be just the first of many films he hoped to make in Florida. "This section [Tampa] is bound to be a moving picture center. Practically all advantages needed to film large pictures are to be had in Florida."[113] Plans were next made to shoot beach scenes on Jacksonville Beach, while the remainder of the production would be filmed at Sulphur Springs and around Tampa Bay.

Even as the producers distanced themselves from support of the African American community in the trade presses, it was, in fact, the Tampa Negro Board of Trade who actively played the role of both backer and liaison between the film's white production staff and the city's large Black community of potential extras (and investors) that helped to finance the remainder of the film.[114] Edwin Barker tapped a white director, Winfield Fernley Kutz, who went by the stage name John W. Noble, a former staffer on D. W. Griffith's *The Birth of a Nation*, to direct the remaining Florida scenes for *The Birth of a Race*.[115]

The addition of John W. Noble eliminated any pretext that *The Birth of a Race* would be a cinematic answer to the racial stereotypes perpetuated by Noble's former boss. A retired U.S. Army lieutenant who served during the Boxer Rebellion and Philippine-American War, Noble expressed his wish to revise the narrative to focus on the exploits of the American Expeditionary Force along the Western Front. The new plot leaned heavily on a story of two white brothers fighting on opposite sides of World War I, as Noble evoked similar themes of "white patriotism" and supposed "universal brotherhood" that D. W. Griffith had emphasized in *The Birth of a Nation*.[116] The convoluted plot overshadowed Emmett Scott's vision and Elaine Sterne's original film treatment, as the film devolved into what *Variety* described as "the most grotesque cinematic chimera in the history of the motion picture business," and "a ghastly example of terrific waste."[117]

Noble and company arrived in Tampa in December 1917 to shoot a biblical sequence that had little to do with the film's initial premise. A production spokesman boasted to the *Tampa Morning Tribune*, "Like all great feature productions, *The Birth of a Race* is a symbolic play going back to the time of Moses, and treating with absolute historic fidelity the magnificent Egyptian civilization, the great drama will trace the effects of man's prejudice down to modern civilization," adding that, in "the crowning feature of the work, . . . a vision of a better age will be glimpsed."[118] A follow-up article published in January 1918 that chronicled the recent filming of the film's Egyptian sequences expressed that it was, "Well worth a trip to the [Sulphur] springs, in order to see a gang of darkies . . . dressed up in a pocket handkerchief and nothing else as they fought the fleeing Jews. This Jews' flight marked the beginning of the ascendancy of the white race and the decline of the brown."[119] Given such conditions, it is remarkable that the picture was finished at all.[120]

Ultimately, Noble's lack of drive and focus, combined with the production's malicious move away from the film's original intent, all but sealed the fate of *The Birth of a Race* long before its December 1918 premiere. A review in *Billboard* condemned the film for violating "its own teachings and vitiat[ing] its own purpose" and declared that *The Birth of a Race* "was perhaps the worst conglomeration of mixed purposes and attempts ever thrown together."[121] *Variety* was even more scathing: "After the stockholders have seen the picture, its day will be done, and it will go that bourne [sic] from whence no photoplays come back."[122] *The Birth of a Race* did receive a slightly more favorable reception in Tampa, where Barker and company rented the Blackstone Theater at the cost of $6,000 per month to regularly run the film for the next eleven months until October 1919.[123] This could also in part be due to Tampa's increasing interest in building up its local film industry out of the shadow of Jacksonville's ill-fated production studios.[124]

As disappointing as the final product turned out to be, a silver lining can be found from the tumultuous production of *The Birth of a Race*. Before the production of *The Birth of a Race* was hijacked by an incompetent producer and incognizant director, African Americans had successfully initiated a film project on their own behalf in the effort to produce a countervailing force against white presumption. According to Thomas Cripps, the ill-fated production of *The Birth of a Race* also "marshaled the NAACP into a national voice and force; had entered the ranks of moviemakers with such vigor (and bungling) as to inspire other black firms, first among them the Lincoln Motion Picture Company, to take up 'race movies' designed to speak to black audiences unmediated by Hollywood stereotypes," and "learned at great cost the art of bargaining with white people, both their presumed enemies and putative friends."[125]

The Birth of a Race also failed to recover the hundreds of thousands of dollars that were invested in the film by Tampa's African American community in a shameless exploitation of financially precarious Black Floridians, who had placed their hopes and savings into a film that offered its viewers nothing. The failure of *The Birth of a Race* left Black Floridians desperate for "films that would speak to their particular cultural experiences and offer effective visual models of race ambition and uplift."[126] In the years following *The Birth of a Race* debacle, Florida did become a haven for filmmakers who sought to tell Black stories on film, with an audience eager to see their stories projected on the silver screen.

"The Harlem of the South"

Jacksonville's LaVilla neighborhood was once an independent city that was drafted into the City of Jacksonville in 1887, with none other than J.E.T. Bowden as the city's last mayor before its annexation. Added as Jacksonville's Sixth Ward, this African American majority neighborhood became a center of civic organizing and political activity over the next twenty years until the white-supremacist takeover of Jacksonville's City Council in 1907, which redrew the city's voting map and removed the last elected citywide Black officials from office until the 1960s.¹²⁷ Yet in the midst of this era of political repression, the four-block strip that ran along LaVilla's Ashley Street would become the center for Black cultural life and political organizing in North Florida. Nicknamed "the Harlem of the South," LaVilla served as ground zero for the Florida Movement, a civil rights campaign that set out "to defeat white supremacy, economic oppression, and one-party rule" throughout the state.¹²⁸

At the turn of the twentieth century, Ashley Street boasted a vibrant music and entertainment scene intermingled with a sharp sense of political advocacy and organizing. It was here that Harlem Renaissance luminaries such as Florida natives James Weldon Johnson, John Rosamond Johnson, and Eatonville's Zora Neale Hurston joined with the "Mother and Father of Jazz," Ma Rainey and Jelly Roll Morton, to create a lively space that fostered a culture of Black entertainment and enlightenment. Before Beale Street became "Home of the Blues" and Lenox Avenue inspired the Harlem Renaissance, these same artists and writers graced LaVilla's lively theater district during the 1910s and 1920s. As Ennis Davis of the *Florida Times-Union* has remarked, "LaVilla has been called the Harlem of the South, when it's Harlem that should be called the LaVilla of the North."¹²⁹

Ashley Street's lively music scene and café culture connected LaVilla into the pulse of a national network of African American activists and entertainers. The Colored Airdome located on West Ashley Street boasted an open-air audience capacity of eight hundred seats; the theater was advertised as providing screenings and performances "exclusively for colored people" and offered its audiences "positively the largest, grandest and coolest theater exclusively for colored people in the entire Southland."¹³⁰

Next door to the Colored Airdome was Frank Crowd's Bijou Theater, which may have been the site of one of the first feature film screenings in Florida. In January 1909, the Kalem Company used the Bijou to test one of the first films in their *Florida Series,* shot during the 1908–9 winter season. The success of Kalem's screening that winter led Crowd to negotiate with the Vitagraph Company to exhibit their fifty-minute feature *The Life of Moses* (1909). In an interview with the *Evening Metropolis* promoting the screening, Crowd conveyed his hopes for a similar arrangement between his theater and Kalem. The ten-cent cost of admission (five cents for women and children) offered audiences an environment for "refined, substantial, and wholesome amusement" where the "moving pictures are colored by hand, the management so by nature."¹³¹ Unable to compete with the newly opened Colored Airdome, Crowd closed the Bijou later that same year.

Down but not out, Crowd invested the $25,000 he earned from the sale of his theater to add new inclined floors, a balcony, private boxes, and an

Figure 13. Frank Crowd's Globe Theatre, 1915. Frank Crowd was an important early African American film exhibitor and theater promoter whose Globe Theatre in Jacksonville became a regular stop along the vaudeville circuit in the 1910s, and where film studios such as Kalem and Vitagraph exhibited the first cuts of their films. Courtesy of *Metro Jacksonville*.

all-tungsten lighting system and rechristened it the Globe Theatre. Crowd's revamped Globe contracted with the Russell-Owens Stock Company, a broad network of Black stock performers that toured across the country. The Globe was considered so important to the Russell-Owens circuit and other traveling performers that it was known as the "anchor to the southern [vaudeville] road shows" and served as an important starting point in the careers of up-and-coming jazz virtuosos Ma Rainey and Louis Armstrong, among others.[132]

The crown jewel of Ashley Street's entertainment district was the Strand Theatre, which opened in June 1915 "amid the glare of blazing lights, a blaring of brass bands and a crowd in gala attire."[133] The nationally syndicated newspaper *Indianapolis Freeman* reported that at the premiere Strand patrons "lined Ashley Street, and pushed and surged like a rolling sea."[134] By the time the Strand opened, the segregated social reality of movie exhibition had already made its impact on the entertainment profession. This shift in the industry attracted white entrepreneurs such as H. S. Walker, who formed the Strand Amusement Company. With his deep pockets and connections to white-owned "combines" (organized theatrical circuits), Walker was able to tap into a broad network of traveling stock companies, musicians, and film distributors to ensure that the Strand outperformed any of its rivals on Ashley Street.[135]

Competition from well-financed exhibitors like H. S. Walker, combined with increased pressure from Jacksonville's [white] women's clubs on the city government to issue Sunday blue laws against motion picture exhibitions, caused many of the Black-owned theaters in Jacksonville to buckle under financial and political pressure. By 1915, the Colored Airdome had been all but run out of business by its competitors, and its owners disappeared from the public record. Frank Crowd's Globe Theatre experienced a similar decline after the Russell-Owens Stock Company disbanded in 1916, and it, too, closed its doors.[136]

That same year, approximately twelve thousand African Americans had left Florida to find better working conditions and wages farther north.[137] James Weldon Johnson, who had himself fled Jacksonville in 1901 after barely surviving an attempted lynching, asserted that "The exodus of Negroes to the North . . . was in full motion; the tremors of the war in Europe were shaking in America with increasing intensity," and [. . .] "all these forces had a quickening effect that was running through the entire mass of the race."[138]

A deciding factor in the sudden departure of so many African Americans from Florida came in response to the inauguration of Sidney Catts as Florida governor in 1917. During his insurgent third-party campaign for the Prohibition Party during the 1916 governor's race, the self-anointed "Cracker Messiah" openly defended to his supporters the necessity of lynch mobs and regularly engaged with publicly antagonistic exchanges with civil rights organizers and the NAACP.[139] Perhaps most infamously, Catts boasted at a campaign rally that he had killed a Black man before and then intimidated a "witness" to testify on the stand in his favor.[140]

The labor shortage caused by the migration out of Florida of tens of thousands of African Americans forced Catts to adjust his rhetoric. In a halfhearted appeal to Black Floridians, Catts utilized the racist "climate theory of racial difference" in his reasoning why African Americans should remain in the state. According to Catts, "The colored people . . . should live in the warm climates and where they leave and try to live in cold climates they are going against destiny."[141] In response to the excessively authoritarian nature of the Catts administration, Eartha White—the voting rights activist who was viciously satirized by Arthur Hotaling in his "Colored Comedies"—formed the Jacksonville Colored Citizens Protective League with the express goal of enfranchising Black voters across Duval County.

The inevitable showdown between Sidney Catts and Black Jacksonvillians would occur at the Duval Theatre on the night of July 16, 1918.[142] The event was promoted as an "Encouragement Meeting Between the Races" to celebrate the financial contributions Black moviegoers had made in the Ashley Street theater district through Liberty Loan subscriptions, Red Cross drives, and War Saving Stamp programs for the war effort. Abraham Lincoln Lewis, Florida's first Black millionaire, hosted the event, while Governor Catts delivered the keynote address upon the urging of his advisors to "make amends" with the state's declining African American population.[143] James Weldon Johnson leaves an account of what came next:

> So, Governor Catts began bullying the gathering. He told African Americans to get jobs, stop loafing, and cease selling bootleg whiskey. Catts boasted: "You are looking into the face of the most powerful man in Florida," and warned them that he was going to force them to work harder. At one place in his speech the Governor seemed to imagine that he was talking to a crowd of gamblers and loose women . . . He enlightened his audience as to why the Indian had vanished. He said it was because the Indian would not bow to the white man, and that no race could hope to survive along with the white man unless it bowed. He also stated that if he were a Negro he would be ashamed to be a brown one or a yellow one, he would be ashamed to be anything but a black one. He spoke of keeping Negro labor in the State as though Negroes were peons. He spoke of soldiers and venereal diseases as though most of the women in the audience were to be held responsible . . . Had he not been the Governor he most likely would have been hissed.[144]

After Governor Catts finished delivering his incendiary diatribe, architect Joseph Haygoood Blodgett, who had been instrumental in the rebuilding of LaVilla after the 1901 Jacksonville fire, rose to provide closing remarks for the evening.[145] Angered and dismayed by the governor's rant, Blodgett "went on to tell the Governor why so many of the faces he looked into were brown and yellow; and he told him why so many Negroes had left and were leaving the State and about lynching and 'Jim Crow' cars and political inequalities."[146] Blodgett attempted to continue, but Governor Catts, blinded with rage, sprang from his seat and shook his fist at one of Jacksonville's most respectable businessmen. He "declared that Blodgett was assailing him, had insulted him, and made him the butt of ridicule," and that he "sensed a challenge to white supremacy in Blodgett's rebuttal."[147] Before matters could escalate further, the mostly Black audience in attendance at the Duval Theatre rose from

Figure 14. In 1916, a one-eyed populist preacher from Alabama named Sidney Catts ran for governor of Florida (and won) as a member of the Prohibition Party, the only time a third-party candidate has won a major office in Florida. Courtesy of State Archives of Florida, Florida Memory.

their seats and started to sing "My Country, 'Tis of Thee," and the meeting was dismissed.

The heated encounter between Governor Catts and Jacksonville's Black business leaders at the Duval Theatre would eventually have significant and ultimately tragic consequences for Black Floridians. According to historian Paul Ortiz, "The fact that the governor felt insulted simply because Blodgett stated the case for Black dignity and citizenship illuminated the unresolved conflict between democracy and white supremacy."[148] Tensions came to their horrendous climax with the election of 1920 in a perfect storm of racial violence that coincided with the recent resurrection of the Ku Klux Klan in Florida and the increased advocacy of Black Floridians for universal suffrage.[149]

The election of 1920 in Florida witnessed the largest increase in Klan activity across the state since Reconstruction. Days before the election, Florida's first chartered "klavern" was incorporated in Jacksonville on October 30. The following night, on Halloween, a cross was burned in downtown Jacksonville "as a warning to Negroes to attempt no lawlessness at the polls on Tuesday."[150] Catts, who was ineligible to run for a second consecutive term due to restrictions in the Florida constitution, attempted to win a seat in the U.S. Senate against incumbent Senator Duncan U. Fletcher, himself a staunch supporter of segregation and states' rights. Fletcher, being the "less extreme" of the primary candidates, soundly defeated Catts in the Democratic primary and went on to win in the general election.

Although Sidney Catts was soundly defeated in the 1920 election, Florida Klan members won elections in races for local offices across the state. The election instigated racial violence that Paul Ortiz describes as "genocidal in scope and scale."[151] In Jacksonville alone, three thousand to four thousand African American men and women were turned away from the polls by this form of mass intimidation.[152] While the Central Florida town of Ocoee witnessed a horrific outbreak of violence where Klan members threw dynamite into the homes of its African American inhabitants and ultimately destroyed the entire settlement, killing as many as sixty of its inhabitants.[153]

In January 1923, Klan members from across the state descended into the town of Rosewood in Levy County following accusations that a white woman in the adjacent town of Sumner had been raped by a Black drifter. A mob of several hundred white men descended on the community, burned almost every freestanding structure in Rosewood, and attempted to hunt down and kill as many of its inhabitants as could be found. To this day the death toll of the Rosewood Massacre remains highly disputed; officially six Blacks and two whites were recorded as killed in the violence, but eyewitness testimony places the numbers at between 26 and 150.[154] The totality of the destruction (not a single inhabitant ever returned to Rosewood) further accelerated the departure of the state's African American population as the 1920s and 1930s progressed.[155] The silence surrounding the massacre would finally be broken in July 1982, when journalist Gary Moore of the *St. Petersburg Times* published a series of interviews he conducted with survivors, which gained nationwide attention when Moore's research was featured on *60 Minutes* in December 1983.[156]

In 1997, acclaimed filmmaker John Singleton collaborated with screenwriter Gregory Poirier to develop a dramatized telling of the atrocities that occurred in Rosewood in January 1923. Extensive creative liberties were taken in *Rosewood* (1997), including the creation of the fictional character of Mann, portrayed by Ving Raines, who steps in to rescue survivors from further violence inflicted by a white posse. In essence, the film attempts to invert the horrific portrayal of white-supremacist terror as seen in the early Jacksonville films of Kalem, Selig, Lubin, and, later, D. W. Griffith's *The Birth of a Nation*. Where John Noble's *The Birth of a Race* proved to be a retort to such stereotypes on screen, John Singleton's *Rosewood* completely flips the script.

Gary Moore, who had first brought the events of Rosewood into the public spotlight, criticized Singleton's version of the events that transpired in Rosewood, expressing that the imposition of the Mann character in the film was condescending to survivors who had come forward to tell the details of the most traumatic day of their lives.[157] Historian David Colburn at the University of Florida took a more accommodating stance toward the creative license Singleton and Poirier took in their depiction of the Rosewood Massacre. According to Colburn, "Why attack John Singleton's movie? What led to the killing and destruction of the community? No one can be sure."[158] Although *Rosewood* was critically lauded, the film was a financial failure that left Singleton to reflect on whether Americans were truly ready to confront their nation's troubled past:

> People say it's violent. I don't think it is, and certainly not as violent as it was being there. I wanted to make you feel you were there. But then maybe Americans are afraid of it because of their own racial problems. They're all fucked up over race, you know.[159]

A "Lily White" Syndicate "Tough on Black Asses"

The deteriorating social and political conditions for Black Floridians had a profound impact on the continued viability of the businesses along Jacksonville's Ashley Street. Competition between Jacksonville's Colored Airdome and the Globe Theatre helped nurture a local audience that had adopted increasingly "sophisticated" tastes. In the void left by the disappearance of Ashley Street's Black-owned theaters, a consortium of primarily white theater owners began laying claim to Jacksonville's African American theatrical industry. Ashley Street's theaters were bought out by the Theater Owners Booking Association (TOBA), with the officers and owners in the syndicate either white Floridians or white theater owners with a rapidly expanding circuit of their own. In 1920, a white TOBA officer and theater owner from Savannah named W. J. Stiles purchased the by then abandoned Strand Theatre. The Strand was added as the southernmost stop along the TOBA circuit, as Stiles worked to establish the theater as the centerpiece of cultural life in LaVilla.

In need of both homegrown talent and entertainers familiar with the cultural atmosphere along Ashley Street, Stiles teamed up with S. A. "Buddy" Austin, a Jacksonville native and seasoned vaudeville comedian on the TOBA circuit. Austin had originally come to Jacksonville to find work in the Afro-American Life Insurance Company but soon was swayed to purchase a stake in the Strand. He had gained previous managerial experience during his time as a traveling showman, and prior to coming to Jacksonville he had worked an extended engagement as stage manager at Bailey's 81 in Atlanta.[160] The unlikely partnership between Stiles and Austin was a refreshing exception to other theaters along the TOBA circuit. For most theaters under the TOBA banner, profits remained firmly in the hands of its primarily white owners. A January 1921 editorial in *Billboard* describes the organization as "a 'Lily White' syndicate of houses and managers whose patronage is Negro."[161] The disparity between the revenue received by TOBA's white officers and the work demanded of its performers soon gave the organization's acronym another meaning within Black vaudeville circles as being "Tough on Black Actors" or, more frequently, "Tough on Black Asses."[162]

Under Austin's direction as manager, the Strand became among one of the most profitable theaters on the TOBA circuit.[163] The Strand would go on to play a central role in Jacksonville Black life during the 1920s, and it established itself as among the most important stopping points in the South for African American performers and aspirational film exhibitors in search of new audiences.[164] In 1922, Stiles and Austin founded the Strand Amusement Company in Jacksonville, "with a capitalization of $100,000 for the purpose of owning and operating theatres, motion picture houses and producing motion pictures."[165]

Following the dismantling of Henry Klutho's proposed Fine Arts City, Austin and Stiles set out to purchase the properties of Jacksonville's former production studios for bottom-dollar prices. The timing of the formation of the Strand Amusement Company would itself provide serendipitous. Yet, just as TOBA consolidated its control along the Ashley Street theater district, an itinerant filmmaker and Florida native by the name of Richard Norman had returned home to Florida intent on establishing the only film studio in the United States that would be wholly dedicated to the production of race films.

Richard Norman Studios

By the early 1920s, the center of gravity for the Florida film industry gradually began to shift from Jacksonville toward Tampa and Miami. Jacksonville's film colony, once considered the "World's Winter Film Capital," had been all but abandoned by 1922. That same year, Richard Norman Jr. returned to North Florida after nearly a decade on the road. He hoped to build a feature film production studio of his own in the hollowed-out ruins of Arlington's once lively film district. Born and raised in Middleburg, Florida, located twenty-six miles southwest of Jacksonville, Norman first gravitated to filmmaking while attending college in Tampa.

In the early 1910s, Norman moved to Des Moines, Iowa, where he set up his own independent production operation. During his time in Iowa, Norman developed a novel approach toward film production and exhibition called "home-talent" productions, which would go on to become quite popular, especially among rural moviegoers. Home-talent films were often short two-reel films that followed a simple prewritten scenario and included previously filmed sequences that would also incorporate scenes featuring town leaders, the sons and daughters of local business owners and politicians, as well as prominent town landmarks such as shops and churches. When filming "wrapped," Norman would take the reel back to his lab, process the new footage, and return to town with a final cut to show. He would then negotiate a contract with a local theater owner to show the film at a slightly marked-up admission price of fifteen cents, and then split the profits of the film's exhibition sixty-forty (sixty for Norman, forty for the theater owner). After the premiere, the town retained the rights to the film for its own promotional purposes, while Norman received a share of the profits of any repeat viewings.[166]

The most popular and widely exhibited of Norman's home-talent films was *The Wrecker* (1916–19). During the three-year stretch when these two films were shown, Norman moved his base of operations from Des Moines to Chicago, renaming his company the Richard Norman Manufacturing Company (RNMC). Over the next three years he would exhibit *The Wrecker* in small towns and hamlets across the Midwest and South. The film featured prerecorded footage that included "A sensational head-on collision, train wreck, automobile collision, thrilling mail race, stirring fight between hero and villain, [and] pistol battle on Main Street!"[167] In total, Norman shot forty different versions of the same film, often spending up to two weeks in a town he had contracted with to film additional sequences that featured local actors and landmarks. Although each version of the film followed a mostly similar pattern, every town would add its own unique nuances to the productions. A description of Norman's process for making his home-talent films in Manistee, Michigan, can be found an article in the *Manistee News* from October 1918:

> An automobile collision, an injured girl, excited people, an ambulance dashing up to the scene, more excitement—it all looked like a good story . . . The reporter saw a motion picture camera and its operator preparing for another "scene" and he knew it was but a play accident. The camera was set up at another angle, the girl resumed her position on the stretcher and the young man's face took on the frightened look again, at a word the officers lifted the stretcher into the ambulance, the young man climbed in behind, the ambulance driver jumped into his seat and the ambulance dashed up the street with the camera faithfully filming its flight. The girl was Miss Hester Johnson, and the young man was Gordon McLarty, while the ambulance was the property of a local undertaking establishment and was loaned for the occasion. These scenes among many others being made here are a part of a railroad picture *The Wrecker*, which is being filmed with a local cast by the Norman Film Manufacturing Company of Chicago.[168]

It was during his time in Chicago that Norman first discovered the FPC. As discussed earlier in this chapter, William Foster had attempted, with little success, to build a studio dedicated to the making of race films in Jacksonville during the 1910s. It is unclear whether Norman corresponded with Foster directly or may have attended an FPC screening while in Chicago, but the connection is intriguing. According to Richard Norman biographer Barbara Tepa Lupack, "Norman never commented specifically on what attracted him to race filmmaking, [although] he no doubt observed the crowds of enthusiastic Black filmgoers at the midnight rambles and special 'colored showings' in the towns and cities he visited during his home-talent productions."[169] Regardless, after years of uninterrupted travel, experiencing biting cold Chicago winters, and perhaps a bit homesick for his native Florida, Norman was eager to come home. He briefly returned to North Florida to produce a promotional film for the Jacksonville Chamber of Commerce but soon decided to stay and build his own independent film studio.[170]

Norman's decision to return to Florida coincided with the exodus of film producers from the state, which meant there was plenty of studio space available. Cheap real estate, combined with the commercial potential of exhibiting race films to African American audiences, had the makings of a lucrative business. Aside from the financial benefits, it does seem that Richard Norman's goals for his studio may have gone beyond the bottom line. Norman's son, Captain Richard Norman III, recalled that his father hoped his films could "do something constructive to better race relations. Through his films he was committed to helping the Black players live up to their potential and show what they were capable of as performers and human beings."[171]

By the early 1920s, the race film industry Richard Norman sought to enter into was quite tenuous and fraught. Between 1921 and 1922, there were only 354 theaters in the United States in twenty-eight of forty-eight states that were openly available to Black audiences, and of those theaters, only 120 had the capability to show films.[172] In Jacksonville, the Strand Amusement Company hoped to capitalize on the increased interest Black audiences had expressed toward motion pictures by exploring options to establish a motion picture production studio solely dedicated to the production of race movies. At the present time, no surviving correspondence between either W. J. Stiles or Buddy Austin is available to indicate how far either man had gotten in negotiating the purchase of studio space, nor is there a record of any film produced by Strand. That said, it is possible that the Strand at the very least formed an unofficial partnership with the RNMC as Norman planned to distribute his first feature-length race film.

After founding the RNMC in 1919, Norman established close ties with LaVilla's theatrical community and soon formed an acting troupe, which also starred Buddy Austin, who received top billing in the film and was paid twenty-five dollars per day for his efforts.[173] Taking advantage of Austin's local celebrity and his connections with the Ashley Street theater district, Norman retooled the original plot of *The Wrecker*, taking care to also recycle his previously recorded car crash and train wreck sequences, and set to work. The only notable difference was a short comedic sequence modeled after the vaudeville performances that regularly appeared along Ashley Street.

Norman retitled the film *The Green-Eyed Monster* (1919), which he advertised in the African American presses as, "spectacular and stupendous: the thrilling scenes were even more interesting than the usual 'thrillers' because of the fact that characters are colored people, splendidly assuming the different roles of Railroad President, Financial backer, Traffic Manager, Directors, Superintendent, Railroad Contractor representing the cream of the colored race."[174] After the audience at a test screening showed their displeasure at the film's vaudeville sequence, Norman removed the scenes, which he later reformatted into a separate short titled *The Love Bug* (1919). He would later show this short as an add-on during screenings of *The Green-Eyed Monster*.[175]

Norman's first venture into race filmmaking was an enormous success both in terms of revenue and critical reviews in the African American presses. The *Chicago Defender* lauded *The Green-Eyed Monster* as "one of the most spectacular productions ever shown at a local house," while the *Pittsburgh Courier* praised the film's star, Edna Morton, as "our Mary Pickford' for her work."[176] Unfortunately, there are no clues in Norman's correspondence or contracts with his actors for *The Green-Eyed Monster* that can provide deeper insights into what went on behind scenes while the film was being made. Barbra Tepa Lupack acknowledges the success of "*The Love Bug* and *The Green-Eyed Monster* gave Norman credibility as a successful and serious producer of 'colored motion pictures' and, in turn, allowed him to explore other innovative themes and approaches in his subsequent films."[177]

Using the profits from *The Green-Eyed Monster* and *Love Bug*, Norman decided to leave Jacksonville for the "All-Colored City of Boley, Oklahoma."[178] Why Norman set out for Oklahoma is not yet fully apparent. Thomas Cripps claims that it was because, at the time, Jacksonville was "strangled by the paucity of money, audiences, technicians, and equipment," although Richard Alan Nelson contests this statement as a "highly questionable assumption."[179] In truth, it is likely that Norman ran into the same difficulties that Buddy Austin and W. J. Stiles had experienced when attempting to purchase studio space for the Strand. It is known that Norman was able to purchase studio and laboratory equipment from Henry Klutho at his Fine Arts City and had even discussed the possibility of erecting a separate facility for Norman's use nearby.

Henry Klutho's financial losses proved to be too severe, and Norman apparently was unable to purchase the studio outright, so for the time being he hit the road and had to put his dreams of owning his own film studio on hold.[180] Using Klutho's equipment, Norman was able to produce two films during his time in Oklahoma: *The Bulldogger* and *The Crimson Skull* (1922), both starring famed African American cowboy and Wild West performer Bill Pickett. Each film had a tremendously popular run, which increased Richard Norman's reputation as an emerging race filmmaker and empowered him to at last set out to establish a permanent base of operations in Jacksonville.[181]

In 1922, Norman's dream of owning a studio finally came to fruition when he purchased the abandoned shell of Eagle Studios located in Jacksonville's Arlington neighborhood. As discussed in chapter 1, Eagle Studios was founded by Harry Kelly in 1915 and was one among a slew of studio properties that came to the city during Mayor J.E.T. Bowden's "quit Los Angeles" campaign. After failing to produce a single film on the property during Bowden's tenure as mayor, Kelly relinquished his stake in Eagle and sold the property to Henry Klutho in 1917.[182] Klutho, for his part, incorporated the Eagle property as part of his vision for his Fine Arts City, but he abandoned the project when financing fell through. That same year Klutho threw in the towel and sold the property to Norman.

With the profits from the exhibition of his Western films, Richard Norman at last had enough capital to purchase the former Eagle property outright from Klutho. Located on a little over an acre of land, the now retitled Norman Film Studio consisted of five buildings in all, with staging laboratories, interior and exterior lighting systems, and an on-site power plant.[183] The paint had hardly dried from the improvements Henry Klutho had invested in the buildings before he opted to sell the studio. This gave Norman a decided advantage that all but assured that he "controlled the finest studio lay-out in the country."[184] Norman's connections with Jacksonville's local network of film exhibitors in African American theaters, combined with the contacts he had made in ethnic theaters across the Midwest and Northeast, helped to establish one of the first fully realized national distribution networks for sending his films to Black film exhibitors far and wide.[185]

Between the escalating racial violence in Florida during the 1920s and an outbreak of another wave of Spanish influenza in 1923, many Black-owned and Black-oriented theaters were forced to close. This added to the logistical challenges for the distribution of Norman's films. By 1923, former Kalem producer D. Ireland Thomas noted that the national race film industry had narrowed to three manufacturing companies: the Lincoln Motion Picture Company in Los Angeles, the Oscar Micheaux Film Corporation in Chicago, and Norman Studios in Jacksonville.[186] That Norman Studios was able to produce any films at all is testament to the resiliency of Black Floridian moviegoers and the tenacity of Norman's dream of creating a "Black Star System" that could produce quality Black actors and actresses with visibility in name recognition.[187]

Over the next five years, Norman Studios produced three feature-length films at his studio in Jacksonville: *Regeneration* (1923), *A Debtor to the Law* (1924), and *The Flying Ace* (1926).[188] Ever the dreamer, Norman had throughout this period sought to experiment with new technical and commercial approaches to his films, with mixed success. Norman's *Colored Serial Supreme*

Figure 15. *The Flying Ace*, Richard Norman Studios (1926). Richard Norman's *The Flying Ace* was one of several "race films" produced at Norman Studios between 1919 and 1928. In 2021, the film was selected for preservation in the United States National Film Registry by the Library of Congress as being "culturally, historically, or aesthetically significant." Courtesy of State Archives of Florida, Florida Memory.

series was envisioned as a significant opportunity to showcase Black characters in serious starring roles rather than in the low comic supporting parts that had previously been presented in mainstream films of the period. He also developed an ingenious way to meet the costs of producing the series through a nationwide profit-sharing enterprise that would establish a viable distribution network for the country's fledgling race theaters.[189] The *Colored Serial Supreme* eventually fell by the wayside after he failed to secure the necessary financial backing. *Regeneration* and *The Flying Ace* were sensations in segregated theaters across the South from Alabama to Texas and were regularly screened in African Methodist Episcopal (AME) churches and at community schools throughout the Midwest.[190]

Building on the popularity and financial success of his feature films produced in Jacksonville, Norman decided to return to Oklahoma to film his next feature, *Black Gold* (1928). After shooting several interior sequences at his Arlington studio, Norman and company set out for the all-Black town of

Tatums, Oklahoma, to complete the rest of his location shooting. The film is based on the true-life story of John Cripps, an African American oil man from Tatums who steadfastly stood up against encroaching ranchers and oil drillers to become one of the most influential landowners in the state. *Black Gold* was supposed to be, like *Flying Ace* before it, part of a series of feature films that "would inspire ambition and members of the colored race to accomplish things achieved by their leaders."[191] Although only fragments of the film survive, it appears that with *Black Gold*, Norman was at the top of his game as a filmmaker and marketer. Showings of the film broke records in many of theaters it played in, especially in movie houses where leads Lawrence Crimer and Kathryn Boyd would appear and perform a fifteen-minute sketch show before the screening.[192]

Despite the critical success and positive audience reception for the movies made at Norman Studios, the continued decline of race film theaters across the country (except in Jacksonville) meant that *Black Gold* would be Norman Studios' swan song. Although Richard Norman accurately anticipated the motion picture industry's shift to all-sound filmmaking, he placed his entire savings and the profits from *Black Gold* into the wrong technology. Warner Brothers had caused a sensation in the film industry with its debut of the Vitaphone in *The Jazz Singer* (1927), starring Al Jolson. However, Richard Norman invested in a different sound synchronization device called the Camera-Phone. Norman was able to sell over a dozen projection units compatible with Camera-Phone to the theaters he had worked most frequently with over the past five years, in the hopes of screening sound films by the end of the decade. Unfortunately, just as he was on the cusp of establishing his own alternative sound unit in Jacksonville, Western Electric unveiled its own sound-on-film system that proved to be technologically superior and cheaper than the Camera-Phone. The failure of Camera-Phone was Norman's undoing.[193]

Unlike the filmmakers during Jacksonville's movie boom in the 1910s who either joined in the exodus to California or left the industry entirely, Richard Norman remained involved in the Florida film industry for the rest of his life. After the loans he took out to install Camera-Phone projectors were recalled, Norman Studios was reduced to a one-man and one-woman (Norman's wife, Gloria) operation. Years later, Norman wrote to *Regeneration* star M. C. Maxwell, "I am road showing everything now, and like yourself taking a projector along and showing in churches and schools where there is no colored theater. Many of the theaters have not been able to put it in sound equipment or pay the high licenses and as a result are shut down, many for good."[194] During the 1930s, Norman traveled across Florida and neighboring states, where he took to the road not only his own films but the films of Oscar Micheaux, along with what he described as "fine clean entertainment" and, later, footage of "Brown Bomber" Joe Lewis's meteoric rise in the boxing ring. He sought to bring these images to communities that had limited or no access to a movie house of their own.[195]

Richard Norman continued to hold onto his Arlington studio for years after RNMC went defunct, at one point attempting to rent the property to produce industrial films and commercials for North Florida businesses. In 1935, Gloria Norman opened a dance studio on the property. After retiring from the roadshow circuits in 1946, Norman's career came full circle as he and Gloria opened two African American theaters in Central Florida, the Ace Theater in Apopka and the Famous Theatre in Winter Park, which they operated into the 1950s.

After her husband's death in 1960, Gloria Norman continued to lease the Arlington studio for various uses for over a decade until selling the location in the mid-1970s.[196] In the interceding years, the property changed hands, with one of the five buildings leased out to Circle of Faith Ministries, which as of this writing, continues to operate in the former dance studio. In 2002, the City of Jacksonville purchased the remaining four buildings that comprised of Norman Studios for $250,000 and in 2004 received a state grant to begin exterior renovations on the project.[197]

Since its incorporation in 2007, the Norman Studios Silent Film Museum has diligently fought to carry out their mission to protect and preserve the history of silent film and to celebrate the African American experience and the role Richard E. Norman played in the early days of the movie industry. The passionate fundraising drive carried out by the Norman Studios Silent Film Museum and Jacksonvillians has helped to bring about a better understanding of Florida's troubled racial past.

In 2015, Norman Studios found an ally in the University of Central Florida, when a graduate course led by Dr. Anne Lindsay assisted in ensuring the property would be designated as a National Historic Landmark. The subsequent efforts to turn the former film studio over to the National Park Service will further aid in the much-needed interior renovations, as well allow for the purchase of all five buildings on the property.[198] The work to preserve the Norman Studio site is still ongoing, but the hope is to build a lasting film museum and educational site that can provide a significant and lasting connection to Florida's film heritage.

Despite Florida's regressive racial politics during the early twentieth century, which many producers active in the Florida film industry were complicit in perpetuating, Florida also gave rise to a vibrant and dynamic race entertainment industry that mounted a monumental campaign against the malicious stereotypes expressed through minstrelsy and pro-Confederate Lost Cause propaganda. Whether Jacksonville's Ashley Street's role as "the Harlem of the South," *The Birth of a Race*'s ill-fated attempt to counter D. W. Griffith's *The Birth of a Nation* in Tampa Bay, or Richard Norman's quixotic dream of turning North Florida into the center of production for the race film industry, both sides of the coin to Florida's role in shaping perceptions of race during cinema's silent era have endless fascinating dimensions still left to be explored. The relationship between Florida and the American motion picture industry certainly did not end with the closing of Richard Norman Studios. The transition to sound and the onset of the Great Depression would once more give Florida film boosters hope that Hollywood producers' studios might just "quit Los Angeles," after all, and return home to the Sunshine State.

3

"Motion Pictures at a Great Saving!"

Florida Attempts to Build a "Second Los Angeles," 1922–1945

> What the picture industry has done for Los Angeles and the State of California it will do for the State of Florida. Where the production of motion pictures is located, the population increases as if by magic. It will indeed bring new life to the state. I am convinced that motion pictures can be produced in Florida at a great saving!
>
> Edward Alexander, producer/director of United Films, 1932

"Ghostly Rhetorics and Melodramatics"

On the night of June 25, 1963, the sky across Tampa Bay was engulfed in smoke as a fire broke out along a stretch of near-forgotten industrial ruins on Weedon Island. That evening seven fire units raced to contain the blaze as it consumed a large warehouse owned by the Florida Power Corporation. Although the firefighters arrived on the scene less than fifteen minutes after the fire was first reported, the warehouse had by then already completely burned to the ground. St. Petersburg fire chief W. B. Thompkins reported the following day that, even if his unit had made it to the building earlier, nothing could have been done since there were no fire hydrants on Weedon Island. In an interview given to the *St. Petersburg Times*, the property's owner complained that the warehouse was "dry as tinder and a disaster in the making."[1] The fire on Weedon Island reportedly could be seen as far as Tampa, and it attracted hundreds of onlookers who drove to the island to witness the spectacle.

Weedon Island had not experienced such a flurry of activity in decades. By 1963, it had been decades since this neglected part of the Pinellas Peninsula had made any major headlines. In the 1930s, however, this collection of derelict buildings was home to Sun Haven Studios, a production complex that aspired to turn Florida's West Coast into a "second Los Angeles."[2] Sun Haven Studios was supposed to signal Florida's dramatic return to the silver screen. Instead, as Fred Wright of the *St. Petersburg Independent* wrote several years after the property was destroyed, "All that remained of Tampa Bay's movie heritage are the ghostly rhetorics and melodramatics of movie actors and camera men who had the dubious honor of making the worst movies in cinema history."[3] Richard Alan Nelson describes this period in equally bleak terms as "essentially a dreary story of stock fraud, studio failure, and over optimistic hopes."[4]

The enthusiasm Tampans felt toward the studio cities that were being built along Florida's Gulf Coast in the 1930s was in part fueled by growing political tensions in California between the Hollywood studios and the state government. With the increased demand for soundstages and expanded studio lots, the Hollywood studios were met with higher property taxes, restrictions on zoning, and a renewed effort by so-called moral crusaders to regulate the industry, leaving studio executives to consider relocating their backlots to another state. During this tumultuous moment in California's film history, a Tampa-based real estate executive named Trenton Collins led an at times one-man crusade to move Hollywood from California's West Coast to Florida's West Coast. Collins's gallant campaign to attract film producers to the state would gain a collection of unlikely allies that included several major Hollywood studio heads, a down-and-out Buster Keaton, and even the governor of Florida.

As Florida grappled with the onset of the Great Depression, a period remembered as "Florida's desperate years," Governors Doyle Carlton (1929–33) and David Sholtz (1933–37) started to explore how to create incentives that could bring the movies back to Florida.[5] Over the course of the 1930s, Trenton Collins and a dedicated group of Florida movie boosters set out to reinvigorate the Florida film industry from the effects of the state government's ongoing "benign neglect" under the Sidney Catts, Cary Hardee, and John Martin administrations.[6] Yet, just as Florida was once again thrust into the spotlight, a series of mishaps caused by limited government support, poor planning, and bad investments made by unscrupulous grifters would put an abrupt end to Florida's film ambitions once again. The abandonment of Sun Haven Studios in the summer of 1934 seemingly marked an end to any hope of rebooting the Florida film industry.

The story behind the rise and fall of Florida's studio cities during the 1920s and 1930s offers a cautionary tale that highlights the limits of individual ambition, as well as the innate challenges that government officials faced in incentivizing filmmakers to establish permanent residence in the state. Although state-sponsored organizations such as the Committee for the Development of the Motion Picture (CDMP) and the Special Motion Picture Committee

(SMPC) inspired film producers, local businessmen, and politicians to harmonize the entertainment industry with broader economic recovery efforts, by the mid-1930s, Florida had once again faded into the background. The hard lessons learned by community organizers and state politicians would go on to serve as a playbook for corporate and government collaboration across the state in decades to come.

This chapter will examine the efforts made at both the state and city level to convince Hollywood to come to Florida and build studio cities throughout the state. Hollywood always loves a comeback story. Even though this comeback ultimately fell short, it established a template for how a statewide film industry can operate and also helped set the stage for Florida's rise as a film and television capital in the 1960s.

"If You Lived in Florida, You Could Be Here By Now"

In the aftermath of World War I and Spanish influenza pandemic, the United States experienced a downturn in manufacturing and production with an estimated decline in gross domestic product (GDP) of between 6 to 8 percent.[7] The sudden drop in wages and decreased revenue across most industries devastated workers across the country, while the reduced prices on goods and services caused by the postwar recession proved to be a boon for an increasing number of white-collar Americans.[8] In Florida, an economic slowdown in the agricultural and industrial sectors left community leaders and state politicians to seek new sources of revenue. Since Florida's stunning natural environment and warm winter weather cost nothing to produce and the state's open frontiers remained widely accessible for newcomers, a series of promotions were geared specifically toward tourists with a disposable income.

Even before the Great Depression, Florida was no longer just a playland for the extraordinarily wealthy who could afford to ride along Plant and Flagler's railways and winter in millionaire-row mansions and perfectly manicured resort communities.[9] As a network of auto-trails connected previously disparate parts of the country, thousands of auto-tourists began to flock southward to Florida in the winter months along the Dixie and Atlantic Highways.[10] These self-described "tin can tourists" would modify their automobiles to allow for roadside camping and carry food and supplies into pockets of the country where roadside stopovers were few and far between. As auto-tourism began to take off nationwide, a national Tin Can Tourist Association (TCT) formed as a loosely organized group of highway travelers. Typically, the TCT would have summer meetings in Michigan, with winter meetings at campgrounds in places such as Tampa, Sarasota, Ocala, and Eustis, sparking "the first statewide invasion of tourism."[11]

The pocketbooks of the tin can tourists soon became a preferred target of unscrupulous real estate developers and ambitious community organizers alike. As more tourists than ever arrived in Florida, land speculators approached incoming visitors with a proposition that they could cover the cost of their winter vacation by purchasing a lot of unused and undeveloped acreage as an "investment," that they would then sell off at the end of their tour to a local "property plunger" for a tidy profit.[12] Across Florida's East and West Coasts, new cities sprouted from the ground up from what was previously just sand and swampland.[13] The overinflated value put into rising property prices throughout the state sparked the construction of a series of overnight subdivision communities such as Harry Kelly's ill-fated effort to build a studio city in Tampa during the 1910s (see chapter 1). Between 1910 and 1920, Florida's population increased by 28.7 percent, surpassing California as the fastest-developing state in country.[14]

Migration and tourism fanned the flames of the sensation caused by land speculation across the state. This whirl of investments in Florida land would go on to become one of the most consequential financial manias in American history.[15] The Florida Land Boom of the 1920s transformed sleepy frontier communities like Orlando and Miami into burgeoning metropolises. With such rampant overspeculation in real estate, it was only a matter of time before ambitious filmmakers and aspirational businessmen set out to cash in on "tinsel-spangled dreams" of their own.[16] In quick succession, developers and speculators soon mobilized newspaper advertising, brochures, films, photographs, and billboards that were strategically placed across northern cities with the slogan, "If You Lived in Florida, You Could Be Here by Now."[17]

Miami Tries to Build a "Second Universal City in Florida"

The first movie booster outside of North Florida to make a conscientious effort to convince producers to relocate from California to Florida was Miami Chamber of Commerce president Everett George (E. G.) Sewell. Through a series of promotions in his personally financed monthly magazine called the *Miamian*, Sewell started concentrated ad campaigns to turn what he saw as "North America's youngest and newest frontier" into "a second Universal City in Florida."[18] According to historian Frank Sessa, South Florida in the 1920s served as a "projection screen" for national and global imaginings, while 1920s Miami was considered by local real estate speculators to be "on the threshold

Figure 16. Theda Bara playing Zara, a South Sea Island princess romantically involved with a missionary, played by actor William B. Davidson. The image is taken from the shoot of the Fox Company film *A Woman There Was* (1919), filmed at Collins and Twenty-Sixth Street in Miami. Courtesy of State Archives of Florida, Florida Memory.

of its first great period of expansion, its boom."[19] Sewell's promotions sought to sell Miami to as "a curious combination of the serious, the artistic, and the bizarre."[20]

As Miami continued to invent itself in the first years of the 1920s, E. G. Sewell teamed up with famed air pioneer Glenn Curtiss and lawyer "Colonel" Frank Shutts, who was also the owner of the *Miami Herald,* to found Miami Studios Incorporated in March 1922. The new studio was announced in the *Miami Herald* as a superb combination of "Personnel with Personality and Pep and Punch and Pluck."[21] The groundbreaking for the 140-acre studio facility took place on March 21, 1922, and was attended by 1,500 Miamians. The event was hailed in the *Herald* as "A significant landmark in the development of this section, and a forecast of a tremendous industry which will mean more to Miami than any other one thing which has happened in many years."[22]

One month later, the New York–based Syracuse Moving Pictures Company responded to one of E. G. Sewell's ads in the trade presses and journeyed to Miami Studios to film an adventure feature called *The Isle of Doubt* (1922).[23] By June, the studio's president, Glenn Curtiss, began talks with British film producer John Brunton to come manage the Miami facility. Brunton agreed to take up the challenge under the condition "that the organization put in its own producing company and also organize a production financing corporation to aid independents."[24] The carte blanche promised by the board of Miami Studios convinced the seasoned producer to uproot to Miami and become "the supreme head of the motion picture industry in Florida."[25]

While film productions made in California and New York still comprised over 96 percent of all films made in the United States in 1922 and 1923, E. G. Sewell helped South Florida to eke out a seemingly comfortable place as a humble regional production center with fourteen feature films completed in 1922 and twenty-one features produced in 1923.[26] Hoping to gain a greater share of the market, John Brunton initiated a new advertising campaign to "talk up" Miami Studios and get "a well-known producer here and by doing so prove to the satisfaction of the entire motion picture-producing world that things could be done in Florida."[27] Brunton followed through on this promise by inviting to director Rex Ingram of Metro Company to shoot his next picture at Miami Studios. Fresh off the enormous financial success of the Rudolph Valentino vehicle *The Four Horsemen of the Apocalypse* (1921), Ingram emerged as one of the most prolific epic filmmakers of the silent era.[28] For his next project, Brunton proposed Ingram film his proposed adaptation of John Russell's South Seas romance *Where the Pavement Ends* (1923) on location in South Florida. Ingram agreed and set out to start location shooting at Miami Studios in December 1922.

Hoping that landing such a high-profile feature film could put South Florida on the map, Brunton remarked to the *Miami Herald* that following the premiere of *Where the Pavement Ends*, it would only be a matter of time before there would be "a general exodus of the motion picture companies of the Pacific slope to Miami, and we must exert every influence to keep them here and make them permanent additions to our community."[29] Soon after this announcement, a cadre of Fort Lauderdale–based realtors purchased ten acres to build a proposed $3 million studio facility near Miami's Oakland Park, along with three hundred housing lots to create a "Greenwich type village for motion picture people."[30] The studio was also supposed to serve as the home for *Miami Movie Magazine*, with the surrounding actors' village becoming yet another jewel in the crown of South Florida's emerging film colony.[31]

The problem was that Miami did not have the resources it needed to build a fully self-sufficient studio city. While South Florida had proven to be quite suitable as a secondary location for major film productions and could provide an affordable backdrop for low-budget and midrange independent films, the infrastructure needed to support a major studio project—especially in South Florida—was not yet there. After arriving in Miami to begin production on

Where the Pavement Ends, Rex Ingram and his wife, Alice Terry (the film's star and his codirector), expressed their anger and frustration at Brunton's false advertising.

From its outset, the production was marred by bad weather and poor community relations. Once location shooting wrapped, Ingram and Terry took the first train they could out of Miami. Returning to Los Angeles, the couple complained to the trade presses about the "unprofessionalism on the part of 'raw' local technicians at the studios."[32] There appeared to be little love lost between Miamians and Ingram either. In response to the Ingram's smear campaign in the trade presses, Miami Studio cofounder Frank Shutts remarked in the *Miami Herald* that "considerable resentment has been caused among the moving picture people of Miami by a published statement attributed to Rex Ingram."[33]

Rex Ingram's statements to the trade presses brought on a public relations disaster that led to the studio's closure. With productions marred by technical and logistical difficulties, Miami Studios had earned an increasingly unfavorable reputation in the industry. The crisis continued to escalate after production wrapped. The film's photoplay writer, Ernest Lebrel, remarked to the *Miami Herald,* "Those of us who had any extensive experience in this intricate and high art, were either utterly unacquainted with each other or made subordinate to the most helpless incompetents."[34] Lebrel's statement also circulated in several major trade presses, and following the negative publicity attached to *Where the Pavement Ends,* all the earlier bids made by studios to film at Miami Studios were withdrawn. John Brunton resigned under pressure from the board soon afterward.

Miami Studios went completely dark by the end of 1923. Although both E. G. Sewell and Miami mayor B. L. Smith continued to pitch Miami as a "Second Hollywood," the poor press associated with South Florida tarnished their efforts. By 1925, the studio facilities were "ballyhooed" and stood as an empty reminder of a faded dream, which, according to Richard Alan Nelson, served "as a stark reminder to future Florida film boosters that the simple existence of a fully equipped local movie studio could not guarantee that Hollywood would come to stay."[35]

Hobe Sound's Picture City: "The Los Angeles of Florida"

In the first half of the 1920s, real estate developers across Florida proposed their own studio cities in the hope of winning over major studio producers and turning Florida into a "Hollywood East." Frank Sessa describes the frenzy for land in Florida, which "had all of the elements of a major land boom in a country of vast expanses of arable but uncultivated or unoccupied lands. Such booms are no novelty."[36] At the height of the Florida Land Boom, Florida had more than fifty thousand unlicensed real estate agents promoting an endless multitude of different land purchase schemes for buyers who likely would never set foot on a piece of property that could change hands several times over the course of a single day.[37] A 1925 state-sponsored survey boldly predicted that "by the middle of the twentieth century Florida is destined to be one of the three or four most densely populated states in the Union, with at least ten million permanent inhabitants and a winter population of as many more."[38]

As Florida's population continued to experience exponential expansion in terms of population growth and economic development, the increased demand for housing and business properties were unable to meet supply.[39] So-called piker promoters were known to pursue all types of gimmicks to propose to would-be buyers of South Florida's still sparsely inhabited hinterlands, which inevitably brought to the state a slew of what Richard Alan Nelson described as "oil-tongued strangers who promised to their gullible investors millions to be made in producing motion pictures in Florida" and soon "crisscrossed the state from Miami to Orlando, and Palatka."[40] A 1927 report on the Florida Land Boom by economist Homer Vanderblue described the situation in even more cutting terms:

> As the speculation spread, or was carried over the country, Florida became "news"; and "special stories" filled the daily newspapers everywhere, telling of the latest "gold rush," and featuring stories of fabulous wealth almost miraculously secured. Pictures of bathing beauties, of coconut palms on moonlight nights, and occasionally of islands and peninsulas which had been pumped out of the sea by enterprising promoters, who thereby reaped "miraculous" paper profits, filled the papers of the North.[41]

The piker promoters found an unlikely ally in recently elected Governor John Wellborn Martin, who promised that his self-proclaimed "businessman's administration" would bring new capital and industries to the state.[42] As discussed in chapter 1, it was Martin's stunning victory over "Movie Mayor" J.E.T. Bowden in Jacksonville's 1917 mayor's race that contributed to the downfall of Jacksonville's emerging film industry.

In his first address before the Florida Legislature, given in January 1925, Governor Martin pledged to work with anyone who could bring investments and new industry to the state. Governor Martin remarked, "Florida needs capital, and must have it, in the building and establishing of her industries.

She needs labor, also, and must have it. One without the other, though in abundance, will not suffice . . . No statute should be enacted inimical to either."[43] Through subsidizing an ambitious roadbuilding initiative and formulating the foundations of a tax incentive initiative that would be modeled in the decades to come, Martin created a favorable environment for large conglomerations like the film studios that had seemingly begun to outstay their welcome in Southern California.[44] John W. Martin's inaugural address indicated Florida was open for business, and producer Carl Laemmle of Universal Studios expressed his interest in building a second Universal City in Florida. Laemmle purchased a tract on the shore of Old Tampa Bay, known locally as Rocky Point, which he envisioned would be the site of a studio-laboratory for what would have been Universal Studios' "Made-in-Tampa Pictures."[45]

Meanwhile on Florida's East Coast, real estate developer Charles L. Apfel partnered with movie mogul Lewis J. Selznick to develop a film community along Hobe Sound in Martin County. In his initial bid for the property, Apfel proposed to Selznick that a nearby development owned by the Olympia Improvement Company be renamed "Picture City." He added that Florida was destined to become a production center since "a treacherous arctic current had been discovered off the coast of California and in a few years would freeze the California climate so severely that filmmakers would have to quit Hollywood and ship their studios to Florida."[46] Even though the studio was founded on the outlandish claim that "an abrupt change in California's climate would precipitate Los Angeles–based producers to seek refuge in Florida," the Hobe Sound Picture City seemed to have gained the attention of investors.[47]

By October 1925, Apfel and Selznick presented to investors $1 million proposal to build what would have been the largest studio complex in the world at the time. Selznick boldly proclaimed that the studio project would turn Picture City into the "Los Angeles of Florida." The following winter, the roads connecting Picture City to the rest of Florida were completed as part of Governor Martin's infrastructure initiative. Although the blueprints for the homes and studio lots had been laid out, none of the parties involved had figured out how or where the money for the venture would ultimately be raised. Without the needed financial backing or a plan for recovering a return on the initial investment in Picture City, the entire venture soon fizzled out. In the end, the dream of Picture City soon collided with reality, and the project collapsed along with the land boom that had originally sustained it.[48]

The Rise and Fall of Sun City Studios

While South Florida's brief movie boom was fragmented and limited to the interests of specific realtors and investors, the communities along the Gulf Coast would come together and make one of the most concerted attempts yet to win over Hollywood and create a true "Second Los Angeles" in Florida. By the end of 1925, Tampa surpassed Jacksonville to become Florida's most populous city.[49] Across the bay in St. Petersburg, the cost of building permits effectively increased from $2.8 million in 1920 to $24 million in 1925.[50] While the boom extended across the state—Miami especially experienced its own dramatic transformation during this same period—developers in that other Florida metropolis looked on with envy. The *Miami Herald* declared, "More fortunes have been made in these last six months on Tampa real estate than all the acquaintances of our lifetime made until six months ago," declaring, "Tampa is the luckiest of the Florida cities and she is bettering her luck by making the most of it."[51]

Hoping to capitalize on Tampa's rising influence in the midst of the statewide land boom, real estate developer J. H. Meyer, the head of sales for the Sun City Holding Company, proposed to build a $300,000 studio complex he envisioned as "a departure from the conventional studio" that would include a "visitor's gallery from which guests may witness the filming of the silver screen celebrities and any studio work."[52] The studio grounds were also supposed to include a "lofty tower [that] affords a splendid view of the entire town, the glistening waters of Tampa Bay and the Little Manatee and of the surrounding woodlands in all directions."[53] In the local papers, Meyer expressed that he was certain that, by "Building a movie studio in Ross," by year's end he believed that he could "create a thriving community that had every element needed for the building of a formidable city."[54]

To secure a proper return on investment to help finance Meyer's self-described "open to public studio," Meyer drafted a grid of streets and boulevards in honor of well-known stars and directors, which he hoped would serve as an enticement for them to invest in Sun City. Meyer appointed industry veteran Ernest Shipman to serve as the president and manager of Sun City Motion Picture Studios, with acclaimed director David M. Hartford as supervisor of productions. Shipman had previously worked at the defunct Klutho Studios in Jacksonville and was understandably hesitant to get involved in another film venture in Florida. However, after receiving a glowing endorsement of Sun City from the Tampa Board of Trade that described the studio city as "amply financed for all needs," he was compelled to join the venture.[55]

Meyer assured investors that his company would rely solely on outside investment and "would not allow any speculative stock promotion in connection with any Sun City activities."[56]

At first, it appeared the only investment that members of the Gulf Coast community were asked to make in the new studio was an emotional one. More than 1,500 people attended Sun City's groundbreaking ceremony on October 8, 1925. The event was followed up with a special oration given by Tampa mayor-commissioner Perry G. Wall. In the hope of improving relations between Sun City and the Tampa community, producer W. E. Macarton announced his intention that the "members of the company will live in Tampa and will make daily trips to the Sun City studio."[57]

In December 1925, Meyer commissioned a series of full-page advertisements in newspapers across Florida. The promotion promised speculators an exclusive tour of the development property on January 5, 1926, with assurances that interested buyers would "not be embarrassed by 'high pressure' sales methods as we do not permit this."[58] The excitement of the moment soon caused Meyer to overplay his hand. Without a functioning studio yet completed, he promised the *St. Petersburg Times* that plans "are now being made for the beginning of activities on a large scale and at an early date, a picture producer of national reputation will be producing pictures at Sun City."[59] The sanguine effort made by Sun City Holding to build community ties to the Gulf Coast was successful in attracting hundreds of prospective buyers from the Tampa and St. Petersburg region. Closer inspection of the press releases issued during this time makes it seem likely that these proposals were a creative loophole Meyer used to get around the regulatory legislation and avoid regional corporation laws.

The enthusiasm of investment-hungry Floridians during Governor Martin's "businessman's administration" seems to have blinded them to glaring problems with Meyer's increasingly bold promises. As the landscape surrounding the Little Manatee River began to be cleared, Meyer commissioned the construction of his proposed studio complex to be designed in Spanish-Moorish architecture with fireproof steel construction and tile overlaid in the stucco for an attractive mother-of-pearl finish. Meyer saw to it that the streets were laid out with names like Griffith Avenue, Gish Drive, Chaplin Drive, Vidor Avenue, Universal Drive, and Pathé Place.[60] Land prices around Sun City surged, and so did the pricing demand for deposits on the surrounding lots. An advertisement for Sun City published in the *Tampa Morning Tribune* on October 29, 1925, announced the availability of two hundred lots for purchase at $1,500, with a $375 minimum deposit up front for buyers "who wanted to live among the stars."[61]

In response to the sensation caused by the Sun City promotions, the St. Petersburg City Council granted permission to Harry P. Carver, a New York–based producer, to build a film city of his own. Intended to be located two miles north of downtown St. Petersburg, Carver's Studio Park was announced in the *Tampa Morning Tribune* to be "predicated upon the motion picture industry at Hollywood, California, Culver City and Universal City."[62] In a series of promises very similar to those that had been put forward in Meyer's Sun City bid, Carver told city organizers of his desire to connect Studio Park directly to St. Petersburg, which, he noted in the press, "seems destined to be the metropolis of the Southland."[63] To show his commitment to turning St. Petersburg into a film center, Carver promised a personal touch, where he would "offer practical, efficient, complete production facilities."[64] But just as interest began to build along both sides of Tampa Bay over the prospect of becoming the next "West Coast," the bottom began to drop out from under the Florida Land Boom.

As late as February 1926, just months before the Florida Land Boom fully collapsed, enthusiasm for Sun City seemed unwavering. That same month, the town of Ross officially changed its name to Sun City and boasted that "countless residential and business lots adjacent to the shiny new Spanish-styled studio had been bought and sold repeatedly, almost every time at a profit."[65] Since there are no surviving records from either J. H. Meyer's correspondences with the Sun City Holding Company, it is difficult to guess how serious the company's intentions were in the film manufacturing portion of their land holdings. Based on information available in newspaper promotions of the time, it could be likely that Meyer viewed his production studio as nothing more than a gimmick to increase property values.

The ploy initially seemed to have worked as a series of homes priced at between $35,000 to $75,000 were built on the Sun City grounds, and the Hillsborough County government approved Meyer's proposal to build an adjacent school and power plant facility. For the rest of the year, partially built homes and empty lots passed through countless hands without any buyers making Sun City their home. All the while, Meyer and boosters for Sun City kept up the ruse that high-profile Hollywood stars would "flock to the development and turn this sleepy corner of Florida into the next movie capital."[66] In a 1970 retrospective published in the *Tampa Tribune*, reporter Gene Fernett describes the moment when Floridians realized that Meyer's promises were wholly undeliverable:

> Once Tom Mix, Rin-Tin-Tin, Marie Dressler and all the other top stars found out about Sun City, its advocates were saying, any lot near the

gates of the new Hollywood would be worth a princely sum. That optimism fixed firmly in their minds, the citizens of the cinema capital of the East sat back and waited. And waited. As the days turned into weeks, the tinsel-spangled dreams slowly began [fading], just as was the stucco façade of the huge, still empty studio. Before long, even the most optimistic of the dreamers began to drift away from the little town, leaving its streets to be lost amid weeds and palmetto bushes, and its carefully surveyed lots merged into the anonymity of woods and pasture.[67]

By the summer of 1926, not only had investors' enthusiasm for Sun City turned cold, but the scandals attached to the Davis Islands project sparked a statewide collapse of the Florida Land Boom. In light of revelations of fraudulent real estate speculation along with a general lack of any serious investment in related studio projects, Ernest Shipman and David Hartford both resigned from the Sun City Motion Picture Company, leaving Meyer not only with an unsettled residential community but now an empty studio complex to go with it. By the following year, the Sun City studio facilities had gone almost entirely untouched, except for two short comedies (the titles of which are seemingly lost to history) that Meyer begrudgingly produced to protect himself from fraud charges.[68] The fallout from the Florida Land Boom ultimately left many of the properties at Sun City in receivership. Unable to pay even the local property taxes, Meyer declared bankruptcy in 1929, and the entire community eventually went up for sale on public auction in 1932 for one hundred dollars. Shortly after the property changed hands, the studio facility "mysteriously" burned to the ground, and its bricks were sold for a paltry $1,500.[69]

Unlike Jacksonville, where the collapse of the city's film industry in the 1910s was caused by a shift in regional politics, Tampa Bay in the 1920s had a supportive political and economic environment perfectly conducive to motion picture production. What the region severely lacked during this time were producers or filmmakers who had the skills, know-how, or business acumen required to attract productions to Florida. Just as interest was piqued, Florida was rocked by the abrupt collapse of its land boom, and investors soon balked. As property values throughout the state continued to fall, any further attempts to build production studios near Tampa Bay ended in empty promises.

The Committee for the Development of the Motion Picture

The economic meltdown that followed the end of the Florida Land Boom in 1926 effectively upended Governor John Martin's hope of turning Florida into "one of the richest, most populous, and influential in the whole family of commonwealths which make up our nation."[70] The situation in Florida only got worse in the fall, when a string of several natural disasters brought the state's surging economy and infrastructure to an abrupt halt. On September 11, 1926, the "Great Miami Hurricane" struck the state, causing over $100 million in damages and up to 1,000 casualties. The storm surge in Biscayne Bay ravaged the city and all but wiped out the former grounds of Miami Studios.[71] The devastation caused by the 1926 hurricane would be overshadowed two years later in what is considered one of the deadliest hurricanes in American history.

With over 4,000 total fatalities, with over 2,500 people killed in South Florida alone, the 1928 Okeechobee Hurricane cut an unimaginable trail of destruction across Florida. The path of the storm crossed directly over Lake Okeechobee and let out an inland tidal wave that desolated the surrounding basin.[72] Three-quarters of the victims were Black migrant farmworkers, leaving lasting shock on the state's African American population.[73] The impact of the hurricane was so pervasive that nearly a decade later, the storm's aftermath was sublimely recalled in Zora Neale Hurston's landmark 1937 novel *Their Eyes Were Watching God*.

> Ten feet higher and far as they could see the muttering wall advanced before the braced-up waters like a road crusher on a cosmic scale. The monstropolous beast had left his bed. Two hundred miles an hour wind had loosed his chains. He seized hold of his dikes and ran forward until he met the quarters; uprooted them like grass and rushed on after his supposed-to-be conquerors, rolling the dikes, rolling the houses, rolling the people in the houses along with other timbers. The sea was walking the earth with a heavy heel.[74]

The 1926 and 1928 hurricanes each caused thousands of deaths and hundreds of millions of dollars' worth of damage, severely tarnishing Florida's long-standing reputation as "a year-round playground."[75] The combined blow dealt to finances and morale brought much of the unbridled enthusiasm surrounding the boom years to a crashing standstill.

Reconstruction from the Okeechobee Hurricane had barely commenced when, on July 17, 1929, what little remained of the real estate bubble that ballooned during the Florida Land Boom burst entirely. In what would be remembered as the "blackest day in the history of Tampa," the Citizens Bank and Trust Company, one of Florida's largest banking institutions, refused to open for business after speculators in the area's failed movie city projects withdrew their remaining deposits. Once Citizens Bank closed its doors, five more banks across Tampa followed its lead, causing a financial frenzy as depositors lost their life savings and more than $10 million in assets disappeared overnight.[76] The collapse of Citizens Bank sent shock waves across Florida's financial intuitions, bringing on a statewide depression a full three months before Wall Street's infamous Black Thursday stock market crash on October 24, which led to the Great Depression.

Just six months into the job, John Martin's successor, newly elected Governor Doyle Carlton, had his work cut out for him. In response to the tumult caused by the Citizens Bank crisis, Governor Carlton set out to establish a more pragmatic approach toward rebuilding the state's fledgling economy. Several months earlier, in Governor Carlton's inaugural address given in January 1929, he seemed to anticipate the financial challenges the state would face during his term: "In order to keep the state financially solvent, industrial development must be encouraged."[77] The governor went further to suggest that one possible solution to stem the hemorrhaging of depositors and investors from state banks would be to entice new businesses to come and set up shop in Florida. According to Carlton, the best way to bring business to the state would be to offer an extended tax remission, which would in turn create "a home market for our produce and employment for labor."[78]

During John Martin's so-called businessman's administration, the Florida government was committed to building the state's transportation network and finding new ways to lure land speculators and encourage tourism. Following the land bust and the destruction caused by the 1926 and 1928 hurricanes, such appeals had lost their luster. Still, one industry that John Martin confoundingly continued to ignore during his time as governor was the film industry. Although several film producers did get swept up in the frenzy of the land boom, Governor Martin did not attempt to offer any incentives that would have kept production companies in the state.

In a break from his predecessor's prejudice against the motion picture industry, Doyle Carlton issued a statement in June 1929, just weeks before the Citizens Bank crisis. In this statement, the governor announced his hope that the state government could work to build a "third motion picture center located in Florida at any cost the movie executives decide is best for the purpose."[79] To make this happen, Carlton approached his former colleague, a Tampa-based real estate developer named Trenton C. Collins, to initiate a statewide publicity campaign to let big-time Hollywood producers know that Florida was open for the film production business.

Collins got his first bite almost right away from director Henry King, who was in search of a tropical environment to film his forthcoming "talkie" *Hell Harbor* (1930), starring Lupe Vélez.[80] Working on behalf of the Inspiration Company Unit of United Artists, King initially planned to shoot on a secluded island in the West Indies, but, acutely aware of past challenges suffered by earlier United Artists Caribbean-based productions such as D. W. Griffith's *The Idol Dancer* and *The Love Flower* (1920), he was swayed by Collins to shoot entirely on location in Tampa.[81]

An agreement was struck between Collins and United Artists in August 1929. King arrived in Tampa's Rocky Point and immediately started scouting locations for his South Seas romance. During this exploratory visit, King and his casting director met with the swashbuckling performers who participated in the Gasparilla Pirate Festival. Joining the Gasparilla pirates were another 120 Tampans for a dress rehearsal to shoot a scene set inside a pirate's den. In his remarks to the *Tampa Morning Tribune*, Henry King explained how impressed he was that "when attired in character garb, the Tampans working on the studio lot were almost perfect counterparts of the riff-raff and human jetsam found in any Caribbean seaport."[82]

Henry King quickly won over skeptical Tampans, who, after being hoodwinked by film producers in the past, were rightfully suspicious of the seeming good intentions of the *Hell Harbor* crew. While producers such as Harry Kelly seemed only to scheme different ways to siphon money from the surrounding community, by the end of his first week of preproduction King invited the public to join his cast and crew in watching the dress rehearsals for the film's opening sequence featuring the Gasparilla pirates. To sweeten the deal, King opened a makeshift "honky tonk" and purchased cases of bootlegged Cuban rum to be enjoyed by his production team, pirate extras, and local revelers alike.[83] Following another week of shooting location footage along the surrounding breakers, King was ready for the star of his film to come to Tampa. To stir up more interest for Lupe Vélez's impending arrival in Florida, Trenton Collins coordinated with Carl Brorein, the president of the Tampa Chamber of Commerce, to host a citywide celebration that would end in a massive reception at Tampa's Floridian Hotel.

Tampa was in a stir as Collins received inquiries from across the state concerning the banquet. A press release to the *Tampa Morning Tribune* reported, "Motorcades will come from every principal city of the west coast section to join thousands of Tampans in giving Miss Vélez an enthusiastic greeting."[84]

Figure 17. Photo taken at Tampa Union Station in September 1929 at the start of production for *Hell Harbor. Left to right:* Henry King (director), Lupe Vélez (star), Josefina Vélez (her mother), and Governor Doyle Carlton. Courtesy of State Archives of Florida, Florida Memory.

Governor Doyle Carlton was also swept up in the excitement as he arranged to greet Vélez at Tampa's Union Station. On Sunday, September 15, Governor Carlton, Tampa mayor D. B. McKay, along with leaders of the city's Chamber of Commerce came together to revel in Vélez's star power.

As Miss Vélez disembarked from her Seacoast sleeper train and was ushered into a motorcade, she sparkled with a radiant smile in her jade-green dress as the bright September sun shined on the five thousand Floridians who had gathered to give her "the biggest, most cordial greeting of all her life."[85] Surprised at the attention given to her arrival, Vélez remarked at the greeting ceremony that this was the first time she had ever been officially greeted by a governor, while Governor Carlton expressed "how glad he was that she had come to Tampa to star in the first big sound picture made in this state."[86] Carl Brorein closed the proceedings by announcing to the governor and the thousands of well-wishers his personal hope that *Hell Harbor* would become "the state's debut into the motion picture industry."[87]

Henry King marveled over the instant support established between Tampa and United Artists. In a statement that surely has not aged well, the director compared his experience of shooting in Tampa to filming *The White Sister*

(1923) in Italy, where "Mussolini gave us the run of the kingdom. We thought the limit of cooperation had been reached. But Tampa has gone even further."[88]

Over the following ten weeks, the Tampa community continued to roll out the red carpet for the cast and crew of *Hell Harbor*. Despite the goodwill established between Tampans and their Hollywood visitors, the experience did not translate on the screen. Ultimately, *Hell Harbor* received mixed reviews and a lukewarm box-office reception. In one of the film's more unflattering reviews, Mordaunt Hall of the *New York Times* criticized the film's sluggish pacing and erratic use of sound gimmicks, "together with the frequent stretches of ineffectual and intrusive comedy, [which] causes the film to be somewhat tedious."[89] Even the most negative reviews still made a special mention of the film's location, noting that, with "Glimpses of the shore and sea, it is never so hopeless," and that the film is better when viewed as "a series of beautifully photographed scenes rather than a drama of greed for gold and pearls."[90] The trade presses were similarly critical of the film's pacing and plot but also made sure to put out special mention to *Hell Harbor* for "the distinction of having been made completely outside studio walls, most of the scenes having been shot in a romantic setting outside of Tampa."[91]

The only national newspaper that wholeheartedly endorsed the plot and premise of *Hell Harbor* was the *Tampa Morning Tribune*. Even if the critical and financial reception of *Hell Harbor* was lackluster, Tampa Bay finally seemed to catch its big break. Seizing the opportunity that the positive press Tampa generated, Trenton Collins next filed a proposal to the governor's office to form a Committee for the Development of the Motion Picture (CDMP). In his proposal, Collins wrote to Governor Carlton, "Even if *Hell Harbor* did not receive a return on its investment, the City of Tampa had made a tidy profit."[92] By hosting Henry King and the sixty-five staff and cast members, *Hell Harbor* helped to employ hundreds of struggling Floridians for periods that ranged from a few days to almost four months. In total, Inspiration–United Artists spent nearly $1 million on set construction, salaries, and day-to-day expenses in Tampa and St. Petersburg.[93]

Floridians continued to struggle from the economic freefall brought on by the Great Depression, but the financial windfall that could result from bringing film productions to the state became a source of hope. To attract more film producers to Florida, Collins sent dozens of personal petitions directly to independent producers, encouraging them to film their next project in Florida. Collins himself admitted that initially "these efforts brought indifferent results, it did have the advantage of keeping Florida constantly before the producers and directors." His hard press would eventually pay off.[94]

As the United States fell into the worst years of the Great Depression, the motion picture industry started to feel the pinch as well. Between 1930 and 1931 alone, domestic film production fell off by 16 percent, which caused an overall drop in prices for international exports of American films, resulting in a nearly 50 percent decline in revenues for Hollywood major and minor film studios alike.[95] Many small-time independent producers sought to strike out on their own as the industry became increasingly fractured in the volatile economic environment. Encouraged by positive reports from established industry directors such as Henry King, these newly disenfranchised producers relished the hope that relocating to Florida could revitalize their own fledgling careers.

One producer who sensed Florida's potential as a production center amid the rapidly fracturing film industry was Edward Alexander. A former associate of Henry King, Alexander had severed his ties with Inspiration–United Artists and founded his own independent film company, the United Film Corporation. In August 1930, he announced his plans to build "the finest and most up-to-date sound studios and color photography lab on Florida's Gulf Coast."[96] In a letter to CDMP member Samuel Borchard, Alexander expressed his certainty that Florida's West Coast was "admirably adapted to the production of good pictures" and expressed his "firm belief that at least a part of the picture industry can be brought to Florida in the next few years."[97] In his endorsement of the project to Governor Carlton, Borchard wrote, "Mr. Alexander's plan looks to me like a real honest to goodness motion picture studio that Florida will be proud of, and glad to offer to the motion picture world."[98]

Trenton Collins next convinced Tay Garnet of R.K.O.-Pathé to shoot several tropical scenes for his film *Prestige* (1931), staring Adolphe Menjou and Melvyn Douglas in Tampa. In November 1931, Garnet brought his thirty-member cast and crew to film along the Myakka River, near Sarasota. By the time production had wrapped, Garnet had spent over $100,000 while in Florida, with much of the money dispersed among the seventy-five Floridians who were employed as extras and crew members during production. Collins used this financial boon as further evidence to the governor of the seemingly "boundless potential the film industry could offer to the state."[99]

By the end of 1931, Edward Alexander had acquired the capital investment needed to build his proposed studio. To leverage even more support from the state, Collins reported Alexander's preference for Tampa to the governor, but he also noted the need for increased institutional support from the state: "Quite naturally, my own interests are in the West Coast [of Florida], but this is a matter in which personal interest must be forgotten, to get the third mo tion picture center located in Florida, at whatever point the movie executives decide is best for the purpose."[100]

When Henry King came to Tampa to film *Hell Harbor* in 1929, only a handful of small-time producers had any interest whatsoever in establishing their own production headquarters outside of California. As wages nationwide stagnated and the film industry started to experience the full sting of the Great Depression, Florida seemed an attractive alternative for newly unaffiliated independent producers who needed to avoid the enormous cost overhead attributed to California's high labor costs and property values.

Despite the profit potential that the motion picture industry could offer Florida's economy, the state government continually struggled to remain financially afloat. Two and a half years into his term as governor, Doyle Carlton had little to show in terms of providing an economic recovery for the state. In a public address given in 1931, Carlton reiterated his inaugural message and defined his essential task as "one of maintaining government, paying obligations, and reducing property taxes."[101] Creating a home market for film production in Florida fit very well with his laissez-faire approach to business regulation.[102] Perhaps skittish from the overspeculation during the land boom, Carlton often played the role of a cautious realtor determined not to succumb to same type of chicanery that had followed earlier ill-conceived picture-city ventures.

Tampa Bay Becomes "An Independent's Paradise"

Plans for Edward Alexander's Florida studio complex were off to a promising enough start. In December 1931, Governor Carlton formally endorsed Collins's proposal for the formation of the CDMP, though he did not commit to a set dollar amount to finance the organization. Without any financial support from the state government, Trenton Collins invested his own savings to finance a series of promotional travelogues with Edward Alexander that he hoped would pitch Florida to film producers based in New York and California.[103]

Collins then initiated a letter-writing campaign to the State Hotel Commission (SHC) along with the mayors and mayor-commissioners of each of Florida's major cities, drafted several write-ups for the Associated Press, and contacted even more independent producers interested in assessing the conditions in Florida. The first producer to respond to Collins was Lloyd Hammond, an independent who was then based in Detroit. With experience as a filmmaker based in Miami prior to the collapse of the Florida Land Boom,

Hammond offered Collins important advice on how to get more producers to invest in Florida. He advised, "No one or two high powered promoters financing individual productions is going to help the industry in Florida. The foundation must be properly laid and well planned and must have the full cooperation of the State[;] if this is done there is no reason why Florida could not in a few years' time, surpass California in the production of pictures."[104]

Several months later, in March 1932, Collins landed his first whale with Chester Beecroft, an industry veteran with an impressively long résumé that dated back to his time working for Thomas Edison's General Film Company in 1914. Beecroft had the distinction of being the only film producer licensed by the War Trade Board to distribute American films in Europe during World War I and also played an instrumental role in establishing Paramount's supremacy in Hollywood during the 1920s.[105] As with many of his fellow disenfranchised producers, following a contract dispute with the Hearst Cosmopolitan Company, Beecroft described himself as "All dressed up and no place to go."[106]

After breaking his contract with Hearst, Beecroft joined Collins on an extensive tour along Florida's West Coast to scout possible locations to build his own studio complex. During the tour, they surveyed possible studio locations around Clearwater, Bradenton, St. Petersburg, Sarasota, and Tampa. Eventually Beecroft expressed his interest in setting up a studio on the grounds of an abandoned residential community on Davis Islands in Tampa. When he saw the community's derelict coliseum, Beecroft envisioned the building renovated into a sprawling state-of-the-art soundstage facility. Returning to New York, he formed Beecroft-Florida Movie Studios and obtained the lease with the option of purchase two unfinished facilities on Davis Islands valued at $100,000. Echoing the promotions that took place during Jacksonville's movie boom in the 1910s, Beecroft boasted that the studio's relative proximity to New York (twelve hours by air and thirty-six by train) "will make a special bid for activities by eastern independents who cannot go to the coast and who cannot produce up north during the winter because of winter conditions."[107]

The speed with which the land purchases were made and the sudden, newfound interest of well-connected and serious producers had far outpaced Trenton Collins's wildest expectations. In a confidential letter to John H. Brown, owner of the Suwannee Hotel in St. Petersburg, Collins admitted that his campaign had "progressed to a point which none of us had expected to attain for two or three years."[108] Despite the governor's endorsement of the CDMP and the Davis Islands project, fiscal conservatives in the Florida State Legislature were unwilling to provide any further state-sponsored support.

At the very moment Collins and the CDMP needed momentum on their side, the Florida Legislature pumped the brakes. When the Florida Chamber of Commerce declined a request for $1,700 to help fund a promotional travelogue to help attract producers based in New York and California, Collins went on the offensive with an appeal to the Florida League of Municipalities to take the lead in funding support to the CDMP. In the April 1932 edition of the *Florida Municipal Record,* Collins penned an article both expressing his annoyance at the lack of financial support and touting the economic potential that Beecroft-Florida Movie Studios could bring to the state: "The motion picture industry recognizes there must be a third production center somewhere between California and New York. There are no state funds which can immediately be diverted to the cause, but the work must be carried on unceasingly for the next six or eight months, by which time the committee is confident that enough permanent studios will be in actual production in the State to influence other producers and directors to do likewise." Aware of Florida's history of missed opportunities in courting film producers in the past, Collins adeptly added a warning, "In places where the industry was previously active[,] a grasping public has formed the habit of extracting very sizeable fees if a private home, estate, or acreage is to be used in the filming of a scene."[109]

In Trenton Collins's personal correspondences with film producers, he lambasted the shortsightedness of Tampa municipal politicians and skeptical businessmen who failed to recognize that "a picture filmed in a temporary Florida location would release sums ranging anywhere from $25,000 to $300,000 in the locality chosen for the production of that particular picture."[110] Without the needed municipal cooperation from the Tampa City Council and with limited support from Tallahassee, Collins felt his best hope would be to reach out to other Florida towns interested building their own studio city.

It seems that helming the governor's mansion during Great Depression had taken an extensive physical and mental toll on Doyle Carlton. At the end of his term as governor, Governor Carlton's enthusiasm for bringing motion picture producers to the state seemed to have faded, leaving Collins with what he privately described as "an indication of ineffectiveness within the administration."[111] Sensing the urgency, Collins wrote to the governor in March 1932, "New York and California are deeply interested[;] the longer we wait the more chance we are giving their enthusiasm to cool off."[112]

In an exchange of letters between Collins and J. C. Huskisson, Doyle Carlton's personal secretary, Huskisson wrote that he understood Collins's frustration toward the governor: "Just between you and me, this city [Tallahassee] will freely tell you how very proud we are and how very interested they are in the state institutions located here, but conversation is cheap and when it comes to putting out money they are very slow to do so, though they may come through eventually."[113] Collins responded by sending another appeal to the governor outlining the need for state cooperation and the appearance of support to encourage other investments. He argued that if his promotion campaign continued to develop "as I anticipate, there will be a vital need for a 'Will Hays' in Florida and you are the logical Will."[114] Will Hays, who was soon to be the first chairman of the Motion Picture Producers and Distributors of America (MPPDA), was a name that surely caught the governor's attention.

In April 1932, Governor Carlton joined Collins at a Movie Ball held at Chester Beecroft's recently completed Florida Studio. The governor immersed himself in the proceedings, even presiding as a judge at a bathing-beauty contest that Beecroft had organized.[115] Two weeks later, Carlton called for a meeting in Orlando with the mayors of six Florida cities to discuss locations for film studios to be built throughout the state. Since the state budget was primarily tied up in Depression-related relief programs, Carlton suggested each community offer their own incentives such as a special plane service, bargain prices on local real estate, and direct investment in the studios from local banks and businesses. The meeting ended with the governor boasting, "We took the orange and citrus fruit trade from California because we are nearer the east, now watch us take the studios."[116]

Despite the governor's involvement at fundraisers and public support of the CDMP's efforts, the legislature continued to refuse to provide any funding to the organization. Following up with the governor after the Orlando meeting, Collins sent a series of letters to the mayors of every major Florida city with a plan to divide up the costs to continue to court producers to establish themselves in Florida. Building on assurances from established industry producers such as Lloyd Hammond and Chester Beecroft, Collins repeated his hope that if his campaign continued its current trajectory, by the end of 1932, "Florida should actually have a goodly share of America's third largest industry."[117]

At this point, Trenton Collins had spent nearly $3,000 of his own money hosting visiting producers and making multiple trips to California and New York to take meetings with studio executives. The legislature would not even cover the seventy-five-cent cost for tolls Collins needed to pay for his daily commute across the Gandy Bridge. In his appeal to mayors across the state, Collins wrote, "Your entire citizenry is interested in the early and complete success of this movement. The unselfish cooperation and financial support of every city are needed, if we are to achieve our goal quickly."[118]

After Collins received a less-than-enthusiastic response from Florida's mayors, he pivoted his attention toward the SHC. Collins requested a stipend of $400–$500 per month for eight months, which he argued would "provide a boon for Florida's fledgling tourism industry." He assured his would-be investors, "The work of the Committee is about half done and it seems almost criminally negligent to stop now, but unless funds with which to carry on are provided, that is exactly what will happen."[119] Collins next reached out to executives in the transit industry. In a message to Ross Norton, an executive on the board of Seaboard Air Line, Collins sought to secure funding for his long-proposed travelogue. At the same time, Edward Alexander worked directly with St. Petersburg–based investors to fund "a film survey of Pinellas County that could be distributed to producers across the country."[120]

By the end of the summer of 1932, Collins's options to fund the CDMP had been exhausted. In a desperate last bid, Collins once again reached out to Doyle Carlton. Carlton was at the time in the middle of a prolonged series of pardon board hearings and expressed his regrets at not being able to prioritize a meeting. Without anywhere else to turn, Collins begrudgingly called for a meeting with Tampa mayor Robert Chancey, who had been one of his main roadblocks toward securing local funding. To his surprise, the meeting went better than expected. It ended with a plan of action to turn the defunct Tampa Bay Hotel into a combined studio and hotel for motion picture personnel.[121] Collins suggested that both Mayor Chancey and Governor Carlton join him on his next trip to California at the end of September to meet with producers who might be interested in purchasing the building for a studio. This request was ignored by both Chancey and Carlton, and Collins had to redirect his attention toward appealing directly to producers. Eventually Chancey secured the funding he needed for renovations to the Tampa Bay Hotel after the Works Progress Administration was implemented and had the building converted into what became the present site of the University of Tampa.[122]

Without institutional support and with charlatans appearing on all sides, Trenton Collins was clearly in over his head and cut adrift by even the state's most vocal movie boosters. The last straw came after Collins's self-funded trip to California. While in Hollywood, he met Academy Award–nominated art director Albert D'Agostino from RKO Studios, who suggested Collins take a meeting with producer David O. Selznick to bring RKO to Florida's West Coast. When he returned to Tampa Bay, Mayors Chancey and H. W. Adams of St. Petersburg both refused to meet with Collins or answer the phone when Selznick tried to call their offices. In a follow-up letter to Trenton Collins, D'Agostino wrote of his frustrations in trying to coordinate with the mayors: "Am I taking too much for granted in seeking a producing proposition for your State? I have spent considerable time and a little money on wires, etc., in introducing to producers the idea of Florida and I hope my efforts will not be in vain."¹²³ Several weeks later, Collins traveled to New York and met with several RKO executives to pitch the idea for a Tampa Bay studio next to the Beecroft-Florida Movie Studio on Davis Islands. It seems the meeting did not bear much fruit, as Collins reported to the governor that "the meeting resulted in several new contacts, but little enthusiasm."¹²⁴

At this point, the only thing Carlton and Collins seemed to agree on was that the CDMP was not working the way either had hoped. The soon-to-be former governor promised Collins, "Possibly I can be of more aid when I have cast aside my official duties after the first of the year. I believe there are real possibilities in the motion picture industry and am anxious to see the work carried on."¹²⁵ He also suggested that "probably a State Motion Picture Committee would be a better title than Motion Picture Department, as that legally is something established by the Legislature."¹²⁶

Following the inauguration of Governor David Sholtz in January 1933, the Florida Chamber of Commerce did just that and set up its own Special Motion Picture Committee, as Trenton Collins's place as Florida's preeminent film promoter diminished to little more than a ceremonial title.¹²⁷ In the end, the most significant legacy of the CDMP was the governor's authorization of a fifteen-year exemption from state and local property taxes to provide for filmmakers who decided to film their productions in Florida. This would be the first recorded example outside of California of the use of tax incentives by a state government to draw film productions to their state.¹²⁸

The Special Motion Picture Committee

Doyle Carlton was succeeded by David Sholtz, who defeated two former Florida governors (John Martin and Cary Hardee) in a dramatic runoff election in November 1932. A self-described protégé of Franklin Roosevelt and the son of Jewish German immigrant parents, Sholtz embraced his reputation as Florida's "New Deal Governor." While Doyle Carlton had refused any form of federal assistance from Herbert Hoover's Reconstruction Finance Corporation (RFC), Sholtz actively pursued federal aid by any means necessary. Following the inauguration of Franklin Roosevelt two months later, in March 1933, Sholtz cobbled together a series of grants from a wide variety of Roosevelt's alphabet soup initiatives. Governor Sholtz formed a state employment service, where he sought to reinvigorate businesses across the state. By the end of his time in office, relief cases had been reduced by 75 percent across Florida.

The infusion of government funds and state regulation turned the state's nearly $2 million deficit into a surplus of nearly a half million by 1937.¹²⁹ According to Florida historian William Cash, David Sholtz left Florida in a "considerably better financial condition than it had been since the depression began."[130] Even with the much-needed infusion of government funds dedicated to infrastructure and public relief, the Sholtz administration initially hesitated to follow up on Trenton Collins's extensive effort to bring the motion picture industry to the state.

In a March 1933 *Film Daily* article, Governor Sholtz denied any "printed rumors that the State of Florida is negotiating with Hollywood producers and offering to finance wholesale removel [sic] of film industry to Florida."[131] Less than one month later, the Florida Chamber of Commerce elected to add "motion picture development" to its list of proposed activities. The Chamber appointed St. Petersburg–based real estate developer Fred Blair as its chairman. Although Trenton Collins continued his letter-writing campaign during the transition from the Carlton to Sholtz administrations, it appears that by April 1933 Collins had all but assigned his duties to Blair and the Chamber of Commerce's Special Motion Picture Committee (SMPC).

In a letter to Maurice Kann, editor of *Film Daily*, Trenton Collins expressed his disillusionment at the Florida government's unwillingness to provide adequate support to filmmakers. Collins acknowledged that "there is no financial structure ready to throw quantities of gold into the production pot, but we will assist responsible executives to secure necessary financing, or at least part of it."[132] Although Collins described the "existence of the friendliest feelings between the CDMP and SMPC," it appears that David Sholtz's preference for direct government oversight through the SMPC won out over the unsupervised freedom allotted to Collins and the CDMP.

Either frustrated by the lack of support he received during the Carlton administration or simply ready to move on to another project, by May 1933 Collins had liquidated the CDMP, announcing his plan to return to working full-time at his advertising firm.[133] As for his opinion of Fred Blair and the SMPC, Collins told Maurice Kann that he felt "quite supportive of Blair and his efforts. Mr. Blair has the reputation of going aggressively, but conservatively after anything he undertakes."[134] Yet, just as Collins resigned from his one-man crusade to bring filmmakers to Florida, his efforts had just begun to bear fruit. In July 1933, Collins's fifteen-year exemption from state and local property taxes for film producers who filmed in Florida was adopted by the Florida Legislature. During the 1932 election that swept David Sholtz into office, many fiscal conservatives in the legislature had been replaced with a new class of New Deal progressives.[135]

Nearly as soon as the incentive program was put into place, brothers Max and David Fleischer from Fleischer Studios of *Betty Boop* and *Popeye* fame agreed to relocate their animation lab to South Florida. The Fleischer brothers constructed their state-of-the-art animation studio in Miami and produced two feature-length animated films, *Gulliver's Travels* (1939) and *Mr. Bug Goes to Town* (1941). In December 1941, the Fleischers were bought out by Paramount Studios, and their Miami property was taken over and renamed Famous Studios. Although the animation lab continued to operate briefly under Paramount's ownership, the studio found it too difficult to sustain separate facilities in New York, California, and Florida and opted to consolidate their holdings.[136]

Fred Blair seemingly scored another early success with the SMPC when he announced that a former Paramount producer named Aubrey Kennedy would construct a new state-of-the-art studio on Weedon Island outside of St. Petersburg. The forty-six-year-old Kennedy had been involved with the film industry since the 1910s and was considered by his peers to be "beyond a doubt the best producer in this business when sober."[137] By 1933, Kennedy's reputation for unreliability and drunkenness had exhausted any remaining goodwill he had left in Los Angeles.[138] So when a wave of displaced producers began to arrive in Florida on the wave of the SMPC's promotional campaign, Aubrey Kennedy washed ashore hoping to redeem his reputation and build his own independent studio in Florida.

The Rise and Fall of Kennedy City

Aubrey Kennedy first came to Florida in 1915 as an assistant director working for the Serial Film Company in Jacksonville. During Mayor J.E.T. Bowden's "quit Los Angeles" campaign, Kennedy became one of North Florida's most outspoken movie boosters.[139] After the collapse of local support with the election of John Martin in 1917, however, Kennedy seemed to have soured on his experience in Jacksonville, which he later described in a May 1932 letter to Trenton Collins as "disastrously discouraging."[140] Kennedy complained that the "Jacksonville merchants were prone to exploit filmmakers" with severe price gouging on goods and services and that the "cost of production was exorbitant," noting, "I could hardly wait to get back to New York to cut out my expenses and live up to my budget."[141]

Initially, Aubrey Kennedy ignored Trenton Collins's letter-writing campaign, but when he was ignominiously fired from Paramount in October 1932, he had a sudden change of heart. That same month, Kennedy journeyed to Florida in search of a place to build a soundstage and new studio city. After learning that Kennedy had started to scope out locations, Al D'Agostino wrote a letter of warning to Collins that Aubrey Kennedy had been "mixed up in quite a few production schemes in the past, which never got beyond the money spending stage. I feel this is a bum promotion down there at this time and will do a lot of harm."[142]

Despite D'Agostino's warning, Kennedy' studio city project moved forward when it passed into the hands of Fred Blair and the SMPC. In his April 1933 letter to Maurice Kann of *Film Daily,* Trenton Collins seems to have become aware of Kennedy's unsavory dealings. The reason for the letter was to correct a previous article published in *Film Daily* that included a false claim by Kennedy that he had been appointed as technical advisor to the SMPC by Governor Sholtz. This brazen lie was just one of several misleading statements Kennedy had made in some of the major trade presses in 1933. As Collins prepared to pass the reins of Florida's preeminent film promotions to Fred Blair and the SMPC, he remarked, "Neither committee is interested in fly-by-night promoters."[143]

Although Trenton Collins claimed in *Film Daily* that neither of Florida's sanctioned film committees was interested in working with Kennedy, his SMPC counterpart Fred Blair must have missed the memo. In October 1932, Blair wrote a personal letter to Kennedy inviting him to survey the conditions in St. Petersburg for building a studio. Several weeks later, Kennedy replied in a lengthy noncommittal telegram that if the money could be raised, he would transfer his operations to St. Petersburg. Unable to get support from the Chamber of Commerce or local businesses, Blair took out a loan directly from the First National Bank of Tampa.

With money in hand, Kennedy agreed to coordinate with the SMPC and develop his self-proclaimed "Kennedy City" on the site of the abandoned San Remo nightclub on Weedon Island.[144] The only barrier now was the St. Petersburg city government, which had expressed its open suspicion of interlopers since the collapse of the Florida Land Boom. In 1930, the St. Petersburg City Council made known its thoughts on outsiders looking to establish business on the Pinellas Peninsula when it voted to erect signs at the city limits that said, "A Good Place to Visit But Don't Come to Stay."[145] Undeterred, the Kennedy Picture Corporation (KPC) was formed, and St. Petersburg city manager W. M. Cotton promised that his "administration would back up the negotiations by pledging support of the city of St. Petersburg to securing the motion picture industry here."[146]

In the local press, Kennedy further embellished his résumé to such an extent that he claimed to be a cofounder of Universal City in Hollywood and at the same time worked as an executive for MGM Studios. A January 30 press release reflected the excitement surrounding Kennedy's arrival and contained many of the same exaggerations found in promotions in the picture-city project proposals during the Florida Land Boom. In an interview with the *St. Petersburg Independent,* Kennedy remarked, "Florida, which can rival California's locations in everything but the mountain atmosphere, is desirable as a production center because of its proximity to New York City, source of many leading stage stars who have bounded into prominence as screen favorites with box office appeal."[147] The article followed up Kennedy's statement by enthusiastically promising, "Kennedy's enterprise offers more hope to this city for a quick return to prosperity locally than any other industry or type of activity."[148]

Kennedy next sought to bankroll his studio by reaching out to his former industry contacts. One such contact was Pat Powers, a New York–based distributor who Kennedy claimed had agreed to a twenty-four-picture distribution deal with KPC. When Powers learned that it was Kennedy who was behind the proposed studio in St. Petersburg, he responded with an editorial in the *St. Petersburg Times* where he publicly refuted Kennedy's claims.[149] In the article, Powers revealed that Kennedy had indeed worked for Universal Studios in the past as a production manager but was not a cofounder of Universal City in California, as he had claimed. Powers also denied Kennedy's assertion that Universal would pay up front half of the production costs of any picture produced by the KPC. Even following this shady introduction, Powers added that he would be willing to "distribute his pictures and might advance money on negatives, but I have no business connection with the production end of the matter."[150] Following a long-distance phone conversation with Powers, W. M. Cotton ordered the St. Petersburg Chamber of Commerce and advertising board to withhold all funds until Kennedy could prove his project was aboveboard.

Fred Blair came to Kennedy's rescue by securing a $2,000 city building permit to revamp the former San Remo nightclub on Davis Islands into a soundstage. Even though funds for the studio renovation were donated almost exclusively by local investors, Kennedy pocketed the money and used the "investment" to purchase a house on Davis Islands, which he justified so that he could have a "permanent residence in St. Petersburg."[151] This misuse of public funds proved to be the last straw for St. Petersburg's city government, which abruptly withdrew all additional funding it had set aside for the completion of Kennedy City.[152] A combination of poor communication and the siphoning of public funds destroyed all remaining trust between Pinellas politicians and Kennedy.

Just as it appeared the entire Kennedy City project was about to be stopped in its tracks, an angel investor named T. C. Parker, the manager of Coca-Cola's bottling plant in Jacksonville, offered to save the studio and invested the remaining funds needed to finish construction on the complex.[153] In May 1933, with all the necessary pieces in place, Kennedy rented a Cinephone sound truck from Pat Powers and hired Oral Cloakey, a former Universal colleague, to establish a casting office in St. Petersburg. He wrote to former Kalem Company director Marshall Neilan that he found "the most perfect swamp that you could possibly ask for" as the setting for his upcoming feature *Chloe: Love is Calling You* (1934). After receiving this message, Neilan flew to St. Petersburg, and after visiting Weedon Island, he agreed to move his production to Kennedy City.[154]

Through sheer force of will, Aubrey Kennedy somehow managed to attract the support and funding necessary to build his studio. According to John Lodwick of the *St. Petersburg Times,* "May 22, should mark a new era in the history of St. Petersburg. The Sunshine City will make its debut as a motion picture production center as cameras here start grinding out the swampland story of *Chloe.*"[155] Lodwick's hopes were encouraged even further by the end of May, when legendary silent film star Buster Keaton arrived in St. Petersburg and announced plans to film his next three feature films on Weedon Island.[156]

"Anything but a Dead Duck:" Buster Keaton in St. Petersburg

It was a late Tuesday afternoon on May 30, 1933, when a large crowd assembled along the runway of St. Petersburg's Grand Central Airport with an air of excitement that Tampa Bay had not experienced since Lupe Vélez's stay in the area during the filming of *Hell Harbor.* Their movie dreams this time turned toward the legendary stone-faced comedian aboard the Eastern Air Transport plane about to set down. In his memoirs, Keaton recalled he "was in very high spirits as I flew into St. Petersburg. Getting 3,000 miles from the scene of my worst defeats was exhilarating. I was determined to stay off the booze, do a good job, and show everyone that I was anything but a dead duck."[157]

Upon landing at Grand Central Airport, Keaton was swarmed by adoring fans. Greeted by Aubrey Kennedy, W. M. Cotton, M. M. Deadrick of the St. Petersburg Chamber of Commerce, and members of St. Petersburg's Board of Governors, Keaton politely waved and nodded as the crowd continued to press in. The impromptu reception was abruptly cut short as Keaton plowed his way through the crowd and into a waiting car, which took him directly to the Suwannee Hotel, where he immediately hung a "do not disturb" sign on his doorknob.[158]

This inauspicious first encounter between Keaton and St. Petersburgians was excused in the local press by Aubrey Kennedy, who explained that Keaton was "very tired" after his plane journey and "anxious to catch up on much needed sleep."[159] Eager to prove himself after walking away from a near career-ruining contract with MGM Studios, the newly independent Buster Keaton was drawn to Florida by the same promise of reinventing himself and reinvigorating a fledgling career.

By the time Buster Keaton checked into the Suwannee Hotel, filming for Marshall Neilan's *Chloe* at Kennedy City was already well under way. *Chloe* producers Adolph Pollak and Morris Shiller followed up this production announcement with a plan to produce two more films at Kennedy City: *Playthings of Desire* and *The Hired Wife* (1934). Pollak and Shiller instructed director Albert Hiller to stop production in Hollywood and come to St. Petersburg immediately.[160] After spending several days languishing in his room at the Suwannee Hotel, Keaton and his manager, Lew Lipton, held their first press conference. During this short meeting in the hotel lobby, Keaton confirmed to the *Times* that he and Lipton had agreed to a six-picture contract with Aubrey Kennedy.

The next day, Keaton flew to Ocala and met with Marshall Neilan during a location shoot for *Chloe*.[161] Impressed by the production, Keaton returned to St. Petersburg invigorated by the area's burgeoning film prospects. To make up for his curt behavior when he first arrived, Keaton agreed to attend an official welcoming event at Williams Park, where Mayor Henry Adams awarded him the key to the city before the largest crowd "ever to have been gathered in the park for a single event."[162] At the event, however, Keaton was still quite standoffish. When asked to give a speech, he refused. He later made the excuse that the terms of his contract made it illegal for him to speak.

Despite his so-far lukewarm response to the overtures made by St. Petersburg's citizens, Keaton wasted no time in establishing himself in the city. Following the gathering in Williams Park, Keaton traveled with Kennedy, who helped him purchase a house in his neighborhood on Davis Islands, and even joined the community baseball league.[163] Despite his seemingly brisk demeanor at certain public functions, the citizens of St. Petersburg seem to have fond memories Keaton's stay in their city. Emil Latham, manager of the Suwannee Hotel recalls, "Buster used to dive through the windows of streetcars to entertain the kids. His greatest thrill was to do something for the kids. Everybody in town loved him."[164] Casting director Oral Cloakey remembered, "Keaton made full use of his training as an acrobat to make people in town laugh."[165]

On June 18, 1933, Keaton joined with Marshall Neilan and Aubrey Kennedy to file articles of incorporation to form the Flamingo Film Company. In what must have seemed a refreshing change for Floridians from the stock schemes perpetrated during the Sun City debacle, Flamingo's secretary-treasurer, Lew Lipton, announced, "The Flamingo Company being a closed corporation, with all the stock owned by members of the company, no stock will be sold."[166] Shortly after the announcement, they broke ground on a proposed 150-by-140-foot soundstage and office building to house Flamingo's productions.[167] At this point, Aubrey Kennedy had succeeded not only in bringing major star power to Florida's Gulf Coast but also attracting deep-pocketed investors who intrigued producers with verifiable credentials. Over the course of the next month, Keaton and Marshall Neilan traveled across Florida and made a detour to Cuba as they scouted locations for Buster Keaton's first planned Florida talking film: *The Fisherman.*

While production for *The Fisherman* seemed more promising by the day, Marshall Neilan's *Chloe* was marred by tragedy and disaster. The first cut of the film was lost when the Eastern Air Transport flight carrying the print crashed en route to New York, killing the pilot and incinerating the film. Neilan recalled the cast and crew for reshoots, which had to be halted when the film's lead actress Olive Borden nearly drowned while filming a scene in Tarpon Springs. After Neilan made a haphazard set of compromises to make up for lost time, a rough cut of *Chloe* was finally complete in July 1933.[168] As production on *Chloe* came to close, the cast of *Playthings of Desire* also arrived from Los Angeles, with seasoned director George Melford set to helm the film. To help film the cityscape scenes for *Playthings of Desire,* crowds gathered across the city and nearly sixty locals were used for various scenes, with almost 1,400 requests sent to Oral Cloakey and his casting office.[169] After production wrapped, another California producer, E. B. Ring, announced his intent to build another studio on Weedon Island.[170]

With three completed soundstages and several more announced feature films supposedly in preproduction, by the end of the summer of 1933 Kennedy City had sprouted into a formidable independent production center. At his moment of triumph, Aubrey Kennedy traveled to New York to meet with Pat Powers and follow up on his earlier promise to help find additional investors for Kennedy's studio facilities. On his way to the meetings, Kennedy was involved in a car accident that led to an infection in his arm, leaving the producer bedridden in a New York hospital for the rest of the summer. Without Kennedy to keep up morale, SMPC chair Fred Blair was left to preside over the day-to-day promotional efforts as well as to work with Buster Keaton and the Flamingo Company to secure the filming permits needed for *The Fisherman.*[171]

To keep the momentum alive for the Weedon Island studio in Kennedy's absence, Blair personally appealed to all cast and crew members who had come to film in Florida to reach out to their "many thousands of friends throughout the country to come to St. Petersburg" and "really enjoy life."[172]

This surface-level shakedown backfired in a spectacular way, disheartening investors even further. In an open letter to the *St. Petersburg Independent*, Blair resorted to the same mistakes that had plagued Florida film boosters in the past. He assured readers, "You will want to see Kennedy City," and that "the Buster Keaton soundstage is as large as any found in the country. Many screen stars are in St. Petersburg and others will come to take part in the various plays that are being produced by these companies. The Sunshine City [will be] recognized as the Florida Mecca for Movie Stars and Fans."[173]

After Fred Blair's plea was published, interest from investors in Kennedy City all but evaporated. Since the correspondence between Blair and Aubrey Kennedy has not survived, it is difficult to know what factors led to the sudden collapse of Kennedy City just as it started to take off. The timing of Kennedy's car accident and the rapid deterioration of his various deals could be one possible reason. It also could be that interest diminished due to a lack of coordination between Fred Blair and the SMPC. Regardless, by August 1933, enthusiasm for a film center in Tampa Bay had started to wane.

The first blow to Kennedy City Studios came when Buster Keaton and Lew Lipton abruptly abandoned their plans for preproduction on *The Fisherman*, dissolved the Flamingo Film Company, and announced that they would not return to St. Petersburg. In his memoir, Keaton recalled that despite the promise of Florida's sublime weather, after watching Marshall Neilan and George Melford suffer through oppressive summer heat and swarms of insects during their outdoor film shoots, he felt the environment was far too inhospitable for filming in the summer. Keaton recalled, "None of this discouraged our optimistic backers. But I told them the truth when I became convinced that they were only throwing their money away in trying to establish a year-round movie industry there."[174] Lew Lipton was less generous and more critical of the situation. In an August 14 statement to the *Tampa Bay Times,* he claimed, "Misrepresentations made by Kennedy were the basic reasons for the star's sudden exit from the field here."[175] When pressed for details on what misrepresentations Kennedy had made, Lipton was evasive: "They were financial more than anything, but also involved working conditions."[176]

Although the studio complex on Weedon Island was considered by Flamingo's producers to be nicely equipped for midrange productions with a budget between $35,000 and $50,000, it did not have the resources to host projects that demanded a larger budget of $100,000 or higher, the type of film that Keaton was interested in producing. E. B. Ring, who had purchased property near the Flamingo facility, also publicly complained that the facility Kennedy built did not "come close to the expectations promised."[177] In a word of advice after "their realization that the glowing promises of Kennedy had not materialized," Lipton suggested that Florida producers needed "to learn how to make small ones [productions] first. No one can hope to beat Hollywood at its own game in three months. I don't doubt for a minute they will be successful in making productions if they don't overstep themselves."[178]

Either due to Keaton's sudden departure, the extended recuperation time needed after his hospitalization, or the ongoing investigations conducted into his unsavory dealings with the SMPC and the St. Petersburg Chamber of Commerce, Aubrey Kennedy abruptly sold all his holdings on Weedon Island to T. C. Parker. Kennedy announced in the *St. Petersburg Independent* that he planned to take a monthlong vacation with his family in the Adirondacks and would "return to St. Petersburg in two to three months."[179] Aubrey Kennedy never showed his face in Florida again.

Sun Haven Studios: "The Hollywood of Florida"

After taking control of Kennedy City, T. C. Parker tried to reassure the St. Petersburg Chamber of Commerce and the local press that he would continue making films on Weedon Island with George Melford as his head director. The studio complex funded by E. B. Ring had completed construction the very same week as the shake-up caused by Kennedy leaving for his "vacation." As postproduction concluded on Melford's *Playthings of Desire* in a processing facility in New York, production on Melford's next film, *The Hired Wife*, commenced just in time to inaugurate the new studio. T. C. Parker reorganized the fragments of Kennedy's former holdings under a single umbrella, which he renamed Sun Haven Studios, with himself as president and Fred Blair as secretary and treasurer. Parker admitted to the *St. Petersburg Times* that Sun Haven was "his first venture into the film field" and said he was eager to follow up on Lipton's advice to scale down the ambition of Sun Haven's productions.

In his acquisition deal with Kennedy, Parker agreed to produce twelve films at Kennedy City over the next six months. In an interview with the *Times*, Parker presented a far more realistic and less pie-in-the-sky approach to what his newly acquired studio was capable of: "We plan to produce feature and program pictures at reasonably moderate costs. Nothing gigantic like *Gold Diggers* or *42nd Street*, but the best pictures possible for $50,000. Some may run as low as $20,000, with an average of $35,000."[180]

The next day, shooting for *The Hired Wife* started at Sun Haven.[181] Even without Buster Keaton and Aubrey Kennedy, enthusiasm for the Weedon Island studios in St. Petersburg seemed as high as ever. Fredric Chapin, the editor in chief of Sun Haven, set out to file a petition to the SMPC to create a school of dramatic arts in St. Petersburg to help support homegrown talent and reduce the costs of having to import talent from Hollywood.[182] Chapin confidently announced, "Hollywood is in a rut. The same old settings and locations have been used over and over. Florida is new and fresh. Virgin territory, new settings, new talent, spontaneity! Someone is going to make a lot of money in Florida in the motion picture industry . . . I want to be in on the ground floor."[183] Fred Blair followed this statement up several days later by remarking to the *Independent*, "If investors play their cards right St. Petersburg will be the Hollywood of Florida."[184]

When production wrapped for *The Hired Wife* in early September, George Melford's *Playthings of Desire* was ready for its world premiere at the Capitol Theatre in St. Petersburg. The event was promised to "be one of the most outstanding and elaborate theatrical events staged in St. Petersburg" and to "have all the glamour of a Hollywood premiere and be staged like those at Hollywood's famous Chinese Theater."[185] St. Petersburg seemed to have finally gotten its big break.

In the lead-up to the premiere of *Playthings of Desire*, Florida state assessor Chick Owens sent out a glowing report heralding the work being done on Weedon Island: "St. Petersburg's motion picture industry has a payroll as great or greater than any single business concern in the city and promises to dwarf all other commercial activities before it is a year old."[186] He also touted the tens of thousands of dollars the industry had already brought to regional "merchants, building supply houses, public utilities, real estate dealers, and hotels," which were just "a few of the lines that have benefited from the industry's golden touch."[187]

Unfortunately, neither *Playthings of Desire*, *Chloe*, or *The Hired Wife* lived up to the excitement that was stirred up by the local press. *Playthings of Desire* premiered to a less than stellar reception from its Capitol Theatre audience, and the poor press surrounding its first screening made it difficult to negotiate a distribution deal for the film. When the long-delayed *Chloe* was ready for its premiere in December 1933, T. C. Parker decided to host a private event at Weedon Island instead of a gala-style premiere.[188] The lackluster response to the premiere of *Chloe* caused similar difficulties for Marshall Neilan in securing a distributor. As Sun Haven struggled to recover expenses, Parker arranged a meeting with Chester Beecroft, who had yet to produce a single film at his studio complex on Davis Islands. The details of the meeting were not fully disclosed, but afterward they agreed to merge Sun Haven with the Beecroft-Florida Movie Studios. Keeping the name Sun Haven Studios, Parker agreed to step back into an advisory position, while Beecroft became managing director, with Fred Blair of the SMPC as general manager.

With this new arrangement, Beecroft expressed his interest in telling the story of the first three conquistadores to land in Florida—Juan Ponce de León, Pánfilo Narváez, and Hernando de Soto—and chronicle their exploits in a feature film.[189] To raise funds, he attempted partner with William Fox, but after several dead-end meetings, the project failed to materialize. After the Fox deal fell through, Beecroft attempted to secure a seven-picture deal with a New York–based independent company, Showman's Pictures Inc., which also failed to gain traction.[190] After several unsuccessful attempts to make a deal with Fox and Showman's Pictures, Beecroft appears to have abandoned Florida for good, as any further mention of his involvement with either Sun Haven Studios or his facility on Davis Islands disappears from the record.

After *The Hired Wife* wrapped production in 1934, the would-be studio city complex was mostly abandoned until the 1950s. In 1956, Empire Studios Inc., an independent studio based in Winter Park, briefly moved its production unit to the soundstage. According to Ronald Yogman and Thomas Rawlins of the *Times*, then governor LeRoy Collins publicly praised Empire's effort to create "Florida's first major film production company."[191] The goal was to use the site as the location for the filming of *The Osceola Story*. However, producer R. John Hugh's announcement that the production would relocate to Kissimmee instead marked the end of any effort to makes movies on Weedon Island. In early 1956, Empire sold the studio grounds to Florida Power, which held the property until the former studio was razed to the ground in June 1963.[192]

Florida Becomes "The Last Word in the Film World"

By February 1934, T. C. Parker had all but given up on Sun Haven Studios, and he sold the property to Walter C. Martin of the Southeastern Oil Corporation. Although Martin and his associates initially expressed interest in continuing to produce films at Weedon Island, no other project would be produced at Kennedy City.[193] The timing of the collapse of Tampa Bay's movie studios was sadly ill-fated. Had either Sun Haven Studios or the Beecroft-Florida Movie Studio kept going for just a few months longer, they might have succeeded in gaining the attention of the Hollywood moguls.

In the fall of 1934, the author and political activist Upton Sinclair ran an insurgent bid for governor of California. His End Poverty in California (EPIC) movement had a broad appeal with the state's working class but drew the ire of the Hollywood studios. If elected governor, Sinclair promised voters he would hand over idle movie studio lots to unemployed film workers to make movies of their own. The studio heads reacted by financing the campaign of Sinclair's opponent for governor, Frank Merriam.[194] Although Upton Sinclair lost the 1934 California governor's race by a sizable margin, his attacks against the Hollywood studios did capture the attention of some California politicians.

Even though EPIC ended with Sinclair's defeat, in March 1935, the California legislature proposed a bill that would have imposed a 35 percent tax on all motion picture productions made in the state. This proposal was met with a widespread backlash from press agents representing Hollywood studios including MGM, Paramount, and R.K.O., who responded by announcing a plan to raise up to $10 million to relocate their studios to Florida.[195] Sensing a moment of opportunity, Fred Blair responded with his own letter-writing campaign directed to studio executives to follow through on this initiative. However, by the time the movie moguls were able to take the move to Florida seriously, poor publicity surrounding the failure of Weedon Island's Kennedy City and Davis Islands' Beecroft-Florida Movie Studio caused the studios to hesitate. Blair requested that Governor Sholtz sign off on his letter to help garner further support from studios, but Sholtz did not get around to endorsing the SMPC letter until December. By the time the governor started writing letters, the California legislature had drastically revised its proposed tax plan and seemingly had made up with the studios. All that followed from the governor's halfhearted effort was a series of rejection letters.

Even with all its ups and downs, the idea of establishing a statewide film industry remained quite popular with Floridians at the grassroots level. This was most apparent in the November 1934 statewide general election, when Floridians resoundingly approved Trenton Collins's proposed amendment to the state constitution to provide a fifteen-year tax exemption to all "motion picture studios and plants which shall be established in this state on or after July 1, 1935."[196] Public support in Florida for the amendment reinvigorated Governor Sholtz to initiate another letter-writing campaign to film producers during the spring of 1935.

An exchange of letters between Governor Sholtz and E. J. Sparks, the Jacksonville-based owner of United Theaters Inc., shows the sense of encouragement that Florida exhibitors felt about David Sholtz's renewed interest in the film industry. In a letter to the governor, Sparks acknowledged, "It is my opinion that one or more studios will come to this state if the proper inducements are offered, irrespective of any legislative program favorable or unfavorable, in California."[197] Sparks drafted, along with fellow exhibitor Jacob

Barker, a twenty-one-page proposal advising the governor on how he could convince the Hollywood studios to relocate their operations to Florida. The cornerstone of Sparks and Barker's proposal was to raise funds to build "a gigantic film city that will be a Wonderland of Art surpassing anything of its kind," which "will attract thousands of people from an educational standpoint and will be the last word in the Film World."[198]

Regarding how best to raise funds for this suggested film city, C. R. Crandall, of Palm Beach Chamber of Commerce, wrote to the governor, "There are enough 'forward thinking' citizens besides yourself who will give one to five dollars each to underwrite a studio for the industry," while adding, without providing any specifics, "There are many civic organizations any one of which could sponsor such an undertaking as a major state-wide movement."[199] Governor Sholtz also received appeals from film producers who had worked with the Doyle Carlton administration and the CDMP. Lloyd Hammond, who had previously corresponded with Trenton Collins, wrote in a March 11, 1935, letter:

> About two years ago I had considerable correspondence with Mr. Trenton Collins of Tampa, who was then head of the Governor's committee, but nothing came of it. I was invited down there but did not believe the time was right. The set up would require four separate finance companies, a Land company to colonize the land, a Building and Construction co., a Studio co., and a Film Finance co., all self-liquidating with eventual profit, and headed by the best available brains in the state, men with vision.[200]

Between November and December 1935, the governor sent a series of copy-pasted letters of introduction to a total of twenty-four studios, including Warner Brothers, United Artists, and Twentieth Century Fox, among others. In the letter, he emphasized the state's recent tax legislation amendment, assuring them "the sites and physical properties of your company would be tax free." Governor Sholtz signaled many of most often repeated talking points used by Florida film boosters, highlighting Florida's advantages in "climate, scenery, nearness to the population center of the United States, and the hospitality of our people."[201]

This uninspired effort on the part of Governor Sholtz was either ignored by his intended recipients or responded to with generic letters of dismissal or outright rejections. In his response to Sholtz's phishing letter, John Hay Whitney of Pioneer Pictures replied, "We are an independent producing company and so have no studio of our own, but simply rent such space as we need for our physical production from the existing plants. These studios are, of course, still largely located in California where we must perforce remain, unless some day the rumors which from time to time emerge from Hollywood assume factuality."[202] Harry Cohn at Columbia Pictures was even more frank in his response: "I anticipate that our company would not be inclined to move the sites of its production activities except in concert with a substantial group of motion picture producers."[203] W. Ray Johnston of Republic Pictures brushed off the governor by asserting, "We own our own studios in North Hollywood, California, having acquired them only a few months ago and therefore we would not at this time be in a position to consider the suggestion set forth in your letter."[204]

It could be argued that Florida was simply a pawn in a complicated maneuver by studio executives to nullify any proposed tax legislation made against motion picture productions put forth by politicians in Sacramento. For the remainder of Governor Sholtz's term, it does not appear that his office had any further correspondence involving the support of Florida's film industry. In the end, Florida's two Depression-era governors, Doyle Carlton and David Sholtz, had at best shown lukewarm support for building a permanent film production industry in Florida. Both governors were willing to endorse the efforts of Trenton Collins and Fred Blair only as long as their demands for time and money were kept to a minimum. The greatest roadblock for both the CDMP and SMPC was that the Florida Legislature refused to provide anything more than basic operating funds through a cumbersome requisition procedure.[205] Lacking an adequate promotional budget, committees such as the CDMP and SMPC were effectively toothless in their efforts to lobby the state and municipal governments to sponsor major production projects.

When Governor Sholtz's term ended in January 1937, his successors, Fred P. Cone (1937–41) and Spessard Holland (1941–45), represented a return to a more fiscally conservative and less interventionist approach to leadership in the state government. Sixty-five years old and riddled with health problems, Fred Cone was described as "too old for his job" by his successor, as he adopted the role of a hands-off governor.[206] The Cone administration subsequently rolled back regulations and taxes including dissolving the by then defunct SMPC. No other state film committees were sponsored under the Cone administration. Historian Jon S. Evans describes his administration quite bluntly: "He generally believed that the governor should not interfere in operation of state agencies or deliberations of the legislature . . . As a result nothing was accomplished."[207]

The 1937 recession hit Florida especially hard, causing a nearly $4 million deficit to accrue over the course of Fred Cone's four years in office. Governor Cone's successor, Spessard L. Holland, responded by placing an emphasis on tax reform and set out to balance the state's budget. Following the attack on Pearl Harbor on December 7, 1941, Holland coordinated with the Franklin Roosevelt administration to oversee the installment of new military bases across the state, which in turn would eventually serve as the spark to Florida's postwar "Big Bang."[208] By 1950, Florida's population increased by nearly a million residents. Meanwhile, following the U.S. entrance into World War II, restrictions imposed on American film productions led to a decrease in location-based shooting and further consolidation of the national film industry around the Hollywood studio system. Preoccupied by the Second World War, Governor Holland made little effort to attract filmmakers to the state.[209]

The inauguration of Millard Caldwell in January 1945 signaled the return of a "pro-business" administration at the head of Florida's government, along the first efforts to woo filmmakers to the state since the 1930s. In June 1945, the Florida Legislature passed a resolution instructing the governor to appoint a new Motion Picture Industry Committee (MPIC). By July, Caldwell had obliged and named a ten-member advisory board to fill the committee intended to reach out to studios. Like his predecessors' approach to the CDMP and SMPC, Governor Caldwell limited the MPIC's operating funds to a bare-bones advertising campaign and reimbursements for travel expenses. Funding for the MPIC was so uninspired that six months after each member's appointment was made, the committee had yet to hold a single meeting. MPIC members were acutely aware that convincing producers to shoot on location in Florida had become an increasingly hard sell. E. A. Kettle, an MPIC advisory member, warned Governor Caldwell:

> Our good friend Will Hays told me that he was familiar with this matter. He opined that an effort was made several times in the past to secure motion picture studios in the State of Florida, but that no great strides were made in this direction and he pointed out that centralization of the casting bureaus in California, whereby a studio within half an hour could obtain could obtain 300 one-legged red headed girls or 72 camels with or without humps, together with snow and tropics in the immediate offing, was quite an asset to the industry—and which Florida would have a difficulty in matching.[210]

By 1945, even the most ardent movie boosters in Florida admitted their defeat by their West Coast counterparts. Although political support for the film industry in Florida had been reduced to inept futility by the mid-1940s,

Figure 18. *Tarzan Finds a Son!* film crew at Silver Springs, 1939. This was the first of several *Tarzan* sequels filmed partially on location at Silver Springs. Courtesy of State Archives of Florida, Florida Memory.

Florida's environment and landscape still had much to offer producers who were interested in filming on location in the state. As the American film industry consolidated on Hollywood soundstages, Florida's palms, cypresses, springs, beaches, and ocean continued to attract location crews for big-budget feature films.[211] The advent of air travel made it easier to shoot outdoor movie scenes on location. This development, in turn, would set the stage for and raise the curtain on the next exciting act of the story of Florida on film.

4

"The Business Can Kill You Anyway"

Hollywood Comes to Florida, 1938–1971

> We made pictures in Florida once. They don't want 'em. They don't know what they're talking about in Florida. We tried it. In Florida, they got has-beens and never-make-its. They've got the con-boys and operators. There are no producers in Florida. Don't get involved where you're not wanted, the business can kill you anyway.
>
> Adolph Zukor to R. John Hugh, 1966

The "Florida Project" Unveiled

On the night of February 2, 1967, an overcapacity crowd packed into the 900-seat Park West Theater in Winter Park to witness a movie premiere unlike any other in Florida's history. In attendance was recently inaugurated Florida governor Claude Kirk, who was fresh on the heels of the upset victory in the 1966 gubernatorial race that made him the first Republican to be elected governor of Florida since the end of Reconstruction. That evening, Governor Kirk was accompanied by four of his cabinet members, nearly half the members of the Florida Legislature, as well as dozens of mayors, commissioners, and civic leaders from across the state who had managed to wangle a ticket. The special event was without question the largest assemblage of Florida politicians at an entertainment venue in the state's history. To document the occasion, press from local, state, and national media outlets converged at the Park West to witness the resurrection of a beloved entrepreneur, animator, and filmmaker who had one last surprise message for his audience. This announcement would dramatically shape the future of Florida's entertainment and tourism industry for generations to come.

Following a brief introduction given by General William Everett Potter, the former governor of the Panama Canal Zone and executive vice president of the 1964 World's Fair, the lights were dimmed and a flash of light burst from the projector to illuminate the room.¹ The audience was then immersed in a series of sweeping vistas accompanied by a voice-over extolling the virtues and engineering achievements of California's Disneyland Park and lauding the attraction as "the greatest piece of urban design in the United States today." As the montage of monorails and aerial views of the park came to an end, the voice-over exclaimed, "Yesterday, Disneyland and the New York World's Fair. Tomorrow a project so vast it has been called a whole new Disney World."² The screen next dissolved to a map of Florida filled with the veiny intersections of its major highways, as the camera slowly zoomed in on the place where all roads in the state meet: Orlando. Another dissolve, and then Walt Disney magically appeared, resurrected from beyond the grave. Uncle Walt is seen beaming from ear to ear as he sits casually on the edge of a conference table filled with blueprints, presentation pointer in hand. Behind him were a collection of maps and concept art that contained what he hoped would become his last and greatest legacy.

Although the featurette was filmed on October 27, 1966, just weeks before his death, Walt Disney appears as vibrant and energetic as ever as he announced to the top leadership in Florida's government and to the world at large his plans for his proposed "Florida project." A cornerstone of his vision was for Central Florida to become home to his projected Experimental Prototype Community of Tomorrow (EPCOT).³ The ambitious and ever-forward-thinking visionary further assured his viewers, "Here in Florida, we have something special we never enjoyed at Disneyland . . . the blessing of size. There's enough land here to hold all the ideas and plans we can possibly imagine . . . This city will be visited by millions every year—a showcase to the world."⁴

The premiere of Disney's *E.P.C.O.T. Florida Film* (1966) at the Park West Theater has since divided Florida history into two distinct periods: "B.D." (Before Disney) and "A.D." (After Disney).⁵ The gathering in Winter Park would be remembered as "Orlando's coming-out party, heralding its transformation into a world-class travel destination."⁶ The front page of the *Orlando Sentinel* on February 3 brimmed with excitement and enthusiasm over the $6.6 billion (in 1967 dollars) in measurable economic benefits Disney would bring to the Florida. The *Sentinel* also made sure to highlight that the new park would provide over 50,000 new full-time jobs to Orange and Osceola Counties alone, and would add an additional 128,000 newcomers to Central Florida within the next decade.⁷ In that same article, Governor Kirk lauded the potential for revenue returns, prestige, and population growth that Disney could bring to the state. Roy Disney—the older brother of Walt and president of the Walt Disney Company since 1945—countered with a more pared-down response to the governor's lofty and unsubstantiated number. Ever the pragmatist, Roy

Disney quipped to the press after Governor Kirk's statement, "I wouldn't go as far as those figures the governor was throwing around."[8]

Despite the optimism fostered by the evening's proceedings, the contrast between the idealistic Claude Kirk and the practical Roy Disney exposed an underlying tension and uncertainty to the public as to whether a productive collaboration between the Walt Disney Company and the Florida state government would ever be possible. Responding to rumblings in the state and national presses, and to alleviate taxpayers' anxieties, Governor Kirk and Roy Disney appeared together and issued a televised "Report to the People of Florida," featuring an introduction by the governor and a special screening of the *E.P.C.O.T. Florida Film* in a direct appeal to Florida voters. The millions and billions of dollars discussed in the broadcast were juxtaposed with the glitz and glamour of the Disney company's prestige, which helped to dispel much of the doubt that had been perpetuated in the press.

On April 17, 1967, two months after Governor Kirk and Roy Disney's televised appeal to Floridians, the Florida Legislature near-unanimously (with one dissenting vote) ratified three separate Disney bills that would give the company unprecedented autonomy and self-determination.[9] Urban design scholars Kevin Archer and Kris Bezdecny argue that in the decades after 1971, "Disney's presence in Orlando became a very powerful agglomerative magnet for similar firms in the tourist-entertainment sectors."[10] The opening of Walt Disney World in October 1971 hit Florida's economy with "the equivalent of a ten-point earthquake," the aftershocks of which are still being felt today.[11]

Disney's arrival in Florida was the culmination of a nearly four-decade-long campaign conducted by businesses, community boosters, and real estate developers to draw entertainers and entrepreneurs to the state. From the mid-1930s, following the failures of Kennedy City and Sun Haven Studios, Florida politicians once again took a step back from applying any form of direct intervention in favor of incentivizing filmmakers to relocate either on a part-time or permanent basis. For much of the 1940s and 1950s, Florida served as a favorite secondary location for Hollywood "prestige pictures," as well as a haven for low-budget filmmakers and television producers on the periphery of the industry as they sought to break into an emerging B-movie market of films that Susan Doll and David Morrow describe as "part sci-fi, part horror, part adventure, and part sexual allegory."[12] This period of seeming dormancy for Florida's film industry, interestingly enough, coincided with a period in state history known as Florida's "Big Bang."[13] This thirty-year stretch of time between the mid-1940s and early 1970s transformed Florida from a far-flung appendage of the continental United States to its modern identity as a tourist empire.[14]

This chapter will examine the implications of Florida's "Big Bang" and how it influenced the development of the state's film and television industry in the mid-twentieth century.[15] As Central Florida was ostensibly "colonized" by the Walt Disney Company, in South Florida, a massive resort development boom turned the state into a premier tourist destination. Advances in transportation and camera technology, which brought about an increase in location-based productions, would also turn Florida into an unofficial Hollywood colony. The arrival of network television studios gave rise to a new wave of production studios and Florida-based producers eager to showcase the state's dynamic landscape and environment. During this period, a small but passionate group of community organizers, business owners, local politicians, and independent producers coordinated to showcase their state to the outside world in a manner that would eventually attract the likes of Walt Disney and others to invent a new form of cultural tourism that would come to define how Florida's image would be shaped in the national imagination by both the big and small screens alike.

Hollywood Comes to Cross Creek

In 1938, MGM Studios under Louis B. Mayer sought to develop a series of big-budget productions to be filmed on location in Florida. Location scouts were first sent to Silver and Wakulla Springs to film second-unit sequences for the latest sequel in the Johnny Weissmuller *Tarzan* series, *Tarzan Finds a Son!* (1939). While at Silver Springs, the scouts reported back to Mayer that they had found the perfect location to film the adaptation of Marjorie Kinnan Rawlings's Pulitzer Prize–winning novel *The Yearling*. Set in post–Civil War Central Florida, Rawlings's breakthrough novel became an instant international literary sensation in the same vein as Margaret Mitchell's *Gone with the Wind*, published two years earlier. Independent producer David O. Selznick entered an unprecedented profit-sharing arrangement with his father-in-law, Louis B. Mayer, to produce an epic film adaptation of Mitchell's novel. To help hedge his bets on the $3.85 million cost of *Gone with the Wind*, Mayer considered acquiring other award-winning literary properties as well.[16] Rawlings's heartfelt telling of the coming-of-age tale of young Jody Baxter set against the bucolic backdrop of the Florida frontier seemed to fit the bill.

After three years of negotiations with Rawlings, MGM arranged a production meeting that included Rawlings's close friend and fellow novelist John Marquand, who was invited to sit in on her behalf. Marquand remarked in his journal that he was amused to find that he was the only person in the entire meeting who had actually read the book. He wrote that "to succeed, the film had to be real and artistic, in Technicolor, long shots of sunsets, plain simple Southern folk with dialect and overalls."[17] The attempt to replicate the deceptively simple setting of *The Yearling*'s Baxter's Island proved to be an even greater challenge than Selznick and Mayer faced when reproducing the sweeping backdrop of Civil War–era Georgia. Unlike *Gone with the Wind*, which was mostly shot on RKO Studios' "Back Forty Acres" studio in Culver City, Mayer intended to shoot the entirety of *The Yearling* on location in Florida. With the help of Marjorie Rawlings, the location scouts elected to carve out a segment of the Juniper Prairie Wilderness in the Ocala National Forest as the setting for "The Scrub."

Rawlings, for her part, insisted to the executives that the production team needed "to do your filming of Baxter's Island right where *I* imagined Baxter's Island to be."[18] Mayer assigned Sidney Franklin to serve as producer and hired Victor Fleming as director. Fleming seemed an excellent fit, having previously directed both *Gone with the Wind* and *The Wizard of Oz* in the same year (1939). However, Rawlings's location demands and the lack of cinematic infrastructure in North Central Florida combined to create a daunting challenge for the seasoned producer-director team. As Rawlings's list of locations grew, the need for more specialists and technicians involved in the production also increased. Furthermore, the challenge presented by the production's need for live animals would, according to film historian William Stephenson, "set the scene for as pretty a showdown between art and nature as anyone could hope to find."[19]

MGM footed the bill for tilling the fields surrounding "The Scrub," hired a couple to live on the farm as the property's caretakers, and spent a small fortune to ship a menagerie of animals from the studio zoo in Hollywood to Florida. To headline *The Yearling*, Fleming cast veteran matinee idols Spencer Tracy and Anne Revere as Penny and Ora Baxter. The production team for *The Yearling* hunkered down into a makeshift village near Silver Glens Springs during the exceedingly hot Florida summer. The cast and crew soon ran into trouble with local Floridians, upon whom they had become reliant for supporting scene work. In one case, the production department hired an eighty-four-year-old master canoe carver to make a hand-hewn cypress log canoe for the film. According to film historian William Stephenson, "The old man made it slowly, with care and love, as he had made all others all his life. As soon as he was finished, the art director took an axe to it and splashed brown paint on it, to make it look aged. After seeing how his careful craftmanship had been torn up, he burst into tears."[20]

Spencer Tracy and director Victor Fleming each found their experience of filming on location in Florida inhospitable and frustrating. The last straw for

Fleming came in his fruitless attempts to wrangle local fawns, who were fed a steady diet of "bourbon and moonshine by the crew to keep them small and docile." The problem was that if the amount of liquor given to the deer was not measured carefully, they turned aggressive and would begin to attack the cast and crew. The run-ins with intoxicated animals only increased feelings of anxiety experienced by Gene Eckman, who was originally cast as Jody. Later in life, Eckman recalled that he had had a deathly fear of the bellicose drunken deer.[21] Eckman, an aspiring child actor from Atlanta, was handpicked by Rawlings to play the role of Jody, but despite the author's endorsement, the boy's thick southern drawl grated on his cantankerous costar Spencer Tracy, who remarked to Fleming that "he was goddamned if he would act with any little boy with an accent like that, that it was too hot anyway and the whole thing was corny and would ruin my reputation."[22]

The combination of heat, humidity, a temperamental lead actor, growing tension with Florida locals, and alcohol-induced animal attacks all contributed to causing Victor Fleming to suffer a nervous breakdown. Once Fleming quit, Tracy followed suit, leaving the "stunned production workers to their own devices in Ocala."[23] Producer Sidney Franklin scrambled to keep the production alive and quickly announced that King Vidor would replace Victor Fleming. Before Spencer Tracy's role could be recast, however, the project was shelved, and the entire cast and crew were recalled to Los Angeles. In total, the three weeks that the MGM team spent in "The Scrub" cost the studio over $500,000 (about $11 million in 2023), and they left without any usable footage.[24] Gene Eckman was so disheartened by the experience that he never acted again.

After the U.S. entrance into World War II in December 1941, production on *The Yearling* was delayed until 1945. For the rebooted production, Clarence Brown was tapped by Sidney Franklin to take over as director, and actors Gregory Peck, Jane Wyman, and Claude Jarman Jr. were recast in the roles of "Pa," "Ma," and Jody Baxter, respectively.[25] With the missteps of the first original production of *The Yearling* fresh in the minds of both cast and crew, this second attempt at filming on location in the Ocala National Forest during the poorly timed months of April and August 1945 somehow did the trick. The reason for the production's resiliency, even though the landscape was as unforgiving as before, was that in the years following the first *Yearling* debacle, Florida had become home to an increasingly confident and competent cadre of local crew members who would help their beleaguered Hollywood colleagues endure the unbearable heat and humidity of the Florida summer.[26]

In a 2011 interview with the *Gainesville Sun*, Claude Jarman Jr. shared memories of the "free vacation" he experienced while filming the outdoor scenes in Florida during the summer of 1945, which included regular visits to Silver Springs. As for the experience of filming, Jarman remarked on director Clarence Brown's perfectionism as he tried to get just the right take, as well as the kind patience of his costar Gregory Peck. Of the experience, he exclaimed, "It was nice being in the film, and I'll always remember winning the Oscar for it."[27]

The Yearling (1946) won three Academy Awards—for art direction, cinematography, as well as the Academy Juvenile Award for Jarman. It was also nominated in nearly every other major category, including Best Picture, Best Director, Best Actor, and Best Actress. The film proved a resounding critical and box-office success, becoming MGM's most successful movie of the 1946–47 season.[28] Despite widespread reports in the trade presses of the turbulent on-again, off-again production of *The Yearling*, its subsequent success reignited industry interest in filming on location in Florida.

Silver Springs Becomes the World's Underwater Film Capital

Located just outside of Ocala, Silver Springs Nature Theme Park is Florida's first tourist attraction and has been a draw for visitors since before the Civil War.[29] In 1924, Ocala-based businessmen W. Carl Ray and W. M. "Shorty" Davidson purchased the property surrounding Silver Springs and set out to turn the park into a roadside attraction for incoming tin can tourists. To lure in more visitors, Ray and Davidson added electric motors to the spring's famous glass-bottom boats and expanded the campgrounds around the park. According to historian Richard Martin, before Ray and Davidson took over the property, "Silver Springs was a sort of glorified picnic park and beach, popular only with the people of this section of Florida."[30]

To convince more tourists to make the detour through Silver Springs, they turned to the movies to persuade would-be vacationers to dive into the spring's crystal-clear waters themselves. After an exchange of letters with Adolph Zukor of Paramount Studios, he sent a location scout to Silver Springs. The scouting report confirmed the sublime clarity of the park's waters, and Paramount agreed to send a production team to shoot a series of vignettes with the 1928 U.S. Olympic swimming and diving teams, which most notably featured the future Tarzan the Ape Man, Johnny Weissmuller.

The water stunts were combined into an eleven-minute documentary reel titled *Crystal Champions* (1929), produced by nationally renowned sportswriter Grantland Rice. Besides including a series of gravity-defying water stunts, the short film also included sequences of the Olympians eating meals underwater as the camera was encased in a waterproof container.[31] In a 1966 interview with Richard Martin, Davidson remarked how he was immediately drawn to the on-screen charisma of the film's breakout star, Johnny Weissmuller. According to Davidson, the short film helped to "put us on the movie map of the world" and assure "our name, and more especially, the remarkable clarity of our water," became known around the world.[32]

Sensing an opportunity to increase the park's visibility and attract more tourists, local herpetologist Ross Allen, who founded the Reptile Institute at Silver Springs in 1929, and Newton "Newt" Perry, the swim coach at Ocala High School, made sure that Grantland Rice had no choice but to turn their cameras on them. In *Crystal Champions,* both Allen and Perry performed as featured divers and during the production made fast friends with Olympian Johnny Weissmuller.[33] When Weissmuller was later tapped by MGM Studios to replace fellow Olympian Herman Brix as the lead in *Tarzan the Ape Man* (1932), he made sure to remember his friends in Florida.[34] Although the first three films in the *Tarzan* series were mostly shot on location in Culver City, California, several vital scenes were shot in and around Silver Springs. Later, *Tarzan Finds a Son!* (1939) and its sequel, *Tarzan's Secret Treasure* (1941), were filmed on location at both Silver and Wakulla Springs in Florida.[35]

Weissmuller's *Tarzan* films produced in the 1930s and 1940s was not Tarzan's debut on the silver screen. During the 1910s, William "Smiling Bill" Parsons and Paul Gilmore secured the rights from *Tarzan*'s author, Edgar Rice Burroughs, to film their own *Tarzan* serials along Crystal River through their company, National Film Corporation of America. The ensuing fraud case (see chapter 1) had so upset Burroughs that he initially hesitated when MGM offered to produce another film adaptation of his book in Florida.[36] Despite Burroughs's reservations about returning to film in Florida, producer Sam Zimbalist and director Richard Thorpe were won over by Allen and Perry, who offered to serve as advisors for the film.[37] Production for *Tarzan Finds a Son!* began in March 1939, with Ross Allen performing stand-in work for Weissmuller during tricky sequences that involved reptiles and amphibians, while Perry earned the nickname "The Human Fish" for his ability to hold his breath for minutes at a time when performing underwater stunts. Perry also served as Weissmuller's stunt double.[38]

According to local legend, during the making of *Tarzan Finds a Son!*, a colony of macaques were set loose in Silver Springs and have made the park their home ever since.[39] Although the production has been blamed for bringing the rogue colony of macaques to Silver Springs, the most likely culprit was a glass-bottom boat tour operator named Colonel Tooey. In 1938, Tooey opened a Jungle Boat Cruise near Silver Springs and to liven up the tour released several macaques onto an island on the Silver River. Tooey didn't realize that they could swim, and they ultimately spread throughout the park grounds.[40] In November 1938, the *Ocala Star-Banner* reported that a "rhesus monkey" named Sourpuss was shot and killed in nearby Anthony, Florida.[41] Since production for *Tarzan Finds a Son!* did not take place until 1939, and reports of "rhesus monkeys" terrorizing the Ocala area were widespread in local papers as early as 1938, it is impossible that the production of *Tarzan Finds a Son!* could have been responsible—yet another example of how the film industry in Florida was unfairly blamed for disturbing the peace.

MGM returned to Florida again in the late 1940s, this time to have the state to serve as a stand-in for an unnamed Hawaiian island in *On an Island with You* (1948), starring Esther Williams, Cyd Charisse, with a special cameo from legendary Cuban bandleader Xavier Cugat. While much of the principal photography was filmed at the MGM backlot in Culver City, California, most of the cast and crew spent the summer of 1947 on location at Anna Maria Island in Manatee County. In an echo of the calamity that actress Clarine Seymour experienced while filming *Idol Dancer* (1920) (see chapter 1), during shooting for *On an Island with You,* lead actress Esther Williams experienced a serious fall after stepping through a camouflaged hole in the jungle floor. Fortunately, Williams sustained only a sprained ankle, and she was able to finish out the remainder of the production on crutches.[42] The fall caused tension between the lead and her director, Richard Thorpe, whom Williams blamed for reckless behavior in navigating outdoor scenes, which also led Williams's costar Cyd Charisse to suffer a torn ligament in her knee during a ceremonial dance sequence. This injury sidelined the actress for the remainder of the film's dance scenes.[43]

On an Island with You went on to become one of the most popular and profitable films for MGM in 1948, with a nearly $1 million profit margin.[44] Esther Williams, seemingly unperturbed by her experience during the making of *On an Island with You,* regularly returned to Florida to show off her aquatic skills. This was perhaps most literally demonstrated in *Easy to Love* (1953), which was set in and partially filmed on location at Cypress Gardens in Winter Haven. During production, Williams even took it upon herself to replicate the water-ski stunts of the park's famous Aqua Maids, and in the final sequence she performed in a spectacular synchronized swimming number in a specially designed pool in the shape of the state of Florida.[45] Williams also returned to Florida to shoot scenes at Silver Springs for a historical set during the Punic Wars, titled *Jupiter's Darling* (1955).[46]

If there is one person who should be most credited for ensuring that Hollywood studios returned to the state time and time again in the 1940s and 1950s, it would be Newt Perry. Following the outbreak of World War II, Perry earned another title in Florida film and tourism circles, the "King of the Spring."[47] By then he had left Silver Springs and accepted a position as manager of Wakulla Springs, located a dozen miles south of Tallahassee. During his tenure as manager of Wakulla Springs, Perry teamed up once more with Grantland Rice to produce up to eighty underwater short films.

One of the most popular of Perry and Rice's shorts was called *What a Picnic!* (n.d.). The film became notorious among Wakulla lifeguards due to the number of young adults who needed to be rescued from the spring after trying to duplicate the short's underwater picnic.[48] Perry and Rice next applied their ever-evolving skills as filmmakers to produce *Amphibious Fighters* (1943), a ten-minute short directed by award-winning director Jack Eaton. For the film, Wakulla Springs was turned into a mock battlefield that simulated the real-life conditions that U.S. Marines had experienced during the invasion of Guadalcanal in 1942. The technical achievements of Rice and Perry's water film sequences, combined with the reality of the reenactment scenes, got the attention of the Academy, and Perry, Rice, and Eaton won the Oscar for Best Short Subject at the 1944 Academy Awards.[49]

Building on the success of his experimental underwater films at Wakulla Springs, Perry decided to create a water-themed tourist attraction of his own. With the money he earned working for MGM Studios, he bought an abandoned swimming hole and adjacent natural spring that the Seminole tribe had named "Weeki Wachee," or "winding river."[50] When Perry purchased Weeki Wachee Springs in 1947, the park grounds were severely neglected and had become little more than a dumping ground, which he described as "full of old rusted refrigerators and abandoned cars."[51] Perry spent that summer clearing the junk out of the abandoned spring, occasionally stealing away for a swim, which was when he first noticed the depth of the underwater caves.

During a dive on one of these swims, Perry came up with the idea to invent a way to let performers breathe underwater through a free-flowing air hose that would supply oxygen from an air compressor. Using the hose, the performing swimmers appeared as if they were indeed able to breathe up to twenty-five feet underwater. To showcase this novel feat, he excavated a portion of the former junkyard and installed an eighteen-seat theater into the limestone, with a glass wall that would allow viewers to take in the show.[52] Perry scouted out local swimmers and trained them to swim with air hoses and smile at the same time. He taught the performers how to drink Grapette, a noncarbonated beverage, eat bananas, and do aquatic ballets; he even enlisted his thirteen-year-old daughter, Margaret Eileen, to perform as one of the youngest mermaids in the spring's history. Within several months, Perry's underwater show had been all but perfected.[53] The thirty-minute shows put

Figure 19. Weeki Wachee mermaid and stunt double Nancy Tribble (later Benda) is awarded the key to the City of Tampa by Mayor Curtis Hixon during a promotion for *Mr. Peabody and the Mermaid* (1948). Nancy Tribble would later produce the popular after-school puppet show *Miss Nancy's Store* (1966–67) on WFSU-TV, which would be the forerunner of and partial inspiration for Fred Rogers's *Mister Rogers' Neighborhood* (1968–2001) on PBS. Courtesy of State Archives of Florida, Florida Memory.

on by the Weeki Wachee mermaids were a national sensation, as tourists from across the country came to watch the mermaids use a special tunnel that allowed them to appear as though they were swimming up from the depths of the spring.[54]

To raise publicity for his newly built attraction, Newt Perry entered into a partnership with Academy Award–winning screenwriter Nunally Johnson, who had struck out with his own independent studio to shoot his latest screenplay and film, *Mr. Peabody and the Mermaid* (1948), at least partially on location at Weeki Wachee Springs.[55] Similar to *On an Island with You*, most of the interior scenes were filmed on the backlot of Universal Studios in California, but outdoor scenes were shot on location at Perry's underwater theater featuring his star mermaid, Nancy Tribble, who served as a stand-in for lead actress Ann Blyth's underwater dance scenes.[56] Perry was also hired to teach Blyth how to swim for scenes where a body double or stand-in could not be used.[57]

To further showcase Weeki Wachee and his mermaids, Perry coordinated with Universal Studios to fund a roadshow where he and Tribble would visit movie theaters across the South promoting *Mr. Peabody and the Mermaid*, with Tribble performing her stunts in a mobile water tank.[58] As a thanks for her instrumental role in promoting the movie, Tribble was awarded the key to the City of Tampa by Mayor Curtis Hixon.[59]

In 1950, Nancy Tribble married local architect Charles Benda becoming Mrs. Nancy Benda. That same year she was hired as a fifth-grade teacher at Havana Elementary School in Gadsden County. She would not remain in a traditional classroom for long. In 1957, the Florida Legislature, at the urging of Governor LeRoy Collins, created the Florida Educational Television Commission (FETC), with the mission "to provide through educational television a means of extending the powers of teaching in public education and of raising [the] living and educational standards of the citizens and residents of the state."[60] The FETC coordinated with state universities and the Florida Institute for Continuing University Studies (FICUS) to develop a "Florida Television Network," with the goal of producing publicly broadcast programming that would enhance learning opportunities for all levels of public education.

In 1960, WFSU-TV opened its studio on the Florida State University campus, to become one of six featured noncommercial broadcast stations operating across the state. That year Nancy (Tribble) Benda reenrolled at her alma mater to take continuing education classes on the techniques applied to television education. The following year, the Leon County School Board held auditions for an on-air teaching position, for which she easily won the part. Mrs. Benda became "Miss Nancy" as she joined with fellow FSU alumnus Rhett Bryson to produce a live broadcast history-themed puppet show, *Our Nation's Story* (1962–65).[61] The show was so successful that, in 1965, the Florida Department of Education partnered with WFSU-TV to produce an educational program to be broadcast statewide with Miss Nancy at the helm.

The result was *Miss Nancy's Store* (1966–67), an after-school puppet show that aimed to boost children's literacy. During its run, *Miss Nancy's Store* aired on all six public television stations in Florida five nights per week at 5:00 p.m. with an audience of nearly six million viewers.[62] By 1967, *Miss Nancy's Store* ranked number one on WFSU-TV's rating list, receiving more than eleven thousand pieces of fan mail during its first season. To make the show more interactive, she spent the last few minutes of each episode acknowledging viewers' birthdays and reading fan letters. The program was so successful that Florida Commissioner of Education Floyd T. Christian praised Benda and her team at WFSU "for its top-notch instructional content."[63]

WFSU's *Miss Nancy's Store* set the template for children's television learning that would later be adopted by Fred Rogers in *Mr. Rogers' Neighborhood* (1968–2001). Unfortunately for the team behind *Miss Nancy's Store*, a series of budget cuts made during the 1967 legislative session forced the show's abrupt cancellation.[64] Had *Miss Nancy's Store* held out on the Florida broadcast networks for just another year and a half, perhaps it might have found a national distributor through the Public Broadcasting Service (PBS), just like Fred Rogers's more famous Pittsburgh-based show. Benda had no hard feelings after her cancellation, and soon after *Miss Nancy's Store* run ended, she accepted a position with the Florida Department of Education and continued to work as advocate for access to public education for Florida children. Nancy Benda also went on to become one of the state's leading voices in enforcing Title IX sex discrimination laws in the Florida education system.[65]

Miss Nancy was not the only important alumna to graduate from Newt Perry's coterie of performers at Weeki Wachee Springs. Another of Perry's protégés during this time was a U.S. Air Force veteran and lifeguard from Fort Pierce named Ricou Browning. As a teenager, Browning was hired by Perry to work as a lifeguard at the springs, and his superb skills as a swimmer caught Perry's attention. Shortly after arriving at Weeki Wachee, Browning became a featured performer for Perry's "Wonders of Weeki" underwater program. Browning eventually became an attraction himself for his near-superhuman ability to hold his breath for up to four minutes at a time without the use of an air hose.[66] Browning's stunts in the underwater tank ranged from performing fight scenes to carrying out everyday activities like mowing the lawn and cooking on the grill.[67]

Hoping to capitalize on his success at Weeki Wachee, in 1950, Perry and his second wife, Dorothy "Dot" Roederer, an aspiring Olympic diver, relocated to San Marcos, Texas, to open Aquarena Springs, another underwater attraction. Instead of mermaids, Aquarena Springs featured glass-bottom boat tours and underwater performances by the spring's "Aquamaids" and a trained pig aptly named "Ralph the Famous Swimming Pig," all in a "submarine theater."[68] The attraction remained popular with day-trippers from the Austin and San Antonio metro areas for decades until it closed in 1994.

Homesickness for Florida quickly set in for the Perrys, and shortly after Aquarena's opening in 1951, the couple returned to Florida, where they opened a swimming school in Gainesville, and Dot organized a water show program for the Florida School for Girls in Ocala.[69] All the while, "The Human Fish" stayed closely invested in the local film industry, helping location scouts for film and television programs to take full advantage of Florida's diverse landscape.

Florida's Swamps Become a Haven for "Cracker Westerns and Universal Horror"

In 1951, Newt Perry was hired by director Raoul Walsh and producer Milton Sperling to scout locations for their upcoming Seminole War drama *Distant Drums* (1951). Set in the Everglades during the Second Seminole War (1835–42), the film depicts a warped account of the conflict, where Gary Cooper portrays the fictional Captain Wyatt on a mission to destroy a remote "old Spanish fort" that was being used as a base for Spanish gunrunners aiding the Seminoles.

The Castillo San Marcos in St. Augustine starred as the Spanish fort in question, while Perry worked as a location scout and assisted in staging the film's climactic underwater fight to the death between Cooper's Captain Wyatt and a dramatized version of Chief Osceola, renamed Chief Ocala (played by Larry Carper). In the film, Perry performed several of his own stunts, including dying, in three distinct backgrounds where Captain Wyatt's soldiers endured a perilous trek through the Florida swamplands.[70]

During one of Perry's "death" scenes, he performed a stunt where he is dragged underwater and eaten by an alligator. In postproduction, voice actor and singer Sheb Wooley added to the scene by dubbing a long, drawn-out "Aaaaaaaarrrrrrrrgggggghhh!" All the sound effects for the movie were dubbed in a single take, with this particular sound labeled, accurately enough, as, "Man getting bit by an alligator, and he screams." That same take would later be remembered as the iconic "Wilhelm scream," recycled in countless films over the past seventy years—perhaps most famously as the sound made by fallen Stormtroopers in *Star Wars* (1977) and dying Nazis in *Raiders of the Lost Ark* (1981).[71]

The popular success of *Distant Drums* inspired an entire subgenre of films in the 1950s known as "Cracker Westerns."[72] Produced between 1951 and 1966, most of these films were set along the Florida frontier during the nineteenth century.[73] Films such as *The Barefoot Mailman* (1951), set on Florida's East Coast in the 1890s, *Shark River* (1953), *Naked in the Sun* (1957), and *Wind across the Everglades* (1961) brought their own unique takes on the Florida frontier to the silver screen.[74]

Besides *Distant Drums*, perhaps the most consequential "Cracker Western" from this period was Universal Pictures' *Seminole!* (1953), produced by screenwriter Charles J. Peck Jr. The premise of *Seminole!* attempted to correct the controversial portrayal of Chief Osceola and the Seminole Nation in *Distant Drums*. Unlike the "Cowboys and Indians" narrative shown in Raoul Walsh's version of the Seminole Wars, this portrayal of Chief Osceola focused on his betrayal by the U.S. Army.[75] Starring Rock Hudson as the fictional

Lieutenant Lance Caldwell and Anthony Quinn as the historical Chief Osceola, and directed by Budd Boetticher, *Seminole!* was shot primarily on location in Everglades National Park. The film has since been lauded for its far more complex portrayal of the interactions between Native Americans and settlers. It is also relatively unique for the period in that the primary antagonist in the film was a commander in the U.S. Army who was loosely based on the historical General Thomas Jesup. To prevent a libel suit from the descendants of General Jesup, the character was renamed as Major Harland Degan. *Seminole!* focuses intently on the fictional Major Degan's role in both Osceola's imprisonment and eventual death, along with his complicity in the massacre of unarmed Seminole women and children.[76]

The low cost and high financial return that came from "Cracker Westerns" was especially alluring to William Goetz and Leo Spitz, who had taken control of Universal Studios and greenlit the production for *Seminole!* Initially Goetz and Spitz sought to produce "prestige pictures" that would break from the studios' trademark Universal Horror and Arabian Nights series of films. However, the desperate financial situation of the newly formed Universal-International Pictures in the late 1940s forced the producers to make low-budget horror and science fiction films instead. Unable to afford the needed renovations to the soundstages in Universal City, Goetz and Spitz became interested in location filming that could transport their audiences to exotic locales without the Hollywood overhead.

The positive critical reception of *Seminole!* gave Goetz and Spitz their long sought-after "prestige picture," leaving the executives open to what other possibilities filmmaking in Florida could offer their fledgling studio. One of the most important producer-director collaborations in Universal's history was formed during this period between producer William Alland and director Jack Arnold. Their collaboration would be later be credited for "saving Universal Studios."[77] The modest financial success that followed *It Came from Outer Space* (1953) allowed the filmmakers even greater creative control in their next project. Alland suggested that they create the newest monster in the pantheon of Universal's famous horror series: the Creature from the Black Lagoon.

The idea for the Creature first came to Alland at a dinner party hosted by Orson Welles in 1942, who had recently returned from South America after concluding filming for his unfinished feature *It's All True* in Brazil. At the party, the film's cinematographer, George Fanto, a close friend of Welles who worked out of Cinédia studio in Rio de Janeiro, told Alland a legend he had heard about an amphibious humanoid creature who emerged from the Amazon once a year. Each year the creature would take a young woman from a local village and then disappear again. The concept resonated with Alland and twelve years later became the treatment for *Creature from the Black Lagoon* (1954).[78] Without the funds available to transplant an entire production crew to the Amazonian rainforest, Alland and Arnold were able to convince stakeholders to finance what they pitched as an "underwater King Kong" by shooting the film in Florida instead.

While scouting for locations that would best resemble the South American rainforest, director Jack Arnold first met Newt Perry. At forty-seven, Perry felt that he was too old to offer his services as a stuntman.[79] Instead, Perry encouraged Arnold to take a meeting with one of his protégés, Ricou Browning. Browning agreed to perform as the underwater version of Gill Man, the film's titular "Creature," and former Weeki Wachee mermaid Ginger Stanley served as the underwater double for lead actress Julia Adams.[80] Browning remembered his Gill Man suit as "very crude," and commented that he "had no control over [the suit] whatsoever." This lack of control caused at least one comical incident: when Browning needed to take an emergency bathroom break, he frantically emerged from the water in full costume, unintentionally scaring an unsuspecting mother and small child who happened to be on the shore nearby.

Ginger Stanley recalled the resourcefulness she and Browning brought to their "underwater ballet" sequences in the film. In a 2017 interview with the *Orlando Sentinel*, she remarked, "The Hollywood folks were used to seeing people swim underwater like a big breaststroke[;] they hadn't seen anything like [Browning's] underwater crawl, or like [my] ability to hold my breath and maneuver underwater for at least two minutes between gulps of air."[81] Browning and Stanley went on to perform as underwater doubles in both of the *Creature* sequels as well: *Revenge of the Creature* (1955) and *The Creature Walks among Us* (1956).

Shortly after the *Creature* series concluded, television also came to Florida's springs. In 1959, Weeki Wachee Springs was purchased by the American Broadcasting Co. (ABC). ABC built a new theater, which is still in use today, and seats four hundred and is embedded in the side of the spring sixteen feet below the surface. ABC also developed themes for the underwater shows, with elaborate props, lifts, music, and storylines such as Underwater Circus, The Mermaids and the Pirates, and Underwater Follies. The mermaids performed *Alice in Wonderland*, *The Wizard of Oz*, *Snow White*, and *Peter Pan*. The program was so successful that by the early 1960s, swimmers traveled from as far away as Japan to try out for the privilege of becoming a mermaid or stunt performer. The glamorous mermaids performed up to eight shows a day to as many as a half million visitors each year who came to Florida

Figure 20. Promotional photo from Universal Studios including Ricou Browning in his underwater Creature suit and Weeki Wachee Mermaid Ginger Stanley as the underwater stand-in for Julia Adams in *Creature from the Black Lagoon* (1954). Courtesy of State Archives of Florida, Florida Memory.

to see the Weeki Wachee mermaids and Ricou Browning's daring underwater feats. At the height of Weeki Wachee's popularity, the springs employed thirty-five mermaids, who took turns swimming in the shows and captivating the crowds by playing football and having picnics underwater, making it an essential stop on Florida's circuit of renowned roadside attractions.[82]

Newt Perry's fingerprints on Florida's midcentury film and television boom can be found in many productions that filmed in Florida between the 1930s and 1960s. The humble, behind-the-scenes effort of "The Human Fish" to shine a light on the boundless potential Florida could offer to filmmakers remains disappointingly underacknowledged. Until the end of his life, Perry stayed engaged in the goings-on in Florida's film and television industry. In an interview with Patti Griffiths of the *Ocala Star-Banner* given months before his death in 1987, Perry reflected on his role in bringing the movies to Florida. He also discussed his thoughts on seeing *Cross Creek* (1983), a biopic of Marjorie Kinnan Rawlings starring Mary Steenburgen, which was filmed on location in Ocala.[83] Griffiths remarked after speaking with Perry about his feelings of seeing his old stomping grounds through his VCR, "Well it is not the same as canoeing down the Silver Run, or swimming in the spring water, or plunging into activities and projects with the zest and zeal as he once did. But Newt Perry has not stopped living; instead, he has found a new joy in life."[84] Content in his career as an educator, Perry also indicated to Griffiths that his greatest accomplishment was teaching 120,000 students to swim during his lifetime.[85]

Perry's daughter Delee continued to operate the Perry Swim School and boasted in 2021 of having taught over fifteen thousand students herself. In reflecting on her own fifty-plus year career as a swim instructor, Delee Perry recalls, "We have some families where my dad, my mother and I have taught someone to swim in every generation of their family."[86] The century-long multi-generational legacy the Perry family has imparted is another powerful example of the fundamental role that a sense community has played in fostering film in Florida.[87]

Sarasota Hosts "The Greatest Show on Earth"

In 1939, the Federal Writers' Project (FWP) sought to dispel the image of Depression-era Florida as a paradise left untouched by the troubles of the outside world. The guide cautioned visitors and prospective film crews alike that "attempts to romanticize Florida's playground features have resulted in an elaborate painting of the lily," and "coast resorts have been strung into a bejeweled necklace that sparkles on the bosom of a voluptuous sea; all is glamour and superficiality."[88] The criticisms from the FWP and Works Progress Administration were also in part due to their close association with existing writers' unions based in New York and Los Angeles, who were not eager for the added competition that had come from Florida's rising cultural capital.[89] Such naysayers were silenced during World War II, however, when Florida hosted a total of 172 military installations.[90]

Hollywood indirectly helped reinforce the massive government investment made in Florida's military bases. *Thirty Seconds over Tokyo* (1944), starring Spencer Tracy, dramatized the 1942 Doolittle Raid made in retaliation for Pearl Harbor and was filmed almost entirely on location at the Eglin, Hurlburt, and Peel Air Force bases in Okaloosa County.[91] Postwar dramas such as *Twelve O'Clock High* (1949), starring Gregory Peck, were filmed on the Florida Panhandle. The film's director, Henry King, was no stranger to the boundless potential of filming in Florida. Nineteen years earlier King had directed *Hell Harbor* (1930), starring Lupe Vélez, in Tampa Bay (see chapter 3). Now a seasoned award-winning filmmaker, King portrayed the U.S. Eight Air Force's daylight bombing missions in Occupied France, utilizing the open spaces over Okaloosa County to superbly capture the challenges and tribulations of realities such as daylight precision bombing without fighter escort. The authentic detail shown in *Twelve O'clock High* was considered by bombardier veterans "as the only Hollywood film that accurately captured their combat experiences."[92]

The success of locally produced war films, "Cracker Westerns," and Universal's B-Horror movies filmed in Florida also inspired producers to use the state as a backdrop for film noir dramas. Although mostly shot on Warner Brothers' backlot in Burbank, John Huston's *Key Largo* (1948) helped to inspire a string of Florida-set crime thrillers in the 1950s, including *Lady without a Passport* (1950), *Under the Gun* (1951), *Crosswinds* (1951), *Shark River* (1953), *The Miami Story* (1954), *Miami Exposé* (1956), *The Gun Runners* (1958), and *Wind across the Everglades* (1958).[93]

The 1951 tourism season brought to the state a blockbuster spectacle that would prove to Hollywood's studio brass that Florida was at long last ready for its close-up. For three months in the winter of 1951, Sarasota residents and tourists were caught up in the production of Cecil B. DeMille's circus drama *The Greatest Show on Earth* (1952), set in the winter residence of the Ringling and Barnum and Bailey Circus.[94] DeMille had first visited Florida a decade earlier to shoot several underwater scenes in the Florida Keys for his 1840s-set drama *Reap the Wild Wind* (1942). However, the dangers of navigating too close to the coral reefs and the risks of running his ships aground led DeMille to relocate to California to finish the principal photography.[95] When he returned to Florida nine years later, DeMille initially hesitated to shoot in the state again. It was a direct appeal from Governor Fuller Warren that eventually convinced the director to give Florida another chance.[96]

Following the fiscally conservative Millard Caldwell, Governor Warren was far more open to the economic potential of the film industry for the state. To bolster *The Greatest Show on Earth*'s winter stay in Sarasota, Warren commenced a funding drive to renew support for the MPIC. He also utilized the Florida State Employment Service to help cast extras and provide support services for the film. Over the course of production for *The Greatest Show on Earth*, the Sarasota press followed the ups and downs of the production along with its seemingly endless array of cameos on a near daily basis. Along with the film's star-studded cast, more than one thousand Sarasotans were cast as extras, who were each paid seventy-five cents an hour for their time.

Governor Warren's support for the film came full circle in the winter of 1952, when *The Greatest Show on Earth* premiered at the Florida Theater (now the Sarasota Opera House). Like Doyle Carlton before him, who had welcomed the cast and crew of *Hell Harbor* to Tampa in 1929, Governor Warren went all in for Sarasota's debut on the red carpet. Before the film's premiere,

Figure 21. Governor Fuller Warren welcomed several major Hollywood film productions to the state during his tenure as governor, including *The Distant Drums* (1951) and *The Greatest Show on Earth* (1952). Here he is seen carrying film canisters for the premiere of *Distant Drums* in St. Augustine. Courtesy of State Archives of Florida, Florida Memory.

the governor led a parade with one of the film's stars, Emmett Kelly, better known for his clown character "Weary Willy" in the movie, followed in tow by the thousands of Floridians who lined the streets of Sarasota to see their friends and neighbors appear on the silver screen.[97]

South Florida's "Beach Blanket" Craze

Since the first cameras started rolling in Florida at the turn of the twentieth century, the state has consistently maintained an image as a place of escape and fortune just waiting to be discovered. This is perhaps most prevalent in a series of "Gold Digger Tourist Plots" that were filmed in the state between the 1920s and early 1940s. These comedies and musicals typically featured young women on vacation in Florida in search of wealthy men to marry. Such films leaned into what Robert Ingalls and Susan Fernández describe as Florida's image "as a region of natural beauty, leisure, and diverse entertainment," with "beaches that are almost deserted, and lightly traveled roads and highways that snake past sunset-lit beaches."[98]

Hotels were built along Florida's beaches in new, modernist styles of architecture, particularly a local variation that would later become known as "Miami Modernism," or "MiMo."[99] The newly built luxury hotels became the setting for a series of "Gold Digger" films like the Marx Brothers' breakout comedy, *The Cocoanuts* (1929), and Preston Sturges's *The Palm Beach Story* (1942). Although these films were set in Florida, they were filmed almost exclusively on soundstages in New York. Other movies, like *The Golden Arrow* (1936) and *Moon over Miami* (1941), featured secondary location scenes in Florida but were primarily filmed in Southern California.[100]

By 1950, Florida had become third-most-desired place to visit in the United States, behind only Hawaii and California.[101] With over five hundred hotels and clubs built in Miami and Miami Beach over the past decade, what was once a far-flung frontier town had become a tourist haven.[102] Advances in air travel and the completion of Interstate 95 also helped connect South Florida to the rest of the country. It's not surprising then that in the 1950s Hollywood would return to Miami Beach's "Millionaires Row" to shoot lavish musicals and romantic comedies like *Meet Me after the Show* (1951) and *Easy to Love* (1953), which was also partially shot on location at Cypress Gardens.[103]

During the 1950s, the Hollywood studio system was in a period of crisis as it faced increasingly steep competition with television and the continuing fallout from the breakup of the Hollywood studio monopoly following the 1948 *Paramount v. United States* Supreme Court ruling. The same audiences who once packed theaters for "Gold Digger" movies in the 1930s and 1940s were no longer going out but instead staying home and watching TV. At the same time, Miami was experiencing an identity crisis of its own. [104]

Several movies filmed on location and set in South Florida showcased the growing pains that both Miami and the motion picture were undergoing at the beginning of the turbulent 1960s. Frank Capra's *A Hole in the Head* (1959), starring Frank Sinatra as the hotel operator of the fictional Garden of Eden Hotel, featured Miami's Cardozo Hotel as a stand-in for exterior and interior scenes. Filming for *A Hole in the Head* took place between November 1958 and January 1959, and although the production finished ahead of schedule and under budget, the lascivious behavior of its lead star left behind a bitter taste for Miamians.[105] In a November 1958 exposé, journalist Herb Rau of the *Miami News* described chaos caused by Sinatra's excessive drinking and carousing that resulted in two separate lawsuits against the Rat Pack headliner and the production. The first lawsuit came from the Flagler Dog Track after Sinatra failed to make a personal appearance due to a weekend-long bender. A second lawsuit was issued against director Frank Capra and United Artists by the Carlyle Hotel for "the continuing nuisance caused by filming at the neighboring Cardozo Hotel."[106] As Rau remarked, Sinatra "left his mark on Miami for good."[107]

Jerry Lewis's *The Bellboy* (1960) was filmed a year later, between February and March 1960, and was met with a very different reception from Miamians. Filmed almost entirely inside the Fontainebleau Hotel, *The Bellboy* was more self-contained than the disruptive production of *A Hole in the Head*. Jerry Lewis arrived in Miami during a heated actors' strike, which escalated following a series of stalled negotiations between the Motion Picture Producers of America (MPPA) and Ronald Reagan, president of the Screen Actors Guild. Without a fixed plan for the project, Lewis called Paramount and requested eight truckloads of equipment to be sent to Miami Beach so that production would not be interrupted in case the strike dragged on. Working closely with the Fontainebleau staff and community vendors, Lewis was able to complete filming in under twenty-nine days, just before the actors' strike began. *The Bellboy*'s $2 million in expenditures contributed to the local economy during February 1960. Lewis's evening stand-up shows also helped line the pockets of hoteliers, business owners, and local politicians.[108]

While *A Hole in the Head* and *The Bellboy* tried to appeal to the nostalgia of older audiences, *Where the Boys Are* (1960) set out to attract a younger audiences by taking advantage of the recent "beach blanket film craze."[109] Although nearly three hundred Fort Lauderdale beachgoers reveled as extras during the three weeks of on-location shooting during the making of *Where the Boys Are*, cast member Connie Francis later remarked to *Seventeen Magazine* that her experience of filming in Florida was: "Awful. We were miles out on a country road and the bugs! Ugh! We had those trailers to change clothes in—it was hotter inside than out. I was happy to get back to the studio."[110] The contrast between the scenes shot on location in Florida and those filmed on soundstages was quite jarring. Film historian Thomas Lisanti describes the awkward way in which the different scenes in the film transitioned into one another:

> The movie captures the craziness of Fort Lauderdale wonderfully from the crowded beaches to the packed sidewalks and traffic-laden streets. The on-location photography elevates the film immensely. However,

the scenes with the principals on the sand were obviously filmed on the MGM backlot and none of the actors were made to wade into the water on screen.[111]

Where the Boys Are proved to Hollywood executives films made in Florida could have cross-generational appeal. The next year, Elvis Presley was set to film the musical *Follow That Dream* (1962) in Ocala and Inverness. The making of the film would change the life of an eleven-year-old Gainesville native named Tom Petty. During the 1950s and 1960s, Petty's uncle Earl Jernigan owned a film-development lab and worked closely with films shot near Ocala, including the *Creature* series. Jernigan was even given Ricou Browning's underwater Creature suit as a token of appreciation after shooting wrapped for *Revenge of the Creature* (1955). When Elvis came to town that summer morning in 1961, Petty and his uncle drove over to downtown Ocala to see him.[112] In a 2005 interview, Petty recalled the moment he first saw Elvis perform behind the camera:

> There was a huge crowd when we got there. The biggest crowd I've ever seen in the streets of Ocala. And we were driven through the crowd and around the back into the film set. They were filming on the street, where Elvis pulled up in his car and walked into a bank. A simple scene. So, they had set up a bunch of trailers with a chain link fence around it for a dressing room . . . And then suddenly I go, "*That's* Elvis!" He stepped out radiant as an angel. He seemed to glow and walk above the ground. It was like *nothing* I'd ever seen in my life . . . It took them hours just to shoot this little scene of him getting out of the car and walking in the door. Because they couldn't control the crowd; they were just *insane*. And I thought at the time, "That is one hell of a job to have. That's a great gig."[113]

Elvis returned to Florida during the summer of 1964 to shoot *Girl Happy* (1965), another "beach blanket" film set in Fort Lauderdale. MGM Studios advertised the latest of its beach party films with, "Elvis brings his beat to the beach! Elvis jumps with the campus crowd to make the beach 'ball' bounce!"[114] Compared to the other Florida-based "beach blanket" films, *Girl Happy* was strangely landlocked, with most of the scenes shot on the MGM backlot; in fact, Elvis is never even seen wearing shorts or a bathing suit in the movie.[115] Two years later, when Elvis was cast as a Miami-based water-ski instructor in *Clambake* (1967), most of his scenes were filmed on soundstages in California. To compensate for the lack of location footage, *Clambake* depended mostly

Figure 22. Premiere of *Follow That Dream* (1962), Ocala. Although many of Elvis Presley's Florida-set "beach blanket films" were mostly filmed on the MGM backlot in Culver City, California, Elvis came to Ocala to shoot *Follow That Dream* (1962) on location. Courtesy of State Archives of Florida, Florida Memory.

on stock footage from Miami Marine Stadium, which included several gaffes where the sun is seen setting over the ocean in the east, while the outskirts of Miami are shown with oil fields and mountains in the background.[116]

By the mid-1960s, Florida's shoreline had become an essential backdrop for a wide range of blockbuster productions. As seen with Elvis's later beach party films, Hollywood studios were reluctant to utilize Florida on the screen for anything more than as a backdrop. For example, South Florida was featured prominently in the back-to-back James Bond films *Goldfinger* (1964) and *Thunderball* (1965), but aside from the use of secondary stock footage, no scenes featuring Sean Connery's Bond were actually filmed in Florida.[117] While *Midnight Cowboy* (1969), includes just one short scene at the end of the film with Miami's buildings reflected in a bus window, as if flashing by like a mirage.[118]

In 1967, Frank Sinatra returned to Miami Beach, eight years after "leaving his mark" on the city while filming for *A Hole in the Head*. This time he came to shoot a hard-boiled detective story, *Tony Rome* (1967). To win over Miamians who were still sore over his last stay in their city, Sinatra agreed to give performances at the Fontainebleau on evenings when he was not filming. The arrangement seemed to work out quite well for both Sinatra and the Fontainebleau, since he returned to Miami the following year to film *Lady in Cement* (1968), a sequel to *Tony Rome*.[119] Sinatra's *Lady in Cement* costar Raquel Welch recalled in a 1982 interview, "It was a revelation to see him in front of an audience. To completely hold an audience like Frank did is a remarkable thing. I decided right there, I'm going to keep that part of my talent alive."[120] Despite Florida's growing reputation as an attractive place to shoot movies of all genres, the state remained mostly a satellite to the Hollywood studios.

Florida Becomes the "Grade-B Movie Capital of the World"

By the 1950s and 1960s, Central Florida was a frequently used location to shoot syndicated television shows and middle-budget films looking to escape the overhead associated with New York and Los Angeles. The overcrowded film production market in Ocala and Miami brought some low-budget independent filmmakers to the Orlando metro area instead. In 1953, Empire Studios in Orlando and Avalon Film Productions in Winter Park were two independent production companies eager to take advantage of the growing demand from exhibitors to make cheaply produced films that would serve as the "bottom half" of a double feature exhibition. These second features were often compared to the B side of a record and soon earned the nickname "B movies." With audiences draining away to television and studios scaling back their production schedules, the classic double feature vanished from many American theaters during the 1950s.[121]

For young producers in search of their first big break in the film industry, making B movies were a way to get their foot in the door. To twenty-nine-year-old English-born filmmaker R. John Hugh, Orlando seemed the perfect place to break into the industry by making low-cost and atmosphere-rich films. After spending the better part of his twenties drifting through the cutthroat world of the New York radio and television industry, Hugh decided to make the leap to film. According to Hugh, it was a meeting with former Paramount founder Adolph Zukor in 1952 that had the most lasting impact on his career. During this meeting, they discussed the television industry in New York and Hugh's plan to make his own movies in Florida. Upon hearing the word "Florida," Zukor responded, "There's only one place for pictures: Hollywood."[122] Undeterred, one year later Hugh landed in Orlando and founded his own independent studio: Empire Studios.

It should be noted that there are several glaring factual errors in Hugh's account that need to be addressed. Hugh states that Adolph Zukor died in 1960, even though the ninety-three-year-old movie mogul was still very much alive in 1966, when Hugh had his interview with the *Orlando Evening Star:*

> He [Zukor] died in a time of radical change and was lucky enough to live into a new post-television era for motion pictures. If he had lived a few years longer he would have seen Florida become part of it; in spite of the fact that everything Mr. Zukor said about film production in Florida was true. What he said about my not believing his advice was true, too. At least, I didn't take it.[123]

What can be gathered is that in June 1953, R. John Hugh founded Empire Studios, set up an office in Orlando, and started his search for a soundstage to make his first proposed film, *The Osceola Story.* The plan was to make a Seminole War "Cracker Western" in a similar vein as *Distant Drums* (1951) and *Seminole!* (1953). Although the authenticity of Hugh's alleged meeting with Adolph Zukor is debatable, he did seem to be acutely aware of the abandoned Kennedy City facilities on Weedon Island and attempted to gain backers to help bring the defunct studio grounds back to life. Ultimately, Hugh faced quite a bit of trouble finding financial backers for the film in the area.

Even twenty years after Aubrey Kennedy's departure, most would-be investors in Pinellas County remained leery of any outsider promising movie glamour. After receiving a cold reception from the St. Petersburg Board of Trade, along with witnessing firsthand the decrepit condition of the abandoned Weedon Island facility, Hugh was forced to abandon the project.[124] Upon returning to Orlando, Hugh dreamed up another adventure story and this time raised enough funding to produce *Yellowneck* (1955). Filmed at Wekiva Springs, just outside of Orlando, during the summer of 1954, *Yellowneck* told the story of five Confederate army deserters as they attempt to trek through hostile Seminole territory in the Florida Everglades with the goal of reaching safety in Cuba.[125] Even with *Yellowneck* in the can, Hugh struggled to find a distributor, eventually connecting with the fledgling Republic Pictures, which had by the 1950s been relegated to one of six so-called poverty row studios operated by investor Herbert J. Yates.[126]

In 1955, the Splendora Film Corporation hired R. John Hugh's longtime director of photographer Charles O'Rork to film what the company hoped would be a breakthrough "race film" called *Carib Gold* (1956), filmed on location at the Miami Seaquarium and Key West. *Carib Gold* told the story of a group of Black and white Florida shrimpers who work together to recover a sunken treasure but fall victim to treachery and murder.[127] The movie starred legendary singer and actress Ethel Waters, with a script written by Charles

Gossett, a Key West native and former U.S. Navy Frogman who was previously featured in Jack Eaton's *Amphibious Landing* (1943).

Gossett hoped his film would elevate opportunities for Black storytellers and actors to get on screen. In a December 1955 interview in the *Key West Citizen*, Waters explained, "It's a colored enterprise, and the reason I am here and have a part in it is because I want to help prove that colored will work for colored with colored . . . This picture has got to be right, because the aim is right."[128] In the same article, producer Coley Wallace outlined his hope that the film would "integrate on a dignified level the talent of the American Negro performer" but "without trying to stir up strife between the races and without trying to teach tremendous lessons in social integration."[129]

Carib Gold's supposed approach toward "racial uplift" was ultimately undermined by Florida's segregation ordinances. The ordinances required that the film have two separate premieres, one, for Black audiences, at Key West's Monroe Theater and another, for white audiences, at the Strand Theater. Although the twin premieres were considered "a landmark in local history" and accompanied by a parade and welcoming committee for the cast and crew led by the mayor and city council, the film had only a two-day run at both theaters. According to *Key West History*, following the premieres, "for all intents and purposes, *Carib Gold* fell off the face of the earth."[130] It was not until the film's rediscovery in 2008 and subsequent restoration in 2010, that the *Carib Gold*'s historical significance was recognized. According to film historian Amy Turner:

> For fifty years, *Carib Gold* was nothing but an obscure piece of local history, a footnote in the careers of a few performers, and an entry on the lists of forgotten low-budget films. While it languished, the research landscape changed radically, and the disciplines of film studies and African American studies illuminated much of the history of Black filmmaking.[131]

Back in Central Florida, as R. John Hugh struggled to find funding for his next film, a Winter Park–based real estate developer named Thomas Casey received a multimillion-dollar loan from his father, Wilbur, to build the first fully operational film studio in Central Florida. In 1952, the Caseys founded Avalon Pictures Inc., purchasing a warehouse and office space in downtown Winter Park. Thomas Casey used his connections with the Air Photographic and Charting Service at the Orlando Air Force Base to produce training films for U.S. Air Force cadets.[132] The new studio started out by filming spring training games for the New York Giants and Boston Braves, teams that both played at Sanford Memorial Stadium in the 1950s. Avalon Pictures also produced industrial films, short advertisements for businesses throughout Central Florida, and commercials for companies such as Crown Can, Ford Motors, Monsanto, and William Morris.

Expanding on their company's early successes in Central Florida, Wilbur Casey purchased a warehouse at Sixty-Second Street in Miami that would serve as a film processing lab and soundstage.[133] The facility was short-lived, and after a fire gutted the Miami studio in January 1954, to recoup lost expenses, the Caseys decided to double down on their early incursion into television and continue to build up their Winter Park studio.[134] In February 1954, Thomas Casey recruited CBS television pioneer Alexander Leftwich to serve as Avalon's vice president and oversee a feature film and television production unit in Winter Park. Before joining Avalon, Leftwich worked as a writer and producer at CBS on a series of groundbreaking programs including *Arthur Godfrey* (1949–57), *We the People* (1948–52), and *The Fred Waring Show* (1949–54).[135]

A month later, using the insurance money they received from the fire at the Miami Studio, the Caseys bought two acres of land next to the Winter Park Drive-In Theater and broke ground on the new studio. Altogether they invested over $250,000 on what Thomas Casey boasted would one day be "the largest film studios in the East."[136] At the same time that R. John Hugh had kicked off production for *Yellowneck*, the partially completed Avalon Studios started production on the pilot for their first syndicated television series, *Sandy Wright, World Scout* (1955).

The proposed twenty-six-episode half-hour program starred William Gideon as the titular character who would show "the work and adventures of the World Scouts."[137] Produced and directed by Alexander Leftwich, most of the scouts on the show were recruited from the Orlando Players. With the studio's soundstage still under construction, the first episode of *Sandy Wright* was filmed on location at Rainbow Springs.[138] Besides the pilot, no other episodes of *Sandy Wright* appear to have been completed. The show's one and only episode focused on the "horrors of marijuana smoking." It appears the show's message did not resonate with viewers; its single showing on CBS in October 1955 was met with little fanfare and was soon forgotten.[139] Without a syndication deal for *Sandy Wright*, Thomas Casey defaulted on the loans he had received from Leftwich and his producing partner Reed Griffith. Leftwich abandoned the partnership and sued Casey for breach of contract. It is unclear whether the Caseys settled with their disgruntled former partners, as there is no record of how the case was resolved, but Wilbur Casey was able to retain ownership of the Winter Park studio, while plans for their Miami facilities were scrapped.[140]

With mounting legal troubles and their TV pilot DOA, the Caseys dissolved Avalon Pictures in September 1954. However, they quickly consolidated and reincorporated their holdings in April 1955 under a new name: Shamrock Studios. In an interview with the *Orlando Sentinel*, Thomas Casey assured readers his new production company "has no connection whatsoever with the defunct Avalon company."[141] Wilbur Casey bought eight additional lots surrounding Avalon's former Winter Park Studio with plans to build a studio compound three city blocks long. The Caseys also spent $1.3 million to buy a thirteen-acre site on Miami's bayfront to rebuild their former studio and turn it into a tourist attraction.[142]

The Caseys next moved forward on production of *Swamp Angel*, which was to be Shamrock's first feature produced at their Winter Park studio.[143] With a screenplay by Thomas Casey and Dick Fowler, the movie was described as "an offbeat film with a foreboding atmosphere set on the Florida frontier in the late nineteenth century."[144] *Orlando Sentinel* columnist Jean Yothers heaped lavish praise on Casey and his latest venture:

> Tom Casey is the epitome of a Hollywood producer if such judging follows the clothes' line. Seated in his swish office, he was flashy in a pair of yellow trousers, a brownish sport shirt and green plaid coat . . . minus dark glasses, however. He's also popping with plans for Shamrock Pictures [three films a year is the goal] and hastened to point out that the corporation is "privately financed" and "we have no desire to raise funds locally." He further added that negotiations were underway with United Artists for the distribution of Swamp Angel over the country. "There's a tremendous market now for B pictures," declared Casey, "and Hollywood certainly doesn't have the corner on the movie market."[145]

There is no record of whether a finished version of *Swamp Angel* was completed. If it was made, it never saw the light of day. For Thomas Casey to meet his goal of three features a year, he needed all the local talent he could find. At the time, the only feature filmmaker active in Central Florida was R. John Hugh, who agreed to move the production unit of Empire Studios to Shamrock in March 1956. Casey also hired former Walt Disney and Warner Brothers production manager Glen Lambert to oversee day-to-day activities at the studio.[146] Lambert set to work raising funds for Shamrock's first official feature film. With financial backing from Columbia Pictures and a letter of support from legendary producer Sam Spiegel, Lambert decided for his first feature to produce a treatment of Calder Willingham's controversial novel *End as a Man* (1947), an "adolescent horror" story set around a hazing incident at a fictional southern military college.

Willingham's novel was adapted as *The Strange One* (1957) and directed by Hungarian filmmaker Jakob Garfein. The movie was noteworthy for having an openly gay character at a time when the Hays Code prohibited such characters from appearing on screen. Although the film was well received by international critics and audiences, even garnering praise from French New Wave luminaries including François Truffaut and Marcel Marceau for its "controversial" portrayal of race relations and sexuality, *The Strange One* was barred from distribution in the United States.[147] Following the film's controversy stateside, Columbia Pictures distanced itself from Shamrock Studios.

Sam Spiegel's criticism of *The Strange One* was directed less toward its content and more toward the lack of available resources at the Shamrock facilities. In an interview with the *Orlando Sentinel*, Spiegel remarked on Shamrock Studios' future, "There's no basic reason why Florida can't make movies the same as California, but first it must have larger studios and more equipment to attract picture-making companies here."[148]

Even without additional support from Columbia Pictures, Shamrock still managed to keep the lights on. Following Spiegel's recommendation, the studio expanded their facilities, and the Caseys built two brand-new soundstages, equipped "with enough cable to bring electric power to every home in Winter Park."[149] Independent producer Harold K. Carrington, who purchased a space at the one of the new offices described the facilities as "better than anything this side of New York or Los Angeles."[150] R. John Hugh also used Shamrock's new studio soundstages to make his second feature, *Naked in the Sun* (1957). The following year, independent filmmaker Robert J. Gurney Jr. produced his self-financed *Terror from the Year 5000* (1958), while director Nicholas Ray came to Winter Park to film segments of Warner Brothers' *Wind across the Everglades* (1958).

To cover the costs for its ever-increasing overhead, Shamrock loaned its film processing lab to the Martin Company, which had moved to Orlando in 1957, and raised funds producing commercials and training films for General Motors. With expansion on his mind, Thomas Casey broke his original promise to Orlandoans that his studio would not depend on local investors. In June 1958, Shamrock posted a series of ads in the *Orlando Evening Star* seeking funding for a state-of-the-art soundstage that could "accommodate New York and Hollywood producers who will trek to Shamrock as a motion picture mecca."[151] He followed up on this promotional drive to boast, "Shamrock Studios may be [the] forerunner of other picture units as industry begins to see the advantages of utilizing Florida climate," and that the Caseys "are becoming a vital force in attracting important segments of both the movie and television industries toward Florida, which they find ideal in many ways."[152]

As Shamrock Studios searched for investors to help fund its dreams of becoming a motion picture mecca, political developments across the Straits of Florida presented an opportunity that could very well put Shamrock and Winter Park on the map. The big break that the Caseys were hoping for came on New Year's Eve 1958, when Cuban dictator Fulgencio Batista suddenly fled the country for the Dominican Republic. The collapse of the Batista regime made headlines worldwide, but most Americans gave little thought to who would take charge of Cuba next. This all changed a week later when rebel leader Fidel Castro entered Havana on January 8, 1959. Among the first U.S. reporters on the scene was none other than Ed Sullivan, who traveled to the outpost town of Matanzas to interview the thirty-three-year-old revolutionary leader. The chummy interview left Sullivan to proclaim to nearly fifty million Americans who tuned into his broadcast, "Castro and *los barbudos*"—Spanish for the bearded ones—were "in the real tradition of George Washington." Ten days later, *Life* magazine featured Castro on their magazine cover with endorsements that ranged from describing him as "the bearded scholar," a "dynamic boss," and "the liberator."[153] This led to brief period of fascination with Castro from the American public that was later remembered as "Fidelmania."

At the same time, a diminished but diligent assemblage of screenwriters and filmmakers who had been driven underground during the Hollywood Blacklist sensed an opportunity. For his part, Castro also fully recognized the propaganda value the motion picture could provide in terms of garnering international support for his regime. Castro had placed an open call to film producers interested in developing a working relationship with the new government and becoming its primary provider of film equipment and serving as an intermediary for all American filmmakers interested in filming on location in Cuba.

Thomas Casey closely followed events as they unfolded in Cuba throughout the winter of 1959. When Castro initiated his open call to producers, Casey jumped on the opportunity and pitched to the Cuban government a feature film that would dramatize Castro's rise to power. He pitched the project to Ed Cole, an executive at General Motors and general manager of Chevrolet, who had previously worked with Shamrock Studios in making training films. Casey overplayed his hand by suggesting that he had cast heartthrob actor Van Johnson and jazz legend Nat King Cole in the lead roles of his proposed feature, *Los Barbudos*.

Casey and his father hoped the film would be remembered as the first English-language telling of the Cuban Revolution and its immediate aftermath. The Caseys received a guarantee of close to $1 million from General Motors and the Martin Company, as Shamrock became the first American studio to establish a working relationship with the Castro government. In an added gesture of goodwill to their Cuban counterparts, Casey agreed to ship the lion's share of Shamrock's studio equipment from Winter Park to Havana right away. Casey and Ed Cole traveled with a small crew to collect establishing footage for the film, while the treatment for *Los Barbudos* was finalized.

As the supposed contract negotiations between Van Johnson and Nat King Cole stalled in California, the production also came into trouble with the Cuban government. After attempting to film several unauthorized street scenes in Havana, the producers were ordered by Raul Castro, who headed the Ministry for the Recovery of Misappropriated Assets (MRMA), to leave the country. Thomas Casey obliged, but Ed Cole ignored the warning and stayed on in Cuba, relocating the production to an American expatriate community on the Isle of Pines (today Isla de la Juventud). Cole initially had received permission from a constabulary to film on the island, but upon his arriving, shooting was interrupted again, and this time all of Shamrock's equipment was seized by the MRMA. Several locals involved in the production were arrested and imprisoned in the island's infamous Presidio Modelo prison, while Cole managed to flee his would-be arresters and arrived safely in South Carolina. In a June 25 report in the *Orlando Sentinel*, both Casey and Cole confidently explained that the situation with the equipment was simply a misunderstanding and that they planned to fly to Havana to meet with Fidel Castro at a prearranged cocktail party to straighten things out.[154] It is highly unlikely that this meeting occurred or that Shamrock was reimbursed for the seized equipment.

Following the *Los Barbudos* debacle, the Caseys were unable to repay their investors. Several months later, in January 1960, the Caseys leased Shamrock Studios to Robert Stambler of Filmaster Productions Inc. Stabler appointed Colonel Robert E. Kearney, the head of aerial photographic and charting services at Orlando Air Force Base, as the company's vice president and to oversee day-to-day operations of the facility.[155] After clarifying several days later in the *Orlando Sentinel* that the studio had not been sold "lock, stock, and barrel" as previously reported, Thomas Casey assured readers, "this entry by a major Hollywood studio into the Central Florida area marks the first big step in making a movie capital here."[156]

Robert Stambler went right to work at the studio, producing *The Beachcomber* (1962) for the British based Incorporated Television Company (ITC). *The Beachcomber*'s thirty-nine-episode run ended abruptly after the series star, Cameron Mitchell, was arrested for falling behind on his alimony payments and held at the Orange County jail on a $60,000 bond he was unable to pay. The four days Mitchell spent in prison apparently took its toll on the actor, and according to his attorney, "has done immeasurable damage to his career."[157] Plans for the show's second season were scrapped following Mitchell's arrest and subsequent court hearing in March 1961.

Following the cancellation of *The Beachcomber,* the Caseys sold their remaining stake in Shamrock Studios. Thomas Casey appears to have relocated to Miami after abandoning his Winter Park studio. In 1962, he began part-time work as a photographer and contributor to the *Miami Herald Sunday Magazine* and periodically worked as a consultant for independent filmmakers in the area. In November 1969, Casey joined comedian Dick Gregory to produce the documentary *It's a Revolution Mother* (1969), which covered a series of teach-ins affiliated with the Moratorium to End the Vietnam War. Reinvigorated in his film career, Casey leveraged his limited finances to produce *Flesh Feast* (1970), a horror movie about a ring of Florida Nazis who recover Adolf Hitler's body and resurrect him from the dead. *Flesh Feast* also had the distinction of being one of the last film credits for the former blonde bombshell Veronica Lake, becoming a midnight drive-in favorite.[158] Casey followed up *Flesh Feast* by going behind the camera for the only other time in his career to produce *Sometimes Aunt Martha Does Dreadful Things* (1971), a chase film where two fugitives resort to disguising themselves in drag to avoid the Miami police. Both movies are currently available on the Screambox streaming platform, rife with commentary from grind-house aficionados. After he finished filming *Aunt Martha,* Casey remained mostly out of the public record until his death in May 1992.[159]

Even after the dissolution of Shamrock Studios, the Winter Park soundstages remained busy. In November 1959, just before the facilities transferred over to Filmaster, R. John Hugh started production on his next film, *A Crowd for Lisette* (1961). Hugh's Empire Studios would pick up where Shamrock left off by convincing down-on-their-luck movie and TV stars to come reinvent themselves in Winter Park. Hugh also coordinated with the Orlando Players to form his own local acting troupe.[160] Hugh's best-known film is the Florida Western *Johnny Tiger* (1966), which starred a down-and-out Robert Taylor as a widowed schoolteacher on a Seminole Reservation who instructs a strong-willed mixed-race Seminole named Johnny Tiger, played by Chad Everett, and Hugh hired former *Playhouse 90* (1956–60) director Paul Wendkos to direct. The film was seen by Robert Taylor as an opportunity to break away from the typecast roles that had caused his career to stagnate. According to Rodney Cavin, who assisted on the production:

It was Robert Taylor's last feature, and this he looked for as a crowning change in his career. He said, "I'm fifty years old, why am I making love to twenty-two-year-olds in these pictures? This is my change from a romantic lead to a character lead." He was willing to do anything to promote the movie and thrilled about the change.[161]

Johnny Tiger was the last feature film made on the Shamrock Studio grounds. Shortly after production wrapped, Filmaster sold the property to Palmer Electric, and the property has since been kept as a warehouse with little inkling of its movie past.[162] Hugh went on to serve as chairman of the Cultural Events Committee for the Winter Park Chamber of Commerce and diligently worked to place Central Florida at the heart of the motion picture industry.[163] To achieve this goal, Hugh led the first statewide movie booster drive since the 1930s.[164] In the years to come, R. John Hugh regularly visited Tallahassee to lobby the Florida Legislature and Governor's Office to provide financial support for a statewide film organization.

Ivan Tors Brings "Underwater Productions" to Florida

When the Fleischer brothers left Miami in the early 1940s (see chapter 3), South Florida lost its last remaining production studio. Although Hollywood came and went during the 1940s and 1950s, local television stations gradually started to appear throughout Florida. In 1949, WTVJ-TV in Miami and WJXT-TV in Jacksonville became the first TV stations to open in the state.[165] Construction on more television studios halted after the Federal Communications Commission (FCC) placed a "freeze" on the number of new stations allowed to open. Three years later, in 1952, the freeze was lifted and more than two thousand new stations opened nationwide.[166] Within five years following the "lifting of the freeze," TV stations had popped up in Fort Lauderdale, Gainesville, Orlando, Pensacola, St. Petersburg, Tampa, Tallahassee, and West Palm Beach.

Florida's breakthrough in the national television industry came in 1959 with ABC's live broadcasts from Weeki Wachee Springs. A year later, ABC greenlit *Surfside 6* (1960–62), a sixty-minute detective drama that was mostly filmed on location at Warner Brothers Television Studios in Burbank, using recycled sets from its other detective series such as *77 Sunset Strip* (1958–64), *Bourbon Street Beat* (1959–60) and *Hawaiian Eye* (1959–63). Although the series was mostly filmed on set in California, its occasional location work and use of actual Miami locales helped bring Florida to the small screen. Smaller networks such as United Artists' Ziv Television and Screen Gems did film on location in Florida. Ziv's *Miami Undercover* (1961) starred former middleweight champion Rocky Graziano and was mostly filmed on location in Miami.[167] Screen Gem's *Tallahassee 7000* (1961), starring Walter Matthau, was filmed on location throughout Florida. Following the show's premiere, the *St. Petersburg Times* excitedly reported what the series could mean for bringing more shows to the state soon:

> Because the entire series has been filmed within the state of Florida, *Tallahassee 7000* capitalizes on the abundance of colorful settings and a scenic variety that is unsurpassed by any other state in the union. There are of course, the typical towns and cities, universities and farms (even cattle ranches) . . . But there is also the exotic, the unusual, the out-of-the-ordinary that is peculiar to the Sunshine State.[168]

Although *Miami Undercover* and *Tallahassee 7000* helped bring Florida into people's living rooms every week for the first time, it would be up to a Hungarian-born former OSS spy named Ivan Tors to help Florida stay on prime time.[169] After his espionage career ended in 1945, the contacts Ivan Tors made while working with members of the Glenn Miller Orchestra during the war convinced him to take a screenwriting job at MGM Studios. In 1953, Tors struck out on his own to produce a series of B-budget science fiction films he called his "Office of Scientific Investigation Trilogy." The films included in the trilogy were *The Magnetic Monster* (1953), *Rider to the Stars* (1954), and *Gog* (1954). The modest success of these films helped to land him a showrunner contract with Ziv Television to produce *Science Fiction Theater* (1955–57), a half-hour anthology series that set the template for Rod Serling's *The Twilight Zone* (1959–64) on CBS two years later.[170]

After *Science Fiction Theater* was canceled, Tors pitched to Ziv executives a passion project that was in part inspired by his experiences serving in the U.S. Army Air Corps during World War II. The series he pitched was *Sea Hunt* (1958–61), starring Lloyd Bridges as a retired U.S. Navy Frogman who travels on his boat, the *Argonaut,* running salvage and rescue missions. As one of the most-watched syndicated programs in television history, *Sea Hunt* helped keep the fledgling television studio afloat as it faced growing competition from ABC, CBS, and NBC.[171] The first season of *Sea Hunt* was filmed at Marineland of the Pacific in Los Angeles, but the program required several scenes to be filmed on location in The Bahamas. It was during a short stopover in Miami on his way to Nassau that Tors "completely fell in love with South Florida."[172]

When production began for *Sea Hunt*'s second and third season, Tors returned to The Bahamas, but he also ventured to Silver Springs and Cypress

Gardens to shoot vital underwater fight scenes for the series. To help choreograph the underwater sequences, Tors turned to none other than Ricou Browning, who was then working as the public relations director for Silver Springs. The two men soon formed a fast friendship. In a 2012 interview, Browning recalled their first meeting: "Ivan saw me swimming and said, 'Hey how'd you like to swim for me?'"[173] Tors also recruited Browning to double for the different villains in several underwater action scenes. The former Gill Man made enough of an impression on Ivan Tors that when *Sea Hunt* returned to film in The Bahamas for its third season, both men formed Underwater Productions, a film company that fittingly enough specialized in underwater cinematography. Based in Nassau, the niche studio found regular work in developing deep underwater action footage for feature films and television alike.[174]

After *Sea Hunt* was canceled in 1961, Ivan Tors chose to relocate to South Florida, where Ziv's production of *Miami Undercover* was already under way. Once in Florida, Tors and Browning pitched to Ziv an idea for a crime-adventure series set in the Everglades, aptly named *The Everglades* (1961–62). The concept for the series came from Fort Lauderdale resident Albert Wilmore, who shared with Browning and Tors his passion for wildlife conversation and capturing the perils of the South Florida swamps. Because the show was on a tight budget (each episode was completed in two and a half days), it also relied heavily on local Seminoles who ran airboat tours in the area.

Portions of the series were filmed in Winter Park at Thomas Casey's Shamrock Studios, while outdoor scenes were filmed on location in the Everglades National Park and Tamiami Trail. *The Everglades* starred Ron Hayes as Constable Lincoln Vail of the fictional Everglades County Patrol, who traveled the Florida Everglades in an airboat, a vehicle that was often the main plot point of each episode.[175] Eventually Hayes became a near-professional at navigating the boats thanks to the guidance of Seminole airboat operators who worked on the show as technicians and extras.[176] The show also is noteworthy for recruiting a Florida State University halfback named Burt Reynolds who had recently been ousted from his twenty-episode run costarring in NBC's *Riverboat* (1959–61) and returned to guest-star in *The Everglades* for two episodes.[177]

The Everglades only ran for one season before United Artists phased out all of Ziv's active television series.[178] With his partnership with Ziv at an end, Ivan Tors decided to return to making feature films. The idea for Tors's first feature came from none other than Ricou Browning. While working at Silver Springs, Browning had toyed with writing a children's book about a boy who befriends a wild dolphin. He pitched his idea for the book as a "sort of *Lassie* on the water."[179] Browning recalled how the idea for *Flipper* (1963) first came to be:

> I remembered all this Greek mythology about boys on dolphins, and I'd seen trained dolphins [at water shows]. My brother-in-law, Jack Cowden, and I spent a weekend writing a summary of a book. I took the idea to publishers in New York, and never heard back from any of them. I thought that if I could get a movie producer to say he was interested in producing my story, the publishing houses would get off their rear ends.[180]

Ivan Tors told Browning to send him the proposal, "just for the hell of it."[181] After reading Browning's treatment, Tors recognized a coming-of-age story that could be as popular as Marjorie Kinnan Rawlings's *The Yearling*. "Forget the book," Tors told Browning, "Let's make a movie!"[182] Tors raised over $500,000 from his connections at MGM Studios and produced a feature film based on Browning's story. The result was a children's adventure show that followed a twelve-year-old boy named Sandy Ricks, the son of a Florida Keys fisherman, who befriends a bottlenose dolphin.[183] The next challenge would be to cast the film's titular dolphin. Browning recalls:

> For *Flipper* we tried to get an animal that was already trained, but all the ones we saw were only trained to do tricks [above water]. That's when we [he and Tors] heard of Milton Santini, who ran a "porpoise school" in the Florida Keys. Santini kept a pet dolphin named Mitzi and when I waded into Mitzi's pond, she swam right up to me and we knew we had our leading man, er, lady.[184]

According to Dennis Elster, marketing director for Miami's Seaquarium, Mitzi was not entirely alone in carrying the burden of the program: "At least thirteen dolphins have been used to portray Flipper. When they filmed the Flipper series, seven dolphins were used, and another five or six that perform in shows out here."[185] *Flipper* proved to be an enormous hit, grossing roughly $8 million against its half-million-dollar budget, and Flipper the Dolphin became the most famous marine mammal on the planet.[186] Tors and Browning wasted no time cashing in on a sequel film, *Flipper's New Adventure* (1964), and also contracted with NBC to develop a half-hour prime-time series. Both *Flipper's New Adventure* and the pilot for NBC's *Flipper* (1964–67) were filmed simultaneously in late 1963.[187]

To meet the demands of a double production of both a feature film and major television studio pilot, Tors needed to travel between The Bahamas and Miami, shooting ocean scenes at his studio in The Bahamas and on-land scenes at the Miami Seaquarium and Florida International University's Biscayne campus.[188] The constant back-and-forth between Miami and Nassau proved an enormous strain on the twin productions. Ultimately, Tors decided to consolidate his operations. His proximity to the Seaquarium and Miami's built-in infrastructure for location-based filmmaking made it an easy decision for Tors to relocate Underwater Productions from The Bahamas to Florida. As filming on both Flipper productions continued, Tors quietly purchased a property in North Miami from Charles Courshon, a Miami-based hotel owner and lawyer. Tors renamed the site, originally called Thunderbird Studios, as Ivan Tors Studios.

The next boon for Miami's television industry came in 1964, when comedian Jackie Gleason relocated *The Jackie Gleason Show* (1952–70) from its New York headquarters to broadcast full-time from the Miami Beach Auditorium.[189] To accommodate Gleason, who rarely left Miami during the last twenty-five years of his life, CBS built a state-of-the-art television studio next to his favorite golf course.[190] This development had a decisive impact on the creation of a local television industry in South Florida. According to Ricou Browning, Gleason's presence in Miami "did more to popularize South Florida than a boatload of press agents working overtime could have managed."[191]

With the completion of the CBS soundstage and Ivan Tors Studios, Miami's dormant motion picture industry had at last been resurrected. Unlike the challenges Miami faced in providing productions with trained personnel in the 1910s and 1920s, by the mid-1960s, air travel allowed major studios to import their own crews or turn to the increasing number of set builders, art directors, soundmen, and camera crews to see through production. By 1965, Miami and Fort Lauderdale boasted enough professional equipment and specialists to support up to two feature film productions and five to six television shows at one time.

Florida earned an even brighter shine from the film industry spotlight when Ricou Browning won a special Best Visual Effects Award at the 1966 Academy Awards for his work underwater on *Thunderball* (1965).[192] Building on its growing prestige, Underwater Productions oversaw making a series of expansions to its Miami facilities as Ivan Tors planned his to return to feature films. Tors's next film would be another underwater adventure, *Around the World under the Sea* (1966), starring his former *Sea Hunt* lead Lloyd Bridges. Tors also directed a string of animal-themed adventure feature films and television programs: *Rhino* (1964), *Zebra in the Kitchen* (1965), and *Clarence the Cross-eyed Lion* (1965) all were filmed in Florida, while *Daktari* (1966–69) was filmed on location in Southern California. As the 1967–68 television season approached, Tors decided not to pursue a fourth season for *Flipper,* and the

Figure 23. Aside from performing the underwater scenes in *Creature from the Black Lagoon* (1954) and its sequels, FSU graduate Ricou Browning frequently collaborated with Newt Perry and Ivan Tors. In 1963, Browning pitched to Ivan Tors an idea for what would eventually become *Flipper*. Here Browning (*left*) is seen with the dolphin Mitzi and animal trainer Ric Barry O'Feldman (*right*). Courtesy of State Archives of Florida, Florida Memory.

series finale aired on April 15, 1967.[193] Tors instead chose to develop another animal adventure program that closely followed the formula he had perfected with his flagship film-and-television combination.

Ivan Tors found his next breakout star in the form of a seven-foot-tall, 700-pound black bear named Bruno. In an April 1966 *TV Guide* article,

Bruno was described as "the biggest working bear in the world, yet so gentle children can ride him."[194] Bruno got his first big break in *Zebra in the Kitchen* and later performed a scene-stealing guest spot on *Daktari*. With his star already chosen, Tors set out to adapt Walt Morey's popular 1965 children's novel *Gentle Ben*, a story of a friendship between a boy and a grizzly bear in the Alaska wilderness. He adjusted the setting from Alaska to the Florida Everglades and changed Ben from a grizzly to an American black bear to better fit with the local geography.[195]

Like his work on *Flipper*, Tors simultaneously set to work on a feature film, *Gentle Giant* (1967), and a series premiere for the TV show *Gentle Ben* (1967–69). Both the movie and show starred Clint Howard (brother of Ron Howard) and were filmed at Ivan Tors Studios, with outdoor scenes shot at Homosassa Springs and the Fairchild Tropical Botanic Garden. The topics of the episodes ranged from animal management, lost children, disasters such as hurricanes or fires, and poaching or other illegal activities that took place in the region. *Gentle Ben* finished number two in the Nielsen ratings for the 1967–68 television season, and a line of creatively promoted tie-in merchandise brought in additional revenue.[196] Both the movie and series turned out to be surprise sleeper hits. The series' unexpected high ratings led CBS executives to move *Gentle Ben* to compete in the same time slot as *Walt Disney's Wonderful World of Color* (1961–69) on NBC during the 1968–69 season. Unfortunately, since *Gentle Ben* now had to fight for the attention of the same young adult demographic, its ratings plummeted, and the show was not renewed for a third season.[197]

In the prime-time matchup between Ivan Tors and Walt Disney, family audiences chose Disney. Although Ivan Tors was considered a possible heir to Disney's legacy, he wanted little to do with the Disney brand. When asked about this comparison with Walt Disney, Tors responded, "I don't want to be the second Walt Disney. I want to be the first Ivan Tors."[198] John Hill of the *Orlando Sentinel* added that had it not been for a series of unfortunate turns in Tors's later career, "Walt Disney might have been known as the Ivan Tors of Central Florida."[199]

With the coinciding cancellations of *Gentle Ben* and *Daktari*, Tors refocused his efforts on an outdoor game show called *Treasure Isle* (1967). Even with his unencumbered efforts, the series was both a critical and ratings flop. The poor reception of *Treasure Isle* was followed by the sudden death of his wife, Constantine, in October 1969. His wife's death, the failure of *Treasure Isle*, and the unceremonious cancellation of *Gentle Ben* and *Daktari* pushed Tors to the brink of a breakdown.[200] To take time to recover, he stepped back from his workload.

Two years later, when Tors returned to producing, he treaded into familiar territory with the undersea adventure series *Primus* (1971), which showed promise with critics but never gained traction with audiences. The show was canceled after just one season, and Tors was forced to abandon his namesake studio and left Miami. According to his son David, his father spent the rest of the decade "pitching ideas to young punk executives, with predictable results."[201] By the time *Primus* aired, Tors relied on loans that he struggled to pay back, which forced to him to lease studio space to other production companies. Although Ivan Tors stayed active as a producer up until his death in 1983, he never seemed to capture the same lightning in a bottle that he had with his underwater and animal adventure programs of the late 1950s and 1960s.[202] Ricou Browning took over as president of Ivan Tors Studios and oversaw the new leases at the Miami facilities. In the end, Ivan Tors's vision of the entertainment industry could never fully escape the long shadow cast by Walt Disney.

The *Florida Standard Agreement:* Florida Filmmakers and Politicians Unite!

The winter of 1959 was one of the snowiest in New York City's history. During the winter of 1908, Gene Gauntier and the Kalem Players decided to escape New York and seek warmer weather in Florida. Fifty-one years later, a twenty-seven-year-old aspiring cinematographer named James Pergola would follow in Kalem's footsteps. After two back-to-back blizzards buried Pergola's car so completely it took him two days to find it, he decided "to pack all of his worldly belongings and head south in search of sunshine, beaches, balmy breezes, and a job."[203] Similar to his Kalem counterparts in Jacksonville in the 1900s, James Pergola arrived in 1950s Miami at an exciting and dynamic time in the city's history. In order to make the move, he had to quit his job as one of the top camera assistants in New York, becoming only the second card-carrying member of the International Alliance of Theatrical Stage Employees (IATSE) to seek film work in Florida.[204]

Pergola's father, James V. Pergola, had worked as a cameraman for Famous Players Studios (the forerunner of Paramount) during the 1910s and later Fox Movietone News. On October 17, 1937, James Pergola Sr. was hired by Pathé to film a newsreel on the safety of transcontinental flying. Tragically, while Pergola Sr. was recording his flight from New York to Los Angeles, a blizzard blew his plane off course killing everyone on board. Undeterred by his father's death, the younger Pergola "humbly attempted to follow in my father's footsteps but I could never fill them."[205] Pergola would go on to play an essential role in the rise of the Florida film industry in the 1960s and 1970s.

By then, James Pergola Jr. had become an important intermediary in facilitating the exodus of technicians from New York and Los Angeles to Miami. Pergola later recalled in a 2012 interview:

> Prior to this huge boon, friendly Florida provided the gorgeous scenery, but only to local craftsmen. The keys—or team-leaders of the various crews—were still being sent down from New York or east from California. The key-electricians and key-grips brought their top assistants with them from New York City or Hollywood, and hired locals for the third or fourth electrician, camera, grip, or set construction positions.[206]

Through this symbiotic arrangement, local Florida teamsters were trained to become highly skilled technicians, learning from the best teachers in the industry. By the late 1960s, Florida could offer producers with everything a studio needed without shipping in entire crews from either Los Angeles or New York. The homegrown nature of Miami's film industry helped drive down costs at an increasingly sensitive time in both the film and television industry. In Miami there were enough set builders, art directors, soundmen, camera crews, and equipment to "fully stock two films simultaneously."[207] Meanwhile, in New York City the television industry was dying. According to Pergola, "The unions had gotten so demanding and difficult in New York . . . that there was a mass exodus."[208]

To address the range of opportunities available to Florida filmmakers, a group of producers based in Dade County, including Howard B. Chapman, president of Ivan Tors Studios, petitioned the Miami Metropolitan Board of County Commissioners (MBCC) to assist in providing financial relief from excessive regulations that governed the installation of electrical devices on open sets. The MBCC responded enthusiastically and, on May 17, 1966, issued an amendment to Section 10-32 of the Metropolitan Building Code, which provided exemptions for motion picture and television producers. This small victory in Dade County would soon turn into a statewide movement. In the late 1960s, Dade County had a 60-70 percent stake in film and television shows produced in Florida.[209] Still, Florida's share of the national market for film products was about 2 percent. Even so, production companies based in Dade County set their sights on expansion. Governor Haydon Burns and the Florida Legislature soon followed up on this victory by passing Florida Statute 212.08, which specifically exempted films produced for television consumption from the 4 percent sales and use tax.[210]

To help promote the state to producers and protect local cast and crew from undue exploitation, James Pergola, Ricou Browning, and R. John Hugh pooled their resources to form the Florida Motion Picture and Television Association (FMPTA), a broad-based trade association that publicized Florida as a film and video site and organizes efforts in recognizing and lobbying against previous deficiencies. Hugh was elected the FMPTA's first president and Browning became vice president, while Pergola coordinated with producers, directors, and government agencies across Florida to standardize productions to follow the same set start time, end time, and realistic overtime wages for union members across the state. In the organization's first official brochure, Hugh remarked that if the following was achieved, "Florida would become the movie capital of the world."[211] The key goals outlined by Hugh as president of the FMPTA were "to maintain an active program of research and development in all phases of technical production, marketing and distribution of film and video tape productions. To further encourage the use of Florida facilities by out-of-state producers, a constant program of promotion is going to be directed toward the areas of greatest potential."[212]

The Florida Legislature officially recognized the FMPTA's charter and endorsed its mission to "help unite Floridians in cooperative efforts toward the state's development."[213] Following the lead taken by the Miami Chamber of Commerce, Governor Burns, and the Florida Legislature, the FMPTA sought to create a unified set of production policies to be applied statewide. The organization's underlying mission since its creation has been to coordinate the state's "motion picture, television, audio recording, and theater industries, by providing assistance and information to all interested organizations in regard to Florida's skilled personnel, locations, services and fiscal incentive."[214] One key advantage the FMPTA had over its New York City- and Los Angeles–based counterparts was that it had a statewide organization at its disposal that would support productions throughout Florida. Unlike New York and California, where film and television production were consolidated in one major city, Florida's production industry was a truly statewide enterprise that would depend on intercity cooperation between each of the state's different film hubs.

To explain what such cooperation would look like, James Pergola drafted the *Florida Standard Agreement,* which established the basic tenets for how each film commission in the state would coordinate a similar set of tax incentives, permit rates, and labor requirements. According to Pergola, "I sent every producer in the country, in concert with [the] business agents, this standard agreement. As films and television shows came to Florida, they used our Standard Agreement."[215] James Pergola's plan helped open a range of opportunities for local unions to negotiate with the major studios and further build up Florida's profile in the American film industry. At the time, in California or New York, to use, for example, an electric generator, required the production to also hire an electrician, even if one were not really needed.

Under the *Florida Standard Agreement,* both commercial and feature film shoots in Florida were able to operate without redundancy. Unions in Florida were allowed an 85-person crew to do what California would require a 125-person crew to do. As a result, local unions were the first to streamline their contracts and aggressively promote their expertise, while producers who used Florida locations had at their disposal one set of uniform union requirements to comply with. Producers no longer had to worry whether makeup artists needed to take their lunch break, as specified by contract, at a different time from the wardrobe dressers.[216]

As president of the FMPTA, R. John Hugh sought to centralize the statewide film offices in Winter Park. In a March 1967 interview with the *Orlando Sentinel,* he announced plans to move forward with his vision to "make Central Florida the dynamo behind a program designed to attract nation-wide attention."[217] The cornerstone of this plan to turn the Orlando metro area into a haven for creative types across the country would be to start by establishing "a Florida film festival promoted by all the leading motion picture producers and directors in the state."[218]

As R. John Hugh fixated on consolidating Florida's film industry, FMPTA vice president, Ricou Browning, sought to create a decentralized statewide collective of local film offices. This difference in vision would eventually become irreconcilable. On Florida's west coast, Browning coordinated with the Florida Council of 100, a Tampa-based collective of Florida business leaders who advise the governor's office. The Council of 100 was founded in 1961 at the request of then governor Farris Bryant to serve as "a forum of strategic thinkers and leaders having a major positive effect on Florida public policy which enhances the quality of life and economic well-being of all Floridians."[219] On November 13 and 14, 1968, the council sponsored a special conference to address how to further stimulate film and television activity across the state.

Several months later, on January 10, 1969, a joint meeting of the FMPTA and the Florida Council of 100 was held in which Browning outlined a plan for a statewide motion picture advisory board in manner that echoed Trenton Collins and Fred Blair's vision for a statewide film liaison office in the 1930s.[220]

Ricou Browning's vision for a decentralized statewide production industry ultimately won out over R. John Hugh's hope to centralize the industry in Orlando. Browning's plan was for all sixty-seven of Florida's counties to create their own local film council, which would then be united under the banner of a broader statewide entity: the Florida Film Council. Under the council, each Florida county council would send representatives to producers in New York and Los Angeles to "educate" producers on what their county film office could offer in terms of affordable labor, local tax incentives, set pieces, and environment.[221] In other words, instead of having one booster working to field all producer questions about the entire state, there would be sixty-seven county representatives who were each intimately familiar with the strengths, weaknesses, and opportunities that their respective communities could provide for filmmakers. Each county council would have its own offices that would deal with any own local production problems that might occur, while coordinating with the state film council to make sure that wages, incentives, and other accommodations were in sync with the rest of the county offices.[222]

Ricou Browning's ambitious idea for developing a statewide film organization received only tacit support from the governor's office and was not immediately realized. His outline would later lay the groundwork for the Florida Motion Picture and Television Bureau (FMPTB) and the Office of Film and Entertainment (OFE). In the meantime, the state government's interests appeared to have shifted almost exclusively toward the tourism sector. Frustrated by the uptick in red tape raised by local politicians, Browning stepped down from his role as vice president of the FMPTA. A year later, in 1970, he also resigned from his role as president of Ivan Tors Studios, which by then had begun to teeter on the brink of bankruptcy.[223]

One deciding factor as to why the Florida politicians wavered in their support for the film and television industry at this pivotal moment was that its attention had been redirected toward the tourism sector. In 1968, the Florida Legislature voted in favor of making enormous concessions to ensure Walt Disney's proposed "Project X" would come to Orlando. R. John Hugh's efforts to establish a permanent production industry in Central Florida at the same time may have been seen as overkill. Ricou Browning's more attainable goal of aligning county film offices under a single entity did not have the bandwidth it needed either, especially in rural counties that were perennially suspicious of outside influences from the "movie people."

The efforts to consolidate the Florida motion picture industry in South Florida also would have been in vain since, by the late 1960s, Miami's initial film and television boom had started to dissipate. The bureaucratic barricades raised by the Florida Legislature, which in part led to Ricou Browning's resignation from the FMPTA, caused a slowdown in productions across the state, as competition from film liaison offices in other states caused steeper competition. South Florida's tourism industry was equally hard hit by increased in-state competition from Orlando.

After Ricou Browning stepped down as president of Ivan Tors Studios, the property was turned over to Bruce Norris, owner of the Detroit Red Wings, who had purchased a large share of stock in Tors's Underwater Studios. Norris was stuck with the mortgage for a sprawling film studio that he considered "secondary to his other business concerns."[224] Instead, the day-to-day operations of the studio grounds was overseen by William Grefé—nicknamed "Wild Bill." Quentin Tarantino considers Grefé as a major influence on his own career and, in 2011, even hosted a special screening series of Grefé's films at the New Beverly Cinema in Los Angeles.[225]

As a filmmaker based in South Florida, William Grefé directed sixteen South Florida–produced grind-house films, including *Death Curse of Tartu* (1966), *The Devil's Sisters* (1966), *The Naked Zoo* (1970), *Stanley* (1972), and *Mako: Jaws of Death* (1976). The latter, an indie film answer to Steven Spielberg's *Jaws* (1975), managed to avoid the same technical challenges its more famous counterpart faced by using a live detoothed shark, which in at least one scene nearly gummed the lead actress to death. In a later interview, Grefé said he considered the scene "quite effective, as Florida movies go."[226]

In 1980, real estate developer Martin Margulies bought a controlling stake of Ivan Tors Studios, and William Grefé continued to work as studio manager of what became Greenwich Studio City.[227] In a few short years, Greenwich would breathe new life into South Florida as the home for *Miami Vice* (1984–90), but at least for the time being, the region's production industry remained in limbo.

Orlando Becomes the "Action Center of Florida"

November 22, 1963, was a day that not only transformed the nation but also indirectly could be considered one of the most important turning points in Florida history. At 1:00 p.m. Central Standard Time, President John F. Kennedy was pronounced dead at Dallas Parkland Hospital. As the country ground to a halt following the assassination of the president, Walt Disney was several thousand feet above the Ocala National Forest, blissfully unaware of the world-changing news. On that auspicious day, he was scouting the land below to decide the best place to begin what he classified as "Project Winter." As his Gulf Stream jet veered toward Houston, it took a short detour over Orlando where the Florida Turnpike intersected with the recently completed Interstate 4. Looking down at the intersection below him, Disney proclaimed, "This

Figure 24. Governor Haydon Burns with Walt Disney and Roy Disney, 1965. In this press conference held one month before Walt Disney's death, Governor Burns introduced the Disney Brothers Walt and Roy, and Walt discussed their enthusiasm about the new Disney facility in Florida. Courtesy of State Archives of Florida, Florida Memory.

is it!"[228] When Disney landed in Houston several hours later, he was told of Kennedy's shocking murder, still that day he was sure of one thing: Orlando would soon become the "Action Center of Florida."[229]

Governor Haydon Burns was aware of Disney's covert "Project Winter" long before the land purchases were officially publicized. In preparation for the impending announcement, he formed the Florida Development Commission to work with Disney to assist in purchasing the 43-square-mile tract that would become his last great legacy.[230] Governor Burns believed Disney's presence in Orlando would not only be a boon for state tourism but would also help to revitalize Florida's long-dormant entertainment industry. In May 1967, three months after the premiere of Disney's *E.P.C.O.T. Florida Film* in Winter Park, the Florida Legislature met for an extraordinary session to form the Reedy Creek Improvement District for Disney's 28,000 acres. The subsequent passage of three bills with near-unanimous support without debate in either chamber of the legislature forever aligned the state with the tourist economy.[231]

Reedy Creek was intended to be the first step toward fulfilling Walt Disney's vision for EPCOT, which he had posthumously detailed to an overcapacity crowd in Winter Park in February 1967. When Disney World opened on October 1, 1971, Orlando mayor Carl T. Langford exclaimed the coming of Disney was "the greatest thing that's happened since the city got its charter."[232] For Howard Colee, the executive vice president of the Florida Chamber of Commerce, the arrival of Disney signaled an opportunity to resurrect Florida's motion picture industry. On the front page of the September 7, 1965, edition of the *Orlando Sentinel,* Colee shared a quick history lesson on "why 1917 remained the film industry's death year in Florida," though he expressed his hopes that "the Burns administration was on the precipice of developing a more sophisticated approach that may regain a share of this glamorous industry. Our study of the state then was detailed. Our reasoning was sound. But we weren't as knowledgeable about the inner workings of the movie industry then as we are today." According to Colee, Governor Burns was on the precipice of developing a "more sophisticated approach" that "may regain a share of this glamorous industry."[233]

Disney's arrival in Florida not only changed the state's tourism industry but inspired a renewed drive on the part of the state government to capture the attention of the American film and television industry. Ivan Tors had once dreamed of building an amusement park in South Florida where visitors could "ride the movies" and "watch live productions being recorded and performed in real-time."[234] Although Tors's vision never became a reality, in Orlando, Walt Disney World would bring such a park one step closer toward becoming reality, along with sowing the seeds for Florida's rise as a "third coast" alternative for film and television producers.

5

"Assurances of Full Cooperation"

Florida Becomes a National Film and Television Capital, 1971–2005

Once the capital of the silent film industry in the early 1900s, Florida is again emerging as a major production area for this highly desirable industry. Many producers are rediscovering Florida's assets including excellent weather for shooting and a wide variety of locations. As Governor, I would extend a personal invitation for you to take advantage of what Florida offers and assure you of the full cooperation of my office and all state agencies.

Governor Reubin Askew, address to the motion picture
and television industry, 1971

"Programming That We Just Don't Do Anymore"

It was a white-gray afternoon on April 30, 1992, when hundreds of children and their parents assembled in front of Nickelodeon Studios in Orlando to celebrate "G-Day" (Gak Day). On a small platform at the steps of the iconic studio grounds, actor Mike O'Malley, host of the game show *Get the Picture* (1991), stood at the edge of a smoking grate with a large orange capsule with the words "Nickelodeon" written across it. The capsule contained a collection of items suggested by Nickelodeon viewers to show "kids in the future what was important to us in 1992."[1] Orlando native Vicki Horn was invited onstage as a special guest to videotape the ceremony on the Nickelodeon "kids cam." She was helped by Joey Lawrence, the star of the NBC sitcom *Blossom* (1991–95), to press the button that lowered the capsule into the ground. Just as the capsule was about to be lowered, a DeLorean crashed through the crowd and an Emmett Brown impersonator wearing a poorly placed wig jumped out of the vehicle to warn the crowd of a dire "gak" (Nickelodeon's iconic slime) shortage that would occur in the year 2042. The emergency gak was placed inside the capsule, and the phony Doc Brown dashed to his DeLorean to make his escape. Mike O'Malley turned the video camera on himself and then placed it in the time capsule. He then gave a short impromptu speech:

> On this spot in fifty years, the kids of the future will be able to visit this spot, the first world headquarters from kids, and find out what is important to kids today. We hope by then that we have found solutions to our problems, that our dreams have become reality, and that concerned kids of 1992 have become the concerned adults of the year 2042![2]

The Nickelodeon time capsule was then covered with a commemorative plaque that was intended to remain sealed in front of the studio entrance for the next fifty years. Little did the crowd who gathered on that gray Orlando day know that in exactly thirteen years to the day, the doors to Nickelodeon Studios would permanently close.

On April 30, 2005, the studio's iconic slime geyser was capped and the signage in front of the studio's main soundstage was removed. Howard Smith, Nickelodeon's senior vice president, had the soundstage doors locked and officially ordered the transfer of the ten remaining staff members of the Orlando production unit to Los Angeles.[3] The disappearance of this vital Central Florida landmark was met with little public fanfare or commentary. Reports of Nickelodeon's closure did not even make the headlines in local papers until several weeks later. When asked to comment on the studio's sudden closure, Smith remarked to the *Tampa Tribune* that although in the 1990s Nickelodeon's Orlando unit "was home to millions of dollars' worth of production," Nickelodeon's change in programming from game shows with large studio audiences toward animation and sitcoms had reduced the need for two Universal soundstages on opposite sides of the country: "The studio was designed to accommodate programming that we just don't do anymore. We just found that we weren't using the facility. That's the bottom line."[4]

Smith followed this statement with a series of blunt comments to the *Orland Sentinel* about the state of film production in Central Florida, remarking, "The talent pool and the resources that are available to us in Los Angeles are much deeper and broader."[5] *Orlando Sentinel* columnist Susan Strother Clarke, who interviewed Smith about Nickelodeon's decision to leave Orlando, had her own theory:

> Ouch. Smith said that the Orlando studio wasn't built for the type of production Nick does now. But let's face it: A soundstage is nothing more than a big box. If the company wanted to, it could refit its big box in Orlando to look like a big box in New York or a big box in California. A Universal spokesman said his company still thinks film and TV pro-

duction is a "viable business" and that it is looking for new tenants for the Nick space. But the studio's official closing shows, again, that while Orlando will get the occasional TV series or movie, we will never be a long-term hub for big, high-end productions.[6]

Clarke's prediction would prove correct. In the years since Nickelodeon's flight from Orlando, Central Florida's dreams of operating as a supposed "Hollywood East" still remains far from reach. Several days after his interview, Howard Smith announced a $25 million investment toward opening a series of Nickelodeon-themed hotels in partnership with Holiday Inn. Smith remarked, "Orlando is a unique family-market, where such an over-the-top, kid-oriented hotel is most likely to be a huge hit."[7] Just like that, Nickelodeon redirected its attention in Central Florida from its soundstages to its resorts. The closure of Nickelodeon Studios in 2005 was an inevitable end point to a long period of decline for Orlando's ambitious decades-long effort to turn Central Florida into a hub for film and television productions.

The loss of Nickelodeon Studios was all the more devastating for Orlando due to the closure of Disney-MGM's animation studio fifteen months earlier in January 2004. David Stainton, the president of Walt Disney Feature Animation, announced the consolidation of the animation team to Disney's Burbank facilities as a "difficult decision based on what is best strategically for our business both in the short term and the long term."[8] Between 1998 and 2003, the $70 million animation studio had produced the last of the great animated films of the "Disney Renaissance." Films like *Mulan* (1998), *The Emperor's New Groove* (2000), *Lilo and Stich* (2002), and *Brother Bear* (2003) were box-office successes and critical darlings that would also be among the last hand-drawn animated features made by Disney before the industry-wide transition toward computer animation.

As *Brother Bear* wrapped production in 2003, Disney-MGM had become a major chess piece caught in a public dispute between Roy E. Disney (son of Roy O. Disney and nephew of Walt) and CEO Michael Eisner over the future of the studio's animation division.[9] In June 2003, fifty animators were laid off after *Brother Bear* wrapped production, while the studio's next film, *A Few Good Ghosts*, was outright canceled.[10] When Disney announced to its Orlando staff of 258 animators the company's plans to consolidate their animation studios in California, they were given the choice between layoff or reassignment to Los Angeles.[11]

The twin departures of Disney-MGM Animation and Nickelodeon Studios in an eighteen-month period spelled the end of Central Florida movie boosters' dreams of turning Orlando into "Hollywood East." The decline of Central

Florida's motion picture movement coincided with the rise of South Florida as a hub for popular television shows. At Greenwich Studios in North Miami, where Ivan Tors and Ricou Browning first put the city on the television map in the 1960s, a new generation of programming from Florida flashed across the small screen. A new state-of-the-art studio complex built by the city on the site of the former Coconut Grove Convention Center attracted an even greater number of productions to South Florida in the 2000s.[12] Although Disney and Universal had withdrawn from Orlando by then, the opening of a new set of studio complexes in Miami in fact freed up the state to again find its cinematic voice.

Three decades earlier, in 1978, Florida boasted the third-largest statewide motion picture industry, next to New York and California, adding over $500 million to the state economy each decade between 1980 and 2000.[13] The top-down efforts to boost support for tax incentives and state funding for filmmakers that started with Governors Reubin Askew and Bob Graham in the 1970s and 1980s carried over to the Jeb Bush and Charlie Crist administrations in the 2000s. The groundwork laid by Florida film boosters like R. John Hugh and Ricou Browning in the 1960s with the creation of local film offices through the FMPTA led to an unprecedented moment of cooperation between Florida politicians and the motion picture industry (see chapter 4).

James Pergola's *Florida Standard Agreement* provided producers who filmed in Florida an unparalleled degree of intercommunity collaboration across the state, and in the 1980s and 1990s, Florida was one of the most sought-after destinations to film in the United States. In the 1980s, Miami became "America's Casablanca," utilizing its close working relationship with the production team for *Miami Vice* (1984–89) to help revitalize South Beach, which resumed its place as a tourist mecca. In the 1990s, Disney and Universal's newest amusement parks included live film and television sets that would help give rise to Orlando's "Hollywood East" movement.

This chapter will examine the factors that influenced Central and South Florida's rise as a major film and television production center from the 1970s to the early 2000s. During this period, Orlando and Miami each became important film and television cities with drastically different approaches in public relations and advertising. The rise of Florida's production industry presents a fascinating case of contrasts in the collective personalities of both cities.

The story of the motion picture industries in both cities is one of "perfect opposites": where Miami functioned as Florida's gateway city, Orlando has never fully been able to escape from Disney's shadow.[14] The differences between the cities would also play out in the type of projects produced in each region as well as how the aesthetics of each city would be shown on screen. Throughout the 1980s and 1990s, the attention of filmmakers and showrunners rotated back and forth between Central and South Florida, and independent filmmakers on shoestring budgets would capitalize on the state's vibrant landscape to tell increasingly personal and detailed stories of a state at an existential crossroads. Florida's rise as a production center corresponded with broader changes occurring in the American motion picture industry in the late twentieth century. Tensions between the new and old Florida would play out on screen in the last decades of the twentieth century in ways that were both exciting and exasperating.

South Florida Becomes Home to the "Golden Age of Porn"

As discussed in chapter 4, B movies had become a staple of the Florida film industry since the early 1950s, as filmmakers sought to offer audiences cheap thrills with a quick turnaround time on productions. While standard drive-in fare was being produced in Central Florida, some Miami-based filmmakers sought to tap into another exploitation film genre that delivered exactly what it promised to sell: nudist camp films. The first so-called nudie made in Florida was *The Garden of Eden* (1954), which is considered the first color feature film portraying nudism in a natural setting. Set at the Lake Como Family Nudist Resort in Lutz, about fifteen miles north of Tampa, the film proved to be a landmark in challenging the Hays Code censorship laws on the depiction of nudity. The film's producer, Walter Bibo, successfully argued in *Excelsior Pictures v. New York Board of Regents* that since the nudity was portrayed without sexual behavior, "there was nothing sexy or suggestive" about the film, which "did not expose the private parts of adult characters."[15] The New York court's decision helped open the floodgates for a whole new wave of exploitation filmmakers to set up their operations in Florida.

The Chicago-based director-producer team Herschell Lewis and David F. Friedman joined the wave of filmmakers producing "nudies" in Florida. Their first film made in Miami, *Wild Women of Wongo* (1958), did not feature any nudity, but had several scantily clad University of Miami coeds romping around Coral Castle. Friedman was a former publicist for Paramount Studios who started producing low-budget films for adult theaters that adeptly took advantage of loopholes that emerged from the New York court's ruling in favor of *The Garden of Eden*. In a 1991 interview, Friedman reflected on the 150 films he produced in his decades-long career: "Until the mid-'60s, nudist-camp movies were the only way you could show naked women in a movie without getting arrested. You'd have the narrator say, 'Nudity is a happy, wholesome way of life,' and that justified 70 minutes of men and women frolicking in the nude playing volleyball."[16]

According to David Friedman, it was the widespread distribution of European films in the early 1960, which were far more relaxed about casual nudity, that "rendered the smirking tone of the 'nudies' ludicrous."[17] In February 1963, Lewis and Friedman returned to Miami after being offered financing by several Florida-based burlesque houses to produce *Bell, Bare, and Beautiful* (1963), another "nudie" they were able to complete under budget and ahead of schedule. With extra money and a reluctance to return to the Windy City in the dead of winter, Friedman pitched to their backer, burlesque mogul Leroy Griffith, an idea for an entirely different type of exploitation film. As Friedman recalled, "We needed a gimmick that the Hollywood studios could not or would not use. One day I went to the movies and saw a major Hollywood film that was loaded with violence, and yet every time somebody died, he expired with eyes closed and a discreet trickle of blood. I realized then what we could do that the major studios wouldn't and the 'gore movie' was born."[18] The result was *Blood Feast* (1963), the first bona fide "splatter" or "slasher'" film, which has since become a time-honored horror tradition.

Filmed in Miami in just four days on a $24,000 budget, *Blood Feast* tells the story of an Egyptian caterer living in Miami who prowls South Beach dismembering women and taking assorted body parts back to his restaurant.[19] The film was primarily shot at the Suez Hotel in Miami Beach, which also boarded the cast and crew. To receive an extra discount on the room rates, Herschell Lewis agreed to allow the hotel owner to set up chairs and serve drinks to guests as they filmed scenes of actors getting their heads bashed in or tongues ripped out. According to Rodney Kerwin, who starred as the hero in most of the Friedman/Lewis horror films, "There's something about Florida that gives these movies a weird 'aura.' It was just another tourist attraction, perfectly normal."[20]

Since *Blood Feast*'s publicity mostly depended on word of mouth, Friedman decided to attract even more attention by filing an injunction against the screening of his own film in Sarasota and suggesting exhibitors provide vomit bags for their audiences due to the film's excessive gore. *Blood Feast* received overwhelmingly negative reviews, with *Variety* declaring the film "a totally inept shocker," the *Los Angeles Times* proclaiming it as "a blot on the American film industry," and even horror writer extraordinaire Stephen King remarking, "it is the worst horror movie I've ever seen."[21]

Of course, the goal of the film was certainly not to win any awards, and director Herschell Lewis later remarked on his role in creating the modern slasher, "I've often referred to *Blood Feast* as a Walt Whitman poem. It's no good, but it was the first of its type."[22] *Blood Feast* may have been the first of its type, but it certainly was not the last. Between 1963 and 1968, the Friedman/Lewis team would go on to produce twenty more films in Miami during this period alone. The "nudie" and slashers made in South Florida helped open the door for a new wave of exploitation films made throughout the state.

To have a faster turnaround on their films, many low-budget producers chose to take advantage of the decline of censorship that followed the collapse of the Hays Motion Picture Production Code in 1968. These producers made a startling number of R- and X-rated movies, which according to Bill Kelley of the *South Florida Sun Sentinel*, "brought on an endless parade of B-movies with three basic things in common: bad taste, an exploitable title, and a meager budget that wouldn't pay the catering bill on a Hollywood production."[23] Miami-based producer William Grefé reflected in a 2012 interview that such films were made "strictly for shock and awe, and certainly not for the benefit of big-budget studios."[24] Grefé's anti-establishment mindset toward the mainstream film industry came to dominate the outlook of the South Florida film industry in the late 1960s and early 1970s:

> I'm not a Hollywood shill. An independent movie is all about the number of days you have to shoot. I shot in 35mm, which was too expensive, so you've got to get it right in two or three takes or less. You hope you got it right, anyway. I didn't want them to become comparable to Fellini or Bergman because I'm a mercenary. I didn't make these movies for critical acclaim, I did it because it was the right time at the box office.[25]

This transition also coincided with the widespread increase in the number of erotic theaters across the country, with over 750 porn theaters running nationwide in 1970.[26] Much to the chagrin of local politicians, South Florida had become a regular contributor to the sexploitation film industry. Miami, Fort Lauderdale, and Coral Gables soon became familiar settings and backdrops in films made during the "Golden Age of Porn."[27] While amateur porn directors may have been satisfied with the state of their industry's quick and easy turnover, a New York–based hairdresser named Gerard Damiano pondered how to create pornographic films that could appeal to couples with the potential for widespread commercial success.[28] Damiano's vision for a more "refined" porn industry would also later loosely inspire Burt Reynolds's portrayal of the fictional Jack Horner in *Boogie Nights* (1998).

After spending time assisting on the sets of several horror films, Damiano raised $24,000 and cast Linda Lovelace in *Deep Throat* (1972), described as "the *Ben-Hur* of porno pix."²⁹ Filmed in Miami in just six days, *Deep Throat* grossed over $300 million in its first-run release. Damiano followed up *Deep Throat* the next year with *The Devil in Miss Jones* (1973), where he sought to increase the film's "production value" by shooting in 35 millimeter and promoting the film's "glossy photography," along with cultivating its "cultural value" by incorporating a plot based on Jean-Paul Sartre's *No Exit* (1944).³⁰ *The Devil in Miss Jones* was an unexpected box-office and critical success that would spawn a slew of sequels and a seeming "legitimization" of the genre and its "artistic" merits. As the film's review in *Variety* remarked, "Booking a film of this technical quality into a standard sex house is tantamount to throwing it on the trash heap of most current hard-core fare."³¹

The Need for "Practical No-Nonsense Cooperation"

The visible use of South Florida locales and backdrops in pornographic films certainly did not win over any naysayers in the Florida Legislature who were against the film industry. Even without any official encouragement, the potential for large box-office receipts from films such as *Deep Throat* and *The Devil in Miss Jones* soon brought adult filmmakers to Miami in droves. The siphoning of money from South Florida's film and television industry was the result of the redirection of the tourist sector toward Disney World in Orlando in 1971, as Florida-bound tourists turned away from Miami and instead rerouted to Central Florida. Disney World's opening also coincided with a building boom of new Caribbean Island resorts, which also were connected through a network of expanding cruise lines routes, causing a marked decline in the regional economy.³²

Claude Kirk, Florida's first Republican governor since the Reconstruction era, bet his entire political capital on close relations with the Disney Company in the hope that voters would reward his support in the 1970 governor's race. Even at the time, Kirk's close relationship with Disney was seen as controversial by Republicans. The Republican primary challenge he received from drugstore magnate Jack Eckerd became so heated that Kirk later described the vitriol of the campaign to *Time Magazine* as the equivalent of "internecine bloodletting" within the ranks of the Republican Party.³³ Kirk's primary challenge from the disgruntled small-business faction within the Republican ranks, combined with a controversial showdown with the Manatee County school district over its efforts to prevent integrating its schools, opened the door for progressive Democrat Reubin Askew to sweep into office and dash Kirk's hopes for reelection.³⁴

The crux of Reubin Askew's campaign was in line with a broader progressive turn in southern politics, which also coincided with the election of Governor Jimmy Carter in Georgia and the emergence of what would later be called the "Sunbelt South." Inspired by Huey Long's "share the wealth" policies in 1930s Louisiana, Governor Askew railed against the Florida Legislature's corporate concessions. He accused his Republican and Democratic opponents alike of being beholden to special interests such as the Walt Disney Company. In what was intended as a jab against the Reedy Creek Improvement District, during a July 1970 campaign speech Askew remarked, "Too long have the special interests controlled the politicians in Tallahassee, and too long have some of their special interests gotten by without paying taxes on their property, while the rest of us suffer."[35]

Governor Askew's campaign was so aggressive in its focus on attacking special interests that he ran the risk of being perceived as an "anti-business" candidate in a similar mold to the "Anti" politicians in the Democratic Party during the 1910s. Askew shrewdly evaded such criticisms by countering that an overhaul of the state's corporate taxes, criminal justice system, education system, and environmental policies was just as essential for fostering new industries in the state as concessions to the state's largest corporations. Askew's overwhelming showing in both the Democrat primary and the landslide defeat of incumbent Claude Kirk was viewed as a political mandate.[36]

Based on Reubin Askew's rhetoric in the 1970 governor's race, his election could have spelled disaster for organizations like the FMPTA and their efforts toward fostering a statewide film industry. Unlike Governor Jimmy Carter, his counterpart in Georgia who was an avid movie buff, Askew personally had very little interest in the motion picture industry. Phil Ashler, a friend and advisor to the governor, stated in an interview to the *Tampa Tribune* that he "could not recall the last time Askew had seen a movie."[37] The proceedings of the 1971–1973 Florida legislative sessions appeared to be equally dismissive of the state's film and television production industry.

Meanwhile in Georgia, Governor Jimmy Carter, in part motivated by the millions of dollars spent in the state during production of *Deliverance* (1972), starring Florida native Burt Reynolds, set out to turn his state into "Hollywood South" and "pursue the feature film industry with the same vigor used in bringing Japanese zipper making, northeastern bedmaking, and other industries to the state."[38] In contrast, during Florida's 1973 legislative session, the State House of Representatives outright rejected a request from the Florida Industrial Commission to receive a promotional budget that could aid in attracting larger Hollywood productions to the state.[39]

When the Florida Legislature and Governor Askew blinked, the Georgia Film Office took decisive action. The most egregious example of the Florida state government's deteriorating relationship with the film industry can be seen during production of *The Longest Yard* (1974), also starring Burt Reynolds. As a lifelong supporter of the state's film industry, Reynolds initially encouraged director Robert Aldrich and producer Albert Ruddy to shoot his forthcoming prison comedy at Florida State Prison in Raiford. After running into excessive bureaucratic red tape, which caused a significant delay in the film's production, the production team reconsidered. While the Florida government nitpicked with Paramount Pictures over costs and production details, the Georgia Film Office, with the encouragement of Governor Carter, swooped in and offered the production team bottom-dollar prices and unrestricted access to Georgia State Prison in Reidsville. Despite Burt Reynolds's hope to keep *The Longest Yard* in Florida, money spoke louder, and the goodwill Reynolds received from the Carter administration during the filming of *Deliverance* further encouraged the production to move across the border to Georgia.[40]

Two years later, when Reynolds and director Hal Needham began scouting for locations of *Smokey and the Bandit* (1977), the second-highest-grossing film of 1977 (after *Star Wars*), the Georgia Film Office once again outbid Florida to host the film's shooting locations.[41] Richard Alan Nelson lauded the Georgia Film Office for its quick maneuvering, while criticizing the disorganization of Florida's film promoters during the early 1970s: "This practical, no-nonsense cooperation led Florida to lose yet another Reynolds picture written specifically for the state to Georgia. The Burt Reynolds snafu wasn't the only one to vividly bring home the need for change."[42]

Even critically acclaimed films that were made in Florida in the early 1970s were typically met with resistance and occasionally outright hostility. For example, the production of Academy Award–winning film *Lenny* (1974), Bob Fosse's biopic on legendary comedian Lenny Bruce, was kept from filming its trial scenes inside the Dade County Courthouse because one of the judges disapproved of the script. The judge's unlikely explanation for blocking the shoot was that "it would put the court in an awkward position in case the movie was later banned in theaters."[43]

Another lost opportunity came when William Grefé and R. John Hugh opened negotiations with American International Pictures (AIP), an MGM-subsidiary, to film their next five low-budget features at Miami's neglected studio spaces. However, the lack of a clear line of authority to approve the necessary permits caused the deal to fall through. Instead, the AIP answered a call from the recently formed Texas Film Commission and relocated there instead. After the AIP debacle, the production teams behind four more films that were originally slated for South Florida opted for Texas instead.[44]

Unlike the previous lulls in production that followed a decline in industry-government relations during the 1910s, 1930s, or 1950s, where local talent headed toward the exit too, when a similar downturn hit in the 1970s, the organizing efforts of the seven chapters of the FMPTA managed to convince nervous local cast and crew members to stand their ground and remain in the state. James Pergola, who had unified local film offices under the *Florida Standard Agreement*, met with the newly appointed Florida film coordinator, Sunny Fader, to appeal to Governor Askew for a larger promotional budget and to create a statewide film office modeled after the ones formed in Georgia and Texas. Governor Askew initially expressed his reluctance to support additional filmmaking in Florida due the state's emerging reputation for harboring pornography. Despite the tough sell, though, Pergola and Fader did succeed in convincing the governor to sign off on a $50,000 stipend to initiate a state film commission.[45]

The result was a new office formed within the state Department of Commerce called the Florida Motion Picture and Television Bureau (FMPTB), with Ben Harris appointed as the director of what was, at the time, a one-man operation. Harris was charged with the monumental task of using his minuscule budget "to change Florida's filmmaking opportunities and image for the better."[46] To achieve this, the FMPTB worked on two separate fronts: to attract New York– and California-based producers to reconsider Georgia or Texas and consider Florida instead, and to convince the governor that establishing favorable attitudes toward the film and television industry could be used as a means of deflecting his perceived "anti-Corporate" image in time for his upcoming reelection bid in 1974. Harris cultivated his contacts at the FMPTA and compiled the data needed to appeal to the governor to provide additional financial assistance by arguing that nurturing a healthy relationship between regional film offices and Tallahassee—as well as municipal and county governments—could both create jobs and provide much-needed income to the recession-stricken state.[47]

Although Ben Harris's initial proposal was stuck down by the Florida Legislature, he did succeed in convincing Governor Askew of the motion picture industry's economic viability. Similar to the dynamic between Governor Doyle Carlton and Trenton Collins as they tried to bring filmmakers to the state through the Committee for the Development of the Motion Picture during the Great Depression, Askew and Harris formed the Florida Film Commission as a means of alleviating Florida's fledgling economy amid the mid-1970s recession. Shortly after the commission's formation, Governor Askew gave Harris full license to negotiate with producers to relocate to the state. Despite his office's limited budget, Ben Harris succeeded in significant areas where earlier state boosters like Trenton Collins had failed. Within a year, Harris managed to coordinate a network of twenty-two film liaison offices across the state to provide local contacts and follow-up for productions. With careful budgeting and monitoring, the bureau sought to prevent another situation like *The Longest Yard* from happening again.[48]

In the aftermath of Reubin Askew's landslide reelection in 1974, he doubled down in support of the industry he previously neglected. That year, with Askew's endorsement, the Florida Legislature at long last expanded its investment in forming a state office that could successfully serve as a liaison between film and television productions and local civic authorities. In almost no time at all, these efforts brought a significant boon to the state's fledgling motion picture industry. Over the four years of Askew's second term, his administration and the Legislature seemingly worked in lockstep toward expanding support for an industry of which both had previously been highly dismissive. Such initiatives brought between $50 and $60 million into the state coffers from major film and television studios, while local independent productions spent an estimated $30 million in-state.

Although in 1976 Florida still lagged both Georgia and Texas, by the second year of its existence, the FMPTB had assisted at a total of thirty-three companies, while fifteen ultimately filmed in Florida and spent over $7 million during their time in the state in just that one year alone.[49] An example of the lavish spending a film production could bring to the state came with production of the John Frankenheimer thriller *Black Sunday* (1977), which featured a bomb-strapped Goodyear blimp on a direct collision course with Miami's Orange Bowl, which so happened to host Super Bowl X in January 1976. To cut down on costs, Frankenheimer brought a film crew to the Super Bowl matchup between the Pittsburgh Steelers and Dallas Cowboys, shooting several scenes starring the film's principal actors during the game. Several weeks later, Frankenheimer issued a call for thousands of local extras to film inside the Orange Bowl, including players from the 1976 Miami Dolphins, who begrudgingly donned Cowboys and Steelers uniforms for the film's iconic blimp crash sequence. In return for the City of Miami's cooperation, Frankenheimer agreed to direct a commercial for the Miami chapter of the United Way charity, featuring the star of *Black Sunday*, Robert Shaw, as its narrator.[50] This arrangement was overseen directly by none other than Ben Harris, and by the time production on *Black Sunday* wrapped in the spring of 1976, $4 million of the film's $8 million budget had been spent in Dade County. Such spending was still considered a drop in the bucket compared to what the film's budget would have called for if it were produced in California.[51]

The local cooperation that the FMPTB had managed to coordinate with the production of *Black Sunday* became the template for several Florida-themed movies made in 1976 and 1977, including *Joe Panther* (1976), *Airport '77, The Greatest, Empire of the Ants,* and *Thunder and Lightning* (1977). Even Burt Reynolds was finally able to return to Florida to film another football comedy, *Semi-Tough* (1977). Ben Harris and Burt Reynolds were able to make this arrangement happen through coordinating with United Artists executives and Dolphins owner Joe Robbie to shoot at the Orange Bowl for the price of $40,000 a day. Although *Semi-Tough* was supposed to be set during the winter at Denver's Mile High Stadium, the low price that the FMPTB had managed to secure made it a cheaper option to simulate snow in Miami instead.[52] Reynolds was later encouraged to ensure that both sequels to *Smokey and the Bandit* (1980 and 1983) would be filmed mostly near his ranch in Jupiter, with millions of dollars spent in West Palm Beach during production.[53]

In the late 1970s and early 1980s, Florida also emerged as a regular destination for big-budget sequels to Hollywood blockbusters. When production problems riddled the highly anticipated *Jaws II* (1978), resulting in not only a change of director but the need for the production to relocate outside of Massachusetts, the FMPTB acted swiftly. Producer Richard Zanuck rehired the original *Jaws* screenwriter, Carl Gottlieb, to fix the troubled sequel script, and members of the Destin–Fort Walton Beach Film Commission encouraged the screenwriter to work on his rewrites at a specially provided beach house in Okaloosa County.[54] Although Gottlieb chose to keep the film's setting in Martha's Vineyard, while writing *Jaws II*, he incorporated several local quirks into the screenplay that the local film commission was able to leverage to bring the entire production to Florida's Emerald Coast.[55]

Over half of *Jaws II*'s estimated $40 million production cost ultimately was spent on location in the Panhandle, with accounts of the production team spending over $18,000 on paint and brushes alone, while over $200,000 was spent at a nearby lumberyard.[56] According to Ben Anderson, who would later become the tax collector for Okaloosa County and played a small part in *Jaws II*, after being cast in the film his "pay went from $2 an hour to $850 a week," and he used the extra cash to buy an engagement ring for his fiancé.[57]

The FMPTB emphasized Florida's right-to-work laws as an added incentive for not only feature film producers but also television commercials and the home video market, which was then still in its infancy. This reality was best reflected in an FMPTB advertisement that pitched to producers, "all the crew, engineers, and production people you'll need, at ready-to-work, sea-level prices."[58] Ironically, Florida's right-to-work laws benefited low- to no budget independent films more so than the big Hollywood features. This was because lower-budget films were able to draw upon a wider local labor pool that could be hired at premium rates through direct negotiations with Florida-based unions. In less than three years, the promotional campaign that Ben Harris had initiated through the FMPTB had not only brought millions of dollars in local production spending to the state but also avoided the costly crew redundancies that often plagued Hollywood studios at the same time.

A front-page headline for the November 17, 1978, issue of *Backstage* heralded, "Fla. Climbs to 3rd As Nat'l Film & TV Capital." In an impressively short turnaround, Florida had gone from watching its motion picture industry bleed out to Georgia, Texas, and beyond, to becoming the very "third coast" that local movie boosters had hoped for since the 1910s. Interestingly enough, the article echoed many of the same promises of "clear-cut sunshine" first advertised in Jacksonville in the 1910s. According to Carol Pearce, author of the *Backstage* article, Florida's rise was due to "the predictably balmy weather and great variety of locations that became Florida's most saleable assets, as it offered a lower-cost alternative to Hollywood. Motion picture and commercial companies recognized these values and gravitated to the fun-in-the-sun flatlands of Florida."[59]

Bob Graham succeeded Reubin Askew as governor of Florida in January 1979. Unlike his predecessor, who pursued the entertainment industry strictly for its economic benefits, Governor Graham (like then president Jimmy Carter) had a passion for the movies. In an interview with the *St. Petersburg Times*, he expressed how "going to the movies is a very special thing. It's an event and I look forward to it."[60] He fondly recalled the eight-mile drive that he and his parents would take from the family farm to a Hialeah theater to watch Roy Rogers Westerns when he was a boy. During his term as governor, Graham returned to that same theater at least six times each year. Graham also described himself as an enthusiastic subscriber to the latest cable-network phenomenon: the Home Box Office Network (HBO).[61]

While serving as a state senator in the mid-1970s, Graham created a unique way to connect to his constituents through his "Workdays Campaign." "Workdays" was an initiative that involved first State Senator and then later Governor Graham to work "anywhere between eight hours and eighteen weeks on various jobs across the state."[62] Graham showed his support to Florida film crews by dedicating one of his "workdays" to serving as a gaffer on Burt Reynolds's *Stick* (1985).[63]

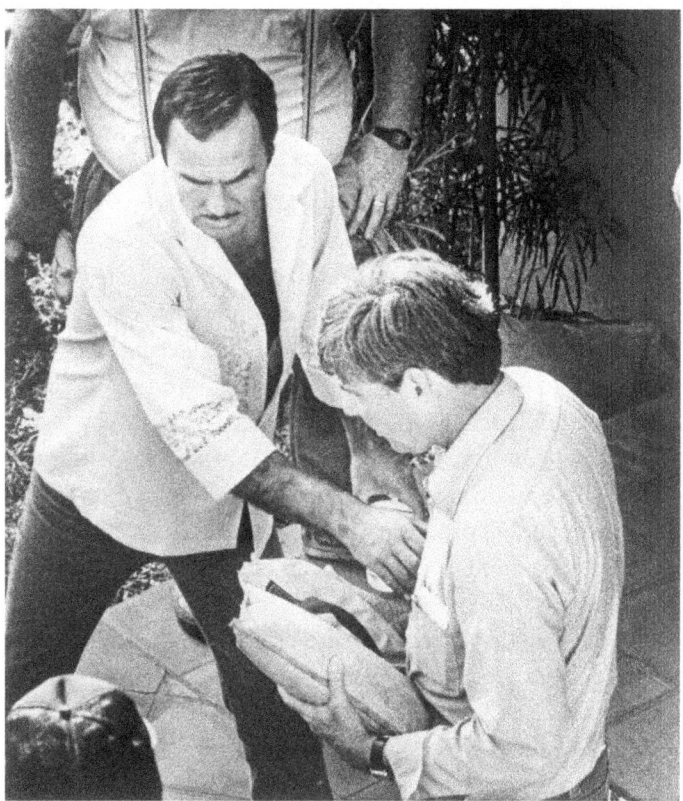

Figure 25. Bob Graham and Burt Reynolds on the set of *Stick* (1985). Governor Graham (*right*) is shown during one of his "workdays." His more than 180 jobs included policeman, railroad engineer, construction worker, sponge fisherman, factory worker, social worker, busboy, teacher, and newsman. *Stick* was directed by and starred FSU graduate Burt Reynolds, along with Candice Bergen and George Segal, and was based on a novel by Elmore Leonard. Released by Universal Studios, it was partly filmed in Miami and Fort Lauderdale. Courtesy of State Archives of Florida, Florida Memory.

One year into Graham's term as governor, Florida experienced a 40 percent increase in commercial and feature film spending, as the state came to compete with New York for the number two place in the American motion picture industry.[64] Although during the Askew administration, the governor's office and legislature endorsed efforts to bring producers to Florida, the state government seldom played a hands-on role in negotiating a given arrangement, instead relying on local film commissioners to work out the details. Bob Graham, on the other hand, both physically worked on film sets and regularly met with Hollywood executives on their home turf in California.[65] Like

Doyle Carlton in the 1930s, Graham's overtures sought to convince California studios to build new soundstages in Florida and relocate at least a portion of their operations to the state.

The most important of Bob Graham's "official state missions to California" occurred on February 23, 1984. The trip to Los Angeles was arranged by Ben Harris and Charles Porretto through the FMPTB, who participated with Graham in dozens of meetings with top-ranking studio executives at Universal, Columbia, Paramount, and Twentieth Century Fox—each studio a long-standing contributor to Florida productions. In a press release to the *St. Petersburg Times,* Graham expressed that this visit could indeed be an opportunity to right a decades-old wrong that that had deprived Florida of its rightful place as a motion picture capital: "The movie industry had a very heavy commitment in Jacksonville in the early 1900s before it moved to California. We're trying to put the best product on the shelf in terms of what Florida has to offer and then let independent producers trying to make quality movies—profitably, within budget, on-time—make the decisions where they best can do that."[66]

After returning to Florida, Governor Graham oversaw the passage of legislation that would provide a special tax exemption applied toward the lease of equipment used by commercial, film, and television productions. Special tax incentives were a key tactic used to lure "runaway productions" to Florida, and if correctly applied, Governor Graham predicted, "By the year 2000, Florida would surpass Hollywood as a filmmaking center."[67] Two directors who took quick advantage of Governor Graham's overtures were Lawrence Kasdan and George Lucas, who in between shooting for *The Empire Strikes Back* (1980) and *Return of the Jedi* (1983), produced *Body Heat* (1981), a neo-noir starring William Hurt that was loosely inspired by Billy Wilder's classic *Double Indemnity* (1944).

Governor Graham's outreach to studio executives during his trips to California, combined with his policies, sought to create a fiscally favorable environment for filmmakers who came to Florida. With popular support at the state and local level, Florida had, by the mid-1980s, become the "third coast" of the American motion picture industry. Between 1974 and 1991, the FMPTB added over $1.25 billion to Florida's economy by bringing an ever-increasing number of commercial, film, and television projects to the state.[68] Although each of the twenty-two film offices active in the state during this period worked diligently toward bringing all types of productions to Florida, it would be the competing bids for studio complexes between Orlando and Miami that sparked an intercity rivalry over where the center of motion picture production in Florida would be located.

Miami Becomes "America's Casablanca"

When designing the cover of *Time Magazine* for its November 23, 1981, issue, illustrator Nicholas Gaetano was charged with depicting in striking detail the ongoing social and political turmoil taking place in South Florida during the early 1980s. Miami had since become a scapegoat in the American mainstream media for the ongoing nationwide "crisis of confidence." The top right corner of the cover displayed a picture of David Stockman, Ronald Reagan's controversial director of the Office of Management and Budget who was later remembered as "the father of Reaganomics," with a line underneath that read, "Economic Woes: Confession and Recession."[69]

Instead of focusing on the bespectacled agent of impending economic woes, the reader's eye is drawn toward a green-and-red map of the Florida coast. The words "Paradise Lost?" blaze across the green—and seemingly unspoiled—Central Florida and blood-red South Florida. Below is a cartoon of the sun wearing sunglasses and a frown. In the boundary between the peaceful green and violent red are the words "South Florida," with each letter filled with apocalyptic imagery of desolate beaches, internment camps, armed officers, drug lords, piles of cash, refugees, and assault.[70] The article that accompanied this shocking cover page certainly would not have been met with much approval from the Miami Chamber of Commerce: "Here is a picture of a policeman leaning over the body of a Miamian whose throat has been slit and wallet emptied. There is a sleek V-planed speedboat, stripped of galleys and bunks and loaded with a half-ton of marijuana, skimming across the waters of Biscayne Bay. Here are a handful of ragged Cuban refugees, living in a tent pitched beneath a highway overpass."[71]

The article, fittingly titled "Trouble in Paradise," addresses the ways in which Miami, once viewed as "America's Favorite Winter Playground," had been overrun by an "epidemic of violent crime, a plague of illicit drugs and a tidal wave of refugees" that had "slammed into South Florida with the destructive power of a hurricane."[72] The November 1981 *Time Magazine* article offers an snapshot into one of the most tumultuous moments in Florida history. Miami had become the "new murder and drug capital of America."[73] Nicholas Gaetano's "Paradise Lost" would go on to become one of the most iconic *Time Magazine* covers of the late twentieth century and serves as a striking showcase of South Florida's troubled recent past.

Media coverage of events such as the Dadeland Massacre in 1979, the McDuffie Rebellion and Mariel Boatlift in 1980, had created a fully unflattering image of what was once the most sought-after tourist destination in the continental United States. Doomsday headlines like *Time Magazine*'s "Paradise Lost" depicted Miami-Dade County to the public as, in the words of architectural historian M. Barron Stofik, "becoming numb with the stress of dealing with overwhelming numbers of refugees, dismayed at the violence in the black community and the rising crime rates. In other words, a county under siege."[74]

By 1981, rising crime rates had become the number-one political issue in South Florida. Francisco Alvarado of the *Miami New Times* recalled how an $800-a-month rental refrigerator truck that was used by the city for storing the city's exorbitant number of murder victims had become "a symbol of Miami's ignominious distinction as the nation's murder capital, largely as a result of shootouts among cocaine cowboys and violent crime committed by Marielitos."[75]

The rise in drug trafficking and violent crime in South Florida escalated to such an extent that Tom Gallagher, the state representative for Florida's 111th District, told local and national newspapers in August 1981, "There is no other issue in Dade County at this point."[76] Jim Dingfelder, the public affairs officer for the United States Customs Service, described the situation in Miami to the *New York Times* as "Dodge City South."[77] A month later, in an attempt to counter the flow of drugs into South Florida, Vice President George H. W. Bush created a special South Florida Drug Task Force charged with bringing together officials from Customs, DEA, the Coast Guard, and the Treasury Department.[78]

As simultaneous economic, social, and political crises in South Florida turned into full-blown emergencies, Miami city officials sought ways to counteract the negative publicity.[79] Such images were juxtaposed against an understanding of Miami's position as the "capital of Latin America" or "the world's most international crossroads of travel, finance, Florida's most influential city."[80] David Rieff of the World Policy Institute observed, "Reporting on a bunch of Colombian dealers peppering each other with Uzis and Mac-10s at every stoplight and across every shopping mall in Dade County was a lot more fun than a story about the SALT talks."[81] Ironically, the state's reputation as a supposed drug den unexpectedly led at least one classic comedy to be filmed in Florida for just that reason.

In the autumn of 1979, producer Doug Kenney started to scout for locations for a follow-up to his wildly successful *Animal House* (1978). Initially, Kenney and director Harold Ramis wanted their next film, *Caddyshack* (1980), to be set somewhere in the Midwest. But they were both concerned that it would be harder to access hard drugs in Iowa than Florida. In a 2010 interview with *Sports Illustrated*, Ramis explained how he settled on a semi pro club in Davie as the setting for the film's fictional Bushwood Golf Resort:

"It was a pretty debauched country at the time. The cocaine business in South Florida was mammoth, and everyone was doing everything."[82] He described the experience as "young people running around South Florida being crazy."[83] Chevy Chase added, in the same interview, "It was pretty fucking nuts on that set. At night we would race golf carts down the fairways, people whacked out having a good time. The crew possessed whatever you needed."[84]

In South Florida, the triptych drama of crime, drugs, and immigration blurred together in the popular media's portrayal of South Florida. Next to *Time Magazine*'s "Paradise Lost," this chaotic period of the city's history is perhaps best showcased by the front cover of the January 1982 issue of *Harper's Magazine*, which gave the city yet another nickname: "America's Casablanca."[85] With such lurid and oddly romantic flourishes attributed to South Florida, it was no surprise that the area soon began to beckon the film industry. When screenwriter Oliver Stone was hired by producer Martin Bregman to pen a remake of the 1930s gangland saga *Scarface: Shame of a Nation* (1932), he decided to relocate the film's original setting in Prohibition-era Chicago to a contemporary setting that best matched the bootlegger period: Miami in the 1980s.

Concerned that the updated *Scarface* (1983) might tarnish the city's image even further, Cuban-born Miami commissioner Demetrio Perez Jr. pledged to halt the production in its tracks. Shortly after Brian DePalma was announced as the film's director and Al Pacino was cast as the titular Marielito, Commissioner Perez introduced a resolution to the city council that would have prohibited the production from getting a permit to shoot on any piece of city property. This way, even if the production team rented private homes and restaurants, they were unable to use city streets to park their equipment trucks. Perez went on the attack even further, accusing the production of the "propagation of pernicious racism" in casting Al Pacino, an Italian American, as a Cuban drug lord.[86] Although the production originally planned to film on location in Miami, the roadblocks initiated by Commissioner Perez ultimately forced the production to shut down. By September of 1982, with only a minimal amount of footage shot in South Florida, Bregman moved the production back to Los Angeles.[87]

Governor Graham and the FMPTA scrambled to find another part of Florida to accommodate *Scarface*, but the public relations campaign against *Scarface* had effectively run the production from the state. FMPTA member Marylee Lander, Miami-Dade's film and television coordinator in 1983, estimated that *Scarface*'s departure cost Dade's economy "at least $10 million," while Commissioner Perez claimed the film's relocation to California as "a victory for the people of Miami."[88] Although the production moved to Los

Angeles, the film's setting and story still exhibited the worst stereotypes associated with South Florida's "Cocaine Cowboys Era." On screen it was impossible for audiences to tell which scenes were filmed on location in Florida and which were shot in California. For example, the film's refugee camp sequence was set below the I-95 overpass in downtown Miami but was filmed beneath Los Angeles's I-5 overpass with no noticeable difference. When *Scarface* premiered in December 1983, Miami still received the bad publicity *and* lost the millions of dollars that would have been spent had the production been filmed on location.

Miami Becomes the "Hippest Hangout on Earth"

Scarface proved to be an important learning experience for both Miami-based film boosters and politicians alike. When producers Anthony Yerkovich and Michael Mann pitched an idea to NBC executives for a series that Mann described as "MTV Cops," they needed a setting that could adequately fit the bill. The proposed series would set out to package the two major pillars of Reaganomics—law and order and conspicuous consumption—into a metanarrative where the location would stand out as a character in its own right. The show's MTV-generation take on procedural cop dramas would need a sleek and sexy locale to match its aesthetic. Michael Mann's motto for the proposed series was said to be, "No earth tones!"[89] Mann hoped that the series would see "sienna, ochre, red and brown eliminated" in favor of "rose, lime, neon, aquamarine, turquoise and peach, [to create] the sensuous feel of pastel and fluorescent colors."[90]

Miami Beach's crumbling art deco architecture, combined with the emerald waterscapes and bright sun, fit Mann's color scheme perfectly. According to John Nicolella, who worked as production manager and director on *Miami Vice*, "Michael was in charge of the whole visual sense of the show, all this slick stuff—which car, what the clothes look like, the colors, the kind of film cutting."[91] In contrast, Anthony Yerkovich was drawn toward the narrative possibilities that the supposed seedy underbelly of Miami could offer to the show's plot. In his initial pitch to set the series in Miami, he invoked the notorious 1982 *Harper's Magazine* depiction of the city as an "American Casablanca."[92] The result was *Miami Vice* (1984–89).

While Mann and Yerkovich pondered whether *Miami Vice* should also be filmed on location in South Florida, local leaders appeared to be far more receptive to hearing the showrunner's pitch than they had with Martin Bregman and Brian DePalma during the production of *Scarface*. Even Commissioner Perez, who had by 1984 become vice-mayor of Miami, remained conspicu-

Figure 26. This NBC-TV ad from the October 13–19, 1984, *TV Guide Magazine* features Don Johnson as Sonny Crockett and Phillip Michael Thomas as Ricardo Tubbs. Initially pitched to the studio as "MTV Cops," *Miami Vice* (1984–89) helped turn South Florida from a "Paradise Lost" into "the hippest hangout on Earth."

ously silent, at least in the public record.[93] Whereas *Scarface* leaned into the worst excesses of Miami in the early 1980s, the show that Mann and Yerkovich promised would "recast a hyper-Miami as a principal character in their cops-versus-drug-lords melodrama."[94]

Concerns over how Miami would be portrayed on-screen went as far as city officials suggesting to producers that the word *Vice* be stricken from the series' title.[95] Author and journalist T. D. Allman observed that many of the show's local critics expressed concern that the real Miami was not accurately depicted on-screen. He remarked that in an ideological sense, "*Miami Vice* got the colors and the rhythms right, but it missed the main point: Miami wasn't just a cauldron of conflicting firepower. It was a cauldron of human possibility."[96] Nonetheless, Mann insisted on his vision, and despite the consternation of local politicians and pundits, production on the show was permitted to move forward. Rather than promoting an image of Miami comparable to Disney's portrayal of Orlando, local politicians feared that Miami's negative image would still be validated by a prime-time chronicle of drug wars, serial murders, shopping mall drug wars, and other assorted mayhem.[97]

Miami in the 1980s certainly had the endemic crime and economic crisis that filmmakers sought to depict a city in desperate need of law and order. The city also offered a fertile environment to extol the virtues of the pursuit of private wealth and conspicuous consumption. Once the political roadblocks against the show's production were lifted, Marylee Lander of the Miami-Dade Film Commission initiated a carefully coordinated public relations campaign to promise a beleaguered public that *Miami Vice* was "the show that could save Miami."[98] She then worked to secure the grounds of Greenwich Studios as the primary backlot for the series. According to Jeff Beal, a producer based at Greenwich Studios in the early 1980s, by the time the series moved in, the grounds had little more than "boarded up storefronts, abandoned buildings . . . *Miami Vice* saved the studio."[99]

With over $5 million spent on the pilot episode and an average of $1 million spent per episode, *Miami Vice* offered Miami a financial windfall that could both resurrect the city's film and television industry and be reinvested in revitalizing communities rocked by civil strife, a financial recession, and an unprecedented urban crime wave.[100] However, the Miami Chamber of Commerce initially winced at the way in which the series "glamorized the very real crime problems the area was suffering."[101] When the two-hour pilot for *Miami Vice* premiered in September 1984, introducing the iconic duo of Crockett and Tubbs, with Jan Hammer's iconic synthesized score, audiences was mesmerized. NBC executives knew they had a hit on their hands. In Miami, concerns over how the series would impact the city's fledgling reputation remained.[102] What they feared most was that the series would be "a bullet in the heart of what was left of the Beach's tourism industry."[103]

Even if *Miami Vice* was supposed to be the proverbial "bullet in the heart" of Miami Beach's Art Deco District, the neighborhood had already been bleeding out for quite some time. Between 1980 and 1984, the number of domestic tourists to South Florida declined from 6.7 million visitors to 5.3 million, while the number of international tourists plummeted by over 15 percent during the same period.[104] As resorts closed and the winter condos were sold off at bottom-dollar prices, the community was inundated with retirees. South Florida had by the early 1980s transformed from "America's Riviera" into "God's Waiting Room."[105] Ultimately, the city's Casablanca-like depiction in *Miami Vice* would almost overnight turn the city into the "capital of cool," a place that "oozed glitz and glamour."[106] By 1995, *Travel and Leisure* would dub the Miami Art Deco District the "hippest hangout on Earth."[107]

Despite initial concerns that *Miami Vice* would bring on another public image fiasco, the series instead provided a sanitized enough version of Miami to inspire its audience to book flights and hotel reservations to catch a glimpse of Michael Mann's vision of South Florida. In a flashback to the heyday of film productions in Jacksonville during the 1910s, the success of the *Miami Vice* aesthetic came as a result of close local cooperation. Mann and his location scouts are credited by *Miami Herald* reporter Andres Viglucci with inventing what he coined as the "*Miami Vice* Effect."[108] He praised the producer's "keen eye for buildings, places, and details that even native Miamians immediately picked up on," and that Mann "depicted those details with an obsessive care unusual for the typically fast-paced production of a television show."[109] Producers had little trouble finding a crowd. Local drama students, models, and musicians could regularly be found milling around in the background of a shoot, according to Fabio Arber, a production assistant and location manager for the show.[110] The production team also paid hotel and storefront owners to repaint their buildings in the Caribbean hues in order to match Michael Mann's pastel vision of South Florida.[111]

Even Miami's criminal element got swept up in the fervor over *Miami Vice*. Drug kingpin Juan Jonny Hernandez became the official cocaine supplier for the cast and crew, who had by then become a mainstay in the city's nightlife scene. In an interview with NPR's Roben Farzad, Hernandez recalled that the unnamed producer "didn't want them out in the mean streets of Miami, dealing with tabloid bound dealers and middlemen to score blow of questionable quality."[112] In exchange, Hernandez was given a two-episode arc on the show, where he depicted a stolen merchandise runner in "Made for Each Other" (1985) and Marco, a goon, in "The Fix" (1986).[113] On the other side of the law, Watergate lawyer G. Gordon Liddy played a retired right-wing renegade general illegally recruiting American mercenaries to fight alongside the Contras in Nicaragua. Then vice president George H. W. Bush was even asked to make a cameo on the show, however a last-minute scheduling conflict prevented him from doing so.[114]

Miami's rehabilitated image had far-reaching implications for the city's tourism and entertainment sector. As tourists came to Miami to see the exotic splendor of the series' locations, businesses invested more and more in renovating South Beach, and city leaders increased their vigilance toward law enforcement.[115] Tours would assemble wherever the crew filmed that day, drawn by the cameras, the lights, and the excitement, and tourists strained to catch a glimpse of the stars. Visitors on tour buses no longer asked about the area's murder rate but instead asked where Don Johnson and Philip Michael Thomas lived.[116] They would also ask where in Miami shows like *The Golden Girls* (1985–92) and *Empty Nest* (1988–95) were shot, not realizing that although these series were set in Florida, they were filmed on soundstages in California.

Miami's transformation became a case of life imitating art as city officials and tourism officials set out to take advantage of the new image of *Miami Vice* and run with it.[117] As prime-time entertainment, *Miami Vice* created a juxta-

Figure 27. "Hollywood Weather without Hollywood Overhead," 1986. Under Governor Bob Graham, Florida became the third-largest motion picture producer in the United States, behind only California and New York. With Los Angeles in their crosshairs, film offices affiliated with the Florida Motion Picture and Television Association encouraged film and television productions to relocate to the state. Courtesy of State Archives of Florida, Florida Memory.

position between criminality and order, combined with grit and glamour.[118] Such contrasts would become a common thread found in the films and television programs that followed *Miami Vice*. When the final season of the series wrapped in 1989, South Florida's reputation in the tourism and entertainment sectors was drastically transformed. By the 1990s, *Miami Vice* had effectively helped to revitalize South Florida, and in the process reinvented the region in the minds of Americans, suggesting fresh, new possibilities for filming.[119] However, a string of short-lived shows like *The 100 Lives of Black Jack Savage* (1991), *Grapevine* (1992), and *South Beach* (1993) all failed to repeat the success of *Miami Vice*.

In the fourteen years between 1995 and 2009, visitors to Miami Beach spent a total of $15 billion on food, drinks, and lodging, while South Beach accounted for nearly 75 percent of tourism dollars spent in the city.[120] After the cancellation of several programs shot at Greenwich Studios, regional production companies scattered across Florida. The completion of soundstages at Disney-MGM and Universal Studios in 1989 and 1990 triggered a push to bring major film and television productions to the Orlando metro area. With the advertised statement, "Hollywood weather without the Hollywood overhead," civic organizers sought to take advantage of a further fracturing of the American motion picture industry to try to create a "Hollywood East" in Central Florida.[121]

"This Doesn't Look Like the Welcome Wagon": Independent Filmmaking in Florida

It is after midnight and the streets of downtown Orlando are empty as a white 1981 Plymouth TC3 rolls down Orange Avenue. Unbeknownst to the drivers, they are being followed. As the Plymouth turns onto Church Street, the road is blocked by an assemblage of Jeeps, trucks, and convertibles with thugs wielding bats and metal pipes. Inside the white Plymouth are students from University of Central Florida who are members of a rock-and-roll band called Dragon Sound, and also happen to be blackbelts in Taekwondo. The thugs are friends of a rival band intent on revenge for losing their coveted place as headliners at a popular local nightclub. One band member remarks, "This doesn't look like the welcome wagon." Tensions grow as the Plymouth is surrounded. One thug approaches them and says, "Have some beer!" as he proceeds to pour beer over the car and drag one of the band members out into the street. Then all hell breaks loose. Against the odds, the five members of Dragon Sound uses their martial arts expertise to fight off over two dozen weapon-wielding goons. As Church Street erupts into chaos, the fighting spills out into the rest of downtown Orlando. At the end of the scene, the hoodlums are beaten back, and Dragon Sound wins the night.

This was among many memorable moments from the cult movie *Miami Connection* (1987). The film's premise involves Dragon Sound's efforts to prevent a motorcycle-riding gang of drug-dealing ninjas from invading Orlando and turning the city into "another Miami." Part martial arts film, part action-musical, *Miami Connection* contained several musical montages with lyrics that sum up the plot perfectly: "Against the ninja . . . evil in their eyes. We will stop the senseless killing . . . stop the evil ways."[122]

The martial arts battle outside Orlando's Church Street unknowingly created a scene reminiscent of James Durkin's *The Clarion* (1916), which included a mock riot in Jacksonville's LaVilla neighborhood. Like Jacksonville during the 1910s, the demands of a large-scale crowd scene in downtown Orlando for a relatively low-budget production depended on a passionate community effort. Originally called *Tae-Kwon-Do,* the film was later renamed *Miami Connection*. It was produced by Korean immigrant Yong Kun Kim, who also starred in the film.[123] Kim had settled in Orlando in 1978 and opened his first Taekwondo studio on Colonial Drive. Kim's ten-student school quickly expanded through his advertising efforts. Denise Smith of the *Orlando Sentinel* remarked, "Competitors say that Kim's marketing has made Taekwondo somewhat of a household word in Central Florida and that the nine schools bearing his name have become kind of a McDonald's of Taekwondo."[124]

Like fellow Orlando-based filmmaker R. John Hugh, Y. K. Kim saw *Miami Connection* as a love letter to the city that had become his adopted home. Raising over $1 million from nearly 1,200 local friends and students—many of whom worked as cast and crew on the film—while risking his Taekwondo franchise as collateral, Kim teamed up with director Richard Park, who pitched the idea for a feature film after seeing Kim on a South Korean talk show.[125] When the first cut of the film screened in late 1986, Kim and Park broke ties over its disastrous reception. According to Kim, when he saw the original version of *Miami Connection,* "the movie turned his stomach" with "too much violence, a depressing plot, and jumbled editing."[126] He used the rest of his savings to buy out Park's share of the film. After reading "eight books on moviemaking," Kim spent the following months reediting the film and dubbing new dialogue along with shooting a new ending. He then tried to sell the rights to film distributors, who according to Kim responded, "This is trash. Don't waste your time."[127] When Kim spent the last of his savings to have *Miami Connection* reviewed for consideration at the 1987 Cannes Film Festival, the response from the screening committee was, "It isn't a movie."[128]

Y. K. Kim persisted, and although he was unable to secure a national distributor, he did connect with Will Henley, an advertising director at the Clark Film Company, based in Jacksonville, who promised *Miami Connection* "would hit most major U.S. cities by Christmas [1988]."[129] In August 1988, Kim's film premiered to a 650-person packed audience at the Plaza Theater in Orlando. Despite an enthusiastic local premiere, once *Miami Connection* expanded to seven theaters across Orlando, the film received a lackluster response from moviegoers who were not immediate friends or family.

Although *Miami Connection* quickly cycled out of theaters, Kim seemed to take the setback in stride. He remarked to the *Orlando Sentinel*, "I know I lost money in the movie, but I do not regret it at all."[130] In time, he lamented that his film failed to put Orlando on the map. In a 2012 interview with *Entertainment Weekly*, he shared that he felt he had let down his students and his adopted city: "My students dedicated themselves to this movie so much. The sheriff's department, the University of [Central] Florida—they support[ed] me so well. I did not lift up the town. It's terrible and terrible. That is what I have to pay back until I [die]."[131]

Decades after *Miami Connection* cycled out of theaters, Y. K. Kim's vision would finally be vindicated. In June 2009, Zack Carlson, a programmer for the Austin-based Alamo Drafthouse, came across a copy of the film on eBay. In April 2010, he screened the first twenty minutes of the film as part of Drafthouse's "Reel One Party" to a small audience free of charge in order to gauge audience response. The word of mouth around just the first twenty minutes was enough that when the film was added to Drafthouse's exploitation series the following month, it played to a sold-out house. Carlson knew he had a hit on his hands.[132] He screened *Miami Connection* to Evan Husney, the creative director for Drafthouse's distribution, who then reached out to Y. K. Kim to discuss a potential rerelease. Kim initially hung up on Husney and dodged his calls for months, believing it all to be a cruel joke. After some cajoling, Kim agreed to a deal that would give his film the national distribution he had long sought.

The rediscovery of *Miami Connection* has tapped into a trend that has emerged since the 2010s toward screening notorious cult titles such as *The Room* (2003) and *Birdemic: Shock and Terror* (2010). According to Husney, "Some people like to refer to films like *The Room* as so-bad-it's-awesome. I think *Miami Connection* fits the category of so-good-it's-awesome."[133] Since its resurgence in the 2010s, *Miami Connection* has achieved a cult status and has been featured at midnight screenings nationwide. Film critics have also reevaluated the film as an ahead-of-its-time commentary on the 1980s action genre that was simply out of step with its own generation. In a 2022 retrospective, film critic Douglas Laman of *Collider* provides an explanation of *Miami Connection*'s appeal for millennial audiences:

> The erratic and sprawling style of this story didn't quite fit in an era of compact narratives like *The Terminator* [1984]. But in the modern world of action films that jump everywhere imaginable, such as in *Everything Everywhere All at Once* [2022], *Miami Connection* feels right at home. Without realizing it, Y. K. Kim and company made a shlocky action movie tailor-made for the sensibilities of the ADD generation.[134]

The initial critical and financial failure of *Miami Connection* is an example of the challenges and high stakes Florida's independent filmmakers would face in their bids to break into the motion picture industry. Despite Governor Graham's efforts to accommodate film and television productions throughout the state, local independent filmmakers were often left behind. In a time when a low-budget production like *Miami Connection* would cost between $1 and $5 million, very few filmmakers were daring or financially secure enough to risk their personal savings on making films. Independent filmmaking in Florida in the 1980s needed to find a careful balance between a strong professional reputation and individual financial finesse as an essential survival factor. Since Florida bankers had little experience at judging whether a project would yield a return on investment, most independent filmmakers were forced to turn to outside investors for their projects.[135]

The story behind the financing of Bob Clark's sex comedy *Porky's* (1981) is a great example of the type of challenges Florida independents had to face in funding their films. Set in the fictional town of Angel Beach, Florida, the movie was inspired by Clark's experiences as a student at Fort Lauderdale High School and a bar called "Porky's Hideaway" in Oakland Park. Clark, who had moved to Toronto, needed to turn to financing from his Canadian contacts to get *Porky's* made.[136] Even with a lukewarm critical reception, the movie became a surprise sleeper hit, earning $100 million in box-office receipts, becoming one of the highest-grossing Canadian-produced films of all time. Two sequels, *Porky's II: The Next Day* (1983) and *Porky's Revenge* (1985), were also poorly received by critics but still turned a profit and laid the template for raunchy teen comedies for decades to come.[137] *Porky's* financial success was an exception to an otherwise difficult period for independent filmmakers in Florida. It should be noted, however, that the film would not have even been made without the nearly $5 million budget Bob Clark was able to raise from his connections in the Canadian film industry.[138]

Another notable independent filmmaker who took advantage of Florida as a backdrop was Jim Jarmusch. His breakthrough film, *Stranger Than Paradise* (1984), was an absurdist comedy shot on a $125,000 budget, with nearly a third of the film's runtime taking place in Melbourne Beach. Jarmusch, who at the time was a recent graduate of the NYU Film School, used his connections with an ailing Nicholas Ray (his thesis advisor at NYU) and German New Wave director Wim Wenders (for whom he worked as an assistant) to get his film made first as a short and, later, as a feature. Unlike Y. K. Kim's *Miami Connection*, Jim Jarmusch's *Stranger Than Paradise* was accepted by the Cannes screening committee and premiered to overwhelming critical acclaim, winning the Caméra d'Or and launching his career as a prolific independent filmmaker.[139] *Stranger Than Paradise* has since appeared near the top of polls of the greatest independent films of all time, been placed on the National Film Registry by the Library of Congress, and even ranked as one of legendary Japanese filmmaker Akira Kurosawa's top 100 favorite films.[140] Jay Boyar of the *Orlando Sentinel* wrote, "Of the feature films that contain substantial Central Florida footage, [*Stranger Than Paradise* was] the finest one I've seen."[141]

Most film and television shows made in Florida in the 1980s and 1990s were financed by out-of-state (or out-of-country) investors, who hired their own crews from outside of Florida. Another challenge was that Florida lacked a postproduction facility that could service high-profile feature films or primetime programs. As was the case for most Florida-filmed productions during the first half of the twentieth century, the movies made in Florida during the 1980s had to be sent for processing and editing in either New York or California. Another challenge facing Florida's motion picture industry was a lack of homegrown talent. As Richard Alan Nelson remarked in his overview of the Florida film industry in the early 1990s, "To move forward, Florida needed to continue solidifying its intrastate pool of producers, directors, writers, editors, and other technical support workers. Many filmmakers are already making a living in-state, but greater attention must be paid to building up the industry within Florida in addition to efforts made to attract out-of-state producers."[142]

Despite such production concerns, there were some notable exceptions. Paul Newman, for example, had such a positive experience during his time working on *Absence of Malice* (1981) in Miami that when he set out to direct *Harry & Son* (1983), he made sure to hire an entirely Florida-based crew. Newman later wrote to Governor Graham complimenting the quality of the crew and assistance provided by the Miami-Dade Film Commission, remarking, "The quality of actors which we interviewed in Florida was equal to that we found in Los Angeles and New York."[143] Such positive word of mouth within industry circles soon encouraged more producers to point their cameras toward Florida.

In 1983, director Ron Howard hired former crew members from Ivan Tors and Ricou Browning's Underwater Productions to assist in filming the most challenging water scenes filmed for the Tom Hanks–Daryl Hannah mermaid comedy *Splash* (1984).[144] Although *Splash* was mostly filmed in New York, Los Angeles, and The Bahamas, the expertise demonstrated by the primarily Florida-based crew during the underwater filmmaking and at-sea shoots made an impression on both Howard and executives at Disney's newly created subsidiary Touchstone Pictures.[145] The following year, when Ron Howard was hired to replace Robert Zemeckis as director for *Cocoon* (1985), he again turned to his Florida connections. Laura Kitzmiller, representative for the FMPTB, met with Howard and producers Richard and Lili Zanuck and provided them with a tour of the greater St. Petersburg area. The tour paid off, and the nearly $20 million production set up in St. Petersburg, giving the city its greatest boost in star power since Buster Keaton's brief stay in 1933.[146]

In the summer of 1984, auditions were held at the Hilton Hotel in St. Petersburg for local talent to appear on the screen along with legendary Hollywood stars Don Ameche, Jack Gifford, Hume Cronyn, Jessica Tandy, Maureen Stapleton, and Gwen Verdon as nursing home residents who are revitalized by a swimming pool in a deserted mansion, with some extraterrestrial help. The production was in full swing between September and December, with Laura Kitzmiller and the St. Petersburg/Clearwater Film Commission working tirelessly to ensure a seamless shoot.[147] Like Trenton Collins and Fred Blair's efforts to sell Florida to Hollywood studios in the 1930s, Kitzmiller made sure the production was at the FMPTB's beck and call.

Cocoon went on to become one of the top-grossing films of 1985, yet Ron Howard did not return to direct the sequel. Regardless, producers Richard and Lili Zanuck opted to return to Florida for the sequel, *Cocoon II: The Return* (1988). Although the sequel was also set in St. Petersburg, by 1988, the buildup of soundstages and facilities in Miami made it easier for Miami-based location manager Mary Morgan to have "South Florida play the role of West Florida."[148] Morgan's pitch to use Coral Gables instead of St. Petersburg represented a broader trend toward the consolidation of Florida's film industry in Miami-Dade County. Morgan assured the Zanucks, "It is very easy to find the Florida 'look' and at the same time not say 'Miami.' We [don't] want the 'Vice' look."[149]

In the mid-1980s, the film and television industry of South Florida reached a pivotal crossroads. The FMPTB cautioned against the construction of facilities that would directly compete with New York and California (and, to a lesser extent, Georgia and Texas). While local boosters had hoped the construction of fully equipped processing labs and larger soundstages would cement Florida's place as a "third coast" in the American motion picture industry, industry insiders "considered the independent studio idea an obsolete white elephant."[150] According to Don Gold, who had worked as a location scout for the original *Hawaii Five-O* (1968–80) and later became a production manager at Greenwich Studios, "When you come to Miami, you don't come to shoot on a soundstage, you come to shoot the city. The city is the third star of the show."[151] Central Florida faced its own challenges in attracting big-budget productions during the 1980s. When *Indiana Jones and the Temple of Doom* (1984) came to Ocala to film a scene where Harrison Ford falls into an alligator-filled swamp, Lucasfilm made no use of nearby soundstages in Florida. Instead, they filmed the scene they needed to shoot and immediately left.[152]

Rather than investing in physical infrastructure, Bob Graham sponsored a contest to encourage local screenwriters to tell Florida-focused stories. In November 1984, Laura Kitzmiller announced the first Governor's Screenwriters Competition, with categories for drama, comedy, and novelettes that had at least 75 percent of their setting in Florida. The six winners would receive a $500 prize and a free trip to Los Angeles for a "pitch" meeting with Hollywood executives. In the press release for the contest, Governor Graham explained, "We want to foster the creative foundation of a Florida film production industry as we continue to grow in the motion picture and television field."[153] In the end, though, none of the contest winners were able to make headway in their pitch meetings with studio executives.

If Florida stories on film were to be told by actual Floridians, local filmmakers in the state had to take matters into their own hands. In 1983, University of Miami Film School graduates George Fernandez and David Nutter approached William Grefé, president of Greenwich Studios, for help producing a screenplay that Fernandez had adapted from his play *Vietnam Trilogy*. With Grefé's support, the twenty-four-year-old filmmakers were raised just shy of $1 million and took a risk on casting a then unknown actor named Don Johnson as the lead.[154]

By the time *Cease Fire* (1985) premiered, Don Johnson had since become a household name playing Sonny Crockett in *Miami Vice*. In fact, the early rushes from *Cease Fire* helped Johnson land the starring role as Crockett in *Miami Vice*.[155] Although *Cease Fire* only had a limited run and box-office receipts, it was able to recoup expenses by preselling the rights to the film following the positive reception to its screening at the Cannes Film Festival.[156] To this day, the film is praised by Vietnam veterans' groups for its portrayal of PTSD and earnest depiction of wartime trauma. Lower-budget films like *Cease Fire* may not have brought much in the way of local spending, but this movie represented an important step toward fostering an increasingly impressive array of homegrown talent in Florida.

Building on the positive reception and financial return surrounding *Cease Fire*, the FMPTB teamed up with the South Florida Film and Tape Producers Association (SFFTPA) to begin hosting seminars on film and videocassette investment opportunities for local investors willing to support local filmmakers. The FMPTB expanded its efforts to foster homegrown talent further by successfully appealing to the state legislature for funds to support film programs at Florida State University, Valencia College, and the University of Central Florida. The FMPTB's advisory council coordinated with Dr. Donald Ungurait, who appealed to the legislature to create an on-the-job-training program that would offer a ten-week apprenticeship for FSU communications students interested in pursuing a career in film.[157] These efforts paid off as the on-the-job apprenticeships often transitioned into full-time industry jobs. The program's success helped support FSU's case to the legislature in 1989 for creating the first film school at a public university in Florida, with Ungurait as its founding dean.[158]

Even before the creation of FSU's College of Motion Picture Arts in 1989, the university's film department was already highly regarded in industry circles. In 1974, Florida native Victor Nuñez, a one-time program director for WFSU-TV—the home of *Miss Nancy's Store* (see chapter 4)—and a professor in FSU's film department, formed his own independent film company. For his first feature, *Gal Young 'Un* (1979), he bought the rights to adapt an eponymous 1932 short story by Marjorie Kinnan Rawlings set during the Prohibition era. Over the next four years, he raised $94,000, with over half the film's budget received from the National Endowment for the Arts and the Florida Fine Arts Council, and the other half from Florida-based investors.[159] Although Nuñez's *Gal Young 'Un* did not receive national distribution, it had an incredibly successful run on the film festival circuit, winning numerous awards and receiving a gross revenue of $500,000 from awards and roadshow screenings.[160]

Nuñez leveraged the critical acclaim and financial success of *Gal Young 'Un* to raise over $1 million to produce *A Flash of Green* (1983), starring Ed Harris in one his earliest lead roles. Nuñez's subsequent films in the 1990s, *Ruby in Paradise* (1993) and *Ulee's Gold* (1997), were also critically acclaimed and, according to film critic Emmanuel Levy, "helped shape regional cinema within the independent movement."[161] Nuñez, for his part, rejects the "regional filmmaker" label, which he considers as "just dumb," and instead argues that his films are simply a way of expressing place. In a 2021 interview with *Film Inquiry*, he elaborates: "So, I figured why not be in film what the writers I've read have done in literature. I hated the term 'regional [filmmaker],' but I was based in a place. One of the things I embraced was this Italian neorealist thing in which it's not just character and story, it's place. You get an energy there that you can't get elsewhere."[162]

By the 1990s, Victor Nuñez's development of unique and incredibly personal place-based films offers a sublime example of Florida-based filmmakers succeeding in dissipating any negative critical associations attached to films labeled "made in Florida." Victor Nuñez's filmography help to demonstrate how even films made on a shoestring budget could play a key role in fostering a flourishing community of local talent. According to Nuñez, "Too much of this effort is wasted on promoting Hollywood-style 'big star' deal making."[163]

Orlando Becomes the "Movieland of the South"

In the mid-1980s, Central Florida's local filmmaking legend, R. John Hugh, continued to hold onto his hope to build a studio city in Winter Park. In the 1960s and 1970s, following the successful run of *Johnny Tiger* (1966), Hugh reveled in his status as a minor local celebrity in the metro Orlando area, where he continued to produce low-budget films such as *Throw out the Anchor* (1974) and *The Meal* (1975). Unlike *Yellowneck*, which won second place at the Venice Film Festival, Hugh's late-career films were not greeted with the same critical acclaim. Local film critics still found it hard to be too rough on Hugh though. In a rectification to his earlier review of Hugh's *The Meal*, Charles Reese, film critic for the *Orlando Sentinel* made sure to give his readers the following disclaimer:

> So, to clear the air, it was *The Meal,* not John Hugh I didn't like . . . Furthermore, Hugh has worked long and hard to bring more of the movie industry to Florida and if his efforts, and those of others, had been supported by some of the short-sighted politicians, they probably would have been successful . . . Everyone from Cecil DeMille on down, has had their *Meal.* I won't let that stop me from seeing Hugh's new movie when it comes to town and I hope it won't deter you.[164]

During his tenure as president of the FMPTA, Hugh went to great lengths to lay the foundations for Florida's movie boom in the late 1970s and early 1980s. Yet, his dream of turning Central Florida into "Hollywood East" remained out of his grasp. Between 1982 and 1983, Hugh worked on developing two feature films, *The Rhino Horn Factor* and *The Neilson Window,* making several trips to Los Angeles to raise funds. Instead of shooting at his usual haunts in Winter Park and Longwood, Hugh hoped gain support to set up a studio in DeLand, which had hosted the cast and crew of *Ghost Story* (1981) at Stetson University. *Ghost Story* was a modest financial success and is best known for being one of the final feature film performances for Fred Astaire and Douglas Fairbanks Jr. R. John Hugh, who had plenty of experience in working with actors in the twilight of their careers, coordinated with Bob Vail of the DeLand Area Chamber of Commerce to bring additional productions to the city.[165]

In February 1983, it appears that filming for *The Rhino Horn Factor* may have been completed, but it is unclear whether the film ever was screened to an audience. Later that year, Hugh prepared for production on *The Neilson Window*, explaining that production had been interrupted by a "false start with some Canadians" but expressing his confidence that "this one would go before cameras soon."[166] In what would be his final interview with the *Orlando Sentinel*, Hugh addressed rumors that Universal Studios would build a studio in Central Florida and make it so "big budget films shot in Florida are no longer a novelty."[167]

R. John Hugh also expressed his hope that his next film would allow him to restore the former Shamrock Studios property to its former glory with a $5 million investment from either Universal Studios or "any other financial backer who will surely follow in setting up operations in Orlando" to make "Central Florida Hollywood East."[168] He followed this statement by remarking on the Sisyphean task of keeping Florida in front of the camera: "What I've been able to market is a track record and stability. I've been here for years, I've done nine pictures, and I'm going to be here tomorrow and hopefully making more and more films. Besides, if Orlando becomes Hollywood East and Reubin Askew is elected President, we could displace California as the state that contributes the most to the nation's fantasy supply."[169]

Reubin Askew did not become president, and R. John Hugh did not live long enough to see the potential that Disney-MGM and Universal Studios would bring to Central Florida's motion picture industry. Hugh's legacy as a champion for Central Florida's film industry and as the first president of the FMPTA was commemorated by its metro Orlando chapter with the R. John Hugh Award, bestowed most recently in 2011.[170]

In 1991, R. John Hugh's decades-long campaign to bring Florida into the international film festival circuit came to fruition. That April, two University of Central Florida graduates, Tim Grayson and Richard Halpern, hosted the first Orlando International Film Festival (OIFF), which over ten days hosted more than 4,300 moviegoers at Orlando's Colonial Promenade and Fashion Square 6 Theaters.[171] As a tribute to Hugh, the festival hosted a special feature screen ing of a recently restored *A Crowd for Lisette* (1961), which had languished "in a closet for twenty-two years."[172] The event was hosted by Richard Owens of the Orlando Opera, who had recovered the film from John Hickman, a local investor who received the only remaining negative of the film to settle a debt Hugh owed to him. After acquiring the distribution rights from Hickman, Owens's screening brought many of Hugh's former cast and crew, along with dozens of extras who had worked on the film, to the OIFF to reminisce.[173]

In the spirit of Hugh's high hopes in supporting his fellow Florida filmmakers, the OIFF also featured several independently made Central Florida films, including the Florida premiere of a sci-fi pulp sequel that Hugh would certainly have approved of being billed alongside: Lloyd Kaufman's *Nuke 'Em High* Part 2: *Subhumanoid Meltdown* (1991).[174] The ten-day event also featured screenwriting and film-financing seminars, along with producer tips on how local filmmakers could break into the business, a concept that he and Ricou Browning had requested the Florida Council of 100 consider as early as November 1968.[175] Even though the first OIFF failed to turn a profit, the event was still considered a win for Orlando film boosters.

The OIFF was featured in multiple articles in *Variety* and the *Hollywood Reporter*, as well as a special report that aired on E! Entertainment Television. Tim Grayson remarked to the *Orlando Sentinel*, "I think all the [movie] distributors are focusing on Orlando this week. I just don't think that's happened before."[176] Grayson and Halpern hoped to leverage the industry publicity that came with the OIFF for a second festival, but as of October 1991, they still had over $10,000 in debt that had lingered from the first festival. Inspired by the community response to the OIFF, Philip and Sigrid Tiedtke, the owners of the Enzian Theater in Maitland, who hosted extended runs of several OIFF films after the festival, announced plans to raise over $400,000 for their own festival in Central Florida "celebrating the modern arts to help its image nationally."[177] Grayson volunteered to assist the Tiedtkes in promoting the new festival and finding sponsors, while a blindsided Richard Halpern, unaware that his partner was working with the Tiedtkes, suggested a merger of the two festivals.[178]

In June 1992, with Grayson and Halpern as promoters, the Tiedtkes moved forward with hosting the first Florida Film Festival at the Enzian Theater. The ten-day event attracted over 10,000 visitors with an impressive list of celebrities in attendance. Guests for the first Florida Film Festival included directors Oliver Stone and Robert Wise, along with actors David Ogden Stiers, Drew Barrymore, and Shannen Doherty.[179] With the theme "Film as Art," the Florida Film Festival hosted twenty-three feature films, along with a special tribute to French New Wave director François Truffaut, and a special showcase of underground and student films from locally based Central Florida filmmakers.[180]

The Florida Film Festival has since not only become an important cultural event in the Orlando metro area but has grown into a major Oscar-qualifying festival and an annual showcase for independent and international films. The resurrection of R. John Hugh's *A Crowd for Lisette* in the 1990s is a poignant illustration of the array of hidden talent and broad audience appeal that independent Florida filmmakers offered audiences in the late twentieth century. The sheer love of storytelling that filmmakers like R. John Hugh can share with their small but loyal local followers has a far-reaching legacy.

By 1991, roughly half of all films and television shows made in Florida were at least partially staffed by local technicians, a development that can be traced back to the state's independent film movement in the 1980s. An example of the legacy of fostering Florida's film community can be seen in the international phenomenon *The Blair Witch Project* (1999), which was produced by two UCF film school graduates, Daniel Myrick and Eduardo Sanchez, and generated over $250 million in box-office receipts. While more recently, in 2017, Miami native and FSU Film School alumnus Barry Jenkins's *Moonlight* (2016) brought him the distinction of being the first Florida filmmaker to take home the Academy Award for Best Picture.

"It's Not Hollywood East, It's Toronto South"

The opening of Disney-MGM and Universal Studios in Orlando in 1989 and 1990, respectively, would not have been possible without the groundwork laid out by independent filmmakers in Florida during the 1980s. As the soundstages went up at Disney and Universal in Orlando, movie boosters across the metro Orlando area worked to appeal to as many producers as possible to bring their films and TV shows to the city. By the mid-1990s, Central Florida's dream of becoming "Hollywood East" led to the state's most serious challenge yet to California's hegemony over the American motion picture industry. Yet, in the decades since the closure of Disney-MGM and Nickelodeon Studios, Orlandoans have been left to wonder, what could have been? Like with Jacksonville's moment in the sun as the "World's Winter Film Capital" during the 1910s, Orlando's moment as "Hollywood East" in the 1990s created a boomtown atmosphere that spread throughout the city. The key difference was that while Jacksonville's film industry was a victim of the regressive policies of local politicians like Governor Sidney Catts and Jacksonville mayor

John Martin, Orlando's motion picture industry was instead undermined by its own ambition.

The 1990s was a decade of unprecedented cooperation in Florida between producers, city leaders, the state legislature, and the governor's office. After Bob Graham concluded his second term in 1987, he continued to champion Florida's film industry during his three consecutive terms in the United States Senate between 1987 and 2005. His successors in the governor's mansion—Bob Martinez (1987–91), a Republican, and Lawton Chiles (1991–98), a Democrat—worked diligently to build on the goodwill that Governor Graham had established with the motion picture industry. In Orlando, Mayors Bill Fredrick (1981–92) a Democrat, and Glenda Hood (1992–2003) a Republican, understood and applied the bipartisan benefits of movie boosterism—along with the enormous economic profits that film and television productions could bring.

The closure of the soundstages at Disney-MGM and Universal Studios in the early 2000s has been a driving factor behind the perceived "failure" of Orlando's bid to become "Hollywood East." Yet, the notion that Orlando "failed" to support a permanent motion picture industry severely discredits the impressive effort carried out by local movie boosters and filmmakers to turn Central Florida into an affordable regional production center. Rather than being seen as a lost opportunity or cautionary tale, Orlando's efforts to become "Hollywood East" can be viewed as an excellent example of how community organizing and local promotion helped Florida's statewide motion picture industry to achieve its greatest heights.

As early as 1989, insiders in the motion picture industry warned that Orlando's production studios would eventually fail if they attempted to go directly head-to-head against major Hollywood studios. Nina Easton of the *Los Angeles Times* observed, "Just as it would be an exaggeration to call Orlando the next Hollywood, it would be shortsighted to underestimate Orlando's threat to film and TV business in Hollywood and elsewhere."[181] The best pathway for success for Orlando would have been to "lure away some of New York's lucrative TV commercial business; and it will become a warm-weather alternative to Canada, where producers have flocked in recent years to take advantage of cheaper labor costs and a weak Canadian dollar."[182] Ted Kaye, the vice president of Disney's Orlando studio operations, seemed to concur: "For the foreseeable future, Orlando will develop into a regional production center. It's not Hollywood East, it's Toronto South."[183]

Orlando's emergence as a regional production powerhouse in the 1990s offers a fascinating snapshot of the wider disruptions that took place throughout the global film industry at the turn of the twenty-first century. The studios that popped up along the I-4 corridor were the sum of the ongoing transformation of Central Florida that had occurred since the opening of Walt Disney World in 1971. In the twenty years since the park's opening, Central Florida experienced a dramatic demographic and economic change. Before the arrival of Disney, the Orlando metro area was known as the "Cow Capital of Florida," with over 40,000 more cows than people in Osceola County's 1970 census.[184] The city that sprouted out of the tourism boom that followed the opening of Disney World simply amplified preexisting trends of industrial growth and development that had been taking place across Central Florida since the end of the Second World War.

The pre–World War II economy in Central Florida was closely tied to citrus and cattle. This started to change when three major military bases—Pinecastle, Orlando Air Base, and Sanford Naval Air Station—also brought new settlement and infrastructure to the region.[185] By the time of Orlando's Centenary in 1977, local historian Eve Bacon considered Disney World as "the single largest factor that accelerated the city's economic development beyond Florida's own rapid pace."[186] In the two decades following Disney's opening, the regional population of the four-county region of Lake, Orange, Osceola, and Seminole Counties tripled from just over a half million in 1970 to over 1.5 million in 1999.[187] It was during this period of accelerated growth that Central Florida managed to capture the attention and imaginations of Florida film boosters and industry workers eager to challenge Hollywood's consolidated control over the motion picture industry.

The first step toward Orlando's rise as a regional production center came in 1982 with the opening of Disney's long-delayed EPCOT (Experimental Prototype Community of Tomorrow) theme park. After years of delays, the project had morphed considerably from Walt Disney's original vision. Indecision by Disney Imagineers on how to effectively create both a technology showcase and an imitation of a world's fairground led to an awkward combination of both, turning the new park into what was then the largest construction project on earth.[188] As EPCOT's original budget of $400 million tripled into $1.2 billion, the Disney corporation subsidized the added cost by allowing sponsored attractions from companies such as General Motors and AT&T in one section, and pavilions offering a taste of different cultures, underwritten by foreign governments, in another.[189] Company vice chairman and senior executive director Roy E. Disney (son of Roy O. Disney) was so unnerved at the cost of EPCOT that he refused to come to the opening ceremonies.[190] After EPCOT opened, attendance at Disney World surged from 12.6 million to 22.7 million in the new attraction's first year of operation.[191] Despite the initial excitement, overall attendance at Disney parks dropped by 10 percent the following year.[192]

In 1983, Disney was in dire financial straits, as the company's moment of weakness created a moment of opportunity for its competitors. One of Disney's longest-standing rivals quickly sensed blood in the water and began a survey on where to build a Florida amusement park. Since 1964, Universal Studios Hollywood had been in competition with Disneyland in California as Los Angeles's cornerstone tourist attraction. Universal hired research economist Harrison "Buzz" Price, who had had also helped Disney choose both Anaheim and Orlando as the location of its American parks, to conduct a feasibility study on the financial potential of a new studio tour. The backlot tour provided by Universal's "glamour trains" soon morphed into a full-fledged amusement park. Amid Disney's shake-up in 1983, Governor Graham met with MCA/Universal executives during one of his visits to Los Angeles and sparked a veritable arms race between Disney and Universal. Although Governor Graham's proposed "Universal City, Florida" did not immediately bear fruit, the concept of a movie-inspired theme park that could compete against Disney's Magic Kingdom and EPCOT would indeed take hold.[193]

The Orange County Commissioners office followed up on Graham's lead and outlined plans with MCA/Universal executives to build a 423-acre, $600 million theme park that would double as a film studio. Initially the talks concentrated on building a so-called Universal City in Florida.[194] At first this idea seemed almost as pie-in-the-sky as Governor Carlton's attempt to build a second Paramount Studios in Tampa during the 1930s (see chapter 3). A survey conducted by Buzz Price concluded that tourists would not visit Orlando "just to visit a new movie studio tour," and although parkgoers might spend less time at Disney's attractions, they "would not bypass either in favor of another park."[195] For their part, Disney officials were even more dismissive of the proposed Universal Studios Florida, calling the idea "an elaborate spin-off of the Hollywood tour Universal offers at its California studios."[196] Although talks over the Universal theme park stalled, it was quite clear that Disney had become increasingly nervous.

To strengthen Disney's ties to Florida, CEO Ron Miller coordinated a $200 million buyout of the Boca Raton–based Arvida Corporation in 1984.[197] After the Arvida-Disney merger, Miller next announced his plans to redirect their focus toward film and television, announcing the creation of the Disney Channel and the establishment of Touchstone Films (later Touchstone Pictures), a feature film outlet that would produce films that had more mature themes targeted to adult audiences.[198] Even with this change in direction for the company, the subsequent fallout from EPCOT's overrun costs and low ticket returns, combined with the high production costs that both the Disney Channel and Touchstone demanded, caused Roy E. Disney to force Ron Miller to step down as CEO. Roy Disney then appointed Michael Eisner as Miller's replacement.[199]

In March 1984, Touchstone's first film, *Splash,* proved a box-office smash and signaled a string of hits for the newly formed studio. In January 1985, the Disney Channel announced it had acquired over two million subscribers as it broke into the black. With a steady source of revenue from Disney's overhauled film and television division, there was an added incentive to produce even more content. Although talks between Orange County and MCA/Universal had since withered, Michael Eisner saw an opportunity to put the nail in the coffin of Universal Studios' plans for Orlando once and for all. In April 1985, Eisner announced plans to build a $300 million Hollywood-style theme park in partnership with MGM Studios. A stipulation in the partnership required a licensing agreement that allowed Disney to utilize characters and scenes from MGM and United Artist films. The partnership also called for "a rendered environmental homage to the art deco/art moderne architecture of Hollywood in the 1930s," in a "park [that] presents a mixture of performances, rides, tours, films, and demonstrations of movie technology and its by-products."[200]

Disney broke ground on Disney-MGM Studios in 1986, offering a studio tour modeled after Universal's, with plans to build four soundstages, an animation building, a backlot of sets and streets, a theater for live game shows, wardrobe rooms, and postproduction facilities. Now that Disney Channel and Touchstone had started to turn a profit, the plan was to film up to fifteen feature-length films, twenty-one made-for-TV movies, and at least one full-length animated feature per year. The plan also called for the rental of the studio facilities to independent producers, with an estimated locally based crew that would provide the area with up to 1,500 jobs. The result was the first successful merger between a popular amusement park and a motion picture production company.

Disney-MGM's founding mission was to create a "living movie set" that could provide a disambiguation for parkgoers between "the 'real world' commercial activity of the film and television studios and the ongoing 'fantasy world' activity of the theme park."[201] The park was to be divided into two distinct sections. The first section was to be a conventional ride-centered amusement park that occupied 40 percent of the park space, while the working studio made up the other 60 percent. Although the studio worked as an active film and television set, with large soundstages, backlots, and postproduction spaces, the facility was designed to allow for a constant flow of tourists who could view scenes as they were filmed in real time.[202] The studio/park was only a small part of the $1.3 billion construction initiative made across all of Disney's properties in Orlando, which also created the Typhoon Lagoon waterpark, Downtown Disney, along with four new hotels that included a total of 4,300 rooms.[203]

Ironically, had it not been for Disney's plans to move ahead with Disney-MGM Studios, Universal Studios Florida likely never would have been built. Since the plans for Disney-MGM required no direct state investment in the interest of the company's special autonomy status, MCA/Universal relied heavily on state funding to have ground broken for their park. After MCA asked the Florida government for a guarantee of $175 million for film projects from the state's $8 billion employee pension holdings, the Florida legislative committee responded by axing a bill that would have permitted such investments. After MCA threatened to pull the plug on the entire project, the state countered with the offer of a $150 million loan to begin construction on the studio in 1987.[204] These funding delays placed construction of Universal Studios Florida roughly one year behind schedule.

On May 1, 1989, visitors were able to glimpse the Disney-MGM's iconic "Earrfel Tower" for the first time. Special guests Kevin Costner, Audrey Hepburn, George Lucas, and Molly Ringwald were among many Hollywood stars who came to Orlando to celebrate the park's grand opening.[205] The three soundstages built at Disney-MGM and four soundstages under construction at Universal Studios suddenly had given Orlando one of the largest concentrations of production facilities in the world outside of Los Angeles. The 444-acre site at Disney-MGM contained an extensive backlot with a hundred different potential production sets that included a New England fishing village, a re-creation of Fisherman's Wharf in San Francisco, a "Wild West" stage, and an animal actor's stage. Once in operation, Disney-MGM became "the largest studio facility on the U.S. East Coast."[206]

Even before Disney and Universal started building their studio parks, Central Florida had begun hosting several high-profile multimillion-dollar productions. Although many of these films were critical and financial failures, such as *Honky Tonk Freeway* (1981), *Jaws 3-D* (1983), and *D.A.R.Y.L.* (1985), *Flight of the Navigator* (1986), and *Rude Awakening* (1989), the extent of local cooperation seemed to have no limits. For example, in 1980, during production of *Honky Tonk Freeway*, the towns of Mount Dora and Fruitville, which stood in for the fictional town of Ticlaw, literally painted themselves pink to fit one of the key plot points of the movie. Many of the film's highway scenes were shot on the still-under-construction I-75 interchange between Sarasota and Fort Myers. The cooperation with the Florida Department of Transportation even allowed the production to dynamite a wooden bridge for the film's climax.²⁰⁷ Although *Honky Tonk Freeway* lost nearly $22 million at the box office, at the time becoming one of the most expensive box-office bombs in film history, the nearly $10 million that the production spent in Central Florida stayed there.²⁰⁸

The premise for *Jaws 3-D* involved a great white shark being set loose inside SeaWorld Orlando. The film cost nearly $20 million, with a large portion of the budget spent on its 3D effects and providing SeaWorld with the world's largest solar pool heater. Clearly the production spent all its funds on effects and location filming at SeaWorld, but the rest of movie did not inspire its audiences. The script was considered so toxic that Roy Scheider, who played Martin Brody in the first two installments, said, "Mephistopheles couldn't talk me into doing it. [The producers] knew better than to even ask."²⁰⁹ His replacement, Dennis Quaid, recalled in a 2015 interview with Andy Cohen of *Watch What Happens Live!* (2009–Present) that *Jaws 3-D* had the largest cocaine budget of any movie he worked on and that he was high in "every frame" in which he appeared on-screen.²¹⁰ Orlandoans did not seem to have nearly the same connection to *Jaws 3-D* as other homegrown productions. James Greene Jr. of the *Orlando Weekly* remarked, "There are Arby's training videos with more spark than most passages in *Jaws 3-D*."²¹¹ Although critic Leonard Maltin's review is slightly more generous, comparing it to another Florida-made 3D horror sequel, *Revenge of the Creature* (1955), *Jaws 3-D* was not only overwhelmingly panned by critics but also suffered what was at the time one the sharpest drop-offs in box-office gross from its opening week in film history.²¹²

Another financial and critical disappointment was Paramount Studios' sci-fi drama *D.A.R.Y.L.* (1985). The supposed family movie about a "Data Analyzing Robot Youth Lifeform" built by the government who learns what it means to be a kid was eclipsed by family releases such as *Back to the Future* (1985), *The Goonies* (1985), and *Pee Wee's Big Adventure* (1985). The film's special effects were produced by the same team that had worked on the original *Star Wars* trilogy at Pinewood Studios. On-location scenes that were shot in Orlando serve as a stand-in for the fictional town of Barkenton, South Carolina. The most recognizable location in the film was the Westinghouse Energy (later Siemens) complex across from the University of Central Florida.²¹³ *D.A.R.Y.L.* failed to make even the top five at the box office on its opening weekend, but much of its $12 million location budget was spent in Central Florida. Critically speaking, *D.A.R.Y.L* did not fare very well either. Jay Boyar of the *Orlando Sentinel* gave the film a little more leeway but criticized the lack of credit given to its Florida hosts:

We have nothing to be ashamed of. *D.A.R.Y.L.,* the first major motion picture to make extensive use of Central Florida locations, may not be *E.T.* [1982], *The Wizard of Oz* [1939], or even *Wargames* [1984], but at least it's not *Jaws 3-D* or *Honky Tonk Freeway* . . . [F]rom a civic perspective, . . . although the moviemakers used our area in the filming, the municipalities of Central Florida aren't mentioned in the dialogue of this science-fiction movie.[214]

Aside from dismissing any mention of Central Florida in the film, the producers at World Film Services also snubbed local editors and did not take advantage of the city's own postproduction services. Orlando's Digital Video Corporation, which rented out their lab to *D.A.R.Y.L.*'s postproduction crew, had to watch as the producers brought in their own editors and equipment.[215] The near exclusive use of outside talent during the making of *D.A.R.Y.L.* foreshadowed many of the challenges later faced by supporters of Florida's "Hollywood East" movement.

In contrast to the troubled productions made in Central Florida, *Flight of the Navigator* was a critical and financial success. Before the Arvida merger in 1984, Michael Eisner originally intended to produce the project, and it was sent to Mark Damon's Producers Sales Organization (PSO).[216] The sci-fi adventure told the story of David Freeman, a twelve-year-old boy from Fort Lauderdale who was abducted by aliens in 1978 and transported to the year 1986. An important landmark in the development of Computer-Generated Imagery (CGI) in movies, *Flight of the Navigator* is most famous today for being the first film to use "reflection mapping" to create realistic reflections on a simulated chrome surface. Disney's distribution deal with PSO turned a tidy profit, giving a greater boost to South Florida's ever-growing film credentials.

Between 1981 and 1989, the Orlando metro area hosted thirty-nine feature-length films, with a median of about $70 million spent by these productions during their time in Central Florida. A carefully coordinated promotional drive carried out by Orlando's Industrial Development Commission ensured that, by 1986, Central Florida was home to 2,400 television commercials and eighteen corporate films with an combined budget of $95.6 million per year. In a 1987 interview with the *Orlando Sentinel,* Les Haskew, vice president of the Kissimmee/Osceola County Chamber of Commerce, expressed his optimism about Central Florida's future as a center for commercial productions: "Coca-Cola Co. recently shot one of its commercials in the Orlando area, and an automaker also shot a truck ad there. Even though there are no studios here, there's still a lot of production going on."[217]

As construction on the soundstages for Universal Studios was finished, the studio had the first test run of its facilities during the winter of 1989, when director Ron Howard returned to Florida to direct the Steve Martin comedy *Parenthood* (1989). Although the movie was set in St. Louis, Orlando offered a far more favorable climate for the winter shoot. Besides christening the still under-construction soundstages at Universal Studios, the production team also took advantage of approximately twenty locations throughout the Orlando area. Some highlights included a showcase of the city's College Park and Pinecastle neighborhoods, along with local landmarks such as Tinker Field, Leu Gardens, and Orlando General Hospital.[218] *Parenthood*'s $20 million budget was almost entirely spent in and around Central Florida.

Parenthood was a critical and financial success, recouping over $100 million on its original budget and landing lead actress Dianne Wiest an Academy Award nomination, proving that Orlando could truly deliver the goods. To capitalize on its success, the movie was adapted into a short-lived series, *Parenthood* (1990–91), which was filmed at the Universal lot in California. Despite praise from TV critics for the show's first season, the high cost of its California-based production caused the show to be canceled after just one season.[219]

The opening of Universal Studios Florida in June 1990, was far less promising. The park's opening ceremony was hosted by Steven Spielberg, who commemorated the event by cutting a celluloid ribbon and announcing, "We're really happy to be here in Florida and we'll be here forever."[220] Spielberg's reassurances did little to relieve the anxieties of shareholders. By the end of that very first day, Spielberg's promise of being in Florida forever may have sounded more like a threat, as one in every ten guests who attended the opening ceremony asked for a refund or rain check. Compared to the fanfare that followed Disney-MGM's opening, Universal's first day was an abject disaster.[221] According to amusement park journalist Jeremy Herbert, "The only thing that worked reliably was live entertainment, but the park's biggest crowd-pleasers were still months, if not years away."[222]

An unexpected opportunity for the fledgling Orlando studio came in November 1990, when the Universal backlot in Los Angeles was set on fire by a disgruntled security guard. The fire destroyed nearly 20 percent of the studio's iconic sets and caused over $50 million in damages. Several features that were in the middle of production had to scramble to relocate.[223] The Touchstone-produced 1930s period-comedy *Oscar* (1991), starring Sylvester Stallone, which was originally slated to be filmed at the Universal Studios Hollywood backlot, had to shift production to Orlando. Columbia Pictures' *My Girl* (1991), also intended to be filmed on the Universal backlot, was relocated to Central Florida, with the towns of Bartow, Sanford, and Winter Haven used

Figure 28. In the 1960s, Ivan Tors originally suggested the idea to build a theme park near Miami where visitors could "ride the movies" and "watch live productions being recorded and performed in real-time." That vision finally became a reality when Disney-MGM and Universal Studios came to Orlando in 1989 and 1990, respectively.

as stand-ins for the fictional town of Madison, Pennsylvania.[224] In the credits for *My Girl*, the producers made sure to give special thanks to Cathy Savino and the Orlando Film Office for her careful efforts in coordinating on-site locations. Even though Twentieth Century Fox was unaffected by the Universal fire, positive word of mouth led producers to decide to shoot *Doc Hollywood* (1991), starring Michael J. Fox, in Micanopy, Florida, to stand in for the fictional town of Grady, South Carolina.[225]

Florida Becomes "*The* East Coast Alternative"

By the early 1990s, there was quite a bit of excitement in Orlando as Disney-MGM and Universal started to put the finishing touches on their respective studios and theme parks. Following the cancellation of *Miami Vice* in 1989 and the subsequent lull in film and television production in South Florida, the timing was ripe for Orlando to become the new center of gravity of Florida's film and television industry. With its theme parks and soundstages in place, a reformed road system and newly minted NBA franchise, Orlando had indeed elevated its reputation as what Larry Guest of the *Orlando Sentinel* called "a great amusement park near a town" into "a major town with a great amusement park."[226] In May 1991, Orlando was featured on the cover of *Time Magazine*, which hailed the growing metropolis as "the boomtown of the South," in a remarkable departure from its "Paradise Lost" cover on South Florida from exactly a decade before.[227] A year later, local film booster James Ponti proclaimed, "Slowly but deliberately, the city of Orlando is developing its image as Movieland South."[228]

Outreach organizations such as the FMPTA-affiliated Metro Orlando Film and Television Office (MOFTO) had all but succeeded in selling Central Florida to the motion picture world as "*The* East Coast Alternative."[229] When ground was struck for the Disney and Universal soundstages in 1987, both Miami and Orlando won their own NBA expansion franchises. It was a time when almost anything seemed possible. State politicians also took close notice of the nearly $200 million a year in spending the motion picture industry brought to the state. In February 1987, recently elected Senator Bob Graham discussed, in his endorsement of Richard Alan Nelson's landmark study on the Florida film industry, *Lights! Camera! Florida!*, the potential that the motion picture industry had to become a "gold mine for those concerned with the economic health of our state."[230] Bob Martinez, Graham's successor as governor, expressed a similar sentiment in his endorsement of Dr. Nelson's work. According to Governor Martinez, the film and television industry in

Florida could "display the vitality, variety, and excitement of life in Florida to a worldwide audience."[231] Samuel Gill, head archivist at the Academy of Motion Picture Arts and Sciences, rounded out the endorsements of *Lights! Camera! Florida!* by acknowledging the unexplored depths of Florida's potential as a production center:

> Florida has, in little over a decade, developed a reputation as one of the country's most desirable centers for filmmaking, due in large part to a highly efficient system of statewide liaison offices, assisted by an active motion picture and television association, and an experienced and knowledgeable industry advisory council . . . Among all the states of the Union, Florida has one of the most colorful "profiles" in all the annals of the American film industry.[232]

Although there was increasing enthusiasm from state and local politicians for expanding film and television production in the state, it was Florida-based filmmakers themselves who expressed their reservations. For example, while nearly $200 million in production expenses were generated in Florida in 1986, a total of $4 billion was spent in in Southern California that same year. Industry veterans like Victor Nuñez believed the state needed to work on its own talent and stories instead of going head-to-head with Hollywood. Nuñez expressed his concerns in a May 1987 interview with *Florida Magazine:* "I hate to think that we will become another Hollywood. Florida needs to develop its own voice as a filmmaking state. We need to explore the talent we have right here."[233]

Bob Allen, a former president of the FMPTA who was hired to become head of television and film production for Walt Disney World, also urged patience: "I usually spend a lot of my time debunking that myth. Florida and Orlando are not going to become a new Hollywood and we don't want them to."[234] Instead, Central Florida's production infrastructure needed to increase substantially to meet motion picture industry standards. Allen predicted that with time, Florida's market share could continue to grow: "I see a ten-year window. I don't think you're going to see it overnight. We'll have to bust our butts."[235]

It could be argued that Orlando's two largest studios, Disney-MGM and Universal, proved the greatest hindrance toward growing its production industry. With most of the available soundstages in Central Florida controlled by Disney and Universal, independent producers and outside studios needed to rent the facilities on both companies' terms. The lack of local alternatives for non-Disney- or Universal-affiliated productions caused runaway productions to simply look elsewhere. Another factor that stunted the growth of Central Florida's production industry was the cost of temporary housing and support for cast and crew. Since most of the creative talent that came to work in Central Florida in the 1980s and 1990s held on to their Los Angeles residences, this added a baked-in expense that proved a significant drain on production budgets that local cooperation or tax incentives could not offset.

Unlike Canada's production boom in the 1990s, Florida was unable to offer the local infrastructure needed to keep filmmakers in the state.[236] Similar to the challenges that producers in the 1910s faced in Jacksonville, which inadvertently became a satellite of New York, Orlando's film and television industry during the 1990s was a satellite of Los Angeles. In the 1910s, most films made in Jacksonville had their cast and crew transported from New York for the winter filming season only to return to the North in the spring. In the 1990s, the lack of local alternatives for producers for non-Disney- or Universal-affiliated productions led most filmmakers to shoot only what they needed on location in Florida, then immediately return to Los Angeles.

Central Florida was seldom the star of its own show, and visiting filmmakers rarely embraced the region's unique architecture and landscape, which often served as a stand-in for other places, *and* only hosted blockbuster productions for little more than a day or two at a time. For example, when *Lethal Weapon 3* (1992) needed to simulate the demolition of a building in downtown Los Angeles for its opening scene, Orlando-based producer Ross Testagrossa jumped on an opportunity to offer Orlando's old City Hall as a tribute to the production. After fielding nearly one hundred calls, Testagrossa was able to get in touch with producer Joel Silver, who agreed to pay $50,000 toward the cost of the building's demolition. Over the next four months, explosives were placed to ensure that the demolition would be as dramatic as possible. After months of preparation, on October 24, 1991, the fateful day came. Once cameras were strategically placed from nearly every conceivable angle of the blast zone, the building crumbled in a manner of seconds. The shot went off without a hitch, and even Mayor Bill Fredrick managed to sneak in a cameo as the police officer who sarcastically claps "Bravo!" at Mel Gibson's Martin Riggs and Danny Glover's Roger Murtaugh.[237]

The Orlando City Hall implosion shined a welcome spotlight on Orlando's commitment to its growing film industry. A portion of the funds Testagrossa raised helped sponsor the first Florida Film Festival the following June (1992). The Office of Film and Entertainment (OFE) also was able to leverage the spectacle to bring *Lethal Weapon 3*'s second unit (along with Gibson and

Glover's stunt doubles) back to Florida in January 1992 to assist with the demolition of the Soreno Hotel in St. Petersburg. Unlike Orlando's City Hall, the Soreno's demolition only appeared in the final credits reel. To add insult to injury, the producers even misspelled the name of the city as "St. Petersberg" in the credits.[238] When production on *Lethal Weapon 3* wrapped, the OFE was tipped off that Testagrossa was severely shortchanged by millions of dollars compared to the compensation demands that would have been made had a similar scene been shot in California. Even if the City Hall demolition demonstrated Orlando's willingness to provide a cheaper alternative to filmmakers, it increased the urgency among the state film offices to create an official liaison office with Hollywood.

In February 1992, a special meeting of the FMPTA was held to address financing concerns and develop an advertising campaign that would sell Central Florida to the industry. John Reitzammer, Florida's film and television commissioner, acknowledged that "several years ago the perception was out in front of the reality as to how quickly Florida's film industry would grow."[239] The slower than anticipated growth in the statewide industry, combined with increased competition between other regional film hubs in British Columbia, Louisiana, North Carolina, Ontario, and Texas, presented another major challenge toward consolidating runaway productions in Florida alone.

To convince more producers to "Film Orlando," MOFTO produced the *Orlando Filmbook*, which outlined to producers all the local accommodations that Orange, Seminole, Lake, and Osceola Counties could offer their productions.[240] The book was intended to be a supplement to a five-minute promotional video developed by Cathy Savino and Kathy Ramsberger of MOFTO. The Screen Actors Guild objected to the video's distribution, however, since the actors featured in it were not paid for their appearances. In the end, the video promo was left to sit unused on the bureau's shelf.[241]

The production challenges encountered in the making of Joe Dante's love letter to B-movie cinema, *Matinee* (1993), starring John Goodman, are especially instructive in understanding the opportunities and limitations non-Disney- or Universal-affiliated productions faced when filming in Florida. *Matinee* was filmed mostly on locations across Central Florida, in Cocoa, Maitland, and on the Universal Studios backlot, with several street scenes shot in Key West, where the movie was set. According to Joe Dante in a 2000 interview with *A.V. Club*, "*Matinee* got made through a fluke. The company that was paying for us went out of business and didn't have any money. Universal, which was the distributor, had put in a little money, and we went to them and begged them to buy into the whole movie, and to their everlasting sorrow they went ahead and did it."[242] Although Florida was an ideal location to film such a thoughtful tribute to a film genre it helped popularize, Universal's takeover of the distribution and poor marketing campaign limited audiences' access to a hidden gem of 1990s cinema.

One of the best incentives that the statewide film and television industry offered producers was easy access to a wide variety of communities and landscapes through coordinating with the FMPTA's film offices. Elsewhere in the South, states such as Georgia, Louisiana, Texas, and North Carolina each had Atlanta, New Orleans, Austin, and Wilmington, respectively, as a center of gravity for their statewide production industries. Unlike Florida, these film centers were not solely dependent on one or two major studios. Although the animation studio at Disney-MGM inspired the "Disney Renaissance" of the 1990s, and Universal's Nickelodeon Studios had its own "Golden Age" of iconic children's programming, neither studio took advantage of the vast well of local talent that was at its disposal. Instead, Disney and Universal preferred to ship in cast and crew from out of state.

James Greene Jr. reflected on this in his 2014 postmortem on "Hollywood East,": "Nick Studio productions rarely if ever wandered out of their Soundstages or the Universal lot; as such, there are no entries where the *Gullah Gullah* tadpole runs afoul of Shaquille O'Neal at Lake Eola, or *Shelby Woo* investigating the case of the missing anything in Longwood or Sanford."[243] Another problem caused by the consolidation around the Disney and Universal soundstages was that filmmakers who were seriously interested in producing their films at the production facilities were turned off by the notion of having tourists look in on them as they worked. According to entertainment writer and Disney scholar Jim Hill:

> It didn't matter that the Imagineers and/or Universal Creative had made these glassed-in viewing areas sound-proof. Or—in some cases—had lined these production corridors with one-way mirrored glass, so that these auteurs wouldn't even know when they were being observed. Just the idea that there were people up there, potentially looking down (figuratively as well as literally) at them working was enough to make some directors and actors deliberately take a pass.[244]

Some perspective should be added in analyzing Orlando's perceived downfall as a production center. The fixation with turning Central Florida into "Hollywood East" was completely out of step with the broader changes that were occurring in the motion picture industry during the 1990s. According to Terri Hartman, publicity director for Universal Studios Florida film and television division, "Houston was supposed to be the third coast. We're not

L.A. We're not New York—never were gonna be. That was never the intention."[245]

Just like with Jacksonville's claims to be "Almost Hollywood" or Tampa Bay's attempt to become a "Second Los Angeles," Orlando's "Hollywood East" movement became a detriment in the long run since it set unrealistic expectations for what Central Florida could provide for producers. According to Billy Manes of the *Orlando Weekly*, "The industry never planted a flag and said, 'We want to be Hollywood East.' That was kind of put upon them as an expectation that was really unfair. It's like taking Simi Valley 'near Hollywood, California' out of Simi Valley and saying, 'We're Simi Detroit.' It just doesn't happen."[246] All it took was an abrupt shift in the priorities of Orlando's flagship studios to bring everything crashing down.

In 1998, the grand opening of Disney's Animal Kingdom was followed by the completion of Universal Studios' Island of Adventure and City Walk in 1999. By the end of the 1990s, both companies had started to disassociate from their mission to have their visitors "ride the movies." According to James Greene Jr., "Suddenly watching some anonymous lunatic mixing up a new batch of Gak had to compete with an Incredible Hulk roller coaster, Popeye-themed river rapids, and a goddamn Starbucks."[247] Billy Manes was even more cutting in his appraisal, lamenting that after Disney and Universal's departure, Orlando was left to "suffer the humiliation of straight-to-DVD sequel infamy, reality television, and commercials."[248] The advent of franchise cinema and continued corporate consolidation also increasingly limited the number of opportunities for middle-budget films and independent producers to get their projects made at all. The cost-saving measures Florida's movie promoters promised to producers had become all but obsolete.

With this in mind, there were still plenty of non-Disney-, Touchstone-, or Universal-associated productions made in Central Florida during the late 1990s. Television shows with multimillion-dollar budgets, like *The Adventures of Superboy* (1988–92), *Thunder in Paradise* (1993–94)—Florida's short-lived answer to *Baywatch* (1989–2001), Ron Howard's *Apollo 13* (1995), and *From Earth to the Moon* (1998), all relied heavily on the local facilities, but were limited in the extent to which their Central Florida backdrop was properly showcased.

Big-budget films made in Florida during the 1990s were mostly shot in South Florida. Unlike the movies produced in Orlando, those made in Miami, such as *Ace Ventura: Pet Detective* (1994), *True Lies* (1994), *Bad Boys* (1995), *The Birdcage* (1996), and *There's Something about Mary* (1998), incorporated their South Florida settings into their plots. In the 1990s, location and economics were the threads common to the success or failure of Florida's entertainment industry. At the same time that Disney and Universal scaled down their activities in Central Florida, increased competition with other regional production hubs created a perfect storm for Florida's film industry.

Soon Orlando and Miami were met with competition not only from other states but also other countries that offered studios favorable exchange rates. This effectively sparked a bidding war where other states also began offering incentives to lure them back. In the arsenal were tax credits, rebates, grants, and sales-tax exemptions. Smaller production centers in the state like in Jacksonville, which had since become a shadow of its former self, collapsed in the face of such competition. North Florida was left to compete with other major southern film centers such as Atlanta, Austin, New Orleans, and Wilmington, cities with better production infrastructure and political support.[249]

By 2003, just as Disney-MGM started to relocate its remaining animation division, Governor Jeb Bush endorsed a 500-page *Film Florida Production Guide* intended to lure film and television productions to the state. This was followed by a series of bills passed by the Florida House providing producers with "easy-to-use permitting forms and an abundance of grants and assistance."[250] The introduction of legislation benefiting filmmakers especially helped to strengthen and reinforce South Florida's production industry.[251]

Within a several years of the *Production Guide*'s release, pilots for Showtime's *Dexter* (2006–13, 2021), the USA's *Burn Notice* (2007–13), and AMC's s *The Glades* (2010–13), began production in South Florida, and Miami also became a regularly sought-after backdrop for reality shows for Bravo, E!, MTV, TLC, and VH1. Many of these programs were filmed at Greenwich Studios in North Miami, where Ivan Tors and Ricou Browning first put the city on the television map in the 1960s, or at a new state-of-the-art studio complex built by the city on the site of the former Coconut Grove Convention Center.[252] When Telemundo Studios consolidated its facilities in Hialeah in 1999, South Florida emerged as one of the largest producers of Spanish-language programming in the world.[253]

At the start of the twenty-first century, it seemed that Florida once again would emerge as a key regional contributor to the American film and television industry. Just as the state's incentive program and outreach initiatives began to hit their stride in the 2010s, however, Florida politics would do yet another about-face that would have far-reaching consequences affecting whether Florida would have any future at all in the motion picture industry.

END CREDITS

"The Flip of a Switch"

The Sun Sets on Florida's Motion Picture Industry (Can It Rise Again?), 2006 to Present

> It was the flip of a switch. The minute we didn't have any tax credits available, the phones rang a lot less. The interest in coming to Florida waned almost immediately.
>
> John Lux, executive director of Film Florida, 2018

"It's a Passion, It's a Memory:" Florida Stays in the Picture

On the night of July 29, 2021, hundreds of cars lined up at the Ocala Drive-In as they had for the past year since the 2020 lockdown placed it in the national spotlight. This evening had an added element of beguilement to it as the drive-in celebrated its tenth anniversary with game and prize stands, a face-painting station, and a raffle for free movie tickets, followed by a special screening of Michael Bay's *Transformers* (2011).

Thursday nights usually did not typically sell out, but that evening, moviegoers came out in droves to celebrate this vital community fixture and to reflect on how the movies had helped with their sense of well-being over the past fifteen months. In an interview with WCJB-TV, John Watzke reflected, "Oh it's great, we come here 10 years ago to a field grown up in weeds, and with the dedication of a few loyal employees and customer support that we've had, we're celebrating 10 years."[1]

Even as the stresses of the pandemic and the moment were momentarily put aside that particular night, even the Ocala Drive-In had not entirely escaped the troubles brought on since the March 2020 lockdown. One week earlier, a white pickup truck whose owner was known by Watzke and staff as a drive-in regular, tore through the parking lot at an extremely high speed, taking down the theater's sixty-foot front fence, destroying several poles, and nearly injuring children who were playing with toys as their parents prepared

Figure 29. John Watzke at the Ocala-Drive-In, 2021. John Watzke, owner of the Ocala Drive-In, provided Floridians a much-needed escape during the COVID-19 pandemic and briefly reigned as the "King of the American Box Office" during the 2020 lockdowns. Photo by Bruce Ackerman/*Ocala Gazette*.

for the evening's screening. The harrowing scene caused over $3,000 worth of damage to the theater, but to Watzke, it was the driver's disregard for the safety of his customers that he found most disconcerting: "This could have been a very serious situation. There was property damage that can be repaired. If he would have run over somebody's child, that could not be repaired or replaced, and that's what has us really shocked here."[2]

Even in the face of such troubling events, the Ocala Drive-In had managed to weather the worse of the COVID-19 pandemic. In fact, despite rising inflation, the Ocala Drive-In has continued to offer its low prices of six dollars entry for adults and three dollars for children, while also offering a unique blend of New Orleans traditional dishes, like the Watzkes' signature muffuletta loaf.[3]

Since the winter of 2021, movie theaters have gradually begun to reopen as audiences have slowly but surely started to immerse themselves in the big screen once again. The movies have been a respite and relief from the darkest moments of our collective history and a reminder that everything will one day be all right. As John Watzke reflected in a 2022 interview to Orlando's WKMG-TV announcing the summer movie season:

> The pandemic was a terrible thing to happen to this country and a lot of businesses didn't make it. On the flip side, the drive-in gave the

younger generation an opportunity to experience a drive-in and the older generation a chance to reminisce on when they were younger, and it became a safe haven for families. If you want to see a movie and you don't mind being stuck in a room with a bunch of people you don't know, the walk-ins are fine. The walk-ins are nothing more than a movie; the drive-in is a memory.[4]

"A Match Made in Heaven, or Rather Paradise"

Now more than ever, Florida should play, if not the lead role, at least an important supporting part in this vital moment in American film history. Unfortunately, for the past decade the state's production industry has seemingly stagnated as neighboring states like Georgia, Louisiana, and North Carolina have not only maintained but dramatically expanded their production industries. To add insult to injury, these states have often also been home to location shoots for films and television programs that are *set in* and *about* Florida. For example, location scouts for Ben Affleck's *Live by Night* (2016), a crime drama set in Tampa's Ybor City in the 1930s, had initially scouted locations to film in Tampa Bay, but without local incentives and governmental support, the production chose to re-create Ybor City across the border in Brunswick, Georgia instead. In other words, it was cheaper and more convenient to build a "fake Ybor City" in Georgia than it was to film at the real deal.[5] Most recently, Netflix's limited series *Florida Man* (2023) was filmed entirely on location in Wilmington, North Carolina.

While plenty of movies and television shows have used Florida's setting and filmed on location elsewhere, such as *Some Like It Hot* (1959), *Surfside 6* (1960–62), *I Dream of Jeannie* (1965–70), *The Love Boat* (1977–86), *The Golden Girls* (1985–92), and, frustratingly, Michael Mann's relatively recent *Miami Vice* (2006) remake, at least these productions were not filmed on location in immediately neighboring states with more favorable incentive policies. For much of the 2010s and 2020s, films and shows like *Eye of the Hurricane* (2012), set in the Everglades but filmed in Georgia; *Paper Towns* (2015), set in Orlando, but filmed in North Carolina; *Baywatch* (2017), set in the fictional Emerald Bay, Florida, but mostly filmed in Georgia; *Gifted* (2017), set in St. Petersburg but filmed in Georgia; *On Becoming a God in Central Florida* (2019), set in Orlando but filmed in Louisiana; and *Killing It* (2022–), set in South Florida but filmed in Louisiana, have used Florida as a setting without taking advantage of the state's unique environment on screen. At the same time, there has been a range of television shows and independent films filmed on location in Florida, including *Bloodline* (2015–17); the first three seasons of *Ballers* (2015–

19); *Walt before Mickey* (2015); *Moonlight* (2016); *The Florida Project* (2017); *The Assassination of Gianni Versace* (2018); *David Makes Man* (2019–2021); and *Zola* (2020). Sadly, at the time of writing, the state's production industry is currently a shadow of what it was during its heyday in the 1980s and 1990s.

What changed? Why has Florida's motion picture industry lost so many productions to other regional film markets? In 2006, just one year after Universal Studios shuttered their soundstages in Orlando, Florida still had the third-largest motion picture industry in the United States.[6] With flagship shows such as CBS's *CSI: Miami* (2002–12); FX's *Nip Tuck* (2003–10); Showtime's *Dexter* (2006–13); and USA's *Burn Notice* (2007–13), along with big-budget franchise films and sequels like *2 Fast 2 Furious* (2003); *Bad Boys II* (2003); *The Punisher* (2004); and *Transporter 2* (2005), Florida was still a top draw for studios. Systemic changes within the motion picture industry at large would act as a deciding factor in the diminishing number of big-budget productions interested in coming to Florida.

An unprecedented degree of corporate consolidation inside the motion picture industry, which itself was a factor in Disney-MGM and Universal Studios' departure from Orlando, caused many major film studios to be absorbed by a handful of international media conglomerates. This consolidation in turn brought on another period of fragmentation in the motion picture industry as disruptive as what was seen in the 1930s with arrival of sound, the 1950s with the challenges brought on by television, the labor unrest of the 1960s, and the advent of megaplexes and the start of the weekly box-office horse race in the 1970s.

Florida is not alone in being impacted by the monopolization of the global media industry. In 2009, on-location filming in Los Angeles fell a record 19 percent, as the permitted number of production days for feature films dropped to their lowest level since the 1990s. To help recoup the state's position as the center of motion picture production in the United States, the California Legislature responded by passing a five-year tax incentive program. In 2012, California governor Jerry Brown signed the legislation into law, but with the stipulation that the incentive program be held at an annual cap of $100 million, while feature film projects with budgets over $75 million were entirely ineligible.[7] Since then, the biggest blockbusters over the past ten years have often looked outside of California for their location shoots or increasingly depend on visual effects and CGI to re-create their on-set locations.

In the ten years between 2012 and 2022, the global film industry has decentered itself from Hollywood. This transition should have been an opportunity for Florida to encourage more filmmakers to come to the state. Unfortunately, as with many other missed opportunities during other moments of disruption in the motion picture industry, Florida once again got in its own way. The major difference between the early twenty-first century and, say, the 1910s, 1930s, 1960s, or 1980s, is that Florida no longer is exclusively fighting to lure productions from California and New York.

As seen in chapter 5, since the mid-1990s, Florida has been faced with competition from other regional production industries, and not just in Georgia and Louisiana. Between 1993 and 2009, the Canadian film industry has morphed into a "Hollywood North" of sorts, with the combination of the low Canadian dollar and a fully refundable tax credit granted in exchange for a percentage of production services helping to prop up the national film industry. Another factor contributing to the decline of Orlando's "Hollywood East" movement in the 1990s was Central Florida's inability to compete with the Canadian government's tax credit program. In recent years, Louisiana has transformed itself into a "Hollywood South," as the state government initiated a series of programs to give runaway film and television productions subsidies for an entire production budget, anything from the first location scout survey on through to catering wrap parties.[8]

The greatest threat to Florida's production industry is Georgia's "Y'allywood," which has since the 2010s implemented a 30 percent tax credit plan and a $4 billion expenditure program. The tradeoff has resulted in the creation of an additional 79,000 jobs across the state and $7 billion added to the state economy.[9] Due to these enticements, nearly 250 television and film productions were shot in Georgia in just 2016 alone. The stunning success of Georgia's incentive program has allowed the state to climb to rank third in the country in the production of film and television programming, behind only California and New York.[10] By 2010, forty U.S. states had each developed their own tax incentives programs to attract film and television productions, while competition with the reduced production costs available in Canada and eastern Europe offers an incredibly diverse array of location possibilities for runaway film and television productions.[11]

To protect Florida's position as the third-largest motion picture production industry during the early 2000s, Governor Jeb Bush (1999–2007) and the Florida Legislature approved $25 million in funding for the 2007–8 fiscal year to sponsor the Florida Entertainment Industry Incentive Program (FEIIP). The program, which was overseen by the OFE and went into full effect in July 2007, was explained as a means to "encourage the use of this state a site for filming and to develop and sustain the workforce and infrastructure for film and entertainment production."[12]

Jeb Bush's successor, Charlie Crist (2007–11), responded to the urgent need for the state to provide additional incentives by increasing funding for the

FEIIP tenfold. In a move that sought to take advantage of Governor Jerry Brown's incentive restrictions in California, in 2010 Governor Crist signed off on a six-year program that allocated $242 million in tax credits for film and television productions active in Florida. In his announcement of the program's ratification, Governor Crist acknowledged the importance of statewide support of its entertainment industry. In a 2009 economic impact survey, the governor remarked, "As we continue to seek growth opportunities for Florida's economy, it is important to remember the significant role film and entertainment plays in our state, directly employing more than 100,000 Floridians . . . These findings highlight how important it is for Florida's business and workforce to ensure this revenue stream continues flowing into our state."[13]

Charlie Crist's successor, Rick Scott (2011–19), at least initially continued his support of the FEIIP and even added $12 million to the program during his first year in office, with another $42 million added in 2012, for a total of $296 million applied to the state's total incentive budget. As impressive as this figure seems, and it should be noted that Florida's entire five-year incentive budget amounted to less than what California spent in six months during this same period.[14] Regardless, the FEIIP helped bring several multimillion-dollar television programs to the state during this time, most notably AMC's *The Glades* (2010–13), Netflix's *Bloodline* (2015–17), and the first three seasons of HBO's *Ballers* (2015–19). The FEIIP incentives also helped land big-budget blockbusters like *Magic Mike* (2012) and smaller independent projects like *Dolphin Tale* (2011) and *Spring Breakers* (2012), which each proved to be a boon for tourism for Tampa and the St. Pete/Clearwater area. The tourism impact from *Dolphin Tale* was so extensive that a 2012 USF St. Petersburg College of Business study estimated 73 percent of all visitors to the Clearwater Marine Aquarium came specifically because of the movie.

A 2013 survey conducted by Visit Florida indicated the film industry helped to induce 22.7 percent of domestic visitors to come to Florida.[15] When *Dolphin Tale 2* (2014) returned to Clearwater in 2013, Governor Scott expressed his enthusiasm for the production's likely stimulation of the local economy on Florida's West Coast: "It's exciting that *Dolphin Tale 2* will be filmed here in Florida. Today's announcement will create more economic activity and opportunities for families living in Pinellas County. This exciting news builds on the economic momentum that Florida is currently experiencing."[16] Pinellas County Senator Jack Latvala and Representatives Ed Hooper and Kathleen Peters each expressly thanked the governor for his support of the production.[17]

In their 2013 assessment of the Florida film industry and its collaboration with the state government, Mary Pergola-Parent and Kevin Govern optimistically predicted that the spirit of cooperation that been created through the FEIIP incentives was "a match made in heaven, or rather paradise. Florida's ineradicable dedication to the needs and desires of the film industry proves her unwavering commitment to this treasured relationship."[18] That same year, the OFE issued a five-year strategic plan for economic development using film incentives. Its opening pitch was reminiscent of the early promotions for Jacksonville's film industry during the 1910s, as well as the efforts to initiate statewide support for the motion picture industry during the 1930s and 1970s:

> Florida's film and entertainment industry is truly unique. It is important to the Florida economy as a major driver of employment and personal income, attracting revenue from other states and countries to be spent locally on wages and film production services. Florida's year-round sunshine, moderate climate, diverse scenery, and business-friendly incentive program give the state an advantage over competitors.[19]

By 2013, it appeared as if Florida had finally managed to strike an effective balance between governmental cooperation and economic encouragement. According to Pergola-Parent and Govern, "As this multi-billion-dollar relationship continues into its second century, with over 120 films and television shows and counting, filmmakers and Floridians can look forward to many more success stories—especially if they focus on diligent collaboration, economic incentives, and absolutely any tale about a bottlenose dolphin."[20] Little did Pergola-Parent and Govern realize that within a year the tide would once again turn against the motion picture and television industry in Florida.

Despite the added $54 million contributed to the FEIIP incentive program during the first two years of Rick Scott's administration, by 2014, the allocated funds were entirely spent. When additional funds were requested, both the Florida Legislature and the Rick Scott administration balked. The last two productions able to take advantage of the funds set aside for incentives were *Bloodline* and *Ballers*. Although the funds were intended to last until 2016, the first-come first served nature of the incentives program allowed productions of all sizes, scopes, and potential economic impact to take advantage of the allotted funds.

Detractors of the tax incentive program expressed their concern that projects would only receive incentives based on when they applied as opposed to their perceived economic impact. An Office of Economic and Demographic Research report published in 2014 claimed Florida received only a forty-three-cent return on each dollar spent on tax credits. Ultimately the Americans for Prosperity–influenced legislature opted not to replenish the incentive program and in 2016 decided to end the initiative entirely.[21] Newly appointed Florida House Speaker Richard Corcoran remarked the day he took the Speaker's gavel in November 2016, "The enemy is us. Left to our own devices, all too often, we'll choose self-interest."[22]

In 2012, four years before he ascended to the Speakership, as a freshman representative, Corcoran drafted an eighty-page manifesto, *Blue Print Florida*, in which he outlined his plans to overhaul the state's legislative culture. Ironically, the manifesto compared the situation in Florida's government in the 2010s to the decline of Blockbuster, which, according to Corcoran, "Explains what happens when an organization simply refuses to face the realities about its circumstances . . . squelching innovative ideas, discounting changing conditions in the industry."[23] Evoking Orson Welles's advice to his *Citizen Kane* (1941) cinematographer Gregg Toland to "Do everything they told us never to do," Corcoran promised a series of solutions "to make the Legislature more efficient, effective, and accountable."[24]

The Florida motion picture industry has since become another casualty of this so-called efficiency in the Florida government. Once it became apparent the FEIIP would not be renewed, several film projects that were initially slated to be filmed in Florida relocated to states offering more lucrative incentives. For example, *Magic Mike XXL* (2015), which had many principal scenes in the original film shot in Tampa Bay, relocated to Savannah, Georgia, and Myrtle Beach, South Carolina. In a 2016 interview with *PoliticoFlorida*, Speaker Corcoran explained his reason for rejecting a $250 million economic incentive program: "The House's position on the issue has been clear. The government engaging in social engineering to pick winners and losers that benefit the 1 percent is a bad deal for Florida taxpayers. There will not be any corporate welfare in the House budget."[25]

Within three years, the extinguishing of FEIIP funds cost Florida nearly $650 million in projects, 110,000 hotel room purchases, and about $1.8 billion in total in-state expenditures.[26] Film Florida's then president Michelle Hillery expressed her frustration toward Florida lawmakers' lack of understanding in regard to the economic benefits such an incentive program could provide: "The legislature's ultimate decision to officially abandon our film, television and digital media professionals has our entire industry and supporters outraged. This is not the message our state wants to send to its longtime industry workers, and the rest of the world after building a reputation for over one hundred successful years in this business."[27]

The collapse of incentives also contributed to the early cancellation of Netflix's *Bloodline*, which had initially planned at least six seasons' worth of storylines. According to series cocreator Todd Kessler, the pivotal role the Florida Keys played in the storyline and the collapse of incentives were the primary reason for the show's early exit: "We decided to set the show there because it's crucial to what the show is, not because of the tax incentive, but it does affect things financially for us and the show will be challenged because of that. It makes things more difficult."[28]

In November 2016, several months after *Bloodline*'s cancellation announcement, HBO revealed its intent to relocate *Ballers* to California. In a statement issued to the *Hollywood Reporter,* the network explained how Florida's lack of incentives informed the decision: "We have a long history of shooting projects in Florida and were obviously disappointed in the recent vote to not renew the incentive program. We will be assessing its impact on any future productions like *Ballers,* who have established Florida as their home."[29]

Although 2016 was a tough year financially for Florida's entertainment industry, several important independent productions helped keep Florida on the map. Barry Jenkins's *Moonlight* (2016) won three Academy Awards including Best Picture. *Moonlight* was filmed on a $1.5 million budget and has the distinction of being the lowest-budget (adjusted for inflation) film to win the Best Picture Oscar. The film was shot in and around Jenkins's former home in Miami's Liberty City, the same neighborhood that was decimated during the 1980 McDuffie Rebellion. Jenkins publicly stated that Miami truly was the only place he could have imagined making his film.[30] Miami Beach film commissioner Graham Winick went as far as to call *Moonlight* "a cultural high-water mark for Miami and Florida, comparable to hosting an international art fair like Art Basel Miami Beach or preserving the area's signature Art Deco architecture."[31] The following year, Sean Baker's Academy Award–nominated *The Florida Project* (2017) was filmed on location in Kissimmee in the shadow of Walt Disney World. According to Baker, his film set out to demonstrate "the juxtaposition of having kids growing up in motels right outside 'the happiest place on earth.'"[32]

While the advent of social problem films like *Moonlight* and *The Florida Project* have helped provide a voice to marginalized communities in Florida, the concerns raised by these films' narratives have yet to inspire any real changes in statewide policy decisions. In an interview with *Time Magazine,* Julio Capo of the University of Massachusetts Amherst lauded *Moonlight*'s depiction of this alternate side of Miami, in particular the film's portrayal of Miami's Liberty City as "a powder keg for such a turmoil following nearly a century of urban violence, displacement and exploitation."[33] The inclusivity that *Moonlight* offers its audiences helps not only to revise Miami's public persona but also to raise important questions about the nature of the city's social structure. Capo adds: "For decades, audiences have had a fairly myopic and often cartoonish view of life in the city, exemplified by crime-focused stories like 1983's *Scarface,* the television show *Miami Vice,* the *Bad Boys* film series and the video game series *Grand Theft Auto* (particularly 'Vice City'). Other stories, such as TV's *Nip/Tuck,* highlighted the city's glitz and glamour to the detriment, if not entire erasure, of the multidimensional worlds of those living in the city's margins."[34]

In contrast, the response to Sean Baker's depiction of Kissimmee's hotel families in *The Florida Project* caused Lake and Osceola County commissioners to express their concerns that the film could "make Kissimmee look bad."[35] In an interview with the *Tampa Bay Times,* Osceola County Commissioner Peggy Choudhury expressed her hope that the film would not stigmatize her district unfairly: "I understand that maybe this is why people are more interested because they're going to say, 'Oh, wow. It's right next to Disney. Oh my god, how could that happen?' Well, it happens everywhere, in the best cities and the best towns."[36] In what could be seen as a possible retaliation for the negative publicity attributed to unflattering cinematic portrayals of the state, the Florida Legislature continued to step up its anti-incentive campaign against the Florida film industry.

As of February 2017, the Florida motion picture industry was considered to be on "life support."[37] In a *Miami Herald* article ironically titled "Paradise Lost?," journalist Rene Rodriguez characterized the film and television industry in Florida as being "unable to compete with other states with generous tax incentives that help studios defray the ballooning budgets of filmed entertainment."[38] That same month, a study conducted by Miami-Dade County's Regulatory and Economic Resources Department indicated that upward of 4,900 jobs, $249 million in personal income, and $20 million in tax revenues were at risk between 2017 and 2022.[39] The tourism impact of *Bloodline* accounted for a total of $95 million, 1,738 jobs, and $9.4 million in state and local taxes.[40]

The following month, in March 2017, the Florida House of Representatives filed a bill that would have closed the offices for Film Florida and OFE completely. Had the bill passed, would have Florida joined Vermont as one of the only two states without a state film office.[41] State Representative Paul Renner proposal called for ceasing the funding for twenty-four economic development programs including Rick Scott's Enterprise Florida jobs initiative and the OFE. According to Representative Renner, these programs were "a misuse of taxpayer dollars or are not effective."[42] Speaker Richard Corcoran expressed his support of the legislation, calling the effort "right on policy, right on principle."[43]

"You Can't Do It Unless the Governor's behind You"

Despite his limited endorsement of the FEIIP incentives during his first term, by the end of his second term, Governor Scott had become all but ambivalent toward Florida's fledgling motion picture industry. Several days after the announcement of the proposed bill that would shut down the Film Florida and OFE offices, Scott faced calls from Florida film industry veterans to veto the legislation. One of the most outspoken supporters for the OFE was film legend Burt Reynolds, who publicly criticized Rick Scott for not doing enough to help Florida's struggling film industry. In an interview with South Florida's Local 10 news station, Reynolds recalled an especially unproductive meeting he had with Governor Scott: "I remember I went in to see him and I said, 'You know, we ought to be shooting more movies down here.' And he said, 'Why?' Then I said, 'How did you get to be governor?' He is dumber than a peach orchard sow for squandering the state's film industry."[44]

Although Reynolds did not explain exactly what a "peach orchard sow" is, he did go on to compare his experience with Rick Scott in the 2010s to the challenges he faced in convincing Governor Reubin Askew to support the Florida film industry in the 1970s: "I did seven pictures in Georgia, because dummy didn't figure it out . . . You can't do it unless the governor's behind you."[45] Less than a week after his remarks criticizing the Scott administration, the governor publicly broke with Speaker Corcoran's proposed incentive cutbacks and suggested that he might veto the bill entirely. After the bill was ratified by the Florida House, Scott criticized the legislation, warning, "A vote for these bills was a vote to kill tourism and jobs in Florida."[46] Ultimately, the veto was not necessary, since the bill died in the Florida Senate.

Through the measured lobby efforts of organizations like Film Florida and OFE, it appears that an increasing number of state legislators had by 2018 started to notice what the state had lost. The debate over how to bring the film and television industry back to Florida would also become a major talking point in the 2018 governor's race. In January 2018, State Senator Annette Taddeo proposed Senate Bill 1606 to provide funding to create the Florida Movie Capital Corporation (FMCC), which would subsidize and promote film and television productions in the state. The bipartisan bill was also cosponsored by State Representative Joe Grunters.[47] Although the use of the word "capital" in this specific bill implies the allotment of cash capital to supplement motion picture production activity, the name was also intended to

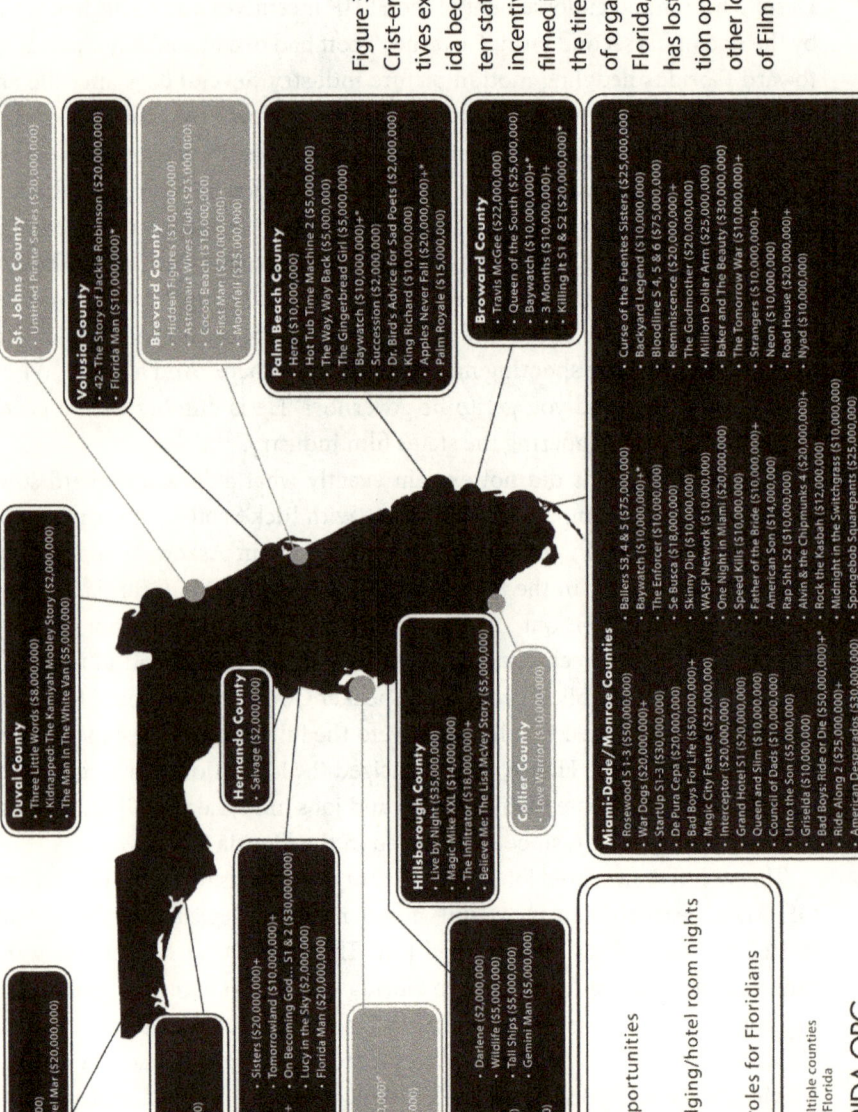

Figure 30. After Bush- and Crist-era film tax incentives expired in 2024, Florida became one of only ten states that do not offer incentives for productions filmed in-state. Despite the tireless lobby efforts of organizations like Film Florida, since 2016, Florida has lost countless production opportunities to other locations. Courtesy of Film Florida.

hark back to an association to Florida's past as the "World's Winter Film Capital," its aspirations toward becoming the "Film Capital of the Nation," and its legacy as a "Forgotten Film Capital."[48]

Senator Taddeo managed to extend support for the FMCC outside of the legislature as well and soon found an important ally in former Miami Beach mayor Philip Levine. In February 2018, with the endorsement of the *Miami Herald*, Levine entered the Democratic primary with the pledge to pursue as governor policies of "environmentalism, living wages, better public schools, gun safety policies and social equality."[49] One area the Levine campaign felt it could immediately help sponsor such initiatives would be through the local spending that film and television productions could bring to the state. At a Seminole County Democratic Party meeting held on February 8, 2018, Levine pledged to work toward ensuring that big-budget motion picture and television productions returned to Florida. In a set of policy proposals reminiscent of Governor Bob Graham (whose daughter Gwen was one of Levine's primary opponents), Levine claimed to have "a lot of contacts in California, I know a lot of studio heads. They're dying to come back. It doesn't take much to get them to come back."[50]

As mayor of Miami Beach between 2013 and 2017, Philip Levine witnessed firsthand the economic consequences of the industry's departure. During his campaign, Levine expressed his frustrations toward the previous administration and Florida's state government's support of regressive economic policies. At a meeting with film industry leaders on July 24, he described the situation as "incredible to me. How do you attract a 21st-century economy when you have a 20th-century government? We're living with a mentality, unfortunately, where they just don't get it."[51]

At the same meeting, several film officials in attendance countered Levine's criticisms by stating that other Republican-led states such as Texas and Georgia have consistently offered incentives. According to journalist Scott Powers, the film officers responded that "their experience has convinced them that Florida appears to be lost in a philosophical position of not offering incentives, and what they called a flawed return-on-investment equation for the film industry."[52] Although Levine finished a distant third behind Gwen Graham and Andrew Gillum in the 2018 Democratic primary, his advocacy for the film industry seemed to carry over into the general election.

While not nearly as outspoken in his endorsement for Florida's film industry as Philip Levine, Andrew Gillum expressed support for SB 1606. An insight into Gillum's position on fostering a film production industry came in February 2018, when as a primary candidate he retweeted a *Deadline Hollywood* article that highlighted how the Marvel blockbuster *Black Panther* (2018) contributed an additional $89.3 million to Georgia's state economy and $26.5 million in wages. In his tweet he added, "This could have been us, Florida. When I'm Governor we're going to bring film tax credits back."[53] *Deadline Hollywood* went as far as to venture that the fate of Florida's film industry could "hinge on the outcome of the 2018 election."[54]

It should be noted that throughout the 2018 governor's race Republican candidate Ron DeSantis did not express any position on the tax incentive debate. Gillum's enthusiasm for incentive policies won him the endorsement of the Congress of Motion Picture Associations of Florida (COMPASS), a trade organization that represents film and television workers.[55] Building on this endorsement, in a recorded statement for Film Florida, Gillum expressed his support for Senator Taddeo's ongoing efforts to "bring back the contract economy where people can make good wages, do good work, produce great products and showcase the beauty and the attractiveness of the state of Florida all across the globe."[56] In one of the closest and most contentious gubernatorial elections in Florida history, Gillum lost the general election to DeSantis by a margin of 0.05 percent, or 32,463 votes.[57]

Several weeks after the 2018 election, Florida TaxWatch published a bleakly titled report, *Is the Sun Setting on Film in Florida?* The report provided a comprehensive review of the factors that influenced the decline of Florida's production industry throughout the 2010s. It also discussed the potential economic impact that film-induced tourism can provide for the state, acknowledging that there is a clear correlation between the decline in motion picture productions and in overall tourism to the state. Florida TaxWatch suggested four possible options for rebuilding Florida's film industry:

1. Retool and relaunch the tax credit incentives program.
2. Have local governments develop their own incentive and subsidy programs.
3. Have the private sector to develop their own incentive and subsidy programs.
4. Develop a new program to reenergize film and television production in Florida.[58]

Senator Taddeo's proposed SB 1606 died in the Approbations Subcommittee on Transportation, Tourism and Economic Development at the end of the 2018 legislative session. In a statement made to Film Florida, Dominic M. Calabro, the president and CEO of Florida TaxWatch, drew on the state's long history of economic development efforts. While he acknowledges that "Florida's business-friendly tax climate, good weather, and beaches have their advantages," Calabro advised that "state policymakers should strongly consider a sound, fiscally-responsible incentive program to help grow targeted industries such as film and television production."[59]

Following his inauguration in January 2019, Governor Ron DeSantis remained taciturn on his support for legislation that could attract film and television productions to Florida. The same month as he took office, Florida state senator and longtime film industry ally Linda Stewart set out to build on Taddeo's initial FMCC policy proposal, with Florida Legislature Senate Bill (SB) 726. The bill proposed to authorize Florida's counties "to use their tax revenues to promote or incentivize film or television productions," as long as each county "require that the production include in its credits the statement 'Created in Florida' or 'Filmed in Florida.'"[60] The bill's purpose was described as "help[ing] prioritize or incentivize film or television productions in this state." According to Senator Stewart, the impetus for SB 726 was that filmmaking in Florida had consistently "gone to Georgia or Louisiana, and they're making a fortune."[61] The bill passed unanimously in the Senate in a series of votes held in March and April 2019. By the end of the March 2020 legislative session, the Florida Legislature still had not approved a state film production program.

According to John Lux of Film Florida, "In order to change the current state of the industry in Florida, we look to the new legislative leadership in Tallahassee to have an open mind, and be willing to consider options that first and foremost helps the entire state, and second, sends a signal to the industry in Florida, the United States, and the world, that Florida is open for business and competing for high-wage jobs in the film, television and digital media industry."[62] As a nonpartisan trade association, Film Florida does not expressly endorse candidates for elected office but instead attempts to work with already elected officials. This suggested change in legislative leadership could take several different forms, from the backing of pro-industry candidates to the continual lobbying for incentivizing producers to come to Florida, along with inspiring content creation within the state.

During the March 2020 session, a series of bills (HB 7039) (SB 1636), similar to the legislation that attempted to repeal the OFE in 2017, was announced and then, following public pressure, amended to include the creation of a special Florida Film and Entertainment Council. *Hollywood Reporter* business correspondent Drew Wilson remarked that these minor protective measures should not be considered "a total loss. In both chambers, more lawmakers signed on to the proposal this year than last, indicating forward progress for the longtime industry priority."[63]

The last day of the 2020 Florida legislative session was March 19. Five days later, Governor DeSantis issued Executive Order 20–83, "urging the public to avoid all social or recreational gatherings of ten or more people and urging those who can work remotely to do so," until "the spread of COVID-19 is slowed."[64] By the end of the March, a statewide stay-at-home order was put into place, and the state soon came to a standstill. Except for one place where the projector kept on rolling: John Watzke's Ocala Drive-In.

The COVID-19 pandemic has left the motion picture industry in a state of disarray it has not experienced since the Great Depression. Yet, as the story of Florida's film industry has helped show, times of extreme crisis have also presented the greatest moments of opportunity. In the 125 years since the first cameramen traveled to Florida and cranked out grainy moving images of the state to wonderstruck audiences, Florida has continued to captivate and inspire visual storytellers in new and challenging ways. As the global entertainment industry continues to recover from the initial shock waves brought on by the 2020 lockdown, Florida once again has an opening to take the lead in shaping the future of the American motion picture industry. What that story will look like is anyone's guess, but one thing is certain: when it is time to shout, "Lights! Camera! Florida!," an incredibly dedicated and accomplished array of filmmakers and movie enthusiasts will be ready to answer to the call.

Notes

Opening Credits

1. Anthony D'Alessandro, "14 Movie Theaters, Mostly Drive-Ins, Remained Open Last Weekend amid the Coronavirus Pandemic," *Deadline,* April 6, 2020.
2. Janet Krajcsik, "Top Grossing Movie Made $1,710 Last Week, All from One Florida Drive-In Theater," *Penn-Live Patriot News,* April 20, 2020, https://www.pennlive.com/coronavirus/2020/04/top-grossing-movie-made-1710-last-week-all-from-one-florida-drive-in-theater.html.
3. Alex Zaragoza, "The Only Theater Screening New Movies Is a Drive-In in Ocala, Florida," *Vice,* April 17, 2020, https://www.vice.com/en_us/article/g5xaj7/the-only-theater-screening-new-movies-is-a-drive-in-in-ocala-florida.
4. Michael Martin, "When It Comes to New Release Showings, a Drive-In Theater Stands Alone," NPR, April 25, 2020, https://www.npr.org/2020/04/25/845026676/when-it-comes-to-new-release-showings-a-drive-in-theater-stands-alone.
5. Zaragoza, "The Only Theater Screening New Movies."
6. "Now Showing," Ocala Drive-In, https://ocaladrivein.info.
7. Jake Schofield, "Ocala Drive-In Theatre Hangs on amid Decades of Nationwide Decline for Drive-Ins," April 26, 2019, https://www.wuft.org/news/2019/04/26/ocala-drive-in-theatre-hangs-on-amid-decades-of-nationwide-decline-for-drive-ins/.
8. Schofield, "Ocala Drive-In Theatre Hangs On."
9. Julia Laude, "Ocala Drive-In Only U.S. Theater Showing New Movies," ABC: WCJB20, April 22, 2020, https://www.wcjb.com/content/news/Ocala-Drive-in-the-only-theater--569868451.html.
10. Hadley Meares, "Closed Movie Theaters and Infected Stars: How the 1918 Flu Halted Hollywood," *Hollywood Reporter,* April 1, 2020, https://www.hollywoodreporter.com/news/how-1918-flu-halted-hollywood-1286640.
11. Laude, "Ocala Drive-In Only U.S. Theater Showing New Movies."
12. Jennifer A. Huber, "Florida's Endangered Species: The Drive-In," *Sun Port Charlotte,* October 11, 2018, https://www.yoursun.com/charlotte/features/florida-s-endangered-species-the-drive-in/article_0d9a6c7c-cc2c-11e8-a675-87fdea3bf684.html.
13. Rick Allen, "Ocala Drive-In Closes," *Ocala Star-Banner* (hereafter *OSB*), October 21, 2002, https://www.ocala.com/news/20021021/ocala-drive-in-closes.
14. Robin T. Reid, "The History of the Drive-In Movie Theater: The Continued Attraction

of Viewing Movies under the Stars," *Smithsonian Magazine*, May 27, 2008, https://www.smithsonianmag.com/arts-culture/the-history-of-the-drive-in-movie-theater-51331221/.
15 Allen, "Ocala Drive-In Closes."
16 Justin Mitchell, "If Business Is Good, New Waveland Cinema's Owner Plans Digital Screen for New Releases," *Sun Herald*, February 27, 2016, https://www.sunherald.com/news/local/counties/hancock-county/article62971712.html.
17 Geoff Belcher, "'Temporary' Drive-In Theater May Be Here to Stay," *Seacoast Echo*, May 14, 2020, https://www.seacoastecho.com/news/temporary-drive-in-theater-may-be-here-to-stay/article_135be11e-960a-11ea-b589-07e1901f3066.html.
18 Belcher, "'Temporary' Drive-In Theater."
19 Pamela McClintock, "AMC Theatres Refuses to Play Universal Films in Wake of 'Trolls: World Tour,'" *Hollywood Reporter*, April 28, 2020, https://www.hollywoodreporter.com/news/amc-theatres-refuses-play-universal-films-wake-trolls-world-tour-1292327.
20 Erich Schwartzel, "'Trolls World Tour' Breaks Digital Records and Charts a New Path for Hollywood," *Wall Street Journal*, April 28, 2020, https://www.wsj.com/articles/trolls-world-tour-breaks-digital-records-and-charts-a-new-path-for-hollywood-11588066202.
21 Anthony D'Alessandro, "'Trolls World Tour': Drive-In Theaters Deliver What They Can during COVID-19 Exhibition Shutdown—Easter Weekend 2020 Box Office," *Deadline*, April 13, 2020, https://deadline.com/2020/04/trolls-world-tour-coronavirus-box-office-vod-easter-weekend-1202907646/. The Ocala Drive-In grossed $2,300 in revenue from the premiere of *Trolls World Tour* on the weekend of April 10.
22 Sandy Schaeffer, "'Trolls World Tour Honest Trailer': The Movie That Killed Theaters," *ScreenRant*, February 28, 2023, https://screenrant.com/trolls-world-tour-honest-trailer/.
23 Laude, "Ocala Drive-In Only U.S. Theater Showing New Movies."
24 Gary Mormino, *Dreams in the New Century: Instant Cities, Shattered Hopes, and Florida's Turning Point* (Gainesville: University Press of Florida, 2022), 4.
25 Both the 1890 and 1900 U.S. Census records Florida as ranked thirty-second. In 1890, Florida was ranked 32/42 with a population of 391,422. In 1900, Florida was ranked 32/45 (with the addition of Idaho, Wyoming, and Utah) and a population of 528,542.
26 U.S. Department of Commerce, "Gross Domestic Product by State, Fourth Quarter and Annual 2018." Florida has the fourth-largest economy in the United States. If Florida were its own country, it would have the sixteenth-largest economy in the world as of 2023.
27 James C. Craig, "Jacksonville: World Film Capital," *Jacksonville Historical Society* 3 (1954): 125; Joel Waldo Finler, *The Hollywood Story* (London: Wallflower, 1988), 16. *The Count of Monte Cristo* was primarily shot in Chicago, but some partial location shooting was completed in Hollywood.
28 Victoria H. McDonell, "The Rise of the 'Businessman's Politician': The Florida Gubernatorial Race," *Florida Historical Quarterly* 52, no. 1 (July 1973): 44–46.
29 William T. Cash, *The Story of Florida* (New York: American Historical Society, 1938), 583.

30 McDonell, "The Rise of the 'Businessman's Politician,'" 50.
31 Frank B. Sessa, "Real Estate Expansion and Boom in Miami and Its Environs during the 1920s" (PhD diss., University of Pittsburgh, 1950), 259.
32 Sessa, "Real Estate Expansion and Boom," 277–78.
33 Raymond A. Mohl and Gary R. Mormino, "The Big Change in the Sunshine State: A Social History of Modern Florida," in *The New History of Florida*, ed. Michael Gannon (Gainesville: University Press of Florida, 1996), 418.
34 Gary R. Mormino, "Sunbelt Dreams and Altered States: A Social and Cultural History of Florida, 1950–2000," *Florida Historical Quarterly* 81, no. 1 (Summer 2002): 3; Mormino, *Land of Sunshine, State of Dreams: A Social History of Modern Florida* (Gainesville: University Press of Florida, 2005), 2.
35 U.S. Department of the Interior, National Register of Historic Places Inventory Nomination Form, *Application of Florida Governor John W. Martin House* (1985), 9; Sessa, "Real Estate Expansion and Boom in Miami and Its Environs during the 1920s," 260.
36 Shawn Bean, *The First Hollywood: Florida and the Golden Age of Silent Filmmaking* (Gainesville: University Press of Florida, 2008), 92. This quote and the previous statement are drawn from a *Florida Metropolis* article clipping included in Bean's book dated May 29, 1916.
37 Bean, *The First Hollywood*, 92.
38 James C. Craig, "Jacksonville: World Film Capital," *Jacksonville Historical Society* 3 (1954): 125.
39 Susan Doll and David Morrow, *Florida on Film: The Essential Guide to Sunshine State Cinema and Locations* (Gainesville: University Press of Florida, 2007), 4.
40 Mary Pergola-Parent and Kevin H. Govern, "Florida and the Film Industry: An Epic Tale of Talent, Landscape, and the Law," *Nova Law Review* 38, no. 43 (2013): 68–69.
41 Jimmy Geurts, "Florida Film Struggles and Successes Post-Tax Incentives," *Sarasota Herald-Tribune*, October 25, 2018, https://www.heraldtribune.com/news/20181021/floridas-film-struggles-and-successes-post-tax-incentives.
42 Joshua Gillin, "PolitiFact Adds New Campaign Promises to the Scott-O-Meter," *Tampa Bay Times*, December 30, 2014, https://www.tampabay.com/politifact-florida-adds-new-campaign-promises-to-the-scott-o-meter/2211869/.
43 David Robb, "How the Power-Broker Koch Brothers Are Killing the Florida Film Business," *Deadline Hollywood*, October 21, 2016, https://deadline.com/2016/10/koch-brothers-florida-film-industry-tax-incentives-lobbying-1201838246/.
44 Robb, "How the Power-Broker Koch Brothers."
45 John Lucas, "50 State Legislators Receive an A+ on AFP-FL's Economic Freedom Scorecard," *Capitolist*, July 25, 2017, https://thecapitolist.com/50-state-legislators-receive-an-a-on-afp-fls-economic-freedom-scorecard/.
46 Lucas, "50 State Legislators."
47 Nelson, *Florida and the Motion Picture Industry*, 96–97.
48 Nelson, *Florida and the Motion Picture Industry*, 97.
49 Nelson, *Florida and the Motion Picture Industry*, 92.
50 Pergola-Parent and Govern, "Florida and the Film Industry," 17.
51 Gene Gauntier, "Blazing the Trail," *Woman's Home Companion* 54, no. 10 (October 1928): 167.

Chapter 1. "This Venture Was Epoch-Making"

1 David Robinson, *From Peep Show to Palace: The Birth of American Film* (New York: Columbia University Press, 1997), 23.
2 Terry Ramsaye, *A Million and One Nights: A History of the Motion Picture* (New York: Touchstone, 1926), 117, 232.
3 Evan Thomas, *The War Lovers: Roosevelt, Lodge, Hearst, and the Rush to Empire, 1898* (New York: Little, Brown, 2010), 48. The Vitascope was the projector used to screen films; the Vitagraph was the camera that recorded film.
4 Oliver Carlson and Ernest Bates, *Hearst: Lord of San Simeon* (Westport, CT: Greenwood, 1970), 97; John D. Stevens, *Sensationalism and the New York Press* (New York: Columbia University Press, 1991), 92; Joyce Milton, *The Yellow Kids: Foreign Correspondents in the Heyday of Yellow Journalism* (New York: Harper and Row, 1989), xii.
5 Thomas A. Edison, Inc., and Paper Print Collection, *Burial of the "Maine" Victims* (West Orange, NJ: Edison Manufacturing Co., 1898), https://www.loc.gov/item/98500963/; Charles Musser, *Before the Nickelodeon: Edwin S. Porter and the Edison Manufacturing Company* (Berkeley: University of California Press, 1991), 127–28.
6 Charles Musser, *The Emergence of Cinema* (New York: Scribner's and Sons, 1990), 224, 261.
7 George W. Simons Jr., *Jacksonville on the St. Johns, 1822–1972* (Jacksonville, FL: Jacksonville Sesquicentennial Commission, 1972), 16; Richard Alan Nelson, *Florida and the American Motion Picture Industry, 1898–1980* (New York: Garland, 1983), 133.
8 James C. Craig, "Jacksonville: World Film Capital," *Jacksonville Historical Society* 3 (1954): 125.
9 See Thomas Hoffer, "Florida's Film History Re-Examined," in *Essays in Florida History* (Tampa: Florida Endowment for the Humanities, 1980), 65; James Ponti, *Hollywood East: Florida's Fabulous Flicks* (Orlando, FL: Tribune, 1992), 6; Shawn Bean, *The First Hollywood: Florida and the Golden Age of Silent Filmmaking* (Gainesville: University Press of Florida, 2008), 95–99; Blair Miller, *Almost Hollywood: The Forgotten Story of Jacksonville, Florida* (Lanham, MD: Hamilton, 2013), 122.
10 Bean, *The First Hollywood*, 2.
11 Wayne W. Wood, *Jacksonville's Architectural Heritage: Landmarks for the Future* (Jacksonville: University of North Florida Press, 1989), 84.
12 Gene Gauntier, "Blazing the Trail," *Woman's Home Companion* 54, no. 10 (October 1928): 169.
13 William T. Cash, *The Story of Florida* (New York: American Historical Society, 1938), 798; Bean, *The First Hollywood*, 23.
14 Robert C. Broward, *The Architecture of Henry John Klutho: The Prairie School in Jacksonville* (Jacksonville: University of North Florida Press, 1983), 107–8; Eileen Bowser, *The Transformation of Cinema, 1907–1915* (New York: Charles Scribner's Sons, 1990), 153; James B. Crooks, "Changing Face of Jacksonville, 1900–1910," *Florida Historical Quarterly* 62, no. 4 (April 1984): 460.
15 Robert S. Birchard, "Kalem Company: Manufacturers of Moving Picture Films," *American Cinematographer* 65 (1984): 34.
16 Bowser, *The Transformation of Cinema*, 24–25.

17 Terry Ramsaye, *A Million and One Nights: A History of the Motion Picture* (New York: Touchstone, 1926), 462–63.
18 Richard Alleman, *The Movie Lover's Guide to New York* (New York: Harper & Row, 1988), 12.
19 Ramsaye, 472; David Robinson, *From Peep Show to Movie Palace: The Birth of the American Film* (New York: Columbia University Press, 1996), 167.
20 "Picture Shows All Put out of Business," *New York Times* (hereafter *NYT*), December 25, 1908, 1; Bowser, *The Transformation of Cinema*, 48; Lee Grieveson, *Policing Cinema: Movies and Censorship in Early-Twentieth Century America* (Berkeley: University of California Press, 2004), 84.
21 Ramsaye, *A Million and One Nights*, 507, 532.
22 Epes Winthrop Sargent, *Technique of the Photoplay* (New York: The Moving Picture World, 1916), 9; Richard Alan Nelson, "Movie Mecca of the South: Jacksonville, Florida, as an Early Rival to Hollywood," *Journal of Popular Film and Television* 8, no. 3 (Fall 1980): 39.
23 Nelson, *Florida and the American Motion Picture Industry*, 86–87.
24 Tony Tracy, "Outside the System: Gene Gauntier and the Consolidation of Early American Cinema," *Film History* 28, no. 1 (2016): 77.
25 Birchard, "Kalem Company," 55.
26 Paul Spehr, "City of Intrigue and Mystery," in *Fort Lee: The Film Town*, ed. Richard Koszarski (Rome: John Libbey, 2004), 5.
27 Bowser, *The Transformation of Cinema*, 152–53.
28 "The Sunny South in Motion Pictures," *Moving Picture World* (hereafter *MPW*), 498.
29 Gauntier, "Blazing the Trail," 169.
30 "The Sunny South in Motion Pictures," 498.
31 Gauntier, "Blazing the Trail," 169.
32 Gauntier, "Blazing the Trail," 169.
33 Davis, *History of Jacksonville*, 500.
34 "Kalem Company," *New York Dramatic Mirror* (hereafter *NYDM*), January 2, 1909, 8; "Florida Feud, Or, Love in the Everglades," *AFI Catalog of Feature Films: The First 100 Years, 1893–1993*, http://catalog.afi.com/Catalog/MovieDetails/35998.
35 "Kalem Films: A Florida Feud," *MPW*, January 2, 1909, 17.
36 "Kalem Films: A Florida Feud," *MPW*, January 2, 1909, 17.
37 Nelson, *Florida and the American Motion Picture Industry*, 140.
38 "Florida Feud, Or, Love in the Everglades"; "Kalem Films: A Florida Feud," 17; Anthony Slide, *Early American Cinema* (Metuchen, NJ: Scarecrow, 1994), 53.
39 "Cracker's Bride," *Variety*, March 27, 1909, 13; Nelson, *Florida and the American Motion Picture Industry*, 50.
40 "New York Picture Theaters Re-Opened," *LA Herald*, December 27, 1908, 4; Charles H. Mills, *The New York Criminal Reports: Reports of Cases Decided in All Courts of the State of New York, Volume 23* (W. C. Little, 1910), 406–7; Rosenbloom, "From Regulation to Censorship: Film and Political Culture in New York in the Early Twentieth Century," *Journal of the Gilded Age and Progressive Era* 3, no. 4 (October 2004): 375.
41 "The Kalem Stock Company," *MPW*, April 17, 1909, 468.
42 Nelson, *Florida and the American Motion Picture Industry*, 126.

43 Nelson, *Florida and the American Motion Picture Industry,* 141.
44 Susan J. Fernández and Robert P. Ingalls, *Sunshine in the Dark: Florida in the Movies* (Gainesville: University Press of Florida, 2006), 3; Thomas Graham, *Silent Films in St. Augustine* (Gainesville: University Press of Florida, 2017), 12–14.
45 "When the Picture Star Rose in the East," *MPW*, March 26, 1927, 360; Nelson, *Florida and the American Motion Picture Industry,* 208.
46 Nelson, *Florida and the American Motion Picture Industry,* 145–46.
47 Graham, *Silent Films in St. Augustine,* 11.
48 Richard Alan Nelson, "Palm Trees, Public Relations, and Promoters: Boosting Southeast Florida a Motion Picture Empire, 1910–1930," *Florida Historical Quarterly* 61, no. 4 (April 1983): 385.
49 Nelson, *Florida and the American Motion Picture Industry,* 145–46; Bean, *The First Hollywood,* 5.
50 Frederick T. Davis, *History of Jacksonville, Florida and Vicinity, 1513 to 1924* (Gainesville: University of Florida Press, 1925), 233.
51 Martin Wallace Nelson, *The Economic Development of Florida, 1870–1930* (Ann Arbor, MI: University Microfilms, 1962), 195.
52 Wood, *Jacksonville's Architectural Heritage,* 251.
53 Glenn Emery, "Dixieland," Jacksonville Historical Society, http://www.jaxhistory.org/portfolio-items/dixieland/.
54 Nelson, *Florida and the American Motion Picture Industry,* 148; Wood, *Jacksonville's Architectural Heritage,* 255.
55 "Motograph Film Company Opens Studio at Dixieland," *Florida Time-Union* (hereafter *FTU*), February 18, 1910, 8; Nelson, *Florida and the American Motion Picture Industry,* 148; Jacksonville Port Authority, "Hooray for Jacksonville," *Port of Jacksonville* (December 1984/January 1985), 11.
56 Wesley W. Stout, "When They Made Movies in Jacksonville," *Orlando Sentinel* (hereafter *OS*), April 21, 1963, 25E; Nelson, *Florida and the American Motion Picture Industry,* 210; Bean, *The First Hollywood,* 66.
57 Nelson, *Florida and the American Motion Picture Industry,* 148–49.
58 "Moving Pictures to Be Made Here," *FTU*, October 23, 1910, 20; Nelson, *Florida and the American Motion Picture Industry,* 150.
59 Nelson, *Florida and the American Motion Picture Industry,* 212.
60 "Selig in Florida," *Nickelodeon,* November 15, 1910, 285.
61 Susan Doll and David Morrow, *Florida on Film: The Essential Guide to Sunshine State Cinema and Locations* (Gainesville: University Press of Florida, 2007), 27–29.
62 "W. N. Selig Shot," *Billboard,* November 4, 1911, 14.
63 Bowser, *The Transformation of Cinema,* 152.
64 Tracy, "Outside the System," 81.
65 James B. Crooks, *Jacksonville after the Fire, 1901–1919* (Jacksonville: University of North Florida Press, 1991), 150.
66 Fernández and Ingalls, *Sunshine in the Dark,* 3.
67 Graham, *Silent Films in St. Augustine,* 8–13.
68 Fredrick E. Wright, "Motion Pictures in the Southland," *FTU,* March 1, 1914, 5; Nel-

son, *Florida and the American Motion Picture Industry*, 161; Graham, *Silent Films in St. Augustine*, 26–28.
69 Nelson, *Florida and the American Motion Picture Industry*, 160.
70 Graham, *Silent Films in St. Augustine*, 13.
71 Nelson, *Florida and the American Motion Picture Industry*, 243–44.
72 Nelson, *Florida and the American Motion Picture Industry*, 243–44. Nelson provides an extended overview of the activities of film companies active in Tampa Bay during the early 1910s on pages 244–69.
73 "Tampa for Picture-Making," *Tampa Morning Tribune* (hereafter *TMT*), May 8, 1913, 4; "Tampa—Moving Picture Company," *FTU*, May 9, 1913, 15; Nelson, *Florida and the American Motion Picture Industry*, 247, 313.
74 "$10,000 Is Subscribed for Moving Pictures," *TMT*, May 1, 1913, 2; Nelson, *Florida and the American Motion Picture Industry*, 244–47.
75 Nelson, *Florida and the American Motion Picture Industry*, 248.
76 Nelson, *Florida and the American Motion Picture Industry*, 249.
77 Hoffer, "Florida's Film History Re-Examined," 66.
78 E. D. Horkheimer, "Some Interesting Financial Facts," *Motography*, December 18, 1913, 1279–80.
79 Horkheimer, "Some Interesting Financial Facts," 1280. Other colorful terms that were widely applied during this period included "Blue Sky Fakes," "Skyrocket Financiers," "Picture Pikers," "Wildcat Schemers," "Quick Buck Artists," and "Movie Fly-by-Nighters."
80 "Comments on the Film: The Wine of Madness," *MPW*, June 14, 1913, 1358.
81 "Board Makes Protest on Libelous Picture," *TMT*, July 24, 1913, 5.
82 "A Victory for Florida," *TMT*, August 26, 1913, 8.
83 Nathan Mayo, *Florida, an Advancing State, 1907–1917–1927: An Industrial Survey* (Tallahassee: Florida Department of Agriculture 1928), 174.
84 Frank B. Sessa, "Real Estate Expansion and Boom in Miami and Its Environs during the 1920s" (PhD diss., University of Pittsburgh, 1950), 4–10.
85 Gregory W. Bush, "Playground of the USA: Miami and the Promotion of Spectacle," *Pacific Historic Review* 69, no. 2 (May 1999): 153.
86 Bush, "Playground of the USA," 154–55.
87 Helen Muir, *Miami, U.S.A.* (Coconut Grove, FL: Hurricane House, 1953), 240–41.
88 Christina Lane, "Forging Florida's Sun Screen: Architecture, Film, Orientalism, and the Settling of America's Final Frontier," *Mississippi Quarterly* 63, no. 3 (Summer 2010): 373.
89 Lane, "Forging Florida's Sun Screen," 374, 375–76.
90 Richard Alan Nelson, "Palm Trees, Public Relations, and Promoters: Boosting Southeast Florida a Motion Picture Empire, 1910–1930," *Florida Historical Quarterly* 61, no. 4 (April 1983): 385.
91 Nelson, "Palm Trees, Public Relations, and Promoters," 386.
92 Nelson, "Palm Trees, Public Relations, and Promoters," 387.
93 "Repeat Miami Pictures Today So All May Have Chance to See Them," *Miami Daily Metropolis* (hereafter *MDM*), December 8, 1914, 1; Nelson, "Palm Trees, Public Relations, and Promoters," 387.

94 Nelson, "Palm Trees, Public Relations, and Promoters," 387.
95 "Big City Scenes Are Needed by Movie Co., Hence Leaving Miami," *MDM,* December 8, 1914, 8; Nelson, "Palm Trees, Public Relations, and Promoters," 387.
96 "Prismatic Film Company to Leave," *Miami Herald* (hereafter *MH*), December 7, 1914, 6; Nelson, *Florida and the American Motion Picture Industry,* 379.
97 "The Prismatic Company to Locate in Miami," *MH,* May 1, 1915, 8; Nelson, *Florida and the American Motion Picture Industry,* 379.
98 "Field Films Make Their Bow," *Motography,* August 16, 1916, 431; Nelson, *Florida and the American Motion Picture Industry,* 379.
99 "Field Films Make Their Bow," 431; Nelson, "Palm Trees, Public Relations, and Promoters," 387.
100 Nelson, "Palm Trees, Public Relations, and Promoters," 389.
101 Nelson, "Palm Trees, Public Relations, and Promoters," 387; Nelson, *Florida and the American Motion Picture Industry,* 354.
102 "The Human Orchid," *Variety,* June 23, 1916, 19; Nelson, "Palm Trees, Public Relations, and Promoters," 387; Nelson, *Florida and the American Motion Picture Industry,* 354.
103 Nelson, *Florida and the American Motion Picture Industry,* 356–57.
104 Nelson, "Palm Trees, Public Relations, and Promoters," 391.
105 John Dorschner, "Lights! Camera! But Where's the Action?," *MH,* November 1, 1970, 14.
106 "Kalem Company Puts up Handsome Studio," *TMT,* January 5, 1914, 2.
107 "'Get in the Movies and Boost Jacksonville,' Is the Slogan," *FTU,* March 16, 1914, 9.
108 "Motion Picture Men Are Invited to the Florida Field," *FTU,* October 17, 1914, 9.
109 Maggie Hennefeld, "Queer Laughter in the Archives of Silent Film," in *The Oxford Handbook of Queer Cinema,* eds. Ronald Gregg and Amy Villarejo (Oxford, U.K.: Oxford University Press, 2021).
110 Melissa Ross and Patrick Donges, "Controversial Silent Film Shot in Jacksonville, St. Augustine Returns to the Silver Screen," *WJCT News,* July 9, 2014, https://news.wjct.org/arts-culture/2014-07-09/controversial-silent-film-shot-in-jacksonville-st-augustine-returns-to-the-silver-screen.
111 Richard Alan Nelson, "Movie Mecca of the South: Jacksonville, Florida, as an Early Rival to Hollywood," *Journal of Popular Film and Television* 8, no. 3 (Fall 1980): 42; "Made in Jacksonville Motion Picture Films," *FTU,* May 6, 1914, sec. 4, p. 23.
112 "Made in Jacksonville Motion Picture Films," 23.
113 "Made in Jacksonville Motion Picture Films," 9.
114 Steve DiMattia, "Latest Pop-Up History Uncovers City's Bawdy Past," *Resident Community News,* October 5, 2012, https://residentnews.net/2012/10/05/latest-pop-up-history-uncovers-citys-bawdy/.
115 Robert Cassanello, *To Render Invisible: Jim Crow and Public Life in New South Jacksonville* (Gainesville: University Press of Florida, 2013), 126; Mark Woods, "One Hundred Years Ago, Jacksonville Had a Mayoral Race for the Ages," *FTU,* September 2, 2021, https://www.jacksonville.com/story/news/history/2021/09/02/1915-jacksonville-mayoral-race-bowden-swearingen-one-ages/5693940001/.
116 Crooks, *Jacksonville after the Fire,* 63.

117 Cash, *The Story of Florida*, 798.
118 Cash, *The Story of Florida*, 38.
119 Broward, *The Architecture of Henry John Klutho*, 200.
120 Davis, *History of Jacksonville*, 390.
121 Nelson, *Florida and the Motion Picture Industry*, 26.
122 Daniel Pleasant Gold, *History of Duval County Florida* (St. Augustine: Record Company, 1929), 208.
123 Nelson, "Movie Mecca of the South," 44.
124 Nelson, *Florida and the Motion Picture Industry*, 164–65; Miller, *Almost Hollywood*, 76–77.
125 "Between 5,000 and 6,000 Saw Gaumont Pictures Made and Well Known Stars Perform," *FTU*, November 29, 1915, 9.
126 Miller, *Almost Hollywood*, 77.
127 "Florida Invites Producers," *Motography*, February 19, 1916, 412.
128 Nelson, *Florida and the American Motion Picture Industry*, 133.
129 H. S. Kealhofer, *Industrial Survey of Jacksonville, Florida* (Jacksonville: Jacksonville Chamber of Commerce, 1915), 3–5.
130 See James Ponti, *Hollywood East: Florida's Fabulous Flicks* (Orlando, FL: Tribune, 1992), 6; Bean, *The First Hollywood*, 95–99; Miller, *Almost Hollywood*, 2013, 122.
131 Gold, *History of Duval County Florida*, 207.
132 "Delegation May Be Sent to New York to Get California Motion Picture Industries," *FTU*, January 12, 1916, n.p.; Nelson, *Florida and the American Motion Picture Industry*, 169.
133 Nelson, *Florida and the American Motion Picture Industry*, 170.
134 Nelson, *Florida and the American Motion Picture Industry*, 169.
135 Lynde Denig, "The Clarion," *Moving Picture World* (hereafter *MPW*), February 26, 1916, 1310; Nelson, *Florida and the American Motion Picture Industry*, 179–80; Woods, "One Hundred Years Ago, Jacksonville Had a Mayoral Race for the Ages."
136 Shawn Bean, *The First Hollywood: Florida and the Golden Age of Silent Filmmaking* (Gainesville: University Press of Florida, 2008), 95.
137 Bean, *The First Hollywood*, 95–96.
138 Nelson, *Florida and the American Motion Picture Industry*, 179–80; Bean, *The First Hollywood*, 96.
139 Bean, *The First Hollywood*, 96.
140 Robert C. Broward, *The Architecture of Henry John Klutho: The Prairie School in Jacksonville* (Jacksonville: University of North Florida Press, 1983), 218.
141 James C. Craig, "Jacksonville: World Film Capital," *Jacksonville Historical Society* 3 (1954): 125.
142 Bean, *The First Hollywood*, 97.
143 "Mob Destroys Brick Building on Davis Street and Then Wrecks a Saloon," *FTU*, January 4, 1916, 3.
144 "Mob Destroys Brick Building," 3.
145 "Mob Destroys Brick Building," 3.
146 Denig, "The Clarion," 1310.
147 "Delegation May Be Sent to New York to Get California Motion Picture Industries,"

FTU, January 12, 1916, sec. 2, p. 13; Nelson, *Florida and the American Motion Picture Industry*, 170; Miller, *Almost Hollywood*, 15–19.

148 "Open Letter to the City of Jacksonville," *Florida Metropolis*, January 22, 1916, 1.

149 Nelson, *Lights! Camera! Florida! Ninety Years of Moviemaking and Television Production in the Sunshine State* (Tampa: Florida Endowment for the Humanities, 1991), 26.

150 Nelson, "Movie Mecca of the South: Jacksonville, Florida, as an Early Rival to Hollywood," *Journal of Popular Film and Television* 8, no. 3 (Fall 1980): 46.

151 "Florida Invites Producers," *Motography*, February 19, 1916, 412.

152 Hoffer, "Florida's Film History Re-Examined," 66.

153 Garth Jowett, "A Capacity for Evil: The 1915 Supreme Court Mutual Decision," in *Controlling Hollywood: Censorship and Regulation in the Studio Era*, ed. Matthew Bernstein (New Brunswick, NJ: Rutgers University Press, 1999), 16; Rosenbloom, "From Regulation to Censorship: Film and Political Culture in New York in the Early Twentieth Century," *Journal of the Gilded Age and Progressive Era* 3, no. 4 (October 2004): 375.

154 Bean, *The First Hollywood*, 94.

155 Nelson, *Florida and the Motion Picture Industry*, 189.

156 Paul Spehr, "City of Intrigue and Mystery," in *Fort Lee: The Film Town*, ed. Richard Koszarski (Rome: John Libbey, 2004), 5.

157 Hoffer, "Florida's Film History Re-Examined," 65.

158 Nelson, *Florida and the American Motion Picture Industry*, 162; Barbara Tepa Lupack, *Richard E. Norman and Race Filmmaking* (Bloomington: Indiana University Press, 2014), 69.

159 Hoffer, "Florida's Film History Re-Examined," 64.

160 "Catts Addresses Voters," *OS*, October 29, 1904, 9.

161 Wayne Flynt, *Cracker Messiah: Governor Sidney J. Catts of Florida* (Baton Rouge: Louisiana State University Press, 1977), 37.

162 Victoria H. McDonell, "The Rise of the 'Businessman's Politician': The 1924 Florida Gubernatorial Race," *Florida Historical Quarterly* 52, no. 1 (July 1973): 44.

163 Flynt, *Cracker Messiah*, 91.

164 Flynt, *Cracker Messiah*, 121–22.

165 William T. Cash, *History of the Democratic Party in Florida* (Tallahassee: Florida Democratic Historical Foundation, 1936), 134.

166 Robert Jackson, *Fade-In, Crossroads: A History of Southern Cinema* (Oxford, UK: Oxford University Press, 2017), 32.

167 Wayne Flynt, "Sidney J. Catts: The Road to Power," *Florida Historical Quarterly* 49, no. 3 (1970): 18.

168 "Open Letter to the People of Jacksonville," *FTU*, January 21, 1917, 8; Miller, *Almost Hollywood*, 114–16.

169 Miller, *Almost Hollywood*, 8, 114–16.

170 "Mayor Bowden Being Villainously Attacked by Candidate Martin in the Same Manner as Martin Attacked United States Senator Fletcher Three Years Ago," *FTU*, February 5, 1917, 3; Bean, *The First Hollywood*, 99; Miller, *Almost Hollywood*, 116–19.

171 Miller, *Almost Hollywood*, 3, 99, 116–19.

172 Davis, *History of Jacksonville*, 304. The final results of the February 6 primary was Martin, 2,890 and Bowden, 2,056.

173 Nelson, *Florida and the American Motion Picture Industry*, 46–47.
174 Nelson, *Florida and the American Motion Picture Industry*, 176, 183–84; Bean, *The First Hollywood*, 99.
175 Nelson, *Florida and the American Motion Picture Industry*, 498.
176 Bean, *The First Hollywood*, 99–102.
177 Broward, *The Architecture of Henry John Klutho*, 222.
178 Broward, *The Architecture of Henry John Klutho*, 236–37; Bean, *The First Hollywood*, 108; Lupack, *Richard E. Norman and Race Filmmaking*, 146–47.
179 Broward, *The Architecture of Henry John Klutho*, 222.
180 Samuel Gill, "Florida Castles in the Air," foreword in Nelson, *Lights! Camera! Florida!*, 5.
181 "Tampa Made Movies," *Tampa Times*, January 11, 1916, 6.
182 See Richard Alan Nelson, "'High Flyer' Movie Finance and the Silver Screen: The Rise and Fall of the National Film Corporation of America," *Film & History* 13, no. 4 (December 1983): 73–83, 93.
183 Nelson, *Florida and the American Motion Picture Industry*, 283.
184 "Superb Film Corp. to Locate in This City," *TMT*, July 23, 1919, 16; Nelson, *Florida and the American Motion Picture Industry*, 285–86.
185 Nelson, *Florida and the American Motion Picture Industry*, 286–88.
186 "A Welcomed Industry," *TMT*, October 14, 1919, 8.
187 Nelson, *Florida and the American Motion Picture Industry*, 288.
188 "Will 'Coast' Mean Florida West Coast?," *MPW*, October 23, 1920, 1066; Nelson, *Florida and the American Motion Picture Industry*, 292.
189 Nelson, *Florida and the American Motion Picture Industry*, 295–97.
190 Hoffer, "Florida's Film History Re-Examined," 66.
191 Gary Mormino, *Land of Sunshine, State of Dreams: A Social History of Modern Florida* (Gainesville: University Press of Florida, 2005), 3.
192 Nelson, *Florida and the American Motion Picture Industry*, 487.
193 "Will Push Studio Plans to Here Soon," *OS*, May 28, 1922, 1.
194 "Work [on] Orlando Movie Studio May Begin in Next 10 Days," *OS*, June 30, 1922, 1.
195 "Stock in Local Motion Picture Co. Selling Fast," *OS*, July 30, 1922, 1.
196 "Company to Begin Work on Its First Movie This Morning," *OS*, October 4, 1922, 1.
197 "An Open Letter of Importance to the People of Orlando," *OS*, October 6, 1922, 3, 11.
198 "An Open Letter of Importance," 11.
199 "Grable Has Unfailing Faith in Orlando's First Venture in the Moving Picture World," *OS*, November 5, 1922, 7.
200 "Grable Has Unfailing Faith," 7.
201 "Grable Has Unfailing Faith," 7.
202 "Beacham Unable to Hold Crowds for 'Broad Road,'" *OS*, January 18, 1923, 7.
203 "Overstreet Is New Head Local Picture Company," *OS*, June 27, 1923, 1.
204 "Overstreet Is New Head," 1.
205 Richard Koszarski, *Hollywood on the Hudson: Film and Television in New York From Griffith to Sarnoff* (Piscataway, NJ: Rutgers University Press, 2008), 16–17.
206 "When Griffith Filmed in Mamaroneck," *NYT*, December 29, 1996, 13.
207 Nelson, *Florida and the American Motion Picture Industry*, 412.

208 Graham, *Silent Films in St. Augustine,* 156–57.
209 "Movie Troupe to Make Films Here," *Fort Lauderdale Sentinel,* November 21, 1919, 1 "David Work [sic] Griffith Is First Name on Hotel Register," *Fort Lauderdale Herald,* November 28, 1919, 1; Nelson, *Florida and the American Motion Picture Industry,* 412.
210 Nelson, *Lights! Camera! Florida!,* 41.
211 Anthony Slide, *The Griffith Actresses* (London: A. S. Barnes, 1973), 136; Eve Golden, *Golden Images: 41 Essays on Silent Film Stars* (Jefferson, NC: McFarland, 2001), 160; Eugene Michael Vazzana, *Silent Film Necrology* (Jefferson, NC: McFarland, 2011), 479.
212 "D. W. Griffith's Trip 'Thro Stormy Seas," *Fort Lauderdale Sentinel,* January 9, 1920, 1; "Griffith's Trip to Nassau Checked by Hector Fuller to Refute 'Fake,'" *MPW,* January 10, 1920, 223; Nelson, *Florida and the American Motion Picture Industry,* 414.
213 Doll and Morrow, *Florida on Film,* 20.
214 Michael Glover Smith, "'Way Down East:' D. W. in HD," *White City Cinema,* December 7, 2011, https://whitecitycinema.com/tag/way-down-east/.
215 Jan Christopher Horak, "Southern Landscapes and the Mind's Eye: Griffith's 'The White Rose,'" *Image* 19, no. 4 (2008): 30.
216 "Story of West Point and the Jungle Starring Richard Barthelmess," *MPW,* November 29, 1924, 450.
217 Doll and Morrow, *Florida on Film,* 36.
218 Doll and Morrow, *Florida on Film,* 37.
219 "Last Dissolve," *Time,* August 2, 1948, http://content.time.com/time/subscriber/article/0,33009,888442-1,00.html.
220 Doll and Morrow, *Florida on Film,* 37.
221 Horak, "Southern Landscapes and the Mind's Eye," 32.
222 Edward Wagenknect and Anthony Slide, *The Films of D. W. Griffith* (New York: Crown, 1975), 194.
223 Nelson, *Florida and the American Motion Picture Industry,* 454.
224 Thomas Cripps, "The Birth of a Race Company: An Early Stride toward a Black Cinema," *Journal of Negro History* 59, no. 1 (January 1974): 30.

Chapter 2. "Of Course They Please the Southern People"

1 Richard Alan Nelson, *Florida and the American Motion Picture Industry, 1898–1980* (New York: Garland, 1983), 44.
2 Abel Bartley, *Keeping the Faith: Race, Politics, and Social Development in Jacksonville Florida, 1940–1970* (Westport, CT: Greenwood, 2000), 19.
3 Paul Ortiz, *Emancipation Betrayed: The Hidden History of Black Organizing and White Violence in Florida from Reconstruction to the Bloody Election of 1920* (Berkeley: University of California Press, 2005), xiv.
4 Holley Snaith, "'The First Lady of Struggle': The Remarkable Mary McCleod Bethune," Herstory Club, July 2, 2021, https://herstory.club/2021/07/02/the-first-lady-of-the-struggle-the-remarkable-mary-mcleod-bethune/.
5 Nelson, *Florida and the American Motion Picture Industry,* 440–41.
6 James B. Crooks, "Changing Face of Jacksonville, 1900–1910," *Florida Historical Quarterly* 62, no. 4 (April 1984): 461; Michael Newton, *The Invisible Empire: The Ku*

Klux Klan in Florida (Gainesville: University Press of Florida, 2001), 28–31; Robert Cassanello, *To Render Invisible: Jim Crow and Public Life in New South Jacksonville* (Gainesville: University Press of Florida, 2013), 103–4.

7 Napoleon Bonaparte Broward, "Race Relations," in Speeches and Writings, George A. Smathers Libraries, University of Florida, https://ufdc.ufl.edu/UF00102915/00012/1; T. D. Allman, *Finding Florida: The True Story of the Sunshine State* (New York: Atlantic Monthly Press, 2013), 337.

8 Newton, *The Invisible Empire*, 31.

9 James B. Crooks, *Jacksonville after the Fire, 1901–1919* (Jacksonville: University of North Florida Press, 1991), 34; Crooks, "Changing Face of Jacksonville," 460.

10 Daniel Bernardi, *The Birth of Whiteness: Race and the Emergence of U.S. Cinema*, ed. Daniel Bernardi (New Brunswick, NJ: Rutgers University Press, 1996), 7.

11 Thomas Cripps, *Slow Fade to Black: The Negro in American Film 1900–1942* (New York: Oxford University Press, 1977), 43.

12 Daniel Bernardi, introduction to *The Birth of Whiteness: Race and the Emergence of U.S. Cinema* (New Brunswick, NJ: Rutgers University Press, 1996), 20.

13 Cara Caddoo, *Envisioning Freedom: Cinema and the Building of Modern Black Life* (Cambridge, MA: Harvard University Press, 2014), 170.

14 Rayford Whittingham Logan, *The Betrayal of the Negro, From Rutherford B. Hayes to Woodrow Wilson* (repr., New York: Da Capo 1997), xxi.

15 Richard Alan Nelson, *Lights! Camera! Florida! Ninety Years of Moviemaking and Television Production in the Sunshine State* (Tampa: Florida Endowment for the Humanities, 1991), 21.

16 Gauntier, "Blazing the Trail," 184.

17 Nelson, *Florida and the American Motion Picture Industry*, 142.

18 Nelson, *Florida and the American Motion Picture Industry*, 138.

19 "Kalem's Florida Series," *MPW*, January 2, 1909, 16–17; Nelson, *Florida and the American Motion Picture Industry*, 139.

20 Nelson, *Florida and the American Motion Picture Industry*, 141.

21 Anthony Slide, *Early American Cinema* (Metuchen, NJ, 1994), 53; Cripps, *Slow Fade to Black*, 25.

22 "The Octoroon," *MPW*, January 23, 1909, 102.

23 "The Octoroon," 102.

24 "The Octoroon," 102.

25 Nelson, *Florida and the American Motion Picture Industry*, 393.

26 John A. Degen, "How to End 'The Octoroon,'" *Educational Theatre Journal* 27, no. 2 (May 1975): 170–78.

27 Nelson, *Florida and the American Motion Picture Industry*, 394.

28 "The Northern Schoolmaster," *MPW*, April 17, 1909, 477.

29 "The Northern Schoolmaster," 477.

30 Mike Konczal, "How Radical Change Occurs: An Interview with Eric Foner," *Nation*, February 3, 2015, https://www.thenation.com/article/archive/how-radical-change-occurs-interview-historian-eric-foner/.

31 Cripps, *Slow Fade to Black*, 30, 32.

32 Nelson, *Florida and the American Motion Picture Industry*, 395.

33. Tony Tracy, "Outside the System: Gene Gauntier and the Consolidation of Early American Cinema," *Film History* 28, no. 1 (2016): 77.
34. "Kalem MFG. Co.," *MPW*, May 15, 1909, 643.
35. "Authentic Equipment for Kalem's War Dramas," *Kalem Kalendar*, December 15, 1911, 8.
36. "Kalem Co.," *MPW*, July 30, 1910, 259.
37. "Kalem Company," February 12, 1910, *The Film Index*, 14–15.
38. Micki McCelya, "The Faithful Slave," *Atlantic*, May 31, 2017, https://www.theatlantic.com/business/archive/2017/05/the-faithful-slave/528630/.
39. Nelson, *Florida and the American Motion Picture Industry*, 393.
40. Crooks, *Jacksonville after the Fire*, 41.
41. Crooks, *Jacksonville after the Fire*, 41.
42. Crooks, *Jacksonville after the Fire*, 94.
43. Crooks, "Changing Face of Jacksonville," *Florida Historical Quarterly* 62, no. 4 (April 1984): 460.
44. James C. Craig, "Jacksonville: World Film Capital," *Jacksonville Historical Society* 3 (1954): 125.
45. Susan Doll and David Morrow, *Florida on Film: The Essential Guide to Sunshine State Cinema and Locations* (Gainesville: University Press of Florida, 2007), 2.
46. Crooks, "Changing Face of Jacksonville," 449–50.
47. Crooks, "Changing Face of Jacksonville," 462–63.
48. Henry T. Sampson, *Blacks in Black and White: A Source Book on Black Films* (Lanham, MD: Scarecrow, 1995), 3; Barbara Tepa Lupack, *Richard E. Norman and Race Filmmaking* (Bloomington: Indiana University Press, 2014), 14.
49. Crooks, "Changing Face of Jacksonville," 461.
50. "Result of Reno Affair Starts Mob Violence in the City," *FTU*, July 5, 1910, 1.
51. Kendall R. Phillips, *Controversial Cinema: The Films That Outraged America* (Westport, CT: Praeger, 2008), 98; Barak Orbach, "The *Johnson–Jefferies Fight* and Censorship of Black Supremacy," *New York University Journal of Law and Liberty* 5, no. 270 (2010): 313–14.
52. Dan Streible, "Race and Reception of Jack Johnson Fight Films," in *The Birth of Whiteness: Race and the Emergence of U.S. Cinema*, ed. Daniel Bernardi (New Brunswick, NJ: Rutgers University Press, 1996), 170.
53. Streible, "Race and Reception of Jack Johnson Fight Films," 194.
54. Devyn Halsted, "The Manliest Man: How Jack Johnson Changed the Relationship of White Supremacy and Masculinity in America," *Footnotes: A Journal of History*, no. 2 (2018): 116–17.
55. Nelson, *Lights! Camera! Florida!*, 16–19.
56. "New Items of the Kalem Companies," *Kalem Kalendar*, April 13, 1912, 4; "Kalem Producing 'The Octoroon,'" *MPW*, May 10, 1913, 602; "The Octoroon," *Kalem Kalendar*, November 15, 1913, 10–11.
57. George Blaisdell, "At the Sign of the Flaming Arcs," *MPW*, May 10, 1913, 601; Tracy, "Outside the System," 89–90.
58. "Gene Gauntier Players Return," *MPW*, May 31, 1913, 926.
59. "Gene Gauntier Players Return," 926.

60 James C. Craig, "Jacksonville World Film Capital," *Jacksonville Historical Society* 3 (1954): 124.
61 Bill Foley, "Today in Jacksonville History: May 4, 1914," *FTU*, May 4, 2019, https://www.jacksonville.com/news/20190504/today-in-jacksonville-history-may-4-1914.
62 Nelson, *Florida and the American Motion Picture* Industry, 156–57, 400.
63 "Rastus in Zululand," *MPW*, May 7, 1910, 740; Nelson, *Florida and the American Motion Picture Industry*, 396.
64 Donald Bogle, *Toms, Coons, Mulattoes, Mamies and Bucks: An Interpretive History of Blacks in American Films* (New York: Ballantine, 1974), 8.
65 Nelson, *Florida and the American Motion Picture Industry*, 398.
66 "Colored Lubin Comedies," *MPW*, May 10, 1913, 600; Nelson, *Florida and the American Motion Picture Industry*, 398–99.
67 "Theatrical Jottings," *New York Age*, March 5, 1914, 6; Daniel J. Leab, *From Sambo to Superspade: The Black Experience in Motion Pictures* (Boston, MA: Houghton Mifflin Co., 1976), 13; Nelson, *Florida and the American Motion Picture Industry*, 397.
68 Cripps, *Slow Fade to Black*, 22–23; Nelson, *Florida and the American Motion Picture Industry*, 432; Lupack, *Richard E. Norman and Race Filmmaking*, 118.
69 Nelson, *Florida and the American Motion Picture Industry*, 149, 400; Shawn Bean, *The First Hollywood: Florida and the Golden Age of Silent Filmmaking* (Gainesville: University Press of Florida, 2008), 20.
70 "Negro Meets Death for 'Movies,'" *TMT*, March 21, 1913, 5.
71 "Colored Lubin Comedies," *MPW*, May 10, 1913, 600.
72 "'Coon Town Suffragettes,'" *MPW*, February 21, 1914, 1012.
73 Carlee Hoffman and Claire Strom, "A Perfect Storm: The Ocoee Riot of 1920," *Florida Historical Quarterly* 93, no. 1 (Summer 2014): 37.
74 Ortiz, *Emancipation Betrayed*, 120.
75 Gregory A. Waller, *Main Street Amusements: Movies and Commercial Entertainment in a Southern City, 1896–1930* (Washington DC: Smithsonian Institute Press, 1995), 179.
76 Michelle Faith Wallace, "The Good Lynching and 'The Birth of a Nation': Discourses and Aesthetics of Jim Crow," *Cinema Journal* 43, no. 1 (Autumn 2003): 86.
77 Ortiz, *Emancipation Betrayed*, 140; James Weldon Johnson to Margaret Downs McCleary, January 10, 1917, Box G41, Folder Jacksonville, Fla. 1915–1917,
78 Nelson, *Florida and the American Film Industry*, 399.
79 Nelson, *Florida and the American Film Industry*, 170.
80 Nelson, *Florida and the American Film Industry*, 5–7.
81 Pearl Bowser and Louise Spence, *Writing Himself into History: Oscar Micheaux, His Silent Films, and His Audiences* (New Brunswick, NJ: Rutgers University Press, 2001), 97; Lupack, *Richard E. Norman and Race Filmmaking*, 9, 13.
82 Jesse Rhines, *Black Film, White Money* (New Brunswick, NJ: Rutgers University Press, 1996), 14.
83 Mark A. Reid, *Redefining Black Film* (Berkeley: University of California Press, 1993), 7.
84 Reid, *Redefining Black Film*, 8–9.
85 Jane M. Gaines, *Fire and Desire: Mixed-Race Movies in the Silent Era* (Chicago: University of Chicago Press, 2001), 95.
86 Cripps, *Slow Fade to Black*, 170.

87 Cripps, *Slow Fade to Black*, 30, 33.
88 Cripps, *Slow Fade to Black*, 72.
89 Cripps, "The Making of 'The Birth of a Race': The Emerging Politics of Identity in Silent Movies," in *The Birth of Whiteness: Race and the Emergence of U.S. Cinema*, ed. Daniel Bernardi (New Brunswick, NJ: Rutgers University Press, 1996), 44; Cripps, "The Birth of a Race Company," 30.
90 Cripps, "The Making of 'The Birth of a Race,'" 44.
91 Cripps, "The Making of 'The Birth of a Race,'" 45.
92 Paul McEwan, *The Birth of a Nation* (London: BFI, 2015), 14.
93 Cripps, "The Birth of a Race Company," 33.
94 Elaine Sterne to Nerney, August 16, 1915, NAACP Records; *NYT*, August 15, 1915; Cripps, "The Birth of a Race Company," 33–34.
95 Cripps, "The Making of 'The Birth of a Race,'" 44.
96 Cripps, "The Birth of a Race Company," 34.
97 Cripps, "The Birth of a Race Company," 33; Nelson, *Florida and the American Motion Picture Industry*, 418, 455.
98 Robert A. Hill, ed., *The Marcus Garvey and Universal Negro Improvement Association Papers*, vol. 1: *1826–August 1919* (Berkeley: University of California Press, 1983), 173–74.
99 Cripps, *Slow Fade to Black*, 77.
100 Nelson, *Florida and the American Motion Picture Industry*, 419.
101 Cripps, *Slow Fade to Black*, 73–74.
102 Nelson, *Florida and the American Motion Picture Industry*, 420.
103 Nelson, *Florida and the American Motion Picture Industry*, 420.
104 Nelson, *Florida and the American Motion Picture Industry*, 456.
105 Cripps, "The Birth of a Race Company," 35.
106 Cripps, "The Birth of a Race Company," 35.
107 Cripps, "The Birth of a Race Company," 35.
108 "'The Birth of a Race,'" *Variety*, December 6, 1918, 38.
109 Nelson, *Florida and the American Motion Picture Industry*, 422.
110 Cripps, *Slow Fade to Black*, 74.
111 Nelson, *Florida and the American Motion Picture Industry*, 422.
112 "Race Film Confusion," *Variety*, October 12, 1917, 29.
113 "Commence Filming 'The Birth of a Race,' Today," *TMT*, December 9, 1917, 9A; Nelson, *Florida and the American Motion Picture Industry*, 457.
114 Nelson, *Florida and the American Motion Picture Industry*, 423.
115 "Jack Noble Goes Mutual," *MPW*, December 27, 1556.
116 Paul Guzzo, "Silent Movie Shot in Tampa Was Supposed to Combat Racism," *Associated Press News*, December 1, 2018, https://apnews.com/article/b2a438cf1b0243c1bff461e3ca94d84c.
117 "'The Birth of a Race,'" *Variety*, December 6, 1918; Nelson, *Florida and the American Motion Picture Industry*, 428.
118 "'Birth of a Race' to Be Magnificent Picture," *TMT*, November 18, 1917, 6A; Nelson, *Florida and the American Motion Picture Industry*, 423.
119 Cripps, "The Making of 'The Birth of a Race,'" 46–47.

120 Nelson, *Florida and the American Motion Picture Industry*, 426.
121 "'Birth of a Race,'" *Billboard*, December 14, 1918, 48; Nelson, *Florida and the American Motion Picture Industry*, 428.
122 "'The Birth of a Race,'" *Variety*, December 6, 1918; Nelson, *Florida and the American Motion Picture Industry*, 428.
123 Nelson, *Florida and the American Motion Picture Industry*, 458.
124 Guzzo, "Silent Movie Shot in Tampa Was Supposed to Combat Racism."
125 Cripps, "The Birth of a Race Company," 51–53.
126 Lupack, *Richard E. Norman and Race Filmmaking*, 8.
127 Ennis Davis, "Ashley Street: The Harlem of the South," MetroJacksonville, May 13, 2009, https://www.metrojacksonville.com/article/2009-may-ashley-street-the-harlem-of-the-south.
128 Ortiz, *Emancipation Betrayed*, xiv.
129 Ennis Davis, "The Rich History of Jacksonville, The One You Probably Didn't Know About," December 17, 2017, https://www.jacksonville.com/j-magazine/2017-12-17/rich-history-jacksonville-one-you-probably-didn-t-know-about.
130 *Jacksonville Evening Metropolis*, May 1, 1909, n.p.; Peter Dunbaugh Smith, "Ashley Street Blues: Racial Uplift and the Commodification of Vernacular Performance in LaVilla, Florida, 1896–1916" (master's thesis, Florida State University, 2006), 76.
131 Smith, "Ashley Street Blues," 75.
132 Kristen Pickrell and Ennis Davis, "The Lost Theaters of LaVilla," *TheJackson*, May 1, 2020, https://www.thejaxsonmag.com/article/the-lost-theatres-of-lavilla-page-2/.
133 Smith, "Ashley Street Blues," 96.
134 Smith, "Ashley Street Blues," 96.
135 Smith, "Ashley Street Blues," 74, 97–98.
136 Pickrell and Davis, "The Lost Theaters of LaVilla."
137 Ortiz, *Emancipation Betrayed*, 140.
138 Ortiz, *Emancipation Betrayed*, 140.
139 Cassanello, *To Render Invisible*, 138–39.
140 Wayne Flynt, *Cracker Messiah: Governor Sidney J. Catts of Florida* (Baton Rouge: Louisiana State University Press, 1977), 86.
141 Ortiz, *Emancipation Betrayed*, 135–36.
142 Ortiz, *Emancipation Betrayed*, 147–49.
143 For more info on A. L. Lewis, see Michael Card, "A. L. Lewis Was a Giant in Jacksonville," *FTU*, February 16, 2020, https://www.jacksonville.com/story/opinion/columns/2020/02/16/al-lewis-was-giant-in-jacksonville/112234934/.
144 Ortiz, *Emancipation Betrayed*, 149.
145 For more info on J. H. Blodgett, see Dreck Spurlock Wilson, *African American Architects: A Biographical Dictionary, 1865–1945* (London: Routledge, 2004), 58–59.
146 Ortiz, *Emancipation Betrayed*, 150.
147 Ortiz, *Emancipation Betrayed*, 150.
148 Ortiz, *Emancipation Betrayed*, 150.
149 Hoffman and Strom, "A Perfect Storm," 28.
150 Newton, *The Invisible Empire*, 49.
151 Ortiz, *Emancipation Betrayed*, 232.

152 Ortiz, *Emancipation Betrayed*, 220.
153 Stephen Hudak, "Official Narrative of the Terror for Decade Was Obscured or Excused by a Whitewashing of Facts," *OS*, October 30, 2020, https://www.orlandosentinel.com/news/ocoee-massacre/os-ne-ocoee-what-happened-20201029-n3k7lqdbafg5re3qwxq2g3wnve-htmlstory.html.
154 Michael D'Orso, *Like Judgement Day: The Ruin and Redemption of a Town Called Rosewood* (New York: Boulevard, 1996), 324–25; David R. Colburn, "Rosewood and America in the Early Twentieth Century," *Florida Historical Quarterly* 76, no. 2 (Fall 1997): 175–92.
155 Lupack, *Richard E. Norman and Race Filmmaking*, 31.
156 Gary Moore, "Rosewood Massacre," *St. Petersburg Times* (hereafter *SPT*) *Floridian*, July 25, 1982, 6–18.
157 Steve Persall, "A Burning Issue," *SPT*, February 17, 1997, 1D.
158 "Rosewood Articles Revisited," *OS*, March 25, 1997, A10.
159 Henri Barber, "John Singleton on 'Rosewood,'" *Film Scouts Interviews*, http://www.filmscouts.com/scripts/interview.cfm?File=joh-sin.
160 Peter Dunbaugh Smith, *A Cultural History of the First Jazz and Blues Communities in Jacksonville, Florida, 1896–1916* (Lewiston, NY: Edwin Mellen, 2015), 161–62.
161 Henry T. Sampson, *Blacks in Blackface: A Sourcebook on Early Black Musical Shows* (Lanham, MD: Scarecrow, 2014), 32.
162 Smith, *A Cultural History of the First Jazz and Blues Communities in Jacksonville*, 161.
163 Smith, "Ashley Street Blues," 99.
164 Monroe N. Work, *Negro Year Book: An Annual Encyclopedia of the Negro, 1921–22* (Tuskegee, AL: Negro Year Book Company, 1922), 305.
165 Nelson, *Florida and the American Motion Picture Industry*, 461.
166 Nelson, *Florida and the American Motion Picture Industry*, 434. Interview of Captain Richard Norman III conducted by Richard Alan Nelson.
167 Richard Norman Studios, "The Wrecker," http://normanstudios.org/films-stars/norman-films/the-wrecker/.
168 Mark Fedder, "'The Wrecker' Commences Filming in Manistee," *Manistee News Advocate*, November 12, 2018, https://www.manisteenews.com/local-history/article/The-Wrecker-commences-filming-in-Manistee-14263467.php.
169 Lupack, *Richard E. Norman and Race Filmmaking*, 71.
170 Nelson, *Florida and the American Motion Picture Industry*, 434.
171 Nelson, *Florida and the American Motion Picture Industry*, 434.
172 Lupack, *Richard E. Norman and Race Filmmaking*, 11.
173 Nelson, *Florida and the American Motion Picture Industry*, 436.
174 Phyllis R. Klotman, "Planes, Trains, and Automobiles: The Flying Ace, the Norman Company, and the Micheaux Connection," in *Oscar Micheaux and His Circle: African Americans and Race Cinema of the Silent Era*, ed. Pearl Bowser, Jane Gaines, and Charles Musser (Bloomington: Indiana University Press, 2001), 167.
175 "The Love Bug," Norman Studios, http://normanstudios.org/films-stars/norman-films/the-love-bug/.
176 Cripps, *Slow Fade to Black*, 177.
177 Lupack, *Richard E. Norman and Race Filmmaking*, 83.

178 Lupack, *Richard E. Norman and Race Filmmaking*, 174.
179 Cripps, *Slow Face to Black*, 183; Nelson, *Florida and the American Motion Picture Industry*, 436.
180 Lupack, *Richard E. Norman and Race Filmmaking*, 146.
181 Lupack, *Richard E. Norman and Race Filmmaking*, 117.
182 Nelson, *Florida and the American Motion Picture Industry*, 286–88.
183 Lupack, *Richard E. Norman and Race Filmmaking*, 147.
184 Nelson, *Florida and the American Motion Picture Industry*, 438.
185 Nelson, *Florida and the American Motion Picture Industry*, 438.
186 Charlene Regester, "The African American Press and Race Movies, 1909–1929," in *Oscar Micheaux and His Circle: African Americans and Race Cinema of the Silent Era*, 41.
187 Lupack, *Richard E. Norman and Race Filmmaking*, 118.
188 Nelson, *Florida and the American Film Industry*, 439.
189 Lupack, *Richard E. Norman and Race Filmmaking*, 120–26.
190 Klotman, "Planes, Trains, and Automobiles," 163.
191 Lupack, *Richard E. Norman and Race Filmmaking*, 190.
192 Lupack, *Richard E. Norman and Race Filmmaking*, 193.
193 Nelson, *Florida and the American Motion Picture Industry*, 440; Lupack, *Richard E. Norman and Race Filmmaking*, 210.
194 Lupack, *Richard E. Norman and Race Filmmaking*, 211.
195 Lupack, *Richard E. Norman and Race Filmmaking*, 211–12.
196 Barbra Tepa Lupack, "Richard E. Norman (1891–1960)," Norman Studios Online Museum, http://normanstudios.org/nsdrc/portfolio/richard-e-norman/.
197 "City Lands Grant for Studio Restoration," *Jacksonville Business Journal*, February 19, 2004, https://www.bizjournals.com/jacksonville/stories/2004/02/16/daily27.html?jst=b_ln_hl; Jacksonville Historic Preservation Commission, *Eagle Film City (Norman Film Studios) Jacksonville Historic Preservation Commission Designation Application for Landmark or Landmark Site*, March 26, 2014, 9–10.
198 Dan Scanlan, "Jacksonville's 100-Year-Old Silent Film Studio Granted National Landmark Status," *FTU*, November 4, 2016, https://www.jacksonville.com/news/2016-11-04/jacksonville-s-100-year-old-silent-film-studio-granted-national-landmark-status.

Chapter 3. "Motion Pictures at a Great Saving!"

1 Ronald Yogman and Thomas Rawlins, "Yesteryear's Suncoast Film Center Goes," *SPT*, June 26, 1963, 13.
2 Richard Alan Nelson, *Lights! Camera! Florida! Ninety Years of Moviemaking and Television Production in the Sunshine State* (Tampa: Florida Endowment for the Humanities, 1991), 44–45.
3 Fred Wright, "It's a Land of Ghosts and Vanishing Landmarks," *St. Petersburg Independent* (hereafter *SPI*), March 26, 1966, 18A.
4 Richard Alan Nelson, *Florida and the American Motion Picture Industry* (New York: Garland, 1980), 487.
5 Hampton Dunn, *Yesterday's Tampa* (Miami, FL: E. A. Seemann, 1972), 23.

6 Nelson, *Florida and the American Motion Picture Industry*, 464.
7 Robert J. Barro, Jose F. Ursua, and Joanna Weng, "The Coronavirus and the Great Influenza Pandemic: Lessons from the Spanish Flu for the Coronavirus' Potential Effects on Mortality and Economic Activity," NBER Working Paper 26866 (Cambridge, MA: National Bureau of Economic Research, 2020), 1.
8 J. R. Vernon, "The 1920–1921 Deflation: The Role of Aggregate Supply," *Economic Inquiry* 29, no. 3 (July 1991): 572–80.
9 Martin Wallace Nelson, *The Economic Development of Florida, 1870–1930* (Ann Arbor, MI: University Microfilms, 1962), 32.
10 American Automobile Association (AAA), *Highways Green Book* (Washington, DC: American Automobile Association, 1922), 418–20.
11 Joshua Cobbs Youngblood, "Following a Trail of Tin Cans: Archival Engagement, 'Tin Can Tourism,' and the Internet Life of Historical Images," *Archival Issues* 36, no. 2 (2015): 36–40; Thomas Graham, *Silent Films in St. Augustine.* (Gainesville: University Press of Florida, 2017), 248–49.
12 Karl H. Grismer, *Tampa: A History of the City of Tampa and the Tampa Bay Region of Florida* (St. Petersburg, FL: St. Petersburg Publishing Company, 1950), 250.
13 Christopher Knowlton, *Bubble in the Sun: The Florida Land Boom of the 1920s and How It Brought on the Great Depression* (New York: Simon and Schuster, 2020), xvi.
14 William T. Cash, *The Story of Florida* (New York: American Historical Society, 1938), 567, 577; Nelson, *The Economic Development of Florida*, 46.
15 Knowlton, *Bubble in the Sun*, xvii.
16 Nelson, *Florida and the American Motion Picture Industry*, 300; Robert Jackson, *Fade-In, Crossroads: A History of Southern Cinema* (Oxford, UK: Oxford University Press, 2017), 34.
17 Christina Lane, "Florida's Sun Screen: Architecture, Film, Orientalism, and the Settling of America's Final Frontier," *Mississippi Quarterly* 63, no. 3 (Summer 2010): 374.
18 Ethan V. Blackman, *Miami and Dade County: Its Settlement, Progress, and Achievement* (Washington, DC: Victor Rainbolt, 1921), 34–35; Richard Alan Nelson, "Palm Trees, Public Relations, and Promoters: Boosting Southeast Florida a Motion Picture Empire, 1910–1930," *Florida Historical Quarterly* 61, no. 4 (April 1983): 393; Lane, "Florida's Sun Screen," 373.
19 Frank B. Sessa, "Real Estate Expansion and Boom in Miami and Its Environs during the 1920s" (PhD diss., University of Pittsburgh, 1950), 64.
20 Sessa, "Real Estate Expansion and Boom in Miami," 64.
21 "Personnel with Personality and Pep and Punch and Pluck," *MH*, April 2, 1922, 1A; Nelson, *Florida and the American Motion Picture*, 359; Nelson, "Palm Trees, Public Relations, and Promoters," 393.
22 "Cine-Miami," *MH*, March 24, 1922, 4A; Nelson, *Florida and the American Motion Picture*, 359–60; Nelson, "Palm Trees, Public Relations, and Promoters," 393–94.
23 Nelson, *Florida and the American Motion Picture*, 359–60; Nelson, "Palm Trees, Public Relations, and Promoters," 393–94.
24 "John Brunton Heads New Miami Studios," *MPW*, June 24, 1922, 703; "John Brunton, Noted Motion Picture Director, Who Has Assumed Charge of the Miami Studios,"

MH, June 30, 1922, 1; Nelson, *Florida and the American Motion Picture*, 361–62; Nelson, "Palm Trees, Public Relations, and Promoters," 394–95.
25 Nelson, "Palm Trees, Public Relations, and Promoters," 395.
26 William Marston Seabury, *The Public and the Motion Picture Industry* (New York: Macmillan, 1926), 278.
27 E. M. Murray, "Will Florida Have a Second Hollywood?," *Florida Magazine* (October–November, 1922), 25; Nelson, *Florida and the American Motion Picture*, 364; Nelson, "Palm Trees, Public Relations, and Promoters," 397.
28 Leonhard Gmür, *Rex Ingram: Hollywood Rebel of the Silver Screen* (Berlin, Germany: epublish, 2016), 473.
29 "Rex Ingram Coming Here to Make Next Big Movie Feature," *MH*, August 17, 1922, 1; Nelson, *Florida and the American Motion Picture*, 363; Nelson, "Palm Trees, Public Relations, and Promoters," 397.
30 Paul Sargis George, *Twentieth Century Journey: A History of the City of Oakland Park* (Fort Lauderdale, FL: Historic Broward County Preservation Board, 1991), 13.
31 "Cattlemen to Build Meat Packing House," *Fort Lauderdale Sentinel*, March 3, 1922, 1.
32 Nelson, *Florida and the American Motion Picture Industry*, 365.
33 Eric Collin, "News of the Motion Picture Industry in Miami," *MH*, December 10, 1922, 7A; Nelson, *Florida and the American Motion Picture*, 365; Nelson, "Palm Trees, Public Relations," 397.
34 Nelson, "Palm Trees, Public Relations, and Promoters," 396.
35 Nelson, "Palm Trees, Public Relations, and Promoters," 398–403.
36 Sessa, "Real Estate Expansion and Boom in Miami," ii.
37 Hampton Dunn, *Yesterday's St. Petersburg* (Miami, FL: E. A. Seemann, 1973), 31.
38 Frank Parker Stockbridge and John Holliday Perry, *Florida in the Making* (New York: de Bower, 1926), 298.
39 Nelson, *The Economic Development of Florida*, 42.
40 Nelson, "Palm Trees, Public Relations, and Promoters," 401.
41 Homer B. Vanderblue, "The Florida Land Boom," *Journal of Land & Public Utility Economics* 3, no. 2 (May 1927): 124.
42 Victoria H. McDonell, "The Rise of the 'Businessman's Politician': The Florida Gubernatorial Race," *Florida Historical Quarterly* 52, no. 1 (July 1973): 44–46.
43 Nelson, *The Economic Development of Florida*, 259.
44 Cash, *The Story of Florida*, 588.
45 Frank G. Heaton, "A Few Florida Facts For 'Bubble Bursters,'" *Suniland* 24, no. 4 (July 1925): 54.
46 Dana L. Thomas, *Lords of the Land: Triumphs and Scandals of America's Real Estate Barons* (New York: Putnam, 1977), 195; Nelson, "Palm Trees, Public Relations, and Promoters," 401.
47 Nelson, "Palm Trees, Public Relations, and Promoters," 401–2.
48 Nelson, "Palm Trees, Public Relations, and Promoters," 401–2.
49 Stockbridge and Perry, *Florida in the Making*, 184.
50 Pinellas County Department of Planning, *Historical Background of Pinellas County, Florida* (Clearwater: Pinellas County Board of County Commissioners and Pinellas County Planning Council, 1968), 27.

51. "Would You Like to Know about the Remarkable Opportunities or Investment in Real Estate in and around the Beautiful and Rapidly Growing City of Tampa, Florida?," *MH*, November 3, 1924, 12c.
52. Margaret Van Petten, ed., *Rinaldi's Official Guide of South Florida, 1925–26* (Tampa, FL: Rinaldi Printing, 1925), 122.
53. Van Petten, *Rinaldi's Official Guide of South Florida*, 122.
54. "Realize Life Ambition at Sun City Building," *Tampa Sunday Tribune* (hereafter *TST*), April 26, 1925, 9F. Ross was located about twenty-four miles south of Tampa.
55. Nelson, *Florida and the American Motion Picture Industry*, 339–40.
56. "This Is Sun City," *SPT*, July 12, 1925, 16.
57. "Movie Studio near City to Be Dedicated," *Tampa Daily Times* (hereafter *TDT*), October 8, 1925, 1.
58. "Reservations Can Now Be Made! For the Opening of Sun City's Motion Picture City," *SPT*, December 6, 1925, sec. 9, p. 1.
59. "Reservations Can Now Be Made!," 1.
60. Van Petten, *Rinaldi's Official Guide*, 122.
61. "Florida's Motion Picture Development," *TMT*, October 29, 1925, 9.
62. "Studio Park at St. Pete Will Be Converted into Moving Picture Colonies," *TMT*, August 16, 1925, 8G.
63. "H. P. Carver Sponsors Move to Make Florida Film Land," *MPW*, October 3, 1925, 382.
64. "H. P. Carver Sponsors Move," 382.
65. Nelson, *Florida and the American Motion Picture Industry*, 301; Todd Underwood and Boris Vasilev, "Florida's Ghost Towns: Sun City," http://www.ghosttowns.com/states/fl/suncity.html.
66. Nelson, *Florida and the American Motion Picture Industry*, 302.
67. Gene Fernett, "Tarnished Tinsel: Sun City, Florida: Film Dream Fades Silently," *TMT*, May 31, 1970, 13.
68. Nelson, *Florida and the American Motion Picture Industry*, 301.
69. Underwood and Vasilev, "Florida's Ghost Town: Sun City."
70. John W. Martin, foreword to *Florida in the Making*, by Frank Parker Stockbridge and John Holliday Perry (New York: de Bower, 1926), vii–viii.
71. Jay Barnes, *Florida's Hurricane History* (Chapel Hill: University of North Carolina Press, 1998), 113.
72. Liz Doup, "1928 Okeechobee," *South Florida Sun Sentinel*, September 11, 1988, https://www.sun-sentinel.com/sfl-1928-hurricane-story.html.
73. Nicole Sterghos Brochu, "Florida's Forgotten Storm: The Hurricane of 1928," *South Florida Sun Sentinel*, September 14, 2003, https://www.sun-sentinel.com/sfl-ahurricane14sep14-story.html.
74. Zora Neal Hurston, *Their Eyes Were Watching God* (1937; New York: HarperCollins, 2013), 161–62.
75. Gregory W. Bush, "Playground of the USA: Miami and the Promotion of Spectacle," *Pacific Historic Review* 69, no. 2 (May 1999): 154–55.
76. Dunn, *Yesterday's Tampa*, 23.
77. Nelson, *The Economic Development of Florida*, 278.
78. Nelson, *The Economic Development of Florida*, 278.

79. Trenton Collins to Doyle Carlton, 19 November 1931, Box 936, Folder 15, Richard Alan Nelson Collection, FSU Library Archives.
80. "Henry King Selects 'Hell Harbor' as Title of Next Film," *Hollywood Filmograph*, August 31, 1929, 26.
81. Trenton Collins to All Members of State Committee for Development of the Motion Picture Industry, 18 May 1932, Box 60, Folder 18, Doyle Carlton Papers, Florida State Archives.
82. "'Hell Harbor' Extras Revel in Honky Tonk," *TMT*, September 13, 1929, 18.
83. "'Hell Harbor' Extras Revel in Honky Tonk," 18.
84. "Jam Expected in Park as Lupe Vélez Is Welcomed Here," *TMT*, September 13, 1929, 18.
85. "Lupe Vélez Gets Big Hand as Thousands Attend Receptions," *TMT*, September 16, 1929, 1.
86. "Governor Greets Fiery Mexican Actress as She Arrives in Tampa," *TMT*, September 16, 1929, 1.
87. "Lupe Vélez Gets Big Hand as Thousands Attend Receptions," 1.
88. "Governor Greets Fiery Mexican Actress as She Arrives in Tampa," 1.
89. Mordaunt Hall, "The Screen; The Girl and the Pearls," *New York Times*, March 28, 1930, https://www.nytimes.com/1930/03/28/archives/the-screen-the-girl-and-the-pearls-fairbankses-not-to-leave-films.html.
90. Hall, "The Screen; The Girl and the Pearls."
91. "Lupe's Latest," *Broadway and Hollywood Movies* (June 1930): 11. For other reviews of *Hell Harbor* in the trade presses, see "Reviews of the Best Pictures," *Screenland* (April 1930): 85; "Henry King's 'Hell Harbor,'" in *Exhibitor's Herald World*, March 22, 1930, 6.
92. Trenton Collins to All Members of State Committee for the Development of the Motion Picture Industry, 18 May 1932, Box 60, Folder 18, Doyle Carlton Papers, Florida State Archives.
93. Trenton Collins to All Members of State Committee for the Development of the Motion Picture Industry, 18 May 1932, Box 60, Folder 18, Doyle Carlton Papers, Florida State Archives.
94. Trenton Collins to All Members of State Committee for the Development of the Motion Picture Industry, 18 May 1932, Box 60, Folder 18, Doyle Carlton Papers, Florida State Archives.
95. Kristin Thompson, *Exporting Entertainment: America and the World Film Market, 1907–1934* (Tonbrige, UK: Whitfriars, 1985), 166.
96. Samuel Borchard to Doyle Carlton, 20 August 1930, Box 936, Folder 14, Richard Alan Nelson Collection, FSU Library Archives.
97. Samuel Borchard to Doyle Carlton, 20 August 1930, Box 936, Folder 14, Richard Alan Nelson Collection, FSU Library Archives.
98. Samuel Borchard to Doyle Carlton, 20 August 1930, Box 936, Folder 14, Richard Alan Nelson Collection, FSU Library Archives.
99. Trenton Collins to Doyle Carlton, 19 November 1931, Box 936, Folder 15, Richard Alan Nelson Collection, FSU Library Archives.
100. Trenton Collins to Doyle Carlton, 19 November 1931, Box 936, Folder 15, Richard Alan Nelson Collection, FSU Library Archives.

101 Grismer, *Tampa: A History*, 262.
102 Grismer, *Tampa: A History*, 256.
103 J. C. Huskisson to Trenton Collins, 19 December 1931, Box 936, Folder 15, Richard Alan Nelson Collection, FSU Library Archives.
104 Lloyd Hammond to Trenton Collins, 26 December 1931, Box 923, Folder 34, Richard Alan Nelson Collection, FSU Library Archives.
105 Robert Grau, *The Theatre of Science: A Volume of Progress and Achievement in the Motion Picture Industry* (New York: Broadway, 1914), 327–28.
106 Trenton Collins to All Members of State Committee for Development of the Motion Picture Industry, 18 May 1932, Box 204, Folder 18, Doyle Carlton Papers, Florida State University Archives.
107 "New Florida Studio Launched by Chester Beecroft," *Film Daily*, March 17, 1932, 1, 8; Jack Alicoate, ed., *The 1933 Film Daily Yearbook* (New York: Film Daily, 1933), 144.
108 Trenton Collins to John H. Brown, 24 March 1932, Box 936, Folder 16, Richard Alan Nelson Collection, FSU Library Archives.
109 Trenton C. Collins, "Florida Seeking New Industry," *Florida Municipal Record* (April 1932): 7.
110 Collins, "Florida Seeking New Industry," 8.
111 Trenton Collins to J. C. Huskisson, 28 March 1932, Box 936, Folder 16, Richard Alan Nelson Collection, FSU Library Archives.
112 Trenton Collins to J. C. Huskisson, 28 March 1932, Box 936, Folder 16, Richard Alan Nelson Collection, FSU Library Archives.
113 J. C. Huskisson to Trenton Collins, 2 April 1932, Box 936, Folder 16, Richard Alan Nelson Collection, FSU Library Archives.
114 Trenton Collins to Doyle Carlton, 5 April 1932, Box 936, Folder 16, Richard Alan Nelson Collection, FSU Library Archives.
115 "Notable to Attend Florida Movie Ball," *Film Daily*, April 29, 1933, 2.
116 "Florida Isn't Kidding," *Variety*, May 10, 1932, 3.
117 Trenton Collins to Mayors of the State of Florida, 18 July 1932, Box 936, Folder 16, Richard Alan Nelson Collection, FSU Library Archives.
118 Trenton Collins to Mayors of the State of Florida, 18 July 1932, Box 936, Folder 16, Richard Alan Nelson Collection, FSU Library Archives.
119 Trenton Collins to Ben Bostein, 18 August 1932, Box 936, Folder 16, Richard Alan Nelson Collection, FSU Library Archives.
120 Trenton Collins to Ben Bostein, 18 August 1932, Box 936, Folder 16, Richard Alan Nelson Collection, FSU Library Archives.
121 Trenton Collins to Doyle Carlton, 2 September 1932, Box 936, Folder 16, Richard Alan Nelson Collection, FSU Library Archives.
122 Dunn, *Yesterday's Tampa*, 24.
123 Al D'Agostino to Trenton Collins, 27 October 1932, Box 936, Folder 16, Richard Alan Nelson Collection, FSU Library Archives.
124 Trenton Collins to Doyle Carlton, 15 November 1932, Box 60, Folder 18, Doyle Carlton Papers, Florida State Archives.
125 Doyle Carlton to Trenton Collins, 15 December 1932, Box 60, Folder 18, Doyle Carlton Papers, Florida State Archives.

126 Doyle Carlton to Trenton Collins, 19 December 1932, Box 60, Folder 18, Doyle Carlton Papers, Florida State Archives.
127 Trenton Collins to Maurice Kann, 17 April 1933, Box 278, Folder 4, Doyle Carlton Papers, Florida State Archives.
128 Nelson, *Lights! Camera! Florida!*, 53.
129 Gene Burnett, "Florida's Dark Horse New Deal Governor," *Florida Trend*, June 6, 2008, https://www.floridatrend.com/article/7492/floridas-dark-horse-new-deal-governor?page=2.
130 Cash, *The Story of Florida,* 590.
131 "Florida Governor Says State Won't Back Film Ventures," *Film Daily*, March 27, 1933, 1.
132 Trenton Collins to Maurice Kann, 17 April 1933, Box 82, Folder 4, Doyle Carlton Papers, Florida State Archives.
133 "Ad Club Here South's Leader," *TDT*, October 9, 1937, 2.
134 Trenton Collins to Maurice Kann, 17 April 1933, Box 82, Folder 4, Doyle Carlton Papers, Florida State Archives.
135 Nelson, *Lights! Camera! Florida!*, 53.
136 Nelson, *Florida and the American Motion Picture Industry*, 466–67.
137 Al D'Agostino to Trenton Collins, 29 October 1932, Box 936, Folder 16, Richard Alan Nelson Collection, FSU Library Archives.
138 Al D'Agostino to Trenton Collins, 29 October 1932, Box 936, Folder 16, Richard Alan Nelson Collection, FSU Library Archives.
139 "Kennedy Declares Jax to Be Logical Producing Center," *Florida Metropolis*, April 9, 1916, 8; Nelson, *Florida and the American Motion Picture Industry*, 172.
140 Trenton Collins to All Members of State Committee for Development of the Motion Picture Industry, 18 May 1932, Box 204, Folder 18, Doyle Carlton Papers, Florida State University Archives.
141 Trenton Collins to All Members of State Committee for Development of the Motion Picture Industry, 18 May 1932, Box 204, Folder 18, Doyle Carlton Papers, Florida State University Archives.
142 Al D'Agostino to Trenton Collins, 29 October, 1932, Box 936, Folder 16, Richard Alan Nelson Collection, FSU Library Archives.
143 Trenton Collins to Maurice Kann, 17 April 1933, Box 82, Folder 4, Doyle Carlton Papers, Florida State Archives.
144 R. M. Markham, "Blair's Work Brought Producer Here," *SPI*, July 29, 1933, 10.
145 Dunn, *Yesterday's St. Petersburg*, 118.
146 "Hollywood Motion Picture Man Plans to Locate in City," *SPI*, January 30, 1933, 1, 8.
147 "Kennedy Buys Property on Weedon's Isle," *SPT*, January 30, 1933, 1–2.
148 "Kennedy Buys Property on Weedon's Isle," 1.
149 "Word from Powers Awaited by City on Movie Project," *SPT*, February 10, 1933, 1.
150 "Powers Prepared to Handle Kennedy's Movies, But Will Not Share Production," *SPT*, February 11, 1933, 1.
151 "Roof Is Raised for Movie Studio," *SPT*, February 22, 1933, 3.
152 "Roof Is Raised for Movie Studio," 3.

153 "T. C. Parker, Chairman of Kennedy Corporation Board, Is Engineer, Sportsman and World War Vet," *SPI*, July 29, 1933, 15.
154 "150 Seeking Jobs in Movies Here," *SPT*, May 17, 1933, 5; "First Movies Are Taken at Local Studio," *SPT*, May 18, 1933, 5; "Weedon's Island Is Ideal Locale," *SPI*, July 29, 1933, 6.
155 John Lodwick, "Local Studios Planning to Shoot First Movie May 22," *SPT*, May 14, 1933, 1.
156 "Buster Keaton Flying to City," *SPT*, May 30, 1933, 1–2.
157 Buster Keaton and Charles Samuels, *My Wonderful World of Slapstick* (San Francisco, CA: Golden Springs, 1960), 244.
158 "Buster Keaton Arrives Here, Too Sleepy to Talk Movies," *SPT*, May 31, 1933, 1.
159 "Buster Keaton Arrives Here," 1.
160 "Movie Company Contracts for 12 Films Here," *SPT*, May 31, 1933, 6.
161 "Keaton Laughs and Smiles but Says Nary a Word as Crowd Welcomes Him as St. Petersburg's Newest Citizen," *SPT*, June 8, 1933, clipping, Box 940, Folder 36, Richard Alan Nelson Collection, FSU Library Archives.
162 "Keaton Laughs and Smiles."
163 "Keaton Laughs and Smiles."
164 "A Legacy of Laughter," *SPT*, February 3, 1966, clipping, Box 940, Folder 36, Richard Alan Nelson Collection, FSU Library Archive.
165 "A Legacy of Laughter."
166 "Buster Keaton Organizes Own Film Company," *SPT*, June 18, 1933, 3.
167 "Buster Keaton Organizes Own Film Company," 3.
168 "'Chloe' Films Burn in Plane," *SPT*, June 7, 1933, 1; "Acting Isn't All Fun, Nerve Needed," *SPI*, July 29, 1933, 11.
169 "1,400 Seek Parts in Local Movies," *SPT*, June 30, 1933, 3; "Local People in Movie Cast," *SPT*, July 4, 1933, 10; "Movie Shooting Gets Underway," *SPT*, July 6, 1933, 2; "Talkies Are Shot at Bayou Farms," *SPT*, July 8, 1933, 6; "Motion Picture Scenes Shot in Clearwater," *SPT*, July 11, 1933, 12.
170 "Film Finished, Players Leave City for East," *SPT*, July 22, 1933, 8.
171 "Film Finished, Players Leave City for East," 8.
172 "All of St. Petersburg Joins Hands with Its Movie Colony in Bidding You Welcome to 'The Sunshine City,'" *SPI*, July 29, 1933, 8–9.
173 "All of St. Petersburg Joins Hands," 9.
174 Keaton and Samuels, *My Wonderful World of Slapstick*, 245.
175 "Keaton Will Not Return to City to Make Movies," *Tampa Bay Times*, August 14, 1933, 1.
176 "Keaton Will Not Return to City," 1.
177 "Keaton Will Not Return to City," 1.
178 "Keaton Will Not Return to City," 1.
179 "Kennedy Sells Out to Parker," *SPI*, August 11, 1933, 15.
180 "Parker Reorganizes Movie Project at Weedon Island; Plans Two Pictures Monthly," *SPT*, August 15, 1933, 1–2.
181 "Movie Cameras Start Shooting 'The Hired Wife,'" *SPT*, August 16, 1933, 3.

182 "Stage and Screen Veteran to Start Dramatic School in Elks Auditorium Here," *SPI*, August 18, 1933, 4.
183 Hazel Winton, "Man Who Began His Stage Career with Belasco Now Working at Studios Here," *SPI*, September 11, 1933, 6.
184 "Stage and Screen Veteran to Start Dramatic School in Elks Auditorium Here," *SPI*, August 18, 1933, 4.
185 "Capitol Arranges Brilliant Premiere for First Locally Made Talkie Picture Tonight," *SPI*, September 2, 1933, 4.
186 Chick Owens, "Enter the Movies: St. Petersburg Takes Place Among Film Producing Centers of Nation," *Florida Municipal Record*, September 1933, 27–28.
187 Owens, "Enter the Movies," 28.
188 "'Chloe' to Get Early Showing," *SPT*, December 12, 1933, 8.
189 "Movie Studios Here in Tampa Enter Merger," *SPT*, December 10, 1933, 6; "Beecroft Takes over Sun Haven Management," *SPT*, December 17, 1933, 7; "Film Adviser Joins Studio," *SPT*, January 2, 1934, 3.
190 "Beecroft Says New Film Work Begins Jan 29," *SPT*, January 19, 1934, 10.
191 Ronald Yogman and Thomas Rawlins, "Yesteryear's Suncoast Film Center Goes," *SPT*, June 26, 1963, 13.
192 Yogman and Rawlins, "Yesteryear's Suncoast Film Center Goes," 13.
193 "Martin Leases Picture Studio," *SPI*, February 16, 1934, 1; "Martin Leases Movie Studio," *SPT*, February 18, 1934, 6.
194 Charles E. Larsen, "The EPIC Campaign of 1934," *Pacific Historical Review* 27 (May 1958): 127–47; Fay M. Blake and H. Morton Newman, "Upton Sinclair's EPIC Campaign," *California History* 63 (Fall 1984): 305–12.
195 "Studios Set for Florida-Schenck," *Motion Picture Herald*, March 9, 1935, 12.
196 "Analysis of Laws Affecting Taxation in Florida," Box 82, Folder 6, David Sholtz Papers, Florida State Archives.
197 E. J. Sparks to David Sholtz, 8 April 1935, Box 82, Folder 6, David Sholtz Papers, Florida State Archives.
198 Jacob Baker to David Sholtz, 22 April 1935, Box 82, Folder 6, David Sholtz Papers, Florida State Archives.
199 C. R. Crandall to David Sholtz, 20 March 1935, Box 82, Folder 6, David Sholtz Papers, Florida State Archives.
200 Lloyd Hammond to David Sholtz, 11 March 1935, Box 82, Folder 6, David Sholtz Papers, Florida State Archives.
201 David Sholtz to Douglas Fairbanks Sr., 5 December 1935, Box 82, Folder 6, David Sholtz Papers, Florida State Archives.
202 John Hay Whitney to David Sholtz, 18 December 1935, Box 82, Folder 6, David Sholtz Papers, Florida State Archives.
203 Harry Cohn to David Sholtz, 19 December 1935, Box 82, Folder 6, David Sholtz Papers, Florida State Archives.
204 W. Ray Johnston to David Sholtz, 21 December 1935, Box 82, Folder 6, David Sholtz Papers, Florida State Archives.
205 Nelson, *Florida and the American Motion Picture Industry*, 466; Nelson, *Lights! Camera! Florida!*, 54–55.

206 David Nelson, "A New Deal for Welfare: Governor Fred Cone and the Florida State Welfare Board," *Florida Historical Quarterly*, 84, no. 2 (Fall 2005): 185.
207 John S. Evans, *Weathering the Storm: Florida Politics during the Administration of Spessard L. Holland in World War II* (Tallahassee: Florida State University Press, 2011), 9–11.
208 Gary R. Mormino, "Sunbelt Dreams and Altered States: A Social and Cultural History of Florida, 1950–2000," *Florida Historical Quarterly* 81, no. 1 (Summer 2002): 4.
209 Nelson, *Florida and the American Motion Picture Industry*, 467.
210 Nelson, *Florida and the American Motion Picture Industry*, 505.
211 Nelson, *Lights! Camera! Florida!*, 59.

Chapter 4. "The Business Can Kill You Anyway"

1 Richard E. Foglesong, *Married to the Mouse: Walt Disney World and Orlando* (New Haven, CT: Yale University Press, 2001), 66.
2 Foglesong, *Married to the Mouse*, 66.
3 The Original EPCOT, "Walt Disney's Original E.P.C.O.T. Film (1966)," YouTube video, 6:04, September 22, 2013, https://www.youtube.com/watch?v=sLCHg9mUBag.
4 "Walt Disney's Quotes on E.P.C.O.T. and the Future," *The Original E.P.C.O.T.*, https://theoriginalepcot/overview/walt-disney?authuser=0.
5 Gary Mormino, "Sunbelt Dreams and Altered States: A Social and Cultural History of Florida, 1950–2000," *Florida Historical Quarterly* 81, no. 1 (Summer 2002): 17.
6 Foglesong, *Married to the Mouse*, 66.
7 Don Rider, "Florida's Disney World Unveiled: Supercalifragilisticexpialidocious," *OS*, February 3, 1967, 1A.
8 Rider, "Florida's Disney World Unveiled," 1A.
9 Foglesong, *Married to the Mouse*, 70–73.
10 Kevin Archer and Kris Bezdecny, "Searching for a New Brand: Reimagining a More Diverse Orlando," *Southeastern Geographer* 49 no. 2 (Summer 2009): 190.
11 Gary Mormino, "Eden to Empire: Florida's Shifting Dreamscape," *Forum: The Magazine of the Florida Humanities Council* (Spring 2001): 10; Gary Mormino, *Land of Sunshine, State of Dreams: A Social History of Modern Florida* (Gainesville: University Press of Florida, 2005), 105.
12 Richard Alan Nelson, *Lights! Camera! Florida! Ninety Years of Moviemaking and Television Production in the Sunshine State* (Tampa: Florida Endowment for the Humanities, 1991), 57–62; Susan Doll and David Morrow, *Florida on Film: The Essential Guide to Sunshine State Cinema and Locations* (Gainesville: University Press of Florida, 2007), 328.
13 Mormino "Sunbelt Dreams and Altered States," 3–4.
14 Mormino "Sunbelt Dreams and Altered States," 4.
15 Mormino "Sunbelt Dreams and Altered States," 4.
16 Otto Friedrich, *City of Nests: A Portrait of Hollywood in the 1940s* (Berkeley: University of California Press, 17–21; Gavin Lambert, "The Making of Gone with the Wind," *Atlantic*, February 1973), https://www.theatlantic.com/magazine/archive/1973/02/the-making-of-gone-with-the-wind-part-i/306455/?single_page=true.

17 William Stephenson, "Fawn Bites Lion: Or, How MGM Tried to Film 'The Yearling' in Florida," in *The Film and the South*, ed. Warren French (Jackson: University of Mississippi Press, 1981), 229.
18 Greg Allen, "On Location: The Central Florida Location of 'The Yearling,'" NPR, July 21, 2011, https://www.npr.org/2011/07/21/138561573/on-location-the-central-florida-of-the-yearling.
19 Stephenson, "Fawn Bites Lion," 230.
20 Stephenson, "Fawn Bites Lion," 234–35.
21 Michael Munn, *Gregory Peck* (Plano, TX: Hale, 1998), 60.
22 Stephenson, "Fawn Bites Lion," 236.
23 Stephenson, "Fawn Bites Lion," 236.
24 Sarah Heiman, "'The Yearling,'" *Turner Classic Movies*, https://www.tcm.com/watchtcm/titles/2523.
25 Crosby Day, "Fine Young Actor Is Highlight of 'Yearling,'" *OS*, July 12, 1998, https://www.orlandosentinel.com/news/os-xpm-1998-07-12-9807090738-story.html.
26 Stephenson, "Fawn Bites Lion," 237–38.
27 Cindy Swirko and Fred Hiers, "After 66 Years, 'Yearling' Star Revisits 'Heart and Soul' of Story," *Gainesville Sun*, February 17, 2011, https://www.gainesville.com/article/LK/20110217/News/ 604132272/GS.
28 "The Eddie Mannix Ledger," Margaret Herrick Library, Center for Motion Picture Study; "Top Grossers of 1947," *Variety*, January 7, 1948, 63.
29 Lily Rockwell, "Spring Woes in Florida," *Florida Trend*, June 20, 2013, https://www.floridatrend.com/article/15745/spring-woes-in-florida.
30 Richard A. Martin, *Eternal Spring: Man's 10,000 Years of History at Florida's Silver Springs* (St. Petersburg, FL: Great Outdoors, 1966), 159.
31 Gary Monroe, *Silver Springs: The Underwater Photography of Bruce Mozert* (Gainesville: University Press of Florida, 2008), 9–10.
32 Martin, *Eternal Spring*, 160.
33 David Cook, "Future Tarzan Makes Film at Silver Springs," *Ocala Star-Banner*, August 31, 2013, https://www.ocala.com/article/LK/20130831/news/604145760/OS.
34 Linda D. Wolfe and Elizabeth H. Peters, "History of the Freeranging Rhesus Monkeys (Macaca Mulatta) of Silver Springs," *Florida Scientist* 50, no. 4 (Autumn 1987): 235; Adam Bernstein, "Film Star and Olympian Herman Brix," *Washington Post*, February 28, 2007, https://www.washingtonpost.com/wp-dyn/content/article/2007/02/27/AR2007022702029.html.
35 Jeffrey Wayne Maulhardt, *Jungleland* (Mount Pleasant, SC: Arcadia, 2011), 7.
36 Richard Alan Nelson, "'High Flyer' Movie Finance and the Silver Screen: The Rise and Fall of the National Film Corporation of America," *Film and History* 13, no. 4 (December 1983): 82.
37 Martin, *Eternal Spring*, 160–61.
38 Ray Washington, "Ocala's Newt Perry: The Human Fish," *OSB*, April 11, 1982, 10C; "Ross Allen's Reptile Institute," *Florida's Lost Attractions*, April 7, 2011, http://lostparks.com/rossal.html.
39 Martin, *Eternal Spring*, 161.
40 Michael Connelly, "Monkey Business Colonel Tooey Was Right: It's a Jungle out There,"

OS, September 14, 1986, https://www.orlandosentinel.com/news/os-xpm-1986-09-14-0250320165-story.html; Annie Roth, "These Wild Monkeys Thrive in Florida—and Carry a Deadly Disease," National Geographic, November 9, 2018, https://www.nationalgeographic.com/animals/article/florida-rhesus-monkeys-herpes-running-wild-invasive-species.

41 Wolfe and Peters, "History of the Freeranging Rhesus Monkeys," 235.
42 Esther Williams and Digby Diehl, *The Million Dollar Mermaid* (New York: Simon and Schuster, 1999), 161.
43 "The Screen: Esther Williams and Peter Lawford Head Cast of 'On an Island with You' at Capitol," *NYT*, July 30, 1948, https://www.nytimes.com/1948/07/30/archives/the-screen-esther-williams-and-peter-lawford-head-cast-of-on-an.html.
44 "The Eddie Mannix Ledger," Margaret Herrick Library, Center for Motion Picture Study.
45 Williams and Diehl, *The Million Dollar Mermaid*, 245–49.
46 Bosley Crowther, "Screen: Hannibal Hooked; And Rome Is Saved By 'Jupiter Darling,'" *NYT*, February 18, 1955, https://www.nytimes.com/1955/02/18/archives/screen-hannibal-hooked-and-rome-is-saved-by-jupiters-darling.html.
47 Washington, "Ocala's Newt Perry," 10C.
48 Tim Hollis, *Glass Bottom Boats and Mermaid Tails: Florida's Tourist Springs* (Mechanicsburg, PA: Stackpole, 2006), 63.
49 Hollis, *Glass Bottom Boats and Mermaid Tails*, 67.
50 "History of Weeki Wachee," Florida State Parks, https://www.floridastateparks.org/learn/history-weeki-wachee.
51 "History of Weeki Wachee."
52 Mary Spicuzza, "Mermaids Make TV Magic in Caribbean," *Tampa Bay Times* (hereafter *TBT*), November 7, 2005, https://www.tampabay.com/archive/2005/10/26/mermaids-make-tv-magic-in-caribbean/; Virginia Sole-Smith, "The Last Mermaid Show," *NYT*, July 5, 2013, http://www.nytimes.com/2013/07/07/magazine/the-last-mermaid-show.html?_r=0.
53 "History of Weeki Wachee."
54 Jakob Schiller, "Professional Mermaids Are Lost Treasure of Florida Park," *Wired*, April 20, 2012, https://www.wired.com/2012/04/professional-mermaids-are-lost-treasure-of-florida-park/#slideid-48041.
55 "The Screen: 'Mr. Peabody and the Mermaid,'" *NYT*, August 14, 1948, https://www.nytimes.com/1948/08/14/archives/the-screen-mr-peabody-and-the-mermaid-with-william-powell-ann-blyth.html. At the 1941 Academy Awards, Johnson won the Oscar in Best Adaptive Screenplay for *The Grapes of Wrath* (1940).
56 Nathaniel Thompson, "Cult Movies in September: 'Mr. Peabody and the Mermaid,'" *Turner Classic Movies*, June 6, 2011, https://www.tcm.com/tcmdb/title/20917/mr-peabody-and-the-mermaid#articles-reviews?articleId=413158.
57 "Swimmer, Educator, Newt Perry Dies at 79," *OSB*, November 23, 1987, 1B.
58 Doll and Morrow, *Florida on Film*, 65.
59 *"Mermaid" Nancy Tribble Receives a Key to the City—Tampa, Florida*, 1948, Florida Memory, State Archives of Florida, https://www.floridamemory.com/items/show/151549.

60 Nancy Tribble Benda Collection (N2016-1), State Archives of Florida; "Miss Nancy's Story," Florida Memory, https://www.floridamemory.com/items/show/332712.
61 Tina Underwood, "'Miss Nancy's Store,'" *Furman University News*, May 24, 2021, https://news.furman.edu/2021/05/24/miss-nancys-store/.
62 Devin Bittner, "'Miss Nancy's Store,' One of WFSU's First Stories," *Local Routes*, May 20, 2021, https://wfsu.org/local-routes/2021-05-20/miss-nancys-store/.
63 Bittner, "'Miss Nancy's Store.'"
64 Bittner, "'Miss Nancy's Store.'"
65 Bittner, "'Miss Nancy's Store.'"
66 Marian Rizzo, "A Silver Springs Story: Ricou Browning Was the Creature," *OSB*, July 13, 2013, https://www.ocala.com/article/LK/20130718/News/604144308/OS.
67 Rizzo, "A Silver Springs Story."
68 Athena Hessong, "Remember Aquarena Springs in San Marcos," *Texas Hill Country*, December 1, 2017, https://texashillcountry.com/aquarena-springs-san-marcos-pictures/.
69 Marian Rizzo, "Human Fish Had a Life Filled with Aquatic Exploits," *OSB*, August 14, 2013, https://www.ocala.com/article/LK/20130814/News/604145183/OS.
70 Cynthia McFarland, "Florida's First Family of Water," *Ocala Style*, June 27, 2013, https://www.ocalastyle.com/floridas-first-family-of-water/.
71 Jack Malvern, "Aaaaaaaarrrrrrrrggggggghhh!," *Sunday Times*, May 21, 2005, https://www.thetimes.co.uk/article/aaaaaaaarrrrrrrrggggggghhh-v62r36ldbvv.
72 "Estimates for This Week," *Variety*, January 9, 1952, 8.
73 James Clark, *200 Quick Looks at Florida History* (Sarasota, FL: Pineapple, 2000), 57–58; Dana Ste. Claire, *Cracker: The Cracker Culture in Florida History* (Gainesville: University Press of Florida, 2006), 17.
74 Nelson, *Lights! Camera! Florida!*, 60.
75 "Charles K. Peck Jr.; Screenwriter, Producer, Nominated for Oscar," *LA Times*, July 27, 1996, https://www.latimes.com/archives/la-xpm-1996-07-27-mn-28449-story.html.
76 Edwin C. Reynold, *The Seminoles* (Norman: University of Oklahoma Press, 1957), 178.
77 James Ponti, *Hollywood East: Florida's Fabulous Flicks* (Orlando, FL: Tribune, 1992), 6; Mary Pergola-Parent and Kevin H. Govern, "Florida and the Film Industry: An Epic Tale of Talent, Landscape, and the Law," *Nova Law Review* 38, no. 43 (2013): 51.
78 Martin, *Eternal Spring*, 162; Jim Knipfel, "A Brief History of the 'Creature from the Black Lagoon' Franchise," Den of Geek, March 8, 2019, https://www.denofgeek.com/movies/a-brief-history-of-the-creature-from-the-black-lagoon-franchise/.
79 Rizzo, "A Silver Springs Story."
80 "Wet and Wild," *People*, April 4, 1994, https://people.com/archive/wet-and-wild-vol-41-no-12/; "Ben Chapman, 'Black Lagoon' Creature, Dies at 79," *NYT*, March 1, 2008, https://www.nytimes.com/2008/03/01/movies/01chapman.html; Lisa MacNeil, "Ricou Browning: Underwater Film Legend," *Hernando Sun*, September 6, 2018, https://www.hernandosun.com/2018/09/06/ricou-browning-underwater-film-legend/.
81 Joy Wallace Dickinson, "Florida Swimmers Made History in 'Creature,'" *OS*, June 11, 2017, https://www.orlandosentinel.com/features/os-joy-wallace-dickinson-0611-story.html.
82 "History of Weeki Wachee."

83 Stephen Farber, "Alligators Weren't the Only Obstacles to 'Cross Creek,'" *NYT*, September 15, 1983, 15.
84 Patti Griffiths, "Newt Perry: Still in the Swim," *OSB*, January 3, 1987, 6B.
85 MacFarland, "Florida's First Family of Water."
86 MacFarland, "Florida's First Family of Water."
87 Sadie Fitzpatrick, "Jump on In, The Tradition Is Fine," *Ocala Gazette*, July 2, 2021, https://www.ocalagazette.com/jump-on-in-the-tradition-is-fine/.
88 Susan J. Fernández and Robert P. Ingalls, *Sunshine in the Dark: Florida in the Movies* (Gainesville: University Press of Florida, 2006), 105.
89 David Kippen, "85 Years Ago, FDR Saved American Writers. Could It Ever Happen Again?," *Los Angeles Times*, May 6, 2020, https://www.latimes.com/entertainment-arts/books/story/2020-05-06/post-coronavirus-federal-writers-project.
90 "Florida during World War II," Florida Memory, https://www.floridamemory.com/learn/classroom/learning-units/wwii/.
91 Bruce Orriss, *When Hollywood Ruled the Skies* (Hawthorne, CA: Aero Associates, 1984), 93–94, 100.
92 Allan T. Duffin and Paul Matheis, *The Twelve O'clock High Logbook* (Albany, GA: Bearmanor Media, 2005), 87.
93 Nelson, *Lights! Camera! Florida!*, 64.
94 Larry Kelleher, "'The Greatest Show on Earth' Was Filmed in Sarasota in the '50s," *Sarasota Magazine*, July 21, 2015, https://www.sarasotamagazine.com/news-and-profiles/2015/07/the-greatest-show-on-earth-was-filmed-in-sarasota-in-the-50s.
95 "'Reap the Wild Wind' THR's 1942 Review," *Hollywood Reporter*, March 18, 1942, https://www.hollywoodreporter.com/movies/movie-news/reap-wild-wind-review-1942-movie-1191606/.
96 David R. Colburn and Richard K. Scher, "Florida Gubernatorial Politics: The Fuller Warren Years," *Florida Historical Quarterly* 53, no. 4 (April 1975): 407.
97 Kelleher, "'The Greatest Show on Earth' Was Filmed in Sarasota in the '50s."
98 Fernández and Ingalls, *Sunshine in the Dark*, 105.
99 Jedediah Drolet and David Listokin, "South Beach, Miami Beach, Florida Case Study: Synthesis of Historic Preservation and Economic Development," in *Economic Impacts of Historic Preservation: Update 2010*, ed. Listokin and Mike L. Lahr (Natchitoches, LA: National Center for the Preservation of Technology), 92.
100 "The 'Cocoanuts,'" *Variety*, May 29, 1929, 14; John Mosher, "The Current Cinema," *New Yorker*, June 1, 1929, 74; "Moon over Miami," *Monthly Film Bulletin*, January 1, 1941, 118; Bosley Crowther, "'The Palm Beach Story' Brings Claudette Colbert and Joel McCrea to the Rivoli," *NYT*, December 11, 1942, 12.
101 Mormino, *Land of Sunshine, State of Dreams*, 83.
102 Mormino, *Land of Sunshine, State of Dreams*, 93.
103 Aubrey Solomon, *Twentieth Century Fox: A Corporate and Financial History* (London: Rowman and Littlefield, 2002), 226; Hal Foust, "The Tribune Traveler's Guide: Make Film of Florida Water Skiing Capital," *Chicago Daily Tribune*, February 22, 1953, D3.
104 Bush, "Playground of the USA," 169.
105 "'A Hole in the Head,'" *Harrison's Reports*, May 23, 1959, 83.
106 Herb Rau, "Sinatra Left His Mark in Miami," *Miami News*, November 23, 1958, 12A.

107 Rau, "Sinatra Left His Mark in Miami," 12A.
108 Ponti, *Hollywood East*, 19; Ily Goyanes, "Celluloid City: Jerry Lewis Is *The Bellboy* at the Fontainebleau Hotel," *Miami New Times*, August 26, 2010, https://www.miaminewtimes.com/arts/celluloid-city-jerry-lewis-is-the-bellboy-at-the-fontainebleau-hotel-6491506; Wayne Federman, "What Reagan Did for Hollywood," *Atlantic*, November 14, 2011, https://www.theatlantic.com/entertainment/archive/2011/11/what-reagan-did-for-hollywood/248391/.
109 Fernández and Ingalls, *Sunshine in the Dark*, 110–12.
110 Fernández and Ingalls, *Sunshine in the Dark*, 44–45.
111 Thomas Lisanti, *Hollywood Surf and Beach Movies: The First Wave, 1959–1969* (Jefferson, NC: MacFarland, 2005), 38.
112 "Ocala Residents Remember the Day Elvis Came to Town," *OSB*, August 11, 2007, https://www.ocala.com/article/LK/20070811/news/604238353/OS; Bill Dean, "Young Tom Petty's Life Changed When He Met Elvis," *Gainesville Sun*, August 16, 2007, https://www.gainesville.com/news/20070816/young-tom-pettys-life-changed-when-he-met-elvis.
113 Paul Zollo, *Conversations with Tom Petty* (London: Omnibus, 2005), 9–11.
114 Thompson Howard, "'Girl Happy' at Forum Has Elvis Presley Singing Again," *NYT*, May 27, 1965, 28.
115 Lisanti, *Hollywood Surf and Beach Movies*, 193.
116 James L. Neibaur, *The Elvis Movies* (Lanham, MD: Rowman and Littlefield, 2014), 219.
117 Nelson, *Lights! Camera! Florida!*, 64–66.
118 Fernández and Ingalls, *Sunshine in the Dark*, 79.
119 David Willis, *The Cinematic Legacy of Frank Sinatra* (New York: St. Martin's, 2016), 20–21.
120 Glenn Collins, "Raquel Welch: I Like a Character with Backbone," *NYT*, May 30, 1982, D1.
121 Linda May Strawn, "Samuel Z. Arkoff Interview," in *King of the Bs: Working within the Hollywood System*, ed. Todd McCarthy and Charles Flynn (New York: Dutton, 1975), 257.
122 Hugh, "How Do You Reach a Movie Goal?," 17B.
123 Hugh, "How Do You Reach a Movie Goal?," 17B.
124 Pinellas County Department of Environmental Education, *The Weedon Island Story* (Tarpon Springs, FL: Department of Environmental Lands Division, 2005), 35.
125 Nelson, *Lights! Camera! Florida!*, 62.
126 Wheeler Winston Dixon, *Death of the Moguls: The End of Classical Hollywood* (New Brunswick, NJ: Rutgers University Press, 2012), 67.
127 Amy Turner, "Recovering 'Carib Gold,'" *Black Camera* 2, no. 1 (Winter 2010): 63.
128 Margert Foresman, "'Caribe Gold' Is Under Way," *Key West Citizen*, December 6, 1955, 1.
129 Foresman, "'Caribe Gold' Is Under Way," 1.
130 Turner, "Recovering 'Carib Gold,'" 66.
131 Turner, "Recovering 'Carib Gold,'" 69.
132 Sid Porter, "California, Here We Come—With Movies," *OS*, August 1, 1954, 25.
133 "Movie Studio Being Built," *OS*, March 9, 1954, 3.

134 "$5,500 Damage in Studio Fire," *MH*, January 9, 1953, 19.
135 "Top TV Director Joins Firm," *Orlando Evening Star* (hereafter *OES*), February 10, 1954, 3.
136 "Top TV Director Joins Firm," 3.
137 "TV Film Studio Here Seeks Talent for Cast," *OS*, June 1, 1954, 15; "Avalon Studios Name Production Official," *OS*, June 8, 1954, 9.
138 "TV Film Series Completed at Rainbow Springs," *Tampa Times*, July 7, 1954, 8.
139 Erkine Johnson, "Hollywood Today," *Spencer Daily Reporter*, October 4, 1955, 5.
140 "Avalon Studios Hit by Suits against Firm, Stockholder," *OS*, May 20, 1955, 11A.
141 "Casey to Make Feature Films," *OS*, April 1, 1955, 3; "Film Firm Seeks Miami Site," *OS*, April 10, 1955, 3; "Avalon Studios Hit by Suits," 11A.
142 "Film Firm Seeks Miami Site," 3.
143 "Casey to Make Feature Films," 3.
144 Jean Yothers, "On the Town," *OS*, April 11, 1955, 14.
145 Yothers, "On the Town," 14.
146 "Florida Studio Gets New Head," *Fort Lauderdale News*, March 29, 1956, 58.
147 Albert Johnson, "Jack Garfien: An Interview," *Film Quarterly*, 17, no. 1 (Autumn 1963): 36–43.
148 Jean Yothers, "Producer Sees Central Florida as Potential Filming Center," *OS*, July 24, 1956, 7.
149 "Commercial Cues," *Billboard*, June 24, 1957, 15.
150 "Filmmaker Choses Winter Park," *Fort Lauderdale News*, May 5, 1957, 62.
151 "Shamrock Studios' Activities Reflect Latest Industry Bid," *OES*, June 14, 1958, 3.
152 "Florida Gets in the Movies," clipping, Box 942, Folder 44, Richard Alan Nelson Collection, FSU Library Archive.
153 Tony Perrottet, "When Americans Loved Fidel Castro," *NYT*, January 24, 2019, https://www.nytimes.com/2019/01/24/opinion/cuba-fidel-castro-1959.html; Perrottet, "When Castro Charmed the United States," Smithsonian.com, January 24, 2019, https://www.smithsonianmag.com/history/when-fidel-castro-charmed-united-states-180971277/.
154 John Clemenston, "Cuban Gov't Halts Shamrock Production of Revolt," *OS*, June 25, 1959, 2A.
155 Henry Balch, "Hush Puppies," *OS*, January 6, 1960, 6B.
156 Balch, "Hush Puppies," *OS*, January 9, 1960, 6B.
157 Todd Persons, "Mitchell Hearing Set for March 6," *OES*, January 31, 1961, 1.
158 Charles P. Mitchell, *The Hitler Filmography: Worldwide Feature Film and Television Miniseries Portrayals 1940 Through 2000* (Jefferson NC: MacFarland, 2002), 69–70.
159 "Obituaries," *OS*, May 28, 1992, B6.
160 "Film Star Arrives to Make Movies," *OS*, November 16, 1959, 1B; "Thespian to Appear in Play," *OS*, February 4, 1960, 15.
161 Ben Brotemarkle, interview by Rodney Cavin, *Florida Frontiers Podcast*, October 2018, https://myfloridahistory.org/frontiers/radio/program/377.
162 Brotemarkle, interview by Rodney Cavin.
163 "Hugh Heads Culture Group," *OS*, March 19, 1967, 6.
164 "Hugh Heads Culture Group," 6.

165 Nelson, *Lights! Camera! Florida!*, 69.
166 "TV Freeze Lifted: 2,053 New Stations to Blanket Nation, F.C.C. Ends 3½ Year Ban," *NYT*, April 14, 1952, 1.
167 Nelson, *Lights! Camera! Florida!*, 69.
168 "Florida Sheriff's Bureau Story Now Told in New TV Crime Series," *SPT*, October 12, 1961, 6D.
169 Gaspar Gonzalez, "The House That Flipper Built: North Miami's Contribution to Popular Culture, From TV's Most Famous Dolphin to 'Miami Vice' and Beyond," *Biscayne Times* 10, no. 1 (March 2012): 35.
170 Martin Grams Jr., *Science Fiction Theater: A History of the Television Program, 1955–1957* (Albany, GA: Bear Manor Media, 2017), 28.
171 Hal Erickson, *Syndicated Television: The First Forty Years, 1947–1987* (Jefferson, NC: McFarland, 2002), 41; Tim Brooks and Earle Marsh, *The Complete Directory to Prime Time Network and Cable TV Shows, 1946–present* (New York: Ballantine, 2003), 1205; Dewayne Bevil, "Return of 'Sea Hunt,'" *OS*, May 24, 2011, D5.
172 Bill Kelley, "Sun, Sleaze and Wild, Wild, Women for 20 Years, a Flood of Sex and Slasher Sagas Made South Florida the Trash-Movie Capital of the World," *South Florida Sun Sentinel*, September 8, 1991, https://www.sun-sentinel.com/news/fl-xpm-1991-09-08-9102040404-story.html.
173 Gonzalez, "The House That Flipper Built," 35.
174 Gonzalez, "The House That Flipper Built," 35.
175 Alex McNeil, *Total Television: The Comprehensive Guide to Programming from 1948 to Present* (New York: Penguin, 1996), 263.
176 McNeil, *Total Television*, 263.
177 Hal Humphrey, "Wait a Minute, Marshal Dillon, What about Me?," *Los Angeles Times*, January 22, 1964, C11.
178 "UA Finally Gets Its Hands on Ziv," *Broadcasting*, March 14, 1960, 84; Linda Vaccariello, "Fred's World," *Cincinnati Magazine*, April 2003, 161–62.
179 Gonzalez, "The House That Flipper Built," 36.
180 Gonzalez, "The House That Flipper Built," 36.
181 Gonzalez, "The House That Flipper Built," 36.
182 Gonzalez, "The House That Flipper Built," 36.
183 "Flipper, the Educated Dolphin, Cavorts in a Seascape Drama," *NYT*, September 19, 1963, 20.
184 Gonzalez, "The House That Flipper Built," 36.
185 "Many Flippers," *Miami Herald*, November 23, 1986, Miami Herald Archives, https://www.miamiherald.com/news/local/community/miami-dade/article235003132.html.
186 "Wet and Wild," *People*, April 4, 1994, https://people.com/archive/wet-and-wild-vol-41-no-12/.
187 "Top Rental Features of 1963," *Variety*, January 8, 1964, 71.
188 Gonzalez, "The House That Flipper Built," 38.
189 M. Barron Stofik, *Saving South Beach* (Gainesville, FL: University Press of Florida, 2005), 107.
190 Nelson, *Lights! Camera! Florida!*, 69.
191 Gonzalez, "The House That Flipper Built," 40.

192 Gonzalez, "The House That Flipper Built," 35.
193 Richard O'Barry and Keith Coulbourn, *Behind the Dolphin Smile* (Chapel Hill, NC: Algonquin, 1988), 200.
194 Cleveland Amory, "Animal Kingdom, USA: Out in California Flourishes a Wild Animal Domain Located Just This Side of Unbelievable," *TV Guide*, April 23, 1966, 4.
195 Bob Foster, "Screenings," *San Mateo County Times*, May 5, 1966, 32; Kenneth White Munden, ed., *American Film Institute Catalog: Feature Films 1961–1970* (Berkeley: University of California Press, 1976), 392.
196 Foster, "Screenings," 32.
197 Paul Mavis, "*Gentle Ben*: Season One," DVD Talk, October 15, 2013, https://www.dvdtalk.com/reviews/62808/gentle-ben-season-one/.
198 Gonzalez, "The House That Flipper Built," 42.
199 John Hill, "Movies Lost Kingdom: Hard Times Hit Father of South Florida Filmmaking Industry," *OS*, November 9, 1987, 24.
200 Gonzalez, "The House That Flipper Built," 42–44.
201 Gonzalez, "The House That Flipper Built," 44.
202 Gonzalez, "The House That Flipper Built," 42–44.
203 Interview with James C. Pergola (September 1, 2012), featured in Mary Pergola-Parent and Kevin H. Govern, "Florida and the Film Industry: An Epic Tale of Talent, Landscape, and the Law," *Nova Law Review* 38, no. 43 (2013): 52.
204 Interview with James C. Pergola, 52–53.
205 James Pergola, "Father's Footsteps: Becoming a Filmmaker Like His Father," *Naples Daily News*, June 21, 2009, https://archive.naplesnews.com/lifestyle/neapolitan/fathers-footsteps-becoming-a-filmmaker-like-his-father-ep-397740634-343889912.html.
206 Pergola-Parent and Govern, "Florida and the Film Industry," 55–56.
207 Pergola-Parent and Govern, "Florida and the Film Industry," 56.
208 Pergola-Parent and Govern, "Florida and the Film Industry," 56.
209 Nelson, *Lights! Camera! Florida!*, 97.
210 Bart Kimball, "The Development of the Television and Film Industry in Dade County, Florida" (master's thesis, University of Florida, 1969), 55.
211 Kimball, "The Development of the Television and Film Industry in Dade County, Florida," 9.
212 Richard Alan Nelson, "Florida: The Forgotten Film Capital," *Journal of the University Film Association* 29, no. 3 (Summer 1977): 9.
213 Kimball, "The Development of the Television and Film Industry in Dade County, Florida," 42.
214 Pergola-Parent and Govern, "Florida and the Film Industry," 57.
215 Pergola-Parent and Govern, "Florida and the Film Industry," 57.
216 Nelson, *Lights! Camera! Florida!*, 83.
217 "Hugh Heads Culture Group," 6.
218 "Hugh Heads Culture Group," 6.
219 "Welcome to The Florida Council of 100," Florida Council of 100, https://fc100.org.
220 Kimball, "The Development of the Television and Film Industry in Dade County, Florida," 57 58.

221 Kimball, "The Development of the Television and Film Industry in Dade County, Florida," 57–58.
222 Kimball, "The Development of the Television and Film Industry in Dade County, Florida," 58.
223 Gonzalez, "The House That Flipper Built," 42.
224 Gonzalez, "The House That Flipper Built," 44.
225 Philip Valys, "A Filmmaker's Schlock to the System," *South Florida Sun Sentinel*, September 19, 2012, 4A.
226 Kelley, "Sun, Sleaze, and Wild, Wild, Women."
227 Gonzalez, "The House That Flipper Built," 42–44.
228 Bailey H. Thompson, "Orlando's Martin Andersen: Power behind the Boom," *Florida Historical Quarterly* 79, no. 4 (Spring 2001): 505.
229 Eve Bacon, *Orlando: A Centennial History, Volume II* (Chuluota, FL: Mickler House, 1977), 267.
230 Richard Foglesong, *Magic Town: Orlando and Disney World* (Los Angeles, CA: Western Political Science Association, 1990), 8.
231 Joe Flower, *Prince of the Magic Kingdom: Michael Eisner and the Re-Making of Disney* (New York: John Wiley and Sons, 1991), 253; Foglesong, *Married to the Mouse*, 73.
232 Bacon, *Orlando: A Centennial History, Volume II*, 267; Mormino, "Sunbelt Dreams and Altered States," 15.
233 "Florida Tries Again to Regain Lost Movie Industry," *OS*, September 7, 1965, 1B.
234 Dan Heaton, "Ride the Movies: The Evolution of Universal Orlando," The Tomorrow Society, July 13, 2015, https://tomorrowsociety.com/ride-the-movies-the-evolution-of-universal-orlando/.

Chapter 5. "Assurances of Full Cooperation"

1 NickRewind, "Footage of 1992 Nickelodeon Time Capsule ft. Joey Lawrence & Mike O'Malley," YouTube video, April 30, 2016, 04:49, https://www.youtube.com/watch?v=W1hxmfi_4J8; Adrienne Crezo, "Every Item in Nickelodeon's Time Capsule," Mentalfloss, June 25, 2012, https://www.mentalfloss.com/article/31016/every-item-inside-time-capsule-nickelodeon-buried-1992.
2 NickRewind, "Footage of 1992 Nickelodeon Time Capsule."
3 Mike Schneider, "Nickelodeon to End Orlando Production," *Tampa Tribune*, May 25, 2005, 4.
4 Schneider, "Nickelodeon to End Orlando Production," 4.
5 Susan Strother Clarke, "Hollywood East Turns Out to Be Just a Dream," *OS*, May 22, 2004, H1.
6 Strother Clarke, "Hollywood East Turns Out to Be Just a Dream," H1.
7 Jerry W. Jackson, "More Nick Hotels May Be in the Works," *OS*, May 28, 2005, C3; Jackson, "A Resort with Character(s)," *OS*, June 9, 2005, X3.
8 "Disney Shutters Florida Studio," CNN Money, January 12, 2004, https://money.cnn.com/2004/01/12/news/companies/disney_layoffs/.
9 Michael McCarthy, "War of Words Erupts at Walt Disney," *USA Today*, December 2,

2003, https://usatoday30.usatoday.com/money/media/2003-12-01-disney-words_x.htm.
10. Walter Isaacson, *Steve Jobs* (New York: Simon and Schuster, 2013), 435–36.
11. James B. Stewart, *DisneyWar: Intrigue, Treachery and Deceit in the Magic Kingdom* (London: Simon and Schuster, 2005), 472–73.
12. Kathleen McGrory, "Burn Notice: We'll Write the Scripts Thanks," *MH*, August 10, 2012, https://www.miamiherald.com/latest-news/article2087595.html.
13. James Ponti, *Hollywood East: Florida's Fabulous Flicks* (Orlando, FL: Tribune, 1992), 8.
14. Gary R. Mormino, "Sunbelt Dreams and Altered States: A Social and Cultural History of Florida, 1950–2000," *Florida Historical Quarterly* 81, no. 1 (Summer 2002): 3; Gary Mormino, *Land of Sunshine, State of Dreams: A Social History of Modern Florida* (Gainesville: University Press of Florida, 2005), 15.
15. Richard Alan Nelson, *Lights! Camera! Florida! Ninety Years of Moviemaking and Television Production in the Sunshine State* (Tampa: Florida Endowment for the Humanities, 1991), 91; Jon Lewis, *Hollywood v. Hardcore: How the Struggle over Censorship Saved the Modern Film Industry* (New York: New York University Press, 2000), 198–201.
16. Bill Kelley, "Sun, Sleaze and Wild, Wild, Women for 20 Years, a Flood of Sex and Slasher Sagas Made South Florida the Trash-Movie Capital of the World," *South Florida Sun Sentinel*, September 8, 1991, https://www.sun-sentinel.com/news/fl-xpm-1991-09-08-9102040404-story.html.
17. Kelley, "Sun, Sleaze and Wild, Wild, Women."
18. Kelley, "Sun, Sleaze and Wild, Wild, Women."
19. Jason Zinoman, *Shock Value: How a Few Eccentric Outsiders Gave Us Nightmares, Conquered Hollywood, and Invented Modern Horror* (New York: Penguin Press, 2011), 33–34
20. Kelley, "Sun, Sleaze, and Wild, Wild, Women."
21. "Blood Feast Arrest: Hold House Manager on Delinquency Angle," *Variety*, April 1, 1964, 8; Kevin Thomas, "'Blood Feast' Grisly, Boring, Movie Trash," *Los Angeles Times*, May 2, 1964, 5; Stephen King, Twitter post, June 29, 2021, 4:53 p.m. https://twitter.com/stephenking/status/1409978287661719556.
22. Randy Palmer, *Herschell Gordon Lewis: Godfather of Gore* (Jefferson, NC: McFarland, 2000), 7.
23. Kelley, "Sun, Sleaze, and Wild, Wild, Women."
24. Philip Valys, "A Filmmaker's Schlock to the System," *South Florida Sun Sentinel*, September 19, 2012, 4A.
25. Valys, "A Filmmaker's Schlock to the System."
26. Linda Williams, *Porn Studies* (Durham, NC: Duke University Press, 2004), 370–400.
27. Susanna Paasonen and Laura Saarenmaa "The Golden Age of Porn: Nostalgia and History in Cinema," in *Pornification: Sex and Sexuality in Media Culture*, ed. Kaarina Nikunen, Paasonen, and Saarenmaa (Oxford, UK: Berg, 2007), 23–32.
28. "Gerard Damiano, 80; Directed Ground-Breaking 'Deep Throat' Film," *Washington Post*, November 1, 2008, https://www.washingtonpost.com/wp-dyn/content/article/2008/10/31/AR2008103103740_pf.html.
29. Nelson, *Lights! Camera! Florida!*, 92.

30 Nelson, *Lights! Camera! Florida!*, 92.
31 Lewis, *Hollywood v. Hardcore*, 211.
32 Jedediah Drolet and David Listokin, "South Beach, Miami Beach, Florida Case Study: Synthesis of Historic Preservation and Economic Development," in *Economic Impacts of Historic Preservation: Update 2010*, ed. Listokin and Mike L. Lahr (Natchitoches, LA: National Center for the Preservation of Technology), 92.
33 "Races: Ain't Nobody Gonna Touch King Claude," *Time*, April 20, 1970, https://content.time.com/time/subscriber/article/0,33009,944015,00.html-Updated link.
34 Gordon E. Harvey, "The Nut with a Huey Long Outlook versus the Goblins of Fear and Distortion: Reubin Askew and the Campaign to Establish the Florida Corporate Profits Tax," *Florida Historical Quarterly* 86, no. 3 (Winter 2008): 312–13.
35 Harvey, "The Nut with a Huey Long Outlook," 312.
36 Text of Askew campaign speech, Sarasota, 24 July 1970; text of Askew campaign speeches, Tallahassee, 5 September 1970, and Tampa, 24 September 1970, all in Askew Campaign Press Files, RG 900000 MSS, M83-8, Box 1, Reubin Askew Campaign Papers, Florida State Archives.
37 Daniel Ruth, "Florida Filmmaking Ripe for Boom," *Tampa Tribune*, July 24, 1977, 3.
38 George Adcock, "In Search of Hollywood South," *The South Magazine* 4 no. 6 (November/December 1977), 63.
39 Nelson, *Lights! Camera! Florida!*, 95.
40 Robert Aldrich, "I Can't Get Jimmy Carter to See My Movie!," *Film Comment* 13, no. 2 (March/April, 1977): 46–52.
41 Surabhi Sabat, "Where Was 'Smokey and the Bandit' Filmed?," *RepublicWorld*, February 1, 2021, https://www.republicworld.com/entertainment-news/hollywood-news/where-was-smokey-and-the-bandit-filmed-see-filming-locations-of-burt-reynolds-starrer.html.
42 Nelson, *Lights! Camera! Florida!*, 95.
43 Ponti, *Hollywood East*, 71.
44 Nelson, *Lights! Camera! Florida!*, 95.
45 Fred Wright, "State Urged to Lure Film-Makers," *Tampa Evening Independent*, May 31, 1973, 5B.
46 Pergola-Parent and Govern, "Florida and the Film Industry," 58.
47 Pergola-Parent and Govern, "Florida and the Film Industry," 58.
48 Nelson, *Lights! Camera! Florida!*, 95–96.
49 "Remarks by Reubin Askew, Governor of Florida to the Florida Motion Picture and Television Advisory Commission," Tallahassee, Florida, September 27, 1977, Box 935, Folder 5, Richard Alan Nelson Collection, FSU Library Archives.
50 Larry Aydlette, "Why Did Thousands of Palm County Residents Appear in a Super Bowl Movie?," *Palm Beach Post*, January 29, 2019, https://www.palmbeachpost.com/story/entertainment/events/2019/01/29/why-did-thousands-of-palm-beach-county-residents-appear-in-super-bowl-movie/6166880007/.
51 Nelson, *Lights! Camera! Florida!*, 74.
52 Ponti, *Hollywood East*, 97–98.
53 "Remembering Burt," *Town of Jupiter*, September 10, 2018, https://www.jupiter.fl.us/1584/20450/Remembering-Burt.

54 Carl Gottlieb, *Jaws Log: 30th Anniversary Edition* (New York: Newmarket, 2014), 221.
55 "Why Film in Destin–Fort Walton Beach?," *Destin–Fort Walton Beach Film Commission*, https://www.filmdestinfwb.com/about/.
56 Nelson, *Lights! Camera! Florida!*, 74.
57 Jennie McKeon, "40 Years of 'Jaws 2': Panhandle Locals Remember Filming of Movie," *Daytona Beach News Journal*, July 21, 2018, https://www.news-journalonline.com/story/news/state/2018/07/21/40-years-of-jaws-2-panhandle-locals-remember-filming-of-movie/11431640007/.
58 Nelson, *Lights! Camera! Florida!*, 83.
59 Carol Pearce, "Fla. Climbs to 3rd," *Backstage*, November 17, 1978, 1.
60 Tom Sabulis, "The Governor Goes to Hollywood," *SPT*, March 18, 1984, 1E, 4E.
61 Sabulis, "The Governor Goes to Hollywood," 4E.
62 Lawrence Mahoney, foreword to *Workdays: Finding Florida on the Job*, by Bob Graham (Miami, FL: Banyan, 1978), 10–11.
63 "Governor Bob Graham Working as a Grip on the Set of Burt Reynolds' Film 'Stick'—Fort Lauderdale, Florida," Florida Memory, https://www.floridamemory.com/items/show/156629.
64 Nelson, *Lights! Camera! Florida!*, 75.
65 Daniel Ruth, "Gov. Graham Hypes Florida to Film Industry Leaders," *Tampa Tribune*, June 19, 1979, 3D.
66 Sabulis, "The Governor Goes to Hollywood," E1.
67 Pat Williams and Larry Guest, *Making Magic: How Orlando Won an NBA Team* (Orlando, FL: Sentinel Communications, 1989), 25.
68 Nelson, *Lights! Camera! Florida!*, 76.
69 William Greider, "The Education of David Stockman," *Atlantic*, December 1981, https://www.theatlantic.com/magazine/archive/1981/12/the-education-of-david-stockman/305760.
70 Nicholas Gaetano, "Paradise Lost? South Florida," *Time*, November 23, 1981, front cover.
71 James Kelly, Bernard Dietrich, and William McWhirter, "Trouble in Paradise," *Time*, November 23, 1981, 24.
72 Kelly, Dietrich, and McWhirter, "Trouble in Paradise," 24.
73 Roben Farzad, *Hotel Scarface: Where Cocaine Cowboys Partied and Plotted to Control Miami* (New York: New American Library, 2017), 9.
74 M. Barron Stofik, *Saving South Beach* (Gainesville: University Press of Florida, 2005), 68.
75 Francisco Alvarado, "1981: Miami's Deadliest Summer," *Miami New Times*, August 10, 2011, https://www.miaminewtimes.com/news/1981-miamis-deadliest-summer-6565290.
76 Gregory Jaynes, "Miami Crime Rises as Drugs Pour In," *NYT*, August 12, 1981, 11; Alison Meek, "Murders and Pastels in Miami: The Role of 'Miami Vice' in Bringing Back Tourists to Miami," *Florida Historical Quarterly* 90, no. 3 (Winter 2012): 288.
77 Meek, "Murders and Pastels in Miami," 288.
78 David Nylan, "Florida Striving to Live with Success," *Los Angeles Times*, September 24, 1981, D1.

79 Meek, "Murders and Pastels in Miami," 289.
80 Mormino, "Sunbelt Dreams and Altered States," 15.
81 David Rieff, *Exiles, Tourists and Refugees in the New America* (Boston: Little, Brown, 1987), 28.
82 Chris Nashawaty, "Caddyshack," *Sports Illustrated*, August 2, 2010, https://vault.si.com/vault/2010/08/02/caddyshack.
83 Nashawaty, "Caddyshack."
84 Nashawaty, "Caddyshack."
85 Fred Weiss, "Miami Does Business: Drugs and Terrorism in America's Casablanca," *Harper's*, January 1982, front cover.
86 Gregory Jaynes, "Miami Official Objects to Cuban Refugee Film," *NYT*, August 24, 1982, A12.
87 Ken Tucker, *Scarface Nation: The Ultimate Gangster Movie and How It Changed America* (New York: St. Martin's, 2008), 53, 55–56.
88 Tucker, *Scarface Nation*, 56.
89 David Buxton, *From "The Avengers" to "Miami Vice": Form and Ideology in Television Series* (Manchester, UK: Manchester University Press, 1990), 141.
90 Buxton, *From "The Avengers" to "Miami Vice,"* 141.
91 Emily Benedek, "Inside 'Miami Vice,'" *Rolling Stone*, March 28, 1985, https://www.rollingstone.com/tv/tv-news/inside-miami-vice-53206/.
92 Meek, "Murders and Pastels in Miami," 291.
93 Trish Janeshutz, *The Making of Miami Vice* (New York: Ballantine, 1986), 12.
94 Andres Viglucci, "The Vice Effect: 30 Years after the Show That Changed Miami," *MH*, September 29, 2014, http://www.miamiherald.com/news/local/community/miami-dade/article2266518.html.
95 Dave Hogerty, "'Miami Vice' (Documentary)," YouTube video, 6:20, September 6, 2014, https://www.youtube.com/watch?v=QC2gF5c9lr8&frags=pl%2Cwn.
96 T. D. Allman, *Miami: City of the Future* (New York: Atlantic Monthly Press, 1987), 93.
97 Meek, "Murders and Pastels in Miami," 293.
98 Gonzalez, "The House That Flipper Built," 44.
99 Gonzalez, "The House That Flipper Built," 44.
100 Benedek, "Inside 'Miami Vice.'"
101 Richard Luscombe, "The Ultimate Makeover," *Christian Science Monitor*, July 31, 2006, 2.
102 Drolet and Listokin, "South Beach, Miami Beach, Florida Case Study," 96.
103 Stofik, *Saving South Beach*, 107.
104 Meek, "Murders and Pastels in Miami," 291.
105 Stofik, *Saving South Beach*, xii.
106 Luscombe, "The Ultimate Makeover," 2.
107 Stofik, *Saving South Beach*, xiv, 195, 240.
108 Viglucci, "The Vice Effect."
109 Viglucci, "The Vice Effect."
110 Meek, "Murders and Pastels in Miami," 305.
111 Stofik, *Saving South Beach*, 107–8.
112 Farzad, *Hotel Scarface*, 193–94.

113 Farzad, *Hotel Scarface*, 194.
114 Meek, "Murders and Pastels in Miami," 292.
115 Pergola-Parent and Govern, "Florida and the Film Industry," 67.
116 Stofik, *Saving South Beach*, 107–8.
117 Meek, "Murders and Pastels in Miami," 305.
118 Mormino, *Land of Sunshine, State of Dreams*, 26.
119 Ponti, *Hollywood East*, 7.
120 Pergola-Parent and Govern, "Florida and the Film Industry," 67.
121 Gary Taylor, "Oviedo Will Be Ready for Lights, Camera, and Action on First Take," *OS*, October 5, 1988, D6.
122 Roger Hurlburt, "Dumb Ninja Saga Will Help You Kick the Habit," *South Florida Sun Sentinel*, September 19, 1988, 7D.
123 Jay Boyar, "Fantasy Extends to Ad Campaigns," *OS*, June 15, 1985, E1.
124 Denise L. Smith, "Grand Master of Daring Moves," *OS Central Florida Business*, September 12–18, 1988, 13.
125 Mike Ayers, "Miami Connection Goes from Flop to Fame," CNN Entertainment, November 8, 2012, https://www.cnn.com/2012/11/08/showbiz/movies/miami-connection-film-ayers/index.html.
126 Smith, "Grand Master of Daring Moves," 13.
127 Erin Sullivan, "Orlando's Grandmaster Y.K. Kim Just Wanted to Make a Good Taekwondo Movie," *Orlando Weekly* (hereafter *OW*), December 11, 2012, https://www.orlandoweekly.com/movies-tv/orlandos-grandmaster-yk-kim-just-wanted-to-make-a-good-taekwondo-movie-2246254.
128 Smith, "Grand Master of Daring Moves," 13.
129 Smith, "Grand Master of Daring Moves," 13.
130 Smith, "Grand Master of Daring Moves," 13.
131 Clark Collis, "'Miami Connection': Ninjas, Cocaine, and Synth Rock!," *Entertainment Weekly*, November 9, 2012, https://ew.com/article/2012/11/09/miami-connection/.
132 Collis, "'Miami Connection.'"
133 Collis, "'Miami Connection.'"
134 Douglas Laman, "Why 'Miami Connection' and Its Endearingly Kind Hearted Vibes Have Aged Like Fine Wine," *Collider*, April 30, 2022, https://collider.com/miami-connection-why-its-good/.
135 Nelson, *Lights! Camera! Florida!*, 78.
136 Peter H. Brown, "We're Talking Gross, Tacky and Dumb," *Los Angeles Times*, January 20, 1985, 6.
137 Ily Goyanes, "Celluloid City: 'Porky's' Trilogy Filmed at Miami Senior High School and Greynolds Park," *Miami New Times*, August 18, 2010, https://www.miaminewtimes.com/arts/celluloid-city-porkys-trilogy-filmed-at-miami-senior-high-school-and-greynolds-park-6510912.
138 Aubrey Solomon, *Twentieth Century Fox: A Corporate and Financial History* (Lanham, MD: Scarecrow, 1988) 195.
139 J. Hoberman, "Paradise Regained," Criterion Collection, September 3, 2007, https://www.criterion.com/current/posts/568.
140 Janet Maslin, "'Stranger Than Paradise' Wins Award," January 3, 1985, *NYT*, C14; Paul

Attanasio, "'Paradise' Lauded by Critics National Society," *Washington Post*, January 4, 1985, https://www.washingtonpost.com/archive/lifestyle/1985/01/04/paradise-lauded-by-critics-national-society-honors-jarmusch-film/e6798f95-0af5-4ab1-95f8-d7ae3bd89c70/; Lee Thomas-Mason, "From Stanley Kubrick to Martin Scorsese: Akira Kurosawa Once Named His Top 100 Favourite Films of All Time," *Far Out Magazine*, May 2021, https://faroutmagazine.co.uk/akira-kurosawa-100-favourite-films-list/.

141 Jay Boyar, "Roadside Hollywood Zips by Central Florida," *OS Calendar*, July 26–August 1, 1991, 6.
142 Nelson, *Lights! Camera! Florida!*, 79.
143 Nelson, *Lights! Camera! Florida!*, 80–81.
144 Nelson, *Lights! Camera! Florida!*, 81.
145 Phil De Semlyen, "Daryl Hanna Reveals the Secrets of 'Splash,'" *Empire Magazine*, May 24, 2016, https://www.empireonline.com/movies/features/daryl-hannah-shares-secrets-splash/.
146 Tom Sabulis, "Ron Howard and 'Cocoon' Write St. Petersburg's Ticket to Hollywood," *TBT*, March 30, 1984, https://www.tampabay.com/features/celebrities/looking-back-ron-howard-writes-st-petersburgs-ticket-to-hollywood-1984-1985/2316799/.
147 Susan Parker, "'Cocoon' Filming a Real Experience for Spring Hill Actor," *Hernando Tribune*, September 1, 1984, 2.
148 Juan Carlos Coto, "Veteran 'Cocoon' Cast back in Florida Swatting out Sequel," *Chicago Tribune*, June 9, 1988, https://www.chicagotribune.com/news/ct-xpm1988-06-09-8801060270-story.html.
149 Coto, "Veteran 'Cocoon' Cast."
150 Nelson, *Lights! Camera! Florida!*, 88.
151 Nelson, *Lights! Camera! Florida!*, 88.
152 Nelson, *Lights! Camera! Florida!*, 88.
153 Greg Tozian, "State Sponsors Screenwriters Competition," *Tampa Tribune*, November 9, 1984, D1.
154 Candice Russell, "Catch Miami-Made 'Cease Fire' at Premiere," *Fort Lauderdale News*, March 15, 1985, 7S.
155 Kevin Thomas, "'Cease Fire:' The Reality of Vietnam," *Los Angeles Times*, November 27, 1985, https://www.latimes.com/archives/la-xpm-1985-11-27-ca-4697-story.html.
156 Nelson, *Lights! Camera! Florida!*, 78.
157 Nelson, *Lights! Camera! Florida!*, 78, 81.
158 Christopher Swendsen, "FSU Film School Founder and Retired Comm Professor, Donald Ungurait Passes Away," *FSU News and Events*, August 16, 2013, https://news.cci.fsu.edu/cci-news/cci-in-the-news/donald-ungurait-passes-away/.
159 Emmanuel Levy, *Cinema of Outsiders: The Rise of American Independent Film* (New York: NYU Press, 2001), 169.
160 Gregory Goodwell, *Independent Feature Film Production: A Complete Guide from Concept through Distribution* (New York: Macmillan, 2003), 22.
161 Levy, *Cinema of Outsiders*, 169.
162 Luke Parker, "Interview with Victor Nuñez, Director of Sundance Classic 'Ruby in Par-

adise,'" *Film Inquiry*, February 24, 2021, https://www.filminquiry.com/victor-nunez-interview/.
163 Nelson, *Lights! Camera! Florida!*, 78–79.
164 Charles Reese, "Winter Park Film Producer: Another Take," *OS*, May 17, 1978, C1.
165 Al Truesdell, "Filmmaker Considering DeLand as Movie Setting," *West Volusia Little Sentinel*, August 5, 1982, 2.
166 Charley Reese, "John Hugh Working toward Making Central Florida Hollywood East," *OS*, February 21, 1983, A14.
167 Reese, "John Hugh Working toward Making Central Florida Hollywood East," A14.
168 Reese, "John Hugh Working toward Making Central Florida Hollywood East," A14.
169 Reese, "John Hugh Working toward Making Central Florida Hollywood East," A14.
170 Gabrielle Sierra, "Eagle Media Corp Receives R. John Hugh Award," November 23, 2011, https://www.broadwayworld.com/miami/article/Eagle-Media-Corp-Receives-R-John-Hugh-Award-20111123.
171 Jay Boyar, "Orlando Film Festival: Not Bad for a First Try," *OS Calendar*, May 10–16, 1991, 4.
172 Catherine Hinman, "Tale of Two Movies Show How Florida Has Changed," *OS Calendar*, April 26–May 2, 4, 6.
173 Boyar, "Orlando Film Festival," 4.
174 Ken Berg, "Exploitation as an Art Form," *OS Calendar*, April 26–May 2, 5.
175 "Movie Insiders Share Secrets of the Trade," *OS Calendar*, April 26–May 2, 6.
176 Boyar, "Orlando Film Festival," 4.
177 Boyar, "New Film Fest Coming to Central Florida," *OS*, October 12, 1991, A2.
178 Boyar, "New Film Fest Coming to Central Florida," A2.
179 Boyar, "10-Day Movie Celebration," *OS*, May 31, 1992, F1, F12.
180 Boyar, "Film Fests, Near Misses on Central Florida's Program," *OS Calendar*, March 20–26, 1992, 21.
181 Nina J. Easton, "Orlando, Florida—Will It Become Hollywood East? Universal and Disney Have Committed a Combined $1 Billion for Production Facilities and Studio Tours," *Los Angeles Times Calendar*, April 9, 1989, 6.
182 Easton, "Orlando, Florida," 6.
183 Easton, "Orlando, Florida," 6.
184 Foglesong, *Married to the Mouse*, 146.
185 Kevin Archer, "Limits of the Imagineered City: Sociospatial Polarization in Orlando," *Economic Geography* 73, no. 3 (July 1997): 323; Kevin Archer and Kris Bezdecny, "Searching for a New Brand: Reimagining a More Diverse Orlando," *Southeastern Geographer* 49, no. 2 (Summer 2009): 185.
186 Eve Bacon, *Orlando: A Centennial History, Volume II* (Chuluota, FL: Mickler House, 1977), 277.
187 Foglesong, *Married to the Mouse*, 5.
188 Jeff Kurtti, *Since the World Began: Walt Disney World, The First 25 Years* (New York: Hyperion, 1996), 89.
189 Foglesong, *Magic Town*, 22; Carl Hiaasen, *Team Rodent: How Disney Devours the World* (New York: Random House, 1998), 50.

190 Joe Flower, *Prince of the Magic Kingdom: Michael Eisner and the Re-Making of Disney* (New York: John Wiley and Sons, 1991), 93–94.
191 Foglesong, *Magic Town*, 22.
192 Kim Masters, *The Keys to the Kingdom: The Rise of Michael Eisner and the Fall of Everyone Else* (New York: HarperCollins, 2000), 189–90.
193 Tozian, "State Sponsors Screenwriters Competition," D1.
194 Dick Marlowe, "Florida's Growing Role in Movies Leads Company to Establish Orlando Headquarters," *OS*, January 18, 1983, D1.
195 Nelson, *Lights! Camera! Florida!*, 90–91; Flower, *Prince of the Magic Kingdom*, 190.
196 Steve Nelson, "Reel Life Performance: The Disney-MGM Studios," *MIT Press* 34, no. 4 (Winter 1990): 77.
197 Thomas C. Hayes, "Disney Agrees to Purchase Arvida," *NYT*, May 18, 1984, D1.
198 Pamela McClintock, "Will Steven Spielberg Drop the DreamWorks Name?," *Hollywood Reporter*, September 24, 2015, https://www.hollywoodreporter.com/movies/movie-news/will-steven-spielberg-drop-dreamworks-826201/.
199 Masters, *The Keys to the Kingdom*, 189–90.
200 Nelson, "Reel Life Performance," 60–61.
201 Nelson, "Reel Life Performance," 61.
202 Nelson, "Reel Life Performance," 60–61.
203 Foglesong, *Magic Town*, 22.
204 Foglesong, *Magic Town*, 91.
205 Gabrielle Russon, "Disney's Hollywood Dream Elusive at Park," *OS*, June 17, 2018, A1.
206 Susan Christopherson, "Divide and Conquer: Regional Competition in a Concentrated Media Industry," in *Contracting Out Hollywood: Runaway Productions and Foreign Location Shooting*, ed. Greg Elmer and Mike Gasher (Lanham, MD: Rowman and Littlefield, 2005), 34.
207 Ramsey Campbell, "Mount Dora Gets Good Reviews by Starring in Movies," *OS*, June 14, 1998, 17.
208 Don Fernandez, "Romantic Comedy to Put City on Movie Map," *OS*, June 14, 1998, 16.
209 Diane C. Kachmar, *Roy Scheider: A Film Biography* (Jefferson, NC: McFarland, 2002), 101.
210 Watch What Happens Live with Andy Cohen, "Which Dennis Quaid Movie Had the Highest Cocaine Budget?," YouTube video, November 18, 2015, 00:51, https://www.youtube.com/watch?v=NYPClgMlkIA&t=51s.
211 James Greene Jr., "Location Matters: SeaWorld from 'Jaws 3-D,'" *OW*, April 4, 2014, https://www.orlandoweekly.com/news/location-matters-seaworld-from-jaws-3-d-2283141.
212 R. M. Hayes, *3D Movies: A History and Filmography of Stereoscopic Cinema* (Jefferson, NC: McFarland, 1998), 101–3.
213 James Greene Jr., "Location Matters: The Government Facility from 'D.A.R.Y.L.,'" *OW*, March 7, 2014, https://www.orlandoweekly.com/news/location-matters-the-government-facility-from-daryl-2282669.
214 Jay Boyar, "'D.A.R.Y.L.' Is Entertaining, But No Classic," *OS*, June 14, 1985, E1.
215 Nelson, *Lights! Camera! Florida!*, 79.

216 Mark Damon and Linda Schreyer, *From Cowboy to Mogul to Monster: The Neverending Story of Film Pioneer Mark Damon* (Bloomington, IN: AuthorHouse, 2008), 376.
217 Chris Carey, "Cinematographer Urges Osceola to Lure Film Industry," *OS: Osceola*, March 8, 1987, 21.
218 Catherine Hinman, "The Scene-Spotter's Guide to 'Parenthood' Locations," *OS*, August 4, 1989, E1, E8.
219 Bill Carter, "Hear about a Film That Became a Hit Series?" *NYT*, December 17, 1990, C11.
220 Jeremy Herbert, "Universal Studios Opening Day Attractions Ranked," *Theme Park Tourist*, November 19, 2021, https://www.themeparktourist.com/features/20211119/32080/universal-studios-florida-opening-day-attractions-ranked.
221 Flower, *Prince of the Magic Kingdom*, 280.
222 Herbert, "Universal Studios Opening Day."
223 Michael Connolly and Tracy Wilkinson, "Guard Is Arrested in Universal Studios Fire," *Los Angeles Times*, November 8, 1990, A1.
224 Ponti, *Hollywood East*, 85–86.
225 Boyar, "Roadside Hollywood," 6.
226 Larry Guest, "One Last Bit of Giving Is Difference for Orlando," *OS*, April 23, 1987, D1.
227 Priscilla Painton, "Fantasy's Reality," *Time*, May 27, 1991, 52–59; Mormino, "Sunbelt Dreams and Altered States," 15.
228 Ponti, *Hollywood East*, 123.
229 Susan G. Strother, "Promoting City's Image: Film Commission Works on Advertising Campaign," *OS*, February 24, 1992, 21.
230 Nelson, *Lights! Camera! Florida!*, 4.
231 Nelson, *Lights! Camera! Florida!*, 4.
232 Samuel Gill, foreword to *Lights! Camera! Florida!*, by Nelson, 7.
233 Michael McCleod, "Where the Films Are: In This Script, Florida Elbows California out of the Picture," *Florida Magazine*, May 3, 1987, 11.
234 John Hill, "A Supporting Role: Studios Won't Bring Hollywood East to Orlando," *OS Central Florida Business*, November 9–15, 1987, 22.
235 Hill, "A Supporting Role," 22.
236 Christopherson, "Divide and Conquer," 33.
237 Ponti, *Hollywood East*, 73.
238 "A History of Implosions in Tampa Bay," *TBT*, February 27, 2012, https://web.archive.org/web/20160223211158/http://www.tampabay.com/blogs/talk/content/history-implosions-tampa-bay.
239 Susan G. Strother, "Promoting City's Image: Film Commission Works on Advertising Campaign," *OS Central Florida Business*, February 24–March 1, 1992, 21.
240 Economic Development Commission of Mid-Florida, *Orlando Filmbook* (Orlando, FL: Metro Orlando Film and Television Office, 1993), 27.
241 Strother, "Promoting City's Image," 21.
242 Joshua Klein, "Joe Dante," A.V. Club, November 29, 2000, https://www.avclub.com/joe-dante-1798208125.
243 Greene, "Location Matters."
244 Jim Hill, "Why For: Central Florida Never Actually Became Hollywood East," Jim Hill

Media, October 13, 2011, https://jimhillmedia.com/why-for-central-florida-never-actually-became-hollywood-east/.
245 Hill, "Why For."
246 Billy Manes, "Back from the Dead," *OW*, February 14, 2008, https://www.orlandoweekly.com/orlando/back-from-the-dead/Content?oid=2257176.
247 Greene, "Location Matters."
248 Manes, "Back from the Dead."
249 Shawn Bean, *The First Hollywood: Florida and the Golden Age of Silent Filmmaking* (Gainesville: University Press of Florida, 2008), 146.
250 Pergola-Parent and Govern, "Florida and the Film Industry," 59–60.
251 Pergola-Parent and Govern, "Florida and the Film Industry," 59–60.
252 McGrory, "Burn Notice."
253 Kevin Baxter, "Telemundo Moves Operations to Florida," *Los Angeles Times*, August 25, 1999, F9.

End Credits

1. "Ocala Drive-In Celebrates 10 Years," ABC: WCJB20, July 29, 2021, https://www.wcjb.com/2021/07/29/ocala-drive-in-celebrates-10-years/.
2. Taylor Simpson, "Ocala Drive-In Damaged after Reckless Driver Knocked down Poles," ABC: WCJB20, July 18, 2021, https://www.wcjb.com/2021/07/18/ocala-drive-in-theatre-damaged-after-reckless-driver-knocked-down-poles-fences-almost-hits-children/; Jeremiah Delgado, "Ocala Drive-In Looking for Pickup Driver Who Sped Through, Damaged Facility," *Ocala-News*, July 20, 2021, https://www.ocala-news.com/2021/07/20/ocala-drive-in-looking-for-pickup-truck-driver-who-sped-through-damaged-facility/.
3. Crystal Moyer, "Moviegoers Get 2 for 1 at This Drive-In Theater in Ocala," ClickOrlando, June 6, 2022, https://www.clickorlando.com/news/local/2022/06/06/moviegoers-get-2-for-1-at-this-drive-in-theater-in-ocala/.
4. Moyer, "Moviegoers Get 2 for 1."
5. Ellie Hensley, "Ben Affleck's 'Live by Night' Building Fake Ybor City in Brunswick," *Atlanta Business Chronicle*, September 29, 2015, https://www.bizjournals.com/atlanta/news/2015/09/29/ben-affleck-s-live-by-night-building-fake-ybor.html.
6. Rene Rodriguez, "Viacom Moves into a New Film Studio in Downtown Miami," *MH*, October 6, 2015, 8A.
7. Heather Gautney and Chris Rhomberg, "The Runaway Production Complex? The Film Industry as a Driver of Urban Economic Revitalization in the United States," *City & Community* 14, no. 3 (September 2015): 266–69.
8. Vicki Mayer, *Almost Hollywood, Nearly New Orleans: The Lure of the Local Film Economy* (Berkeley: University of California Press, 2017), 9–10.
9. Dave Berman, "End of Incentives for Film, TV, Costly," *Pensacola News Journal*, February 27, 2017, A4.
10. William Pate, "Welcome to Y'allywood: Atlanta Is the New Face of the Entertainment Industry," *Atlanta Business Chronicle*, April 24, 2017, https://www.bizjournals.com/atlanta/news/2017/04/24/welcome-to-y-allywood-atlanta-is-the-new-face-of.html.

11 Tara McPherson, "Revamping the South: Thoughts on Labor, Relationality, and Southern Representation," in *American Cinema and Southern Imaginary*, ed. Deborah Barker and Kathryn McKee (Athens: University of Georgia Press, 2011), 345.
12 Mary Pergola-Parent and Kevin H. Govern, "Florida and the Film Industry: An Epic Tale of Talent, Landscape, and the Law," *Nova Law Review* 38, no. 43 (2013): 68–69.
13 Pergola-Parent and Govern, "Florida and the Film Industry," 69–70.
14 David Robb, "How the Power-Broker Koch Brothers Are Killing the Florida Film Business," *Deadline Hollywood*, October 21, 2016, https://deadline.com/2016/10/koch-brothers-florida-film-industry-tax-incentives-lobbying-1201838246/.
15 Kelly O'Connell, "Florida Yells 'CUT' on Film Tax Incentives," *Miami Florida, Blog for Entertainment Law, Business Law, and Public Interest*, July 13, 2016, https://msworldlaw.com/lawyer/2016/07/13/Entertainment-Law/Florida-Yells-CUT-on-Film-Tax-Incentives_bl25725.htm.
16 "Governor Rick Scott Announces *Dolphin Tale 2* to be Filmed in Clearwater," Fl.gov, July 26, 2013, https://www.flgov.com/governor-rick-scott-announces-dolphin-tale-2-to-be-filmed-in-clearwater-2/.
17 "Governor Rick Scott Announces *Dolphin Tale 2*."
18 Pergola-Parent and Govern, "Florida and the Film Industry," 79.
19 Florida Department of Economic Opportunity, *Office of Film and Entertainment Five Year Strategic Plan for Economic Development, 2013–2018* (Tallahassee: Florida Office of Film and Entertainment, 2013), 7.
20 Florida Department of Economic Opportunity, *Office of Film and Entertainment Five Year Strategic Plan*, 80.
21 Geurts, "Florida Film Struggles and Successes Post-Tax Incentives."
22 Steve Bousquet, "This Political Leader Stormed Florida's Capital and Made a Lot of People Angry," *Bradenton Herald*, March 6, 2017, https://www.bradenton.com/news/politics-government/state-politics/article136669278.html.
23 Richard Corcoran, *Blue Print Florida* (2012), 24. https://archive.org/details/2012-blue-print-florida-1
24 Corcoran, *Blue Print Florida*, 66.
25 Matt Dixon, "Scott, Corcoran Spar over Economic Incentives to Companies," *Politico-Florida*, September 29, 2016, https://www.politico.com/states/florida/story/2016/09/scott-corcoran-spar-over-economic-incentives-105938.
26 Monivette Cordeiro, "Orlando Lawmaker Wants to Let Counties Use Tourism Funds to Incentivize Film, TV Production," *OW*, February 6, 2019, https://www.orlandoweekly.com/Blogs/archives/2019/02/06/orlando-lawmaker-wants-to-let-counties-use-tourism-funds-to-incentivize-film-tv-production.
27 "Florida Legislature Allows the Entertainment Industry Financial Program to Sunset," *Film Florida*, March 10, 2016, https://filmflorida.org/news/florida-legislature-allows-entertainment-industry-financial-program-sunset/.
28 Bryn Elise Sandberg and Kim Masters, "'Bloodline' Will End on Netflix after Season 3," *Hollywood Reporter*, September 14, 2016, https://www.hollywoodreporter.com/live-feed/bloodline-will-end-netflix-season-928743.
29 Bryn Elise Sandberg, "HBO's 'Ballers' Moving to California after Two Seasons in Flor-

ida," *Hollywood Reporter*, November 30, 2016, https://www.hollywoodreporter.com/live-feed/hbos-ballers-moving-california-two-seasons-florida-951167.
30 Geurts, "Florida Film Struggles and Successes Post–Tax Incentives."
31 Associated Press, "Oscar Winning 'Moonlight' Shines on Miami's Liberty City," *Florida Politics*, February 28, 2017, https://floridapolitics.com/archives/232922-oscar-winning-moonlight-shines-miamis-liberty-city.
32 Mary Shanklin, "'Florida Project' Film Portrays Life in Kissimmee Hotels," *OS*, October 14, 2017, A1.
33 Julio Capo Jr., "Best Picture Winner 'Moonlight' Is a Window into Florida's Past," *Time*, February 27, 2017, http://time.com/4684596/moonlight-florida-history/.
34 Capo Jr., "Best Picture Winner 'Moonlight.'"
35 Steve Persall, "Intersection of Happy, Homeless," *Tampa Bay Times*, October 24, 2017, A1, 5A.
36 Persall, "Intersection of Happy, Homeless," 5A.
37 Rene Rodriguez, "Paradise Lost?," *MH*, February 6, 2017, 12G.
38 Rodriguez, "Paradise Lost?," 12G.
39 Rodriguez, "Paradise Lost?," 13G. This, of course, did not take the disruptions that would be caused by the COVID-19 pandemic into account.
40 Monroe County Tourist Development Council, *Economic Impacts of the Netflix Original Series 'Bloodline'* (Springfield, MO: H2R Market Research, 2015), 1.
41 Richard Luscombe, "Moonlight's Oscars Shine May Not Be Enough to Save the Florida Film Industry," *Guardian*, March 16, 2017, https://www.theguardian.com/us-news/2017/mar/16/florida-film-industry-bill-moonlight.
42 Jeremy Wallace, "'Moonlight' Cited in Tallahassee as Reason to Keep State Incentives for Filmmakers," *MH*, March 7, 2017, https://www.miamiherald.com/news/local/community/miami-dade/article136880163.html.
43 Luscombe, "Moonlight's Oscars Shine May Not Be Enough to Save Florida Film Industry."
44 Deanna Ferrante, "Burt Reynolds Blames Gov. Rick Scott for Florida's Dying Film Industry," *OW*, March 10, 2017, https://www.orlandoweekly.com/Blogs/archives/2017/03/10/burt-reynolds-blames-gov-rick-scott-for-floridas-dying-film-industry.
45 Peter Burke, "Burt Reynolds Blames Governor for Florida's Floundering Film Industry," Local10.com, March 9, 2017, https://www.local10.com/entertainment/burt-reynolds-blames-governor-for-floridas-floundering-film-industry.
46 Luscombe, "Moonlight's Oscars Shine May Not Be Enough to Save Florida Film Industry."
47 Geurts, "Florida Film Struggles and Successes Post–Tax Incentives."
48 James C. Craig, "Jacksonville: World Film Capital," *Jacksonville Historical Society* 3 (1954): 125; Richard Alan Nelson, *Florida and the American Motion Picture Industry* (New York: Garland, 1980), 301; Nelson, "Florida: The Forgotten Film Capital," *Journal of the University Film Association* 29, no. 3 (Summer 1977): 16.
49 "About Philip Levine," Philip Levine for Governor 2018, https://philiplevine2018.com.
50 Scott Powers, "Philip Levine Vows to Bring Back TV, Movie Production Industry," *Florida Politics*, February 9, 2018, http://floridapolitics.com/archives/

255818-philip-levine-vows-bring-back-tv-movie-productionindustry?fbclid= IwAR3JswptxN8PtfNpp6Z7bt3Ox0pJ4BFTIrOS3QqGUbC1g9adiJRYKkoNAPI.

51. Scott Powers, "Philip Levine: Quest for Film Business Is Part of 21st-Century Economy," *Florida Politics*, July 25, 2018, http://floridapolitics.com/archives/269698-philip-levine-quest-for-film-business-is-part-of-21st-century-economy.

52. Powers, "Philip Levine."

53. Dino-Ray Ramos, "'Black Panther' Generates $89.3 Million for Georgia Economy," *Deadline Hollywood*, February 7, 2018, https://deadline.com/2018/02/black-panther-marvel-studios-georgia-atlanta-economy-1202281118/; Andrew Gillum, Twitter post, February 11, 2018, 10:53 a.m. https://twitter.com/AndrewGillum/status/962761620865847302.

54. Ramos, "'Black Panther' Generates $89.3 Million for Georgia Economy."

55. David Robb, "Fate of Florida's Decimated Film Industry Might Hang on Governor's Race," *Deadline Hollywood*, October 30, 2018, https://deadline.com/2018/10/florida-film-incentives-tax-credits-governors-race-ron-desantis-andrew-gillum-1202492389/.

56. Film Florida, "Andrew Gillum–D (Gov)," YouTube video, 0:37, August 16, 2018, https://www.youtube.com/watch?time_continue=1&v=zqwoeV9mupc.

57. "Governor," Florida Election Watch, https://floridaelectionwatch.gov/StateOffices/Governor.

58. Florida TaxWatch, *Is The Sun Setting on Film in Florida?* (Tallahassee: Florida TaxWatch Research Institute, 2018), 13–14.

59. "Florida TaxWatch Analyzes Florida Film and Television Industry: The Status Quo Is Not a Viable Option," *Film Florida*, February 19, 2019, https://filmflorida.org/news/florida-taxwatch-analyzes-floridas-film-and-television-industry/.

60. Florida Congress, Senate, *Tourism Development Tax*, SB 726, General Bill, 2019 sess., introduced in Senate February 15, 2019, https://www.flsenate.gov/Session/Bill/2019/726/BillText/__/HTML.

61. Steven Lemongello, "'We're Dying Out Here': Will Film Production Ever Return to Florida? A New Bill Would Let Counties Dip into Tourism Funds," *OS*, February 14, 2019, https://www.orlandosentinel.com/news/politics/political-pulse/os-ne-film-video-game-incentives-tourist-tax-20190205-story.html.

62. Robb, "Fate of Florida's Decimated Film Industry Might Hang on Governor's Race."

63. Drew Wilson, "The Industry Still Has Plenty to Celebrate as the 2020 Legislative Session Wraps," *Florida Politics*, March 19, 2020, https://floridapolitics.com/archives/324098-film-industry-quietly-wins-big-continues-to-build-momentum/.

64. Office of the Governor, *State of Florida Executive Order 20–83*, March 24, 2020, 1.

Index

Adams, Henry (St. Petersburg mayor), 137, 144
Adams, Julia, 170–171
Advance Motion Picture Company (AMPC), 92
Affleck, Ben, 257
Alamo Drafthouse, 229–230
Alexander, Edward, 114, 132–133, 137
Allen, Bob, 249
Allen, Ross, 162
American Broadcasting Company (ABC), 170, 188
American International Pictures (AIP), 212
Americans for Prosperity (AFP), 13–15
"America's Casablanca," 206, 219–225
Anna Maria Island, 163
Apfel, Charles L., 122
Apopka, FL, 112
Arlington, Jacksonville, 17, 24, 73, 105, 108–110, 112
Arnold, Jack, 169–171
Art Deco District, Miami Beach, 222–224
Arvida Corporation, 241, 245
Ashley Street, Jacksonville, 73, 97–100, 104–105, 107, 113
Askew, Reubin (governor, 1971–1979), 12, 19, 203, 206, 211–217, 236, 265
Associated Authors Productions, 18, 65–67
Astaire, Fred, 236
Atlantic Coast Line (ACL), 37, 64
Atlantic Highway, 116
Austin, S. A. "Buddy," 104, 107–109
Avalon Film Productions, 179, 181–183

Bahamas, the, 26, 32, 40, 68, 70, 189–192, 232
Baker, Sean, 263–264
Baltimore, MD, 32–33
Bara, Theda, 118
Barker, Edwin L., 92–95
Barrymore, Drew, 237
Batista, Fulgencio, 185

"Beach Blanket Craze," 174–178
Beecroft, Chester, 134–138, 148–149
Beecroft-Florida Movie Studio, 135–136, 148–149
Benda, Nancy (née Tribble), 165–166, 234
Bethune, Mary McLeod, 73, 88
Bijou Theatre, 82, 97
Biograph Studios, 27
Birth of a Race Photoplay Corporation, The, 93
Black Maria, 22
Blair, Fred, 139–142, 145–150, 152, 201
Boggs, Francis, 34–35
Bonavita, Jack, 37–38, 40
Bowden, J.E.T. (Jacksonville mayor), 12, 45–59, 96, 121
Bridges, Lloyd, 189, 192
Briggs Pictures Incorporated, 61
Broward, Napoleon (governor, 1905–1909), 33, 74
Browning, Ricou, 167, 170–171, 190–200, 206, 237, 254
Brunton, John, 118–120
Bryan, William Jennings, 64
Bryant, Farris (governor, 1961–1965), 198
Burns, Haydon (governor, 1965–1967), 196–198, 201–202
Bush, George H. W., 220, 225
Bush, Jeb (governor, 1999–2007), 13–15, 19, 206, 254, 259–260, 267

Caldwell, Millard (governor, 1945–1949), 153–155, 173
Capra, Frank, 176
Cardozo Hotel, 175–176
Carlton, Doyle (governor, 1929–1933), 12, 115, 128–139, 151–152, 173, 213, 218
Carter, Jimmy, 211–212, 216
Carver, Harry P., 125
Casey, Thomas, 181–187, 193

Casey, Wilbur, 181–182
Castro, Fidel, 185–186
Castro, Raul, 186
Catts, Sidney (governor, 1917–1921), 17, 56–59, 62, 99–102, 115, 238
CBS Broadcasting, 18, 182, 189, 192–194
Chancey, Robert (Tampa mayor), 137
Chaplin, Charlie, 67, 124
Chapman, Howard, 196
Charisse, Cyd, 163
Chase, Chevy, 221
Chicago Defender, 87, 108
Citizens Bank and Trust Company, 128
Clark, Bob, 230–231
Clark, Jack J., 84
Clark Film Company, 229
Clearwater, FL, 134, 232, 260
Clearwater Marine Aquarium, 260
"Cocaine Cowboys Era," 220–222
Cohn, Harry, 152
Cole, Ed, 185–186
Cole, Nat King, 185–186
Collins, LeRoy (governor, 1955–1961), 149, 166
Collins, Trenton C., 18, 115, 128–141, 151–152, 198, 232
Columbia Pictures, 152, 183–184, 218, 246
Committee for the Development of the Motion Picture, 115, 131–139, 151–153
Cone, Fred (governor, 1937–1941), 152
Congress of Motion Picture Associations of Florida (COMPASS), 268
Cooper, Gary, 168
Costner, Kevin, 243
Cotton, W. M., 141–143
COVID-19 Pandemic, 1–6, 9, 256, 270
"Cracker Western," 168–169, 180
Cripps, Thomas, 71, 75, 93, 96, 108
Crist, Charlie (governor, 2007–2011), 13–14, 19, 206, 259–260, 266
Cross Creek, 158–161
Crowd, Frank, 97–99
Cuba, 22–23, 26, 28, 32, 145, 180, 185–186
Cugat, Xavier, 163
Curtiss, Glen, 118
Cypress Gardens, 163, 175, 190

Dade County, 196, 212, 214, 220
Dadeland Massacre, 219
D'Agostino, Albert, 137, 140

Damiano, Gerard, 209–210
Davidson, William B, 118
Davidson, W. M. "Shorty," 161–162
Davie, FL, 220–221
Davis Islands, 18, 126, 134, 138, 142, 144, 148–150
Daytona Beach, FL, 73
DeLand, FL, 236
Deland Area Chamber of Commerce, 236
DeMille, Cecil B., 173, 235
DePalma, Brian, 221–222
DeSantis, Ron (governor, 2019–), 268–269
Destin-Fort Walton Beach Film Commission, 215
Dickson, William Kennedy Laurie, 21–22
Disney, Roy E., 205, 240–242
Disney, Roy O., 156–157, 201, 205
Disney, Walt, 19, 156–158, 183, 194–195, 200–202, 205, 240, 249, 263
Disney Channel, 241–242
Disneyland California, 156, 241
Disney-MGM Studios, 13, 19, 205, 227, 236–239, 242–243, 247–249, 252–254, 258
Dixie Highway, 116
Dixieland Amusement Park, 32–34, 48–49, 59, 82
Dixie Theater, 33
Doherty, Shannen, 237–238
Duval County, 84, 99
Duval Theatre, 26, 33, 100–101

Eagle Studios, 62, 108–110
Edison, Thomas, 22–23, 25, 27, 32–35, 43, 54–55, 82, 84–85
Edison Manufacturing Company (EMC), 8, 17–18, 21–24, 28, 82
Eisner, Michael, 205, 242, 245
Equitable Film Company, 50, 53
Everglades National Park, 17, 168–169, 173, 180, 190, 194, 257
Experimental Prototype Community of Tomorrow (EPCOT), 156, 202, 240–242

Fader, Sunny, 213
Fairbanks, Douglas, Jr., 236
Fairbanks, Douglas, Sr., 67
Fairfield, Jacksonville, 24, 29
Federal Communications Commission, 188
Federal Writers Project (FWP), 172

Field, Charles, 40–43
Field Feature Film Company (FFFC), 42–43
Film Florida, 254–255, 264–269
First National Pictures, 62, 66–67, 141
Flagler, Henry, 67
Flagler Depot, 25
Flagler Dog Track, 176
Flamingo Film Company, 144–146
Fleischer, David, 139–140, 188
Fleischer, Max, 139–140, 188
Fleming, Victor, 159–160
Florida Chamber of Commerce, 135, 138–139, 202
Florida Council of 100, 198, 237
Florida East Coast Railway, 32, 36, 62
Florida Educational Television Commission, 166
Florida Entertainment Industry Incentive Program (FEIIP), 259–262, 265
Florida Film and Entertainment Council, 269
Florida Film Council (FFC), 199
Florida Film Festival, 198, 237–238, 250
Florida International University, 192
Florida Land Boom, 11–12, 18, 25, 117, 121, 125–128, 133, 141
Florida League of Municipalities, 135
Florida Magazine, 249
Florida Metropolis, 11, 44, 46, 53, 97
Florida Motion Picture and Television Association (FMPTA), 19, 197–199, 206, 211, 213, 221, 235–236, 248–252
Florida Motion Picture and Television Bureau (FMPTB), 19, 199, 213–218, 232–234
Florida Movement, 97
Florida Movie Capital Corporation (FMCC), 265
"Florida's Big Bang," 153, 157–158
Florida Standard Agreement, 197–200, 206, 213
Florida State University, 166, 190, 234, 238
Florida Times-Union, 16, 33–34, 36, 44–46, 48, 50–51, 53, 57, 72, 78, 82–83, 86, 97
Florida West Coast Association, 63
Ford, Harrison, 233
Fort Lauderdale, FL, 67–71, 119, 176–177, 188–190, 192, 209, 217, 230, 245
Foster, William D., 89–90, 106
Foster Photoplay Company (FPC), 89–90, 106
Fox, William, 24, 28, 31, 149
Frankenheimer, John, 214

Fredrick, Bill (Orlando mayor), 239, 250
Friedman, David F., 207–210
Frohman Amusement Corporation, 94

Gadsden County, 166
Gainesville, FL, 7, 167, 177, 188
Gainesville Sun, 160
Garrick, Richard, 48, 59
Gasparilla Pirate Festival, 129
Gaumont Film Company, 48, 54, 59, 82
Gauntier, Gene, 20–22, 26–30, 36, 59, 76–80, 84–85, 89, 195
Gene Gauntier Players (GGs), 59, 84
Georgia Film Office, 212
Gibson, Mel, 250
Gillum, Andrew, 267–268
Gilmore, Paul, 60–63, 162
Gleason, Jackie, 192
Glenn Miller Orchestra, 189
Globe Theatre, 82, 98–99, 104
Glover, Danny, 250
Goetz, William, 169
"Gold Digger Tourist Plots," 174
Graham, Bob (governor, 1979–1987), 13, 206, 216–221, 226, 231, 233, 239–241, 248, 267
Graham, Gwen, 267
Great Depression, 11, 18, 113, 115–116, 128, 131–135, 213, 270
Greenwich Studio City, 200, 206, 224, 227, 233, 254
Grefé, William, 200, 209, 212, 233
Griffith, D. W., 67–71, 73, 79, 91–92, 95
Griffith, Leroy, 208
Griffith, Reed, 182
Guardians of Liberty, 56, 58

Hammond, Lloyd, 133–134, 136, 151
Hanks, Tom, 232
Hanna, Daryl, 232
Hardee, Cary (governor, 1921–1925), 115, 138
"Harlem of the South," 73, 96–97, 113
Harlem Renaissance, 72, 97
Harris, Ben, 213–218
Harris, Ed, 234
Hartford, David M., 123, 126
Hays, Will, 136, 153, 184, 207, 209
Hearst, William Randolph, 22, 134
Hearst Cosmopolitan Company, 134
Hepburn, Audrey, 243

Hillery, Michelle, 262
Hillsborough County, 125
Hillsborough River, 37–38
Hixon, Curtis (Tampa mayor), 165–166
Hobe Sound Picture City, 122
Holland, Spessard (governor, 1941–1945), 152–153
"Hollywood East," 6, 67, 120, 205–207, 227, 235–236, 238–248, 252–253, 259
Hollywood Reporter, 237, 263, 269
Home Box Office Network (HBO), 216, 263
Homosassa Springs, 194
Hotaling, Arthur, 40, 86–90, 99
Hotel Mason, Jacksonville, 51–53
Howard, Clint, 194
Howard, Ron, 194, 232, 246, 253
Hudson, Rock, 168
Hugh, R. John, 18, 149, 155, 157, 179–184, 187–188, 197–198, 206, 212, 228, 235–238
Hurricanes: Great Miami (1926), 18, 127; Okeechobee (1928), 18, 127
Hurston, Zora Neale, 97, 127
Hurt, William, 218
Huston, John, 173

Incorporated Television Company (ITC), 186
Indianapolis Freeman, 98
Indianapolis Recorder, 87
Ingram, Rex, 119–120
Ivan Tors Studios, 192–195

Jacksonville, FL, 6, 8–9, 11, 17, 20, 24–27, 29–40, 43–64, 67, 72–90, 96–113, 150, 188, 218, 229, 238, 250, 254; Great Fire of 1901, 26, 45–47, 49, 100
Jacksonville Board of Trade, 43–45, 48, 88
Jacksonville Chamber of Commerce (JCC), 48–50, 54–55, 59–60
Jarman, Claude, Jr., 160–161
Jarmusch, Jim, 231
Jenkins, Barry, 238, 263
Jesup, Thomas, 169
Jim Crow system, 18, 75, 79
Johnson, Don, 223, 225, 233
Johnson, Jack, 82–83
Johnson, James Weldon, 72–73, 89, 97, 99–100
Johnson, Van, 185
Jordan, William S. (Jacksonville mayor), 82–83
Jupiter, FL, 215

Kalem's *Florida Series,* 20, 44–45, 54–55, 76, 78–81, 97
Kalem Stock Company, 20–21, 24–36, 43, 54–55, 59, 75–81, 84–86, 88, 97–99, 103, 109, 143, 195
Keaton, Buster, 115, 143–147
Kelly, Emmett "Weary Willy," 174
Kelly, Harry, 62–63, 109–111, 109, 129
Kennedy, Aubrey, 19, 142, 144–149
Kennedy City Studios, 19, 142–150, 157, 180
Kennedy Picture Corporation (KPC), 141–143
Key West, FL, 15, 21–23, 180–181, 251
Key West Citizen, 181
Kim, Yong Kun, 228–230
King, Henry, 129–133, 172
Kirk, Claude (governor, 1967–1971), 12, 155–157, 210–211
Kissimmee, FL, 149, 263–264
Kissimmee/Osceola County Chamber of Commerce, 245
Kitzmiller, Laura, 232–233
Kleine, George, 26–29
Klutho, Henry John, 46, 59–60, 62, 108–109, 123
Klutho Fine Arts City, 59–61, 63–64, 104, 108–109
Ku Klux Klan, 56, 72–74, 79–81, 84, 102
Kurosawa, Akira, 231

Laemmle, Carl, 24, 28, 92, 122
Lake, Veronica, 187
Lake Eola, 252
Lander, Marylee, 221, 224
Langford, Carl (Orlando mayor), 202
LaVilla, Jacksonville, 24, 45, 50, 73, 81, 96–97, 100, 104, 228
Leftwich, Alexander, 182
Leon County, 166
Lewis, Abraham Lincoln, 100
Lewis, Herschell, 207–209
Lewis, Jerry, 176
Lewis, Joe, 112
Lipton, Lew, 146–149
Little Manatee River, 123–124
Loew, Marcus, 24
Long, Samuel, 27, 29
Longwood, FL, 235, 252
Los Angeles Times, 208, 239
Lubin, Siegmund, 32, 40

Lubin Manufacturing Company, 32, 36, 38–40, 43, 55, 60, 76, 84–89
Lucasfilm, 233
Lucas, George, 218, 243
Lux, John, 255, 269

Manatee County, 163, 210
Mann, Michael, 222–223, 225
Mariel Boatlift, 19, 221
Marion, Frank, 27, 29, 35, 76
Marion County, 1
Martin, John W. (governor, 1925–1929), 11–12, 17, 59, 115, 128, 138, 140, 249
Martin, Steve, 246
Martin County, 122
Martinez, Bob (governor, 1987–1991), 239, 248–249
Mayer, Louis B., 158–159
MCA/Universal, 241–243
McCleary, Margaret Downs, 89
McClellan, George, Jr., 28–30
McDuffie Rebellion, 221–222
McKay, Donald B. (Tampa mayor, 1910–1920, 1928–1931), 37, 60, 130
Melbourne Beach, 231
Melford, George, 145–146
Metro-Goldwyn-Mayer (MGM) Studios, 144, 150, 158–164, 177–178, 189, 191, 205–206, 212, 227, 236–239, 242–243, 248–252, 254, 258
Metro Orlando Film and Television Office (MOFTO), 248, 251
Meyer, J. H., 123–126
Miami, FL, 8–9, 13, 17–18, 32, 39–43, 64, 70, 105, 117–120, 123, 127, 139–140, 173, 175–180, 182–183, 187–197, 206–210, 215–217, 219–233, 238, 248, 251, 253–254, 257–258, 263–265, 267
Miami Beach, FL, 175–178, 192, 208, 227, 263, 267
Miami Beach Auditorium, 192
Miami Board of Trade, 40–41, 43
Miami Chamber of Commerce, 117, 197, 219, 224
Miami-Dade County, 223, 227, 236, 267
Miami-Dade Film Commission, 224, 231
Miami Dolphins, 214
Miami Herald, 41, 43, 118–120, 123, 187, 225, 264, 267

Miami Metropolitan Board of County Commissioners (MBCC), 196
Miami Studios, 70, 118–120, 127
Micanopy, FL, 248
Micheaux, Oscar, 89, 109, 111
"Millionaires Row," 175
Ministry for the Recovery of Misappropriated Assets, 186
Mitzi the Dolphin, 191–193
Montgomery, Frank, 86, 88
Montgomery Theater, 37
Motion Picture Industry Committee (MPIC), 153, 173
Motion Picture Patents Company (MPPC), 24–29, 31–34, 43, 49, 54–55, 76
Motion Picture Producers of America (MPPA), 176
Motograph Company, 32–33
Motography Magazine, 38, 41, 54
Mount Dora, FL, 243–244
Music Corporation of America (MCA), 241–243

National Association for the Advancement of Colored People (NAACP), 17, 72–73, 88–89, 91–93, 96, 99
National Broadcasting Company (NBC), 13, 18, 189–191, 194, 203, 222–224
National Film Corporation of America, 60, 162
Neilan, Marshall, 143–146, 148
Nelson, Richard Alan, 16, 32, 87, 108, 115, 120–121, 212, 231
Nerney, Mary Childs, 91–92
New Jersey, 21, 29, 44, 55, 76, 83
Newman, Paul, 231
New York Age, The, 87
New York Times, 44, 56, 131, 220
Nickelodeon (Theater), 28, 30–31
Nickelodeon Studios, 203–205, 238, 252
Noble, John W., 95, 103
Norman, Gloria, 111
Norman, Richard, 17, 60, 73, 105–113
Nuñez, Victor, 234–235, 249

Ocala, FL, 1–6, 8–10, 18, 117, 144, 162, 170, 174, 179–181, 233, 236, 255–256, 270
Ocala Drive-In, 1–5, 9–10, 255–256, 270
Ocala National Forest, 19, 159–160, 200
Ocala Star Banner, 3, 163, 171

Ocoee Massacre, 102
Office of Film and Entertainment (OFE), 199, 250–251, 259, 261, 264–265, 269
Okaloosa County, 172, 215
Olcott, Sidney, 27, 29–31, 59, 78–79, 84–85
O'Loughlin, John, 64–66
O'Neal, Shaquille, 252
Orange Bowl, 214–215
Orange County (Florida), 187, 241–242
Orange County Commissioner's Office, 241
Orlando, FL, 8, 13, 18–19, 64–67, 117, 121, 136, 156–157, 179–184, 186–188, 194, 198–206, 210, 218, 223, 227, 230–254, 257–258
Orlando Air Force Base, 181, 186, 240
Orlando Evening Star, 65, 180, 184
Orlando Film Office, 248
Orlando International Film Festival (OIFF), 236–237
Orlando Sentinel, 65, 156, 170, 183, 186, 194, 198, 202, 204, 228–229, 231, 235–237, 244–245, 248
Orlando Weekly, 244, 253
Orpheum Theatre, 33, 47
Oscar Micheaux Film Corporation, 109, 111
Osceola (chief), 149, 168–169, 180
Osceola County, 156, 240, 245, 251, 264
Ovington, Mary White, 91–92
Owens, Chick, 148
Owens, Richard, 237

Pacino, Al, 221
Palm Beach, 32, 40, 151, 175, 188
Palm Beach Chamber of Commerce, 151
Paramount Studios, 25, 29, 61, 140, 150, 161, 175–176, 179, 195, 207, 212, 218, 241, 244
Paramount v. United States (1948), 175
Parker, T. C., 142, 147–149
Park West Theater, 155–156
Parsons, William "Smiling Bill," 60, 62, 162
Pastime Theatre, 26, 29, 33
Pathé, 36, 48, 65, 124, 132, 195
Peck, Charles, Jr., 168
Peck, Gregory, 160–161, 172
Pensacola, FL, 188
Perez, Demetrio, 221–222
Pergola, James, 195–198, 213
Pergola, James V., 195

Perry, Newton, 162, 164–172, 193
Petty, Tom, 177
Pinellas County, 114, 137, 141–142, 180, 260
Plant, Henry, 37, 116
Ponce de León, Juan, 149
Powers, Pat, 142–143, 145
Presley, Elvis, 177
Prohibition Era, 221, 234
Prohibition Party, 12, 56–57, 99–101
"Project Winter," 200–201
Public Broadcasting Station (PBS), 165, 167

"Ralph the Famous Swimming Pig," 167
Ramsberger, Kathy, 251
Rawlings, Marjorie Kinnan, 158–166, 171, 234
Ray, Nicholas, 184, 231
Ray, W. Carl, 161–162
Reagan, Ronald, 176, 219, 222
Reedy Creek Improvement District, 201–202, 211
Republic Pictures, 152, 180
Reynolds, Burt, 190, 211–212, 215, 217, 265
Richard Norman Manufacturing Company (RNMC), 105, 107, 112
Richard Norman Studios, 17, 105–113
RKO Studios, 137–138, 159
Roosevelt, Franklin, 138, 153
Roosevelt, Theodore, 33–34
Roseland House, 29–30, 54
Rosewood Massacre, 1923, 102–103
Ross, FL, 123–125
Ruddy, Albert, 212
Russell, Lillian, 26
Russell-Owens Stock Company, 98–99

San Antonio, FL, 57
Sanford, FL, 182, 240, 246, 252
Sanford Memorial Stadium, 182
Sanford Naval Air Station, 240
Sarasota, FL, 117, 132, 134, 172–174, 208, 243
Sarasota Opera House, 173
Savino, Cathy, 248, 251
Scheider, Roy, 244
Scott, Emmett, 91–95
Scott, Rick (governor, 2011–2019), 13, 260–261, 265
Screen Actors Guild (SAG), 176, 251
Selig, William, 33–35, 93–94

Index · 327

Selig Polyscope Company, 33–36, 38, 43, 55, 76, 82, 86–89, 93–94, 103
Selznick, David O., 137, 158–159
Selznick, Louis J., 122
Seminole County, 240, 267
Sennett, Mack, 90
Sewell, Everett George, 70, 117–120
Shamrock Studios, 18, 183–188, 190, 236
Sherman Anti-Trust Act, 55
Shipman, Ernest, 123, 126
Sholtz, David (governor, 1933–1937), 12, 115, 138–141, 150–152
Shutts, Frank, 118, 120
Sid Olcott Players, 84–85
Silver Springs, 18, 154, 158, 161–168, 190
Sinatra, Frank, 175–176, 178
Sinclair, Upton, 149
Smith, B. L. (Miami mayor), 120
Smith, Howard, 204–205
Soreno Hotel, 251
South Beach, Miami Beach, 206, 208, 225, 227
Southern Christian Leadership Conference (SCLC), 74
South Florida Film and Tape Producers Association (SFFTPA), 234
South Florida Sun Sentinel, 209
South Jacksonville, FL, 32–34
Spanish-American War, 21–24
Spanish Influenza Pandemic, 3–4, 58, 60, 109, 116
Special Motion Picture Committee (SMPC), 117–118, 141–143, 147, 150, 152, 154–155
Spielberg, Steven, 202, 249
Spitz, Leo, 169
Splendora Film Corporation, 180
Stanley, Ginger, 170–171
State Hotel Commission (SHC), 133, 136
St. Augustine, FL, 32, 35–36, 39, 44, 56, 168, 174
Sterne, Elaine, 92
Stetson University, 236
Stewart, Linda (Florida state senator), 269
Stiles, W. J., 104–105, 107–108
St. Johns River, 29–30, 32, 48, 67
St. Leo Abbey, 57
Stone, Oliver, 221, 237
St. Petersburg, FL, 44, 114–116, 123, 125, 131, 134, 137, 139–149, 180, 188–189, 217–218, 232, 251, 257, 260

St. Petersburg Board of Trade, 182–183
St. Petersburg Chamber of Commerce, 149
St. Petersburg City Council, 125
St. Petersburg/Clearwater Film Commission, 232
St. Petersburg Independent, 115, 125, 142, 146–147
St. Petersburg Times, 103, 114, 124, 143, 147, 189, 216–217
Strand Amusement Company, 98, 104–107
Strand Theater, Key West, 181
Strand Theatre, Jacksonville, 98–99, 104–108, 110
Suez Hotel, 208
Sulphur Springs Park, 37, 94–95
Sun City Studios, 123–126, 144
Sun Haven Studios, 114–115, 147–149, 157
Sunny South Releases, 20, 29–31, 76
Suwannee Hotel, 134, 143–144
Swearingen, Van C. (Jacksonville mayor), 45–47

Taddeo, Annette (Florida state senator), 265–267
Tallahassee, FL, 135, 164, 188–189, 211, 213, 269
Tampa, FL, 6, 8, 12, 17–18, 21–23, 37–40, 57, 60–64, 87, 94–96, 105, 114–117, 122–126, 128–138, 141, 149, 151, 165–166, 172–173, 188, 198, 204, 207, 241, 253, 257, 260, 262
Tampa Bay Hotel, 37–38, 137
Tampa Bay Times, 146, 264
Tampa Board of Trade, 37–40, 60, 63, 123
Tampa Films Incorporated (TFI), 37–39
Tampa Tribune, 62, 125, 204, 211
Taylor, Robert, 187
Telemundo Studios, 254
Testagrossa, Ross, 250–251
Texas Film Commission, 212
Thanhouser, Edwin, 49–50
Thanhouser Film Corporation, 48–50, 82
Theater Owners Booking Association (TOBA), 104–105
Thomas, Ireland D., 109
Thomas, Phillip Michael, 223, 227
Thunderbird Studios, 192
Time Magazine, 210, 219–222, 248, 263
Tors, Ivan, 18, 188–196, 199–200, 202, 206, 232, 254
Touchstone Pictures, 232, 241–242, 246

Tracy, Spencer, 159–160, 172
Trammell, Park (governor, 1913–1917), 86
Tuskegee Institute, 91–93
20th Century Fox, 26, 30, 151, 153, 195, 218, 248

United Artists, 67, 70, 129–132, 151, 176, 183, 189, 190, 215
United Confederate Veterans, 84–86
United States v. Motion Picture Patents Co. (1915), 55
Universal Studios, 5, 92, 117, 122, 124–125, 142–143, 165–166, 168–169, 204–206, 217–218, 227, 236–239, 241, 245–254, 258
Universal Studios Florida (theme park), 13, 19, 206, 227, 236–239, 241–243, 245–254, 258
Universal Studios Hollywood (theme park), 241
University of Central Florida, 112, 227, 234, 236, 244
University of Miami, 207, 233
University of Tampa, 137

Valencia College, 234
Variety, 42, 94–95, 208, 210, 237
Vélez, Lupe, 129–130, 172
Vidor, King, 160
Visit Florida, 260
Vitagraph Company, 22, 44, 70, 83, 97–98

Wakulla Springs, 158, 162, 164
Wall, Perry G., 124
Walsh, Raoul, 168
Walt Disney World, 157, 202, 240, 249, 263
Walters, Elmer, 33
Wargraph, 22–23
Warner, Sam, 85
Warner Brothers, 1, 38, 66, 84, 111, 151, 173, 183–184, 188
Warren, Fuller (governor, 1949–1953), 173–174
Washington, Booker T., 91, 92

Waters, Ethel, 180–181
Watzke, Charlie, 3–5
Watzke, Charles Alexander, 3–4
Watzke, John, 2–5, 7, 255–256, 270
WCJB-TV Gainesville, 7, 255–256
Weedon Island, 19, 114–115, 140–141, 143–150, 180
Weeki Wachee Springs, 164–167, 173, 170–171; mermaids, 165–167, 170–171
Weissmuller, Johnny, 158, 161–162
Welch, Raquel, 179
Welles, Orson, 169, 262
West Orange, NJ, 21–22
West Palm Beach, FL, 188, 215
WFSU-TV Tallahassee, 165–166, 234
Whitman, Frank, 37–39
Williams, Esther, 163
Williams, Kathlyn, 34
Winter Haven, FL, 163, 248–251
Winter Park, FL, 18, 112, 149, 155–156, 179–188, 190, 198, 200–202, 235–236
Winter the Dolphin, 260–261
Wise, Robert, 237
WJXT-TV Jacksonville, 188
WKMG-TV Orlando, 256–257
Works Progress Administration, 137, 172
World War I, 57–60, 90, 94–95, 116, 134
World War II, 11, 153, 160, 163, 172, 189, 240
WTVJ-TV Miami, 188
Wyman, Jane, 160

Ybor City, 257
Yerkovich, Anthony, 222–223

Zanuck, Lili, 232
Zanuck, Richard, 215
Zemeckis, Robert, 232
Ziv Television Programs, 189–190
Zukor, Adolph, 24, 28, 155, 161, 179–180

Index to Films and Television Shows

All works were filmed and set in Florida unless preceded by an asterisk.
* Filmed in Florida, set elsewhere
** Set in Florida, filmed elsewhere
*** Partially filmed in Florida or production relocated
**** Not filmed or set in Florida
***** Animated film
dir. = Director
s.c. = Show creator(s)

Films

Absence of Malice (1981), dir. Sydney Pollack, 231
Ace Ventura: Pet Detective (1994), dir. Tom Shadyac, 253
Airport '77, (1977), dir. Jerry Jameson, 215
Apollo 13, (1995) dir. Ron Howard, 253
**Around the World Under the Sea*, (1966), dirs. Andrew Martin and Ricou Browning, 192
Bad Boys (1995), dir. Michael Bay, 253, 264
Bad Boys II (2003), dir. Michael Bay, 258, 264s
Barefoot Mailman, The (1951), dir. Earl McEvoy, 168
***Baywatch (2017), Seth Gordon 257
Bellboy, The (1951), dir. Jerry Lewis, 176
****Ben Hur (1907), dir. Sidney Olcott, 27
Birdcage, The (1996), dir. Mike Nichols, 253
*****Birth of a Nation, The* (1915), dir. D.W. Griffith, 18, 71, 73, 75, 79, 81, 84, 88–89, 91, 95, 103, 113
**Birth of a Race, The* (1918), dir. John W. Noble, 90–96, 103
****Black Gold (1928), dir. Richard Norman, 110–111
Black Sunday (1977), dir. Jonathan Frankenheimer, 214–215

*****Blair Witch Project, The* (1999), dirs. Daniel Myrick and Eduardo Sánchez, 238
Blood Feast (1963), Herschell Gordon Lewis, 208–209
Body Heat (1981), Lawrence Kasdan, 218
Broad Road, The (1922), dir. John O'Loughlin, 65–67
*****Brother Bear (2003), dirs. Aaron Blaise and Robert Walker, 205
*****Bulldogger, The* (1922), dir. Richard Norman, 108
Burial of the Maine Victims (1898), dir. William Paley, 22–23
*Caddyshack (1980), dir. Harold Ramis, 220–221
Carib Gold (1956), dir. Harold Young, 180–181
Chloe: Love Is Calling You (1933), Marshall Neilan, 143–145, 148
City of Jacksonville (1916), documentary, 89
***Citizen Kane (1941), dir. Orson Welles, 262
**Clambake (1967), dir. Arthur Nadel, 177–178
Clarion, The (1916), dir. James Durkin, 50–53, 228
Classmates (1924), John S. Robertson, 70–71
Confederate Spy, The (1910), dir. Sidney Olcott, 80–81
Cracker's Bride, The (1910), dir. Sidney Olcott, 31, 78
**Creature from the Black Lagoon, The* (1910), dir. Jack Arnold, 18, 169–171
**Creature Walks Among Us, The* (1956), dir. John Sherwood, 170
*****Crimson Skull, The* (1922), dir. Richard Norman, 108
Cross Creek (1983), Martin Ritt, 171
*Crosswinds (1951), Lewis R. Foster, 173
Crowd for Lisette, A (1961), dir. R. John Hugh:187, 237–238

Crystal Champions (1929), dir. Grantland Rice, 161–162
D.A.R.Y.L. (1985), dir. Simon Wincer, 243–245
Daughter of Dixie, A (1910), dir. Sidney Olcott, 80–81
****Days of '61, The* (1907), dir. Sidney Olcott, 77
Death Curse of Tartu (1966), dir. William Grefé, 200
Deep Throat (1972), dir. Jerry Gerard, 209–210
Devil and Miss Jones, The (1973), dir. Gerard Damiano, 213
Devil's Sisters, The (1966), dir. William Grefé, 200
Distant Drums (1951), dir. Raoul Walsh, 168, 174, 180
**Doc Hollywood* (1991), dir. Michael-Caton Jones, 248
Dolphin Tale (2011), dir. Charles Martin Smith, 260
Dolphin Tale 2 (2014), dir. Charles Martin Smith, 260–261
Easy to Love (1953), dir. Charles Walters, 163, 175
*****Emperor's New Groove, The* (2000), dir. Mark Dindal, 205
E.P.C.O.T. Florida Film (1966), dir. Art Vitarelli, 156–157, 201
Eye of the Hurricane (2012), dir. Jesse Wolfe, 257
Flesh Feast (1970), dir. Brad F. Grinter, 187
Flight of the Navigator (1986), dir. Randal Kleiser, 243, 245
Flipper (1963), dir. James B. Clark, 18, 191–194
Flipper's New Adventure (1964), dir. Leon Benson, 191
Florida Feud; Or, Love in the Everglades, A (1909), dir. Sidney Olcott, 30–31, 78
Florida Project, The (2000), dir. Sean Baker, 258, 263–264
Flying Ace, The (1926), dir. Richard Norman, 109–111
Follow That Dream (1962), dir. Gordon Douglas, 177–178
Gal Young Un (1979), dir. Victor Nuñez, 234
Garden of Eden, The (1926), dir. Max Nosseck, 207
Gentle Giant (1967), dir. James Neilson, 194

**Ghost Story* (1981), dir. John Irvin, 236
***Gifted* (2017), dir. Marc Webb, 16, 257
***Girl Happy* (1965), Boris Sagal, 177
Girl Spy, The (1909), dir. Sidney Olcott, 80
****Goldfinger* (1964), dir. Guy Hamilton, 178
Greatest Empire of the Ants, The (1926), dir. Bert I. Gordon, 215
Greatest Show on Earth, The (1952), dir. Cecil B. DeMille, 172–174
Green-Eyed Monster, The (1919) dir. Richard Norman, 107–108
Gun Runners, The (1958), dir. Don Siegel, 173
Harry & Son (1983), dir. Paul Newman, 231
**Hell Harbor* (1930), dir. Henry King, 129–133, 143, 172–173
Hired Wife, The (1934), dir. George Melford, 144, 147–149
Hole in the Head, A (1959), dir. Frank Capra, 175–176, 178
Honeymoon through Snow to Sunshine, A (1910), dir. Arthur Hotaling, 32, 40
Honky Tonk Freeway (1981), dir. John Schlesinger, 243–244
**Idol Dancer, The* (1920), dir. D. W. Griffith, 67–70, 163
****Indiana Jones and the Temple of Doom* (1984), dir. Steven Spielberg, 233
In Old Florida (1911), dir. Sidney Olcott, 36
In the Clutches of the Ku Klux Klan (1913), dir. Sidney Olcott, 84
**Isle of Doubt* (1922), Hamilton Smith, 118–119
Jacksonville in Motion (1914), documentary, 44
****Jaws* (1975), dir. Steven Spielberg, 4, 200, 215
**Jaws II* (1978), dir. Jeannot Szwarc, 215
Jaws 3-D (1983), dir. Joe Alves, 243–245
****Jazz Singer, The* (1927), dir. Alan Crosland, 111
Joe Panther (1976), dir. Paul Kransy, 215
Johnny Tiger (1966), dir. Paul Wendkos, 187, 235
****Johnson-Jeffries Fight* (1910), dir. J. Stuart Blackton, 83
**Jupiter's Darling* (1955): George Sidney, 163
**Key Largo* (1948), dir. John Huston, 173
Lady in Cement (1968), dir. Gordon Douglas, 179

***Lenny* (1974), dir. Bob Fosse, 212
Lethal Weapon 3 (1992), dir. Richard Donner, 250
*****Lilo and Stitch* (2003), dirs. Chris Sanders and Dean DeBlois, 205
**Live By Night* (2016), dir. Ben Affleck, 16, 260
**Longest Yard, The* (1974), dir. Robert Aldrich, 212
Lost in the Jungle (1911), dir. Otis Turner, 34
Love Bug, The (1919), dir. Richard Norman, 108
Love Flower, The (1920), dir. D. W. Griffith, 67–70, 129
Magic City of the South, The (1914), documentary, 40
Magic Mike (2012), dir. Steven Soderbergh, 26
**Magic Mike XXL* (2015), dir. Gregory Jacobs, 262
Mako: Jaws of Death (1976), dir. William Grefé, 200
Meal, The (1975), dir. R. John Hugh, 235
***Meet Me After the Show* (1951), dir. Richard Sale, 175
Miami Connection (1987), dirs. Richard Park and Y. K. Kim, 231–234
Miami Exposé (1956), dir. Fred F. Sears, 173
Miami Story, The (1954), dir. Fred F. Sears, 173
Miami Vice (2006), dir. Michael Mann, 257
Moonlight (2016), dir. Barry Jenkins, 238, 258, 263–264
**Mr. Peabody and the Mermaid* (1948), dir. Irving Pichel, 165–166
*****Mulan* (1998), dirs. Barry Cook and Tony Bancroft, 205
Naked in the Sun (1957), dir. R. John Hugh, 168, 184
Naked Zoo (1970), dir. William Grefé, 200
Northern Schoolmaster, The (1909), Sidney Olcott, 79
Octoroon: A Story of the Turpentine Forest, The (1909), dir. Sidney Olcott, 78–79
Octoroon, The (1913), dir. Sidney Olcott, 79–80
**On an Island with You* (1948), dir. Richard Thorpe, 163, 165
**** *Other Lamb, The* (2020), dir. Małgorzata Szumowska, 1–3
***Palm Beach Story, The* (1942), dir. Preston Sturges, 175
**Parenthood* (1989), dir. Ron Howard, 246
***Paper Towns* (2015), dir. Jake Schreier, 257

Playthings of Desire (1934), dir. George Melford 144–148
Porky's (1981), dir. Bob Clark, 230
Porky's II: The Next Day (1983), dir. Bob Clark, 230
Porky's Revenge (1985), dir. James Komack, 230
Punisher, The (2004), dir. Jonathan Hensleigh, 258
Rastus in Zululand (1910), dir. Arthur Hotaling, 87
Rastus Among the Zulus (1913), dir. Arthur Hotaling, 87
****Reap the Wild Wind* (1942):, dir. Cecil B. DeMille, 173
**Regeneration* (1923), dir. Richard Norman, 109–111
**Revenge of the Creature* (1955), dir. Jack Arnold, 170, 177, 244
Rosewood (1997), dir. John Singleton, 103
Ruby in Paradise (1993), dir. Victor Nuñez, 234
*****Scarface: Shame of a Nation* (1932), dir. Howard Hawks, 221
****Scarface* (1983), dir. Brian DePalma, 221–223, 264
Seminole! (1953), dir. Budd Boetticher, 168–169
**Semi-Tough* (1977), dir. Michael Ritchie, 215
Shark River (1953), dir. John Rawlins, 168, 173
*****Smokey and the Bandit* (1977), dir. Hal Needham, 212, 215
**Smokey and the Bandit II* (1980), dir. Hal Needham, 215
**Smokey and the Bandit III* (1983), dir. Dick Lowry, 215
Sometimes Aunt Martha Does Dreadful Things (1971), dir. Thomas Casey, 187
***Some Like it Hot* (1959), dir. Billy Wilder, 257
South Beach (1993), dirs. Fred Williamson and Alain Zaloum, 227
*****Splash* (1984), dir. Ron Howard, 245
Spring Breakers (2012), dir. Harmony Korine, 260
Stanley (1972), dir. William Grefé, 200
Stick (1985), dir. Burt Reynolds, 216–217
Strange One, The (1957), dir. Jack Garfein, 184
****Stranger Than Paradise* (1984), dir. Jim Jarmusch, 231
**** *Swallow* (2020), dir. Carlo Mirabella-Davis, 1–3
*****Tarzan the Apeman* (1932), dir. W. S. Van Dyke, 161, 162

Tarzan Finds a Son! (1939), dir. Richard Thorpe, 154, 158, 162–163
Tarzan's Secret Treasure (1940), dir. Richard Thorpe, 162
Terror From the Year 5000 (1958), dir. Robert J. Gurney Jr., 184
There's Something about Mary (1998), dirs. Bobby and Peter Farrelly, 253
Throw Out the Anchor (1974), dir. R. John Hugh, 235
Thunder and Lightning (1977), dir. Corey Allen, 215
***Thunderball* (1965), dir. Terence Young, 178, 195
Tony Rome (1967), dir. Gordon Douglas, 178
Transporter 2 (2005), dir. Louis Leterrier, 258
Trip to St. Augustine, A (1906), dir. William Selig, 36
***** *Trolls World Tour* (2020), dir. Walt Dohrn, 5
Twelve O'clock High (1949), dir. Henry King, 172–173
2 Fast 2 Furious (2003), dir. John Singleton, 258
Ulee's Gold (1997), dir. Victor Nuñez, 234
Under the Gun (1951), dir. Ted Tetzlaff, 173
U.S. Calvary Supplies Unloading at Tampa Florida (1898), dir. William Paley, 23
****Way Down East* (1920), dir. D.W. Griffith, 67–70
Where the Boys Are (1960), dir. Henry Levin, 176–177
Where the Pavement Ends (1923), dir. Rex Ingram, 119–120
White Rose, The (1923), dir. D. W. Griffith, 70–71
Wind Across the Everglades (1961), dir. Nicholas Ray, 168, 173, 184
Wine of Madness, The (1913), dir. E. D. Horkheimer, 38–39
Wizard of the Jungle (1913), dir. Howard Shaw, 37, 87
Woman There Was, A (1919), J. Gordon Edwards, 118
Yearling, The (1946), dir. Clarence Brown, 158–161, 191
Yellowneck (1955), dir. R. John Hugh, 180–182
Zeb, Zack and the Zulus (1913), dir. Arthur Hotaling, 87
Zebra in the Kitchen (1965), dir. Ivan Tors, 18, 192, 194
Zulu King (1913), dir. Arthur Hotaling, 87

Television Shows

Adventures of Superboy (1988–1992), s.c. Ilya and Alexander Salkind, 253
Assassination of Gianni Versace, The (2018), s.c. Tom Rob Smith, 258
****Ballers* (2015–2019), s.c. Stephen Levinson, 257–258, 260–261, 263
*****Baywatch* (1989–2001), s.c. Michael Berk, Gregory J. Bonann, and Douglas Schwartz, 253
Beachcomber, The (1962), s.c. Walter Newman, 186–187
Bloodline (2015–2017), s.c. Glenn and Todd Kessler, and Daniel Zelman, 257–258, 260–261, 263–264
Burn Notice (2007–2013), s.c. Matt Nix, 254, 258
****Daktari* (1966–1969), s.c. Art Arthur and Ivan Tors, 192, 194
David Makes Man (2019–2021), s.c. Tarell Alvin McCraney, 258
Dexter (2006–2013, 2021), s.c. James Manos Jr., 254, 258
***Empty Nest* (1988–1995), s.c. Susan Harris, 225
Everglades, The (1961–1962), s.c. Albert Witmore, 190–191
Flipper (1964–1967), s.c. Jack Cowden and Ricou Browning, 191–194
***Florida Man* (2023), s.c. Donald Todd, 16, 257
From Earth to the Moon (1998), s.c. Ron Howard, Brian Grazer, Tom Hanks, and Michael Bostick, 253
Gentle Ben, (1967–1969), s.c. Ivan Tors, 19, 194
Get the Picture (1991), s.c. Marjorie Cohn, 203
Glades, The (2010–2013), s.c. Clifton Campbell, 254, 260
***Golden Girls, The* (1985–1992), s.c. Susan Harris, 225
Grapevine, (1992), s.c. David Frankel, 227
***I Dream of Jeannie* (1965–1970), s.c. Sidney Sheldon, 257
****Jackie Gleason Show, The* (1952–1970), s.c. Jackie Gleason, 192
***Killing It* (2022–Present), s.c. Dan Goor and Luke Del Tredici, 16, 257

*****Love Boat, The* (1952–1970), s.c. Wilford Lloyd Baumes, 257
Miami Undercover (1961), s.c. Howard W. Koch, 189
Miami Vice (1984–1989), s.c. Anthony Yerkovich, 13, 200, 206, 222–227, 233, 248, 257
Miss Nancy's Store (1966–1967), s.c. Nancy Tribble Benda, 166–167, 234
****Nip/Tuck* (2003–2010), s.c. Ryan Murphy, 264
**On Becoming a God in Central Florida* (2019), s.c. Robert Funke and Matt Lutsky, 16, 257
100 Lives of Black Jack Savage, The (1991), s.c. Glen Morgan, James Wong, and Stephen Carnell, 227
Parenthood (1990–1991), s.c. Sascha Schneider, 246
Primus (1971), s.c. Ivan Tors, 195
*****Riverboat* (1959–1961), s.c. Richard Bartlett, 190
Sea Hunt (1958–1961), s.c. Ivan Tors and James Baxbaum, 189–190, 192
******77 Sunset Strip* (1958–1964), s.c. Roy Huggins, 188
***Surfside 6* (1960–1962), s.c. William T. Orr and Hugh Benson, 188, 257
Tallahassee 7000 (1961), s.c. Herbert Leonard, 189
Thunder in Paradise (1993–1994), s.c. Michael Berk, Douglas Schwartz, and Gregory J. Bonann, 253
*****Walt Disney's Wonderful World of Color* (1961–1969), s.c. Walt Disney, 194

David Morton is a lecturer in the Film and History Departments at the University of Central Florida, where he teaches courses in American history and media studies.

Michael V. Gannon Fund

In honor of Michael Gannon's lasting legacy and his dedication to the scholarship of our state's history, the University Press of Florida has established the Michael V. Gannon Fund to provide continued support for first publications in Florida history. Royalties and gifts donated to this fund underwrite the costs of these monographs, helping to keep the price as affordable as possible.

Special thanks to Dr. Gary R. Mormino for his very generous contribution to further publications about the Sunshine State's long and fascinating history.

History of Florida, edited by Michael Gannon (2018)

www.ingramcontent.com/pod-product-compliance
Lightning Source LLC
Chambersburg PA
CBHW020829160426
43192CB00007B/573